2nd Edition

Mr. Cheap's®
New York

Michelle Roy Kelly
and
Jennifer M. Wood

Managing Editor
Steven Graber

Associate Editor
Heidi E. Sampson

Editorial Assistants/Researchers
Susan Joyal
Michelle M. Lang
Alison L. Stankus

Previous edition written by Mark Waldstein

Adams Media Corporation
Holbrook, Massachusetts

Published by Adams Media Corporation
260 Center Street, Holbrook, MA 02343. U.S.A.

Mr. Cheap's® is a registered trademark of Adams Media Corporation.

ISBN: 1-58062-271-2

Printed in Canada.

J I H G F E D C B A

Library of Congress Cataloging-in-Publication Data
are available from the publisher.

Product or brand names used in this book may be trademarks or
registered trademarks. Any use of these names does not convey
endorsement by or other affiliation with the name holder.

Every effort has been made to ensure that all material in this book is
current as of the time of this writing. However, this information is subject to
change. Readers should check with the individual services and products
to find up-to-date information, such as current prices, fees, and features.

This publication is designed to provide accurate and authoritative
information with regard to the subject matter covered. It is sold with the
understanding that the publisher is not engaged in rendering legal,
accounting, or other professional advice. If legal advice or other expert
advice is required, the services of a qualified professional person should be
sought.
—From a *Declaration of Principles* jointly adopted by a Committee of the
American Bar Association and a Committee of Publishers and Associations.

This book is available on standing order and at quantity discounts for
bulk purchases. For information, call 800/872-5627 (in Massachusetts,
781/767-8100) or email at reference@adamsmedia.com.

Visit our Website at www.adamsmedia.com

TABLE OF CONTENTS

MANY THANKS...

First and foremost, we would like to thank Mr. Mark Waldstein, the original author of *Mr. Cheap's®*, for laying the groundwork for this (still) vast undertaking. It is because of his initial parsimony that this second edition has been made possible.

Thank you to all the business owners, managers, and employees who were more than willing to share their stories and information so that this book could be as comprehensive as possible.

Our extreme gratitude also goes out to the many dedicated readers who took the time to write us with leads, feedback, and support. Keep it coming!

Finally, a very special thanks goes to the dynamic duo of Mr. Colin Powers and Mr. Patrick J. Noble, who were unselfish in their willingness to provide leads and accompany the author on an endless number of excursions throughout the city that never sleeps.

Thank you!

A FEW WORDS FROM *MR. CHEAP'S®*...

Ultimately, the world can be divided into two types of people: those who have money to burn, and those who don't. Being of the latter species (and let's face it, most of us are), I have spent considerable time and energy assembling this book. Yet, never one to discriminate, I have compiled this book with both the frugal and the frivolous in mind. Even if you *do* have a money tree germinating in your backyard, we are all united in the fact that nothing feels better than getting something for less!

Before taking a hasty glance at this book and dismissing it simply because you think "Me? *Cheap*? Never!," please bare with me for a moment while I explain that the term "cheap" -- in no way -- should be understood to have a negative connotation. Let me first start off with a few synonyms for my own definition of CHEAP: frugal, thrifty, cost-conscious, economical... The point is, while a "cheap" person may be understood as someone who reuses paper plates and plastic utensils, and brings to mind visions of Ebenezer Scrooge, a *Mr. Cheap's®* reader is someone who only expects or accepts the highest quality products and the highest caliber services, at budget-friendly prices. Again, this does not mean that you insist on paying under $10.00 for *any* article of clothing, or *any* entertainment must be free; Mr. C never sets such stringent guidelines. I simply believe that everyone, no matter what their lifestyle, *can* be and *should* be getting things for less. If you prefer to wear an Armani suit to work, or are strictly all-Donna Karan-clad, that is fine. I'll let you know the best places to buy. But, if you prefer to buy your clothes by the pound at the local thrift store, I'm here to aid you in *your* search as well. No matter what your preference or your budget, this book can help you. And no matter what you're looking to buy, eat, or do, Mr. C has got you covered.

Spend the weekend at a ritzy hotel, take in a show, shop 'til you drop, eat 'til you explode -- then come back tomorrow and do it all over again. Don't worry about the cost, with the money you'll be saving the first time around, you can afford to be excessive. So grab an $.75 cup of coffee (TriBeCa's **Franklin Station Cafe**), slip into something comfortable ($.99 sleepwear at **Canal Jean Company**), bury yourself beneath the covers ($3.50 at **Macy's**), fluff up your pillows ($7.99 at **Webers Closeout Center**), and let *Mr. Cheap's®* show you how to conquer the Big Apple.

WEBSITES

While Mr. C and his staff try their hardest to bring you the best and most in cheap fun, food, and fashion around the city, there are definitely some places that we missed, overlooked, or weren't able to fit into our book. Therefore, if you've read this book cover to cover (and you definitely *should*) and you still can't find exactly what it is that you are looking for, the following list of Websites might provide you with some useful information. Enjoy!

ARE WE THERE YET?
http://www.fieldtrip.com/ny/index_ny.htm
The Lowdown: This site lists an extensive collection of places of interest throughout the state, focusing primarily on museums. Categories include aquaria & marine-related, botanical gardens, children's museums, history museums, science & natural history, and zoos. All suggested visitation spots have detailed write-ups, with information on main attractions and exhibits, prices, hours, reservations, and directions.
Cheap **Tip:** Sign up for the *Are We There Yet?* newsletter. It offers tons of great information on special events happening in and around New York and, best of all, it's FREE!

CUISINENET
http://www.cuisinenet.com
The Lowdown: CuisineNet is a resourceful compendium of places to eat throughout the city, complete with menus and reviews. You can search the alphabetical listing of restaurants, or browse by the type of cuisine. You'll get the skinny on each restaurant including ratings on food, service, and ambiance; average meal prices; acceptable dress; address and phone; and hours.
Cheap **Tip:** You can limit your restaurant search to "Inexpensive (under $20.00)" establishments.

4DINING
http://www.4dining.com
The Lowdown: 4Dining simplifies the task of acquiring information on restaurants throughout the city. Search by area or browse by food type. Restaurant listings (which range from cheap to very expensive) include links if available; user ratings; and basic info such as address, phone number. Some include menus and even allow you to place an order or make a reservation.
Cheap **Tip:** Upon entering the site, go directly to the "Expert Search" option, where you can compile a list of restaurants based on location, food type, star rating, credit cards accepted, and (most importantly) price! Prices range from $ to $$$$.

HOTEL DISCOUNTS
http://www.hoteldiscounts.com
The Lowdown: This service is definitely worth checking out, boasting hotel discounts at rates as high as 65 percent off, and rooms available for sold-out dates. The site allow you to browse hotel rates by punching in the desired date(s), number of nights,

number of beds, and number of occupants. You'll be presented with a list of available hotels, as well as basic statistics including prices, amenities, and hotel star ratings.

Cheap **Tip:** If the dates of your trip are flexible, try playing around with them while researching rates. It's surprising how much the rates of hotel rooms can fluctuate from night to night.

I LOVE THE BRONX
http://www.ilovethebronx.com

The Lowdown: Run by The Bronx Tourism Council, this Website contains dates, times, and prices of events throughout the Bronx. Events listed here are predominantly arts & crafts functions, fairs, poetry readings, and expos. You can search by date and/or keyword, or by the type of event you're seeking (e.g. literary arts, visual arts, outdoors, workshops & classes, etc.).

Cheap **Tip:** The site offers a Bronx Fun Pass (for $.52), which affords you great savings at various Bronx theaters, museums, galleries, zoos, and outdoor events.

I LOVE NY
http://www.iloveny.state.ny.us

The Lowdown: We all know the slogan. This is New York State's official tourism site, compiled by the Department of Economic Development. You can search for information on an abundance of events and attractions, and the site also offers miscellaneous data such as weather and transportation facts for visitors.

Cheap **Tip:** The "Travel Ideas" section offers various creative tips on things to do for fun throughout the state. Check out their "Road Trips" section, where the cost of gas alone will allow you to see all the beauty New York State has to offer.

THE NYC INSIDER
http://www.theinsider.com/nyc

The Lowdown: The NYC Insider has a little bit of everything. A unique feature (and one that warrants multiple visits) is their "New York Tip of the Day." Here, you'll find great insider tips that will let you in on some of the city's hidden treasures.

Cheap **Tip:** The NYC Insider's "Money-Saving Guide" includes advice on beating high prices at the movies (which requires skill, indeed); discount shopping; methods of acquiring discounts on Broadway theater tickets; and the days and hours you can get into top museums for *free*. This section also identifies those museums where admission is always free.

NYSALE
http://www.nysale.com

The Lowdown: NYSale is a valuable research tool for the serious shopper. If you thought you'd missed all the biggest sample sales and designer name clearance extravaganzas, think again! NYSale lets you search for current sales by category, date, or store name. Store categories include apparel; eyewear; jewelry; home accessories/furnishings; maternity; rugs; and much more.

Cheap **Tip:** Register to become a member of the NYSale site and you can receive information on the most current sales via e-mail.

THE NEW YORK CITY CULTURE GUIDE & CALENDAR
http://www.allianceforarts.org

The Lowdown: Created by The Alliance for the Arts, this site features information on an assortment of arts events. Search by name, type of event, or location. Event categories include dance, museums, botanical gardens, music, theater, photography/film/video, children, and more. General profiles are provided, with information such as what type of exhibits are typically offered.

Cheap **Tip:** If your visiting plans entail bringing the family along, this site offers a downloadable "Kids' Culture Calendar." This free guide will let you know the best places to take the kids if you're looking to mix a little culture in with their fun.

NEW YORK CITY WEBSITE
http://www.ci.nyc.ny.us

The Lowdown: As the official New York City government Website, here you'll find links for a plethora of events, attractions, and entertainment venues. Search categories include Current Events, Getting Around, Food & Drink, and Music, Dance, & Theater.

Cheap **Tip:** With the number of movies and television shows being shot in NYC on the rise, it is *always* a possibility that you could bump into your favorite star while walking the streets of the Big Apple. Link to the "City Services & Agencies" section to find out which shows and stars will be filming during your visit.

NEW YORK CITYSEARCH
http://newyork.citysearch.com

The Lowdown: This extensive Website offers information on every aspect of life in the Big Apple. Explore detailed listings in the areas of arts & entertainment, special events, restaurants & bars, shopping, and more. The site includes articles and reviews as well as links to additional reviews on other sites.

Cheap **Tip:** Go to "Visiting the City," which often provides tips on how to tackle New York on a budget. The "Discount Shopping" section allows you to search by categories including flea markets, outlets, thrift shops, and warehouses.

NEW YORK CONVENTION & VISITOR'S BUREAU
http://www.nycvisit.com

The Lowdown: Search a wide list of arts & entertainment, hotels, shopping, restaurants, bars, sports, fitness, and more on this Website. Descriptions and links to official sites are provided, so that you may access full details including addresses, schedules, hours, and prices.

Cheap **Tip:** The site allows you to access a calendar of upcoming events around the city that are often very inexpensive, if not free. Look here for parades, concerts, exhibits, benefits, seasonal events (like the holiday lighting of the Empire State Building), and other traditional New York City activities.

NEW YORK HOTELGUIDE
http://www.newyork.hotelguide.net

The Lowdown: New York HotelGuide is another worthwhile site for your affordable hotel search efforts. Browse by location and view a list of hotels, and click on any given hotel for extensive information including features, location, and rate range. You can then book a hotel room through the site.

Cheap Tip: Lots of research keeps popping up that, although many people choose the Internet as their main source for booking a trip, a good old phone call can sometimes be your best bet. Don't be afraid to research some possible rates and then call the hotel and try to haggle a bit. Maybe you won't get a *lower* rate, but perhaps you can up the room features, like getting a bigger bed. Hey, it can't hurt.

NEW YORK TV SHOW TICKETS INC.
http://www.nytix.com

The Lowdown: Don't let the name fool you! While this site *does* provide an abundance of information on how to get tickets for television talk show tapings in New York City (many for free), they'll also let you know how you can get to the theater on a budget. The site offers tips on how to get tickets to such popular shows as *The Late Show with David Letterman*, *The Rosie O'Donnell Show*, and *Saturday Night Live*. In addition, the site offers tips on how to obtain half-price Broadway show tickets, free guided tours of the city, cheap television studio tours, and $20.00 "Starving Artist Tickets" for top shows like *Rent* (note, you don't really have to be a starving artist to get them). Another section suggests places you can go in New York for under $10.00.

Cheap Tip: If, after following all the tips on this site, you *still* can't get tickets to see your favorite television personalities, take an early morning stroll to Rockefeller Center at 49th Street, where the *Today* show has a storefront studio. You're welcome to look on as they tape.

PAPERLESS GUIDE TO NEW YORK
http://www.ny.com

The Lowdown: This marvelous site offers up an impressive slate of places to go in the city, many of which are cheap (thankfully). Check under the "WOW" section for listings of sporting events, museums, shopping, nightlife, and more. All major categories are broken down into subcategories for convenient browsing (e.g. under "Nightlife", you'll find Jazz Clubs, Bars & Pubs, etc.). Listings include a brief editor's note that describes the place, letting you know what to expect.

Cheap Tip: In "Food & Dining", you can search by food price. Choose the meals "under $15.00" option and see what comes up!

PAPERMAG'S GUIDE TO NYC
http://www.papermag.com/guide

The Lowdown: *Paper Magazine* has gone online, and this Website is the result of that venture. The site offers information on art, fashion, film, music, restaurants, and more. Searches can be conducted by area (Chelsea, East Village, SoHo/TriBeCa, Williamsburg, etc.), or by what you are looking to do (Food, Bars, Beauty, Books, Stage, etc.)

Cheap Tip: While you can't search all categories by price range, Papermag's Guide *does* let you know what to expect as far as prices. The writing style here is fun and, much like Mr. C, they'll let you know what kinds of bargains *they* found.

TIME OUT NEW YORK
http://www.timeoutny.com

The Lowdown: This voluminous online magazine guide to New York City complements the printed version of *Time Out New York*. The Web version comes complete with interesting articles on such designations as Around Town, Art, Books & Talks, Clubs, Dance, Film, Gay & Lesbian, Kids, Music, and Theater. Pertinent information is provided with each listing such as address, phone number, price, and a brief review when applicable.

Cheap **Tip:** The site's "Eating & Drinking" section, allows you to search out places via a lengthy list of criteria including BYOB, After Hours, and (that magical word) *Cheap!* Searching under "Shops" offers an equally extensive list, where the equally magical word *discount* makes its way into the search options.

ZAGAT SURVEY
http://www.zagat.com

The Lowdown: You've read their books, now visit their Website. Zagat.com offers the same information you can find in the best-selling book series. What's best is that it's not just Tim & Nina Zagat who rate these restaurants; ratings are based on hundreds (sometimes thousands) of regular customer experiences. The Zagat lists provide several options for organizing your potential eateries including top service rating and top food rating. The Zagat lists can even rate restaurants by the top female/male traffic or by the popularity with different age groups.

Cheap **Tip:** Aside from seeking out a restaurant based solely on price, Zagat offers a Best Buys section, where you can get the best deal for your dollar. Best Buys combine all the search criteria, allowing you not just the *cheapest* dining experience, but the best overall. Also, if you take advantage of the free online membership, Zagat can provide you with special discounts, maps & driving directions, and over 20,000 reviews and ratings.

SHOPPING
▀▀ Accessories ▀▀

FINE AND KLEIN
119 Orchard Street, New York NY 10002. 212/674-6720.
Description: One of the landmarks of the Lower East Side bargain area, Fine and Klein is known for retailing all kinds of handbags at wholesale prices. The selection includes leather bags, wallets, and evening bags in casual and handwoven styles from well-known designers. All are current styles, first quality, and about 30 percent off retail prices.

GREAT VALUE, INC.
23 East 33rd Street, New York NY 10016. 212/889-5792.
Description: If you're looking for a leather bag, wallet, purse, or belt, they're all available here at great prices. Enormous leather duffel bags were seen for just $100.00. All-leather purses, in any color and/or style imaginable, start at just $30.00. A rack of designer belts were priced 50 percent below retail. For all your leather handbag and accessory needs, this place is -- as the name suggests -- a *great value*.

LEEKAN DESIGNS
93 Mercer Street (between Broome & Spring Streets), New York NY 10012. 212/226-7226. **Description:** This large, beautiful SoHo shop specializes in Asian folk art, making for lots of unique gift options, from the elaborate and expensive to the small and simple; Mr. C, of course, will focus on the latter. My visit to this pseudo-Orient revealed such treasures as enameled porcelain bracelets from $8.00 - $12.00, jade earrings from $16.00, and myriad tiny cases and decorative boxes ranging from $8.00 - $16.00. How about an Indian silk sari bag from $1.50? Pick up a notebook with a heavy cover done over in brightly-colored silk for just $6.00; add a calligraphy brush for $10.00, and see if it gets any creative juices flowing. Or look at all the little handmade toys, from Japanese tin pins for $.50 to a Noh character hand puppet for $12.00. These are all gifts that should certainly make a unique impression on anyone.

LISMORE HOSIERY
334 Grand Street, New York NY 10002. 212/674-3440.
Description: This stretch of Grand Street, from Allen to Essex Streets, is lined with warehouse-style hosiery shops. Each has its specialty, but Lismore is one of the best. For over 50 years, this service-oriented shop has worked to fill every need and preference. They have a huge selection, at 20 - 30 percent off retail prices. They also manufacture their own line, patterned after antique styles, and they have lots of hard-to-find items including support hose for men and women, cotton-lined health socks, and more.

STEUER HOSIERY

31 West 32nd Street, New York NY 10001. 212/563-0052.
Description: This large but humble shop sells first-quality and
irregular hosiery for as little as two-thirds the price of
department stores. They also have first-quality activewear and
leotards at very low prices, all on display for you to look at. The
service is very attentive here; Steuer Hosiery is one of New
York's few wholesale stores where everyday shoppers like you are
welcome to come in and save as well.

TOMPKINS SQUARE STUDIO

147 Avenue A (at 10th Street), New York NY 10009. 212/477-
9578. **Description:** This terrific little East Village storefront is
packed with bargains on handbags, belts, scarves, and other
accessories. These are mainly buyouts on brand-new merchandise;
in perfect condition. A suede bag by Tano was seen here for
$18.00, and a black leather one by Barganza -- originally $120.00 --
was just $25.00. Tompkins Square Studio has the largest selection
of new bags priced from $5.00 - $25.00. The store also has finds
in handcrafted items from around the world, like Indonesian carry
bags made of woven straw, for as little as $7.00; and jewelry, such
as Rosecraft earrings, marked down to $5.00. There's a lot to see
and with new closeouts to be snapped up all the time -- their
selection is always changing.

SHOPPING
💰 Appliances 💰

BERNIE'S DISCOUNT CENTER
821 Avenue of the Americas (between 28th & 29th Streets), New York NY 10001. 212/564-8582. **Description:** Bernie's Discount Center is one of the best places in town for all kinds of household appliances, small and large. They have large-screen TVs from Sony, Mitsubishi, Panasonic, and Toshiba; fax machines; every kind of small kitchen appliance; refrigerators; washers; and more. And while Bernie's is one of the few dealers left selling big-ticket items in midtown, prices remain at just about 10 percent above cost. Bernie himself related the story that employees of Kruger and Macy's were buying coffee machines here because his prices were better than what their own employee discounts afforded. Bernie's is also a great place to get camcorders and blank video tapes at discount prices. The salespeople at Bernie's put no pressure on you -- they know the prices will do the work. Plus, it's always so busy that they don't have time to hassle you. Still, when you are ready to order, they'll give you all the time and attention you need.

BLOOM & KRUP
504 East 14th Street (between Avenues A & B), New York NY 10009. 212/673-2760. **World Wide Web address:** http://www. bloomandkrup.com. **Description:** What began as a basic hardware store back in 1928 has grown to become one of the city's most complete appliance and furniture centers, selling lots of big-name brands at discount prices. They have items large and small for every room in the house. Whether you're looking for a 12-cubic foot Whirlpool refrigerator (retail price $649.00, here $519.00), a 26-inch RCA color TV ($200.00 below retail at $499.00), or a La-Z-Boy recliner (from just $299.00), chances are you'll find it at Bloom & Krup. There are several large showrooms; the store seems to go on and on. In the front, you'll find all the kitchen appliances, like a Welbilt 550-watt microwave oven for $119.00 or a Whirlpool washer for $399.00. But wait, there's more! Head upstairs to the furniture area for beds, mattresses, sofas, and chairs, all at discount prices. You may find a Whitman and Clark loveseat that opens up into a bed, $100.00 off at $449.00. One recent closeout featured a Simmons Maxipedic twin mattress and box spring set for just $299.00. Kitchen tables are here too, like a simple model topped in black or butcher-block formica for $140.00, including two ice-cream parlor chairs. The service here is impeccable; the sales staff will work with you to find just what you need to fit your home's dimensions, and they don't mind if you're just looking. Open Sunday, 11:00 a.m. - 4:00 p.m.; Monday through Saturday, 9:00 a.m. - 6:00 p.m.

EBA WHOLESALE CORPORATION

2361 Nostrand Avenue (at Avenue J), Brooklyn NY 11210. 718/252-3400. **Toll-free phone:** 800/380-2378. **Description:** They do seem to have everything at EBA (Electronics-Bedding-Appliances), from small appliances such as toasters and blenders, to every major appliance by big brand names like GE and Whirlpool. How would you like to save $100.00 or more on an extra-large Maytag washing machine? How about similar savings on a Friederich air conditioner (come on, we all know how hot the Big Apple can be in the summer)? As part of a dealer buying group, EBA is able to get great deals on any appliance and, in turn, pass the savings on to you. Sounds simple enough. Now you're probably wondering what the catch is, right?. Well here's the great part: there is none! All products carry a full manufacturer's warranty, and EBA is an authorized dealer for every product that they carry. They also offer a 30-day price guarantee; if you can find the same item at a lower price within 30 days of your purchase, EBA will pay you double the difference. Really, you've got nothing to lose. EBA carries a full line of electronics and video products too. And let's not forget the "B" in EBA; EBA carries quality orthopedic bedding, and they've just begun carrying furniture as well. The huge (it would have to be), modern showroom is open seven days a week.

GRINGER & SONS INC.

29 First Avenue, New York NY 10003. 212/475-0600. **E-mail address:** gringerman@aol.com. **World Wide Web address:** http://www.gringer.baweb.com. **Description:** For more than 80 years, the Gringer family has been offering Big Applers some very big discounts on major brand appliances. Step inside this showroom to find great prices on refrigerators, dishwashers, air conditioners, washer/dryers, and everything in between by top brand names like Westinghouse, GE, and Maytag. Daily specials bring the prices down to decidedly one of the lowest in the five boroughs.

KRUP'S KITCHEN & BATH

11 West 18th Street, New York NY 10001. 212/243-KRUP. **World Wide Web address:** http://www.krups.baweb.com. **Description:** If you're looking to renovate or refurbish your kitchen or bathroom, Krup's is the place. Krup's offers everyday low prices on major kitchen and bath appliances and hardware including sinks, tubs, dishwashers, refrigerators, and stoves. And Krup's carries all the major brand names including Kohler, American Standard, Friederich, and GE.

P.C. RICHARD AND SON

576 86th Street, Brooklyn NY 11209. 718/745-7300. ♦ 450 Kings Highway, Brooklyn NY. 718/382-5006. ♦ 2259 Ralph Avenue (at Avenue M), Brooklyn NY. 718/968-9631. ♦ 113-14 Queens Boulevard (at 76th Avenue), Queens NY. 718/896-6822. ♦ 103-54 94th Street, Queens NY. 718/848-6700. ♦ 92-63 Queens Boulevard (at Woodhaven Boulevard), Queens NY. 718/268-8155. **World Wide Web address:** http://www. pcrichard.homeappliance. com. **Description:** Long established on

Long Island, P.C. Richard and Son eventually made its way into Brooklyn and Queens through wide-scale expansion. Each store has a huge selection of appliances for the home, and you can save big bucks on such big-ticket items as refrigerators, dishwashers, gas ranges, washers and dryers. They carry all major brands, sometimes featuring special sales on a particular manufacturer. A recent sale found all General Electric items at reduced prices, including a 20.7 cubic-foot refrigerator for $650.00 and an 800-watt microwave/convection oven for $380.00. P.C. Richard and Son guarantees to match the lowest advertised price you can find (even after your purchase) for as long as you own the product. Why not take them up on the offer?

SHOPPING
 Books: New & Used

ACADEMY BOOK STORE
10 West 18th Street, New York NY 10011. 212/242-4848. **Description:** The Flatiron District of lower Fifth Avenue is a great area for used bookstores. Academy can keep you happily browsing for hours. Academy looks almost like a regular bookstore; it's big and bright with good sections on the arts, history, poetry, and philosophy. Most are hardcovers, selling for half the original cover price or less; Mr. C found the hefty *Oxford Companion to the American Theatre*, like new, half-price at $25.00. Also, the companion book to the television series *The Civil War* was reduced from $50.00 to just $15.00.

DROUGAS BOOKS
34 Carmine Street, New York NY 10014. 212/229-0079. **Description:** If this small but surprising shop in Greenwich Village could cast itself as a book, it might be titled *The Little Politically Correct Engine That Could*. With tongue in cheek, Drougas refers to its wares as un-oppressive, non-imperialist discount books. Yes, these do include extensive selections in international relations, philosophy, poetry, and the like; but there are also books on movies and the arts, fiction, travel, and the rest of the sections you'd find in any bookstore. All of these are overstocks at very low prices, with special tables of $3.00 books.

GRYPHON BOOKS & RECORDS
2246 Broadway (between 80th & 81st Streets), New York NY 10024. 212/362-0706. **Description:** A visit to Gryphon Books & Records is like a trip back to the 19th century -- a narrow, handsome shop lined from floor to ceiling with dark wood shelves, rolling ladders, and books on every subject imaginable. Most of these are used, in both paperback and hardcover, and many are rare; especially those in the mezzanine gallery. On my visit, there was a great selection of well-priced African-American writings by Richard Wright, Maya Angelou, and Terry McMillan. A useful section of travel guides were selling for $3.00 apiece. Gryphon also has a large collection of used records and tapes including rock, jazz, and classical selections. Most are priced between $5.00 and $10.00. Mr. C even saw a five-album boxed set of Glenn Miller hits for $15.00. If you like to riffle, this shop (right across from Zabar's) is a good find. Open daily, 10:00 a.m. - 12:00 a.m.

JULIAN'S BOOKS
110 West 25th Street, 9th Floor, New York NY 10001. 212/929-3620. **Toll-free phone:** 888/467-3481. **E-mail address:** julianbook@aol.com. **World Wide Web address:** http://www.julianbook.com. **Description:** Looking for rare and collectible books? This place has a great selection at affordable prices (depending on how rare you want to get). Julian's offers

first, signed, and limited editions... lots for under $50.00. Recently on the shelves: a signed and inscribed copy of Frank McCourt's *Angela's Ashes* ($85.00); a first edition of *Jazz* by Toni Morrison ($40.00); and Margaret Atwood's *Bluebeard's Egg*, also a first edition ($40.00). Open daily, 10:00 a.m. - 6:00 p.m.

MANHATTAN BOOKS

150 Chambers Street, New York NY 10007. 212/385-7395. **Description:** Near Greenwich Street and the campus of Manhattan Community College, Manhattan Books sells used textbooks for about 25 percent less than what you would pay in a college bookstore. A used copy of *The Norton Introduction to Literature by Women* ($30.00 if new) sells for $22.00 here. New editions, including general paperbacks, are discounted by about $1.00 off the cover price; same deal on shelves of used Penguin editions of Shakespeare plays and other literature. You'll also find lots of used computer books at 50 percent off, along with bins of old magazines. Open Monday and Thursday, 9:00 a.m. - 7:00 p.m.; Wednesday, 9:00 a.m. - 8:00 p.m.; Friday, 9:00 a.m. - 6:00 p.m.; Saturday, 11:00 a.m. - 4:00 p.m.

MURDER INK

2486 Broadway (at 92nd Street), New York NY 10025. 212/362-8905. **Toll-free phone:** 800/488-8123. **World Wide Web address:** http://www.murderink.com. **Description:** It really pays to be a mystery-lover in New York, as stores catering to the who-dunnit-crowd are in abundance. Murder Ink is a store for not only those who love to read mysteries, but for those who love to collect them as well. The store has a variety of rare, out-of-print, and signed books. For those who are just looking to read a good mystery, the sales staff will be more than happy to recommend something to you. And prices are more than reasonable; a paperback will run you right around the $6.00 - $7.00 range. How about Jessica Fletcher's *Murder at the Powderhorn Ranch* for $5.99, M. C. Beaton's *Death of a Scriptwriter* for $6.50, or Mary Higgins Clark's *You Belong to Me* for $7.99? Open Sunday, 11:00 a.m. -6:00 p.m.; Monday through Saturday, 10:00 a.m. - 7:30 p.m.

MYSTERIOUS BOOK SHOP

129 West 56th Street (between Avenue of the Americas & Seventh Avenue), New York NY 10019-3808. 212/765-0900. **Description:** It's no mystery why this bookstore is so popular. For lovers of this genre, new and old, this place delivers. Mysterious Book Shop stocks more than 20,000 new, used, and rare titles, with finds in every price range. They also offer a free bookfinding service so, if that rare title you've been looking for is not in stock, they'll try their hardest to find it for you. If you can't get there in person, they issue a free monthly 40-page newsletter listing new books, autographings, and more. Open Monday through Saturday, 11:00 a.m. - 7:00 p.m.

POSMAN BOOKS

One University Place, New York NY 10003. 212/533-2665. ◆ 70 Fifth Avenue (at 13th Street), New York NY 10011. 212/633-2525. ◆ Grand Central Terminal (Vanderbilt Ramp & 42nd Street),

New York NY 10017. 212/983-1111. **World Wide Web address:** http://www.posmanbooks.com. **Description:** Posman Books has become one of the city's top choices for the best in learned literature. With strategic locations near NYU and New School University (the Fifth Avenue location actually serves as the New School's official bookstore), students in particular are drawn to the fantastic selection of academic literature (in a number of different languages, no less) at reasonable prices. The University Place location offers a weekly reading series, and the Grand Central Terminal location does the same. Stop in or call for the most up-to-date schedule of happenings.

RUBY'S BOOK SALE
119 Chambers Street, New York NY 10007. 212/732-8676. **Description:** Ruby's is a downtown mecca for discounts on new and used books and magazines. The new books, sold from open tables, are mostly overstocks and slightly damaged books with review copies thrown into the mix. They include computer, reference, home repair, and children's books, along with art, cooking, and many other subjects. Used paperbacks, sold at half price, and back issue magazines sold at 40 percent off the cover price round out the stock.

SKYLINE BOOKS AND RECORDS
13 West 18th Street, New York NY 10011. 212/759-5463. **Description:** When similar stores gather themselves together, it's good for business and great for shoppers. Skyline Books and Records complements Academy Books (see separate listing) just across the street, rather than competing with it. After all, you never know where that one lost title may turn up. Skyline is cramped and winding, like an eccentric old library, with a vast selection in all subjects, fun and serious. You'll find hardcovers and paperbacks mixed together, at good prices. The record room, way in the back, has lots of well-worn LPs in rock, jazz, and classical music. They start as low as $.75, but most are in the $4.00 - $9.00 range. In good weather you can browse the bins outside the shop, a cherished New York tradition.

THE STRAND BOOKSTORE
828 Broadway (at 12th Street), New York NY 10003. 212/473-1452. **Description:** The Strand is widely known as the mother of all discount book stores, and it well deserves the title. So many titles are here, in fact, that it looks as if several local libraries decided to sell everything off. The sign says, "Eight Miles of Books"; Mr. C says "start jogging". For starters, browse the racks outside the shop; they're filled with fiction and nonfiction, hardcover and soft, for $1.00 and $2.00 apiece. Many are a mere $.48, or five for $2.00. Once inside, you'll find the recent overstocks and publishers' clearances. Mr. C noted David McCullough's best-selling bio of Harry Truman, originally $30.00, reduced to $23.00; and Anne Rice's *Cry to Heaven* in paper for just $4.00. Save $11.00 on a boxed set of Art Speigelman's clever and harrowing *Maus* books, here $25.95. Martin Gottfried's *More Broadway Musicals*, filled with oversized, glossy color photos, sells here for

$45.00, down from $60.00. Move further into the art section and perhaps you'll findsomething like a $70.00 edition on the works of Georges Seurat, for as little as $52.95. And then you come to the shelves and shelves of general categories -- the library part -- with discounted books on every subject: history, drama, politics, science fiction, computer manuals, poetry, television, and everything in between. But wait, there's more! Downstairs, they continue with all the subjects that couldn't fit on the huge main floor. Then there are shelves and shelves of reviewers' copies, tons of recent novels, and other releases in every subject at a straight 50 percent off cover price. Also, this area has the hurt books section, with slightly damaged bindings and such, for up to 80 percent off. You can even find various -- vintage? -- phone books for sale here. The third floor houses rare and antiquarian books, not cheap, but considered to be reasonable amongst collectors' editions. Many are signed editions. The Strand has information desks on each floor, where helpful clerks can assist you in looking up titles. Look for their outdoor bookstalls in parks around town, too. Open Sunday, 11:00 a.m. - 10:30 p.m.; Monday through Saturday, 9:30 a.m. - 10:30 p.m.

TRAVELER'S CHOICE BOOKSTORE

2 Wooster Street, New York NY 10012. 212/941-1535. **Description:** Planning a trip outside of the Big Apple? Then you should probably plan a trip to Traveler's Choice Bookstore, where you'll find everything you need to make your trip great. Travel guides, maps, videos, and language tapes are just a few of the conveniences you'll find here, all at 10 percent below list price. Traveler's Choice Bookstore also offers Tenba travel bags at a discount. So, before you hop aboard that plane, make sure you're prepared with a visit to Traveler's Choice.

SHOPPING

CDs, Records, Tapes, & Videos

ACADEMY RECORDS & CDs
12 West 18th Street, New York NY 10011. 212/242-3000. **E-mail address:** staff@academy-records.com. **World Wide Web address:** http://www.academy-records.com. **Description:** Right next door to the Academy Bookstore (see separate listing), you can continue saving at Academy Records & CDs. This little shop is always crowded with only the finest of music connoisseurs. Academy carries a large stock of classical, pop, jazz, rock, soul, and blues CDs and LPs. Records are priced from $2.00 - $5.00, while CDs are mostly in the $6.00 - $9.00 range. An extensive selection of opera, orchestral and early music recordings are arranged according to composer, artist, and label. With the backup of a helpful and knowledgeable staff, you should be able to find that treasured record. Open Sunday, 11:00 a.m. - 7:00 p.m.; Monday through Saturday, 9:30 a.m. - 9:00 p.m.

DISC-O-RAMA MUSIC WORLD
186 West 4th Street (between Avenue of the Americas & Seventh Avenue), New York NY 10014. 212/206-8417. ♦ Annex Outlet, 40 Union Square East (between 16th & 17th Streets), New York NY. 212/260-8616. ♦ Classical, Used, & Clearance Outlet, 146 West 4th Street (between Avenue of the Americas & MacDougal Street), New York NY. 212/477-9410. **Description:** To say that the main location of Disc-O-Rama is the most expensive one is kind of ironic. At Disc-O-Rama Music World, you'll find new and used CDs, records, tapes, and DVDs, all at unbeatable prices. Where else could you pay under $10.00 for a brand-new CD? Not too many places that I know of, I can assure you of that. For even better deals (yes, they *do* get better), walk a few steps to the Disc-O-Rama Classical, Used, & Clearance Outlet where CDs start at just $5.00. The Annex Outlet offers similarly great bargains. The main store is open Sunday, 11:30 a.m. - 8:00 p.m.; Monday through Thursday, 10:30 a.m. - 10:30 p.m.; Friday, 10:30 a.m. - 11:30 p.m.; Saturday, 10:00 a.m. - 12:30 a.m. The Annex Outlet is open Sunday, 11:00 a.m. - 5:45 p.m.; Monday and Tuesday, 8:30 a.m. - 6:15 p.m.; Wednesday through Friday, 8:30 a.m. - 6:45 p.m.; Saturday, 10:00 a.m. - 6:00 p.m.. Disc-O-Rama's Classical, Used, & Clearance Center is open Sunday, 11:00 a.m. - 8:00 p.m.; Monday through Thursday, 10:00 a.m. - 10:00 p.m.; Friday and Saturday, 10:00 a.m. - 11:00 p.m.

FOOTLIGHT RECORDS
113 East 12th Street, New York NY 10003. 212/533-1572. **World Wide Web address:** http://www.footlight.com. **Description:** Footlight houses one of the city's most extensive selections of show tunes, movie soundtracks, spoken word, and similar recordings -- both American and imported. It's a very impressive shop indeed. Rare albums are priced around $15.00, but you'll find

lots at lower prices. Footlight does buy and sell, so you will find tapes and CDs, mixed in with the vinyl and you will find some rock and pop sections as well. It's definitely worth the trip to look around.

KIM'S UNDERGROUND
144 Bleecker Street (between Thompson Street & La Guardia Place), New York NY 10012. 212/260-1010. ◆ Kim I, 85 Avenue A (between 5th & 6th Streets), New York NY 10009. 212/529-3410. ◆ Kim's West, 350 Bleecker Street, New York NY 10014. 212/675-8996. ◆ Mondo Kim's, 6 St. Marks Place, New York NY. 212/505-0311. **Description:** Kim has made quite a name for herself around New York City. With four stores, each with a different twist and/or specialty, Kim's offers a wide selection of hard to find music and movies. Kim's Underground specializes in new and used records, tapes, and CDs. The selection is geared toward avant-garde. Open daily, 9:00 a.m. - 12:00 a.m. Kim I is one of the last remaining stores that carries laserdiscs for sale and rental. If you have yet to jump on the DVD bandwagon, you better make a quick trip to Kim I before these oldies but goodies are all but obsolete. Open daily, 9:00 a.m. - 12:00 a.m. (until 1:00 a.m. on Friday and Saturday). Kim's West offers a wide range of rare and out of print videos, laserdiscs, and books. Open daily, 9:00 a.m. - 12:00 a.m. Mondo Kim's is just that; it offers the biggest selection of all the Kim's stores. Three floors of pure, non-mainstream bliss make this place a heavily-traveled area. The first floor offers a large selection of new and used compact discs and plays gracious host to the occasional live performance. The second floor is record heaven with used LPs (and movies). The third floor is reserved for video rentals, though you will find a unique laserdisc and comic book selection (for purchase). Open daily, 9:00 a.m. - 12:00 a.m. So if you've been looking for a truly obscure record, CD, video, or laserdisc, there's no excuse not to check with Kim (there *are* four locations after all).

N.Y.C.D.
426 Amsterdam Avenue (between 80th & 81st Streets), New York NY 10024. 212/724-4466. **World Wide Web address:** http://www.nycd.baweb.com. **Description:** Someone better call the *NYPD*, because I've never seen such steals. If you have only dared to dream of a place where CDs start at just $1.99, step into reality, because this is the place where dreams come true. Besides CDs, N.Y.C.D. also offers great deals on used DVDs. Open Monday through Thursday, 10:00 a.m. - 11:00 p.m.; Friday and Saturday, 10:00 a.m. - 12:00 a.m.; Sunday, 11:00 a.m. - 10:00 p.m.

REBEL REBEL RECORDS
319 Bleecker Street, New York NY 10014. 212/989-0770. **Description:** The Bowie reference in this store's name tells you what you need to know: they specialize in rock. That includes alternative sounds and current dance styles such as trip hop. Lots of new and used LPs are priced from $.99, and CDs range from

$1.98 to $9.98. It's a small store, but they certainly manage to pack in a good selection.

RECORD EXPLOSION
142 West 34th Street, New York NY 10001. 212/714-0450. ◆ 176 Broadway, New York NY. 212/693-1510. ◆ 507 Fifth Avenue (between 42nd & 43rd Streets), New York NY. 212/661-6642. **Description:** This discount chain has standard prices on current-release rock and pop music. What is more interesting to Mr. C is their huge stock of closeout bargains. They have table after table of cassette tapes priced at three for $10.00; these are not your usual "never-heard-of-'em" bands, but lots of big names like the Beatles, Genesis, and Motown artists galore. Lots of classical CDs are on hand for as little as $3.99 apiece too. The store also has tons of new and previously viewed movies from $3.99 - $9.99. Mr. C picked up a number of new releases, obviously snatched up from a video rental shelf (it was the "Please Be Kind. Rewind." sticker that tipped me off) for $3.99 apiece. DVDs are well priced too, though the selection is not quite as expansive as the VHS. If you're just browsing, a great thing they do -- besides categorize by genre -- is separate movies by actor and actress.

ROCK'S IN YOUR HEAD
157 Prince Street, New York NY 10012. 212/475-6729. **Description:** A used record shop in SoHo? What's the world coming to? Well, you'll be coming to this store for a small but good variety of music -- mostly rock & roll (naturally). Top-line used CDs go for $7.99 and $8.99; many others are priced at $5.00 each, or three for $10.00. There are some LPs and cassettes as well, but space is limited here, so there's not as much to choose from.

SECOND COMING RECORDS
235 Sullivan Street, New York NY 10012. 212/228-1313. **Description:** Tucked away in a relatively quiet section of the Village, Second Coming has a large selection of used music. Most CDs range from $4.99 to $7.99; New discs are blended in too and are usually priced around $12.00. Cassettes generally go for $2.99 - $4.99. I spotted the Rolling Stones' *Under Cover* for $3.99. And records, of course, are plentiful. Joe Jackson's *Night and Day* was spotted, in good condition, for $2.99. Second Coming also has a good variety of music videos, most of which are in the vicinity of $19.99 or thereabouts.

SECOND HAND ROSE'S RECORD SHOP
525 Avenue of the Americas (at 14th Street), New York NY 10011. 212/675-3735. **Description:** Vinyl is not dead! Of the city's many used music shops, few have as many good old LP record albums as Second Hand Rose's (which, rightfully, has been around for 25 years). The owner is clearly a jazz aficionado, lining the walls with bookcases stuffed with well-worn but well-loved records. Most of these are priced from $7.99 to $9.99 -- not as cheap as the records in other secondhand shops, but then, many of these titles have gone out of print. Along with jazz of all strains, Rose's is

great for soul, R&B, and oldies. And they do have other formats, with most cassettes for $4.99 and $5.99, and compact discs as low as $3.99. For higher-priced CDs, you can get a further discount when you purchase three or more.

SMASH COMPACT DISCS
33 St. Mark's Place, New York NY 10003. 212/473-2200. **Description:** That's not a suggestion, it's the name of this well-stocked shop. Smash has a whole wall of used CDs, mostly rock with some jazz and country mixed in; most of these are priced from $7.99 to $9.99. Mr. C found major albums by Van Morrison, R.E.M., Peter Gabriel, the Beatles, and many more. Even a double-length CD containing 20 hits by Sly and the Family Stone was only $11.99. This is definitely one of the best record shops in the East Village.

TLA VIDEO
52 West 8th Street (between Fifth Avenue & Avenue of the Americas), New York NY 10011. 212/228-8282. **World Wide Web address:** http://www.tlavideo.com. **Description:** TLA's first venture out of the City of Brotherly Love has proven to be a fruitful one. Their Greenwich Village digs have rustled up a bit of excitement from non-mainstream film lovers throughout the city. Originally conceived as an experimental theater group in the early sixties (which included the likes of fellow *Taxi*ers Danny DeVito and Judd Hirsch), TLA caught on to the video craze and opened their first store in 1985. Yet, it wasn't until recently that they branched outside of Pennsylvania. TLA both rents and sells one of the largest collections of independent, foreign, and art films and documentaries anywhere. They *do* carry new releases, but that is not what makes this place so great. What makes it so noteworthy is the selection and the staff (think you know a thing or two about movies? I dare you to try and stump one of these employees). All genres are represented, from the earliest in silent films (*The Birth of a Nation, Battleship Potemkin*); to film noir classics (*Double Indemnity, The Lady From Shanghai*); to New Hollywood landmarks (*Easy Rider, Mean Streets*). Whether you've been looking for that hard to find Barbara Kopple documentary (*American Dream, Harlan County USA*), or those cult heroes from Tromaville (*The Toxic Avenger, Sgt. Kabukiman*), TLA will not let you down. If you're just in the city for a visit, stop in to browse for some good buys. If you live in the city, however, I strongly suggest that you get yourself a membership. For even more free fun, visit TLA's Website. With a seemingly infinite selection of videos and DVDs, and an awful lot of exciting film info (TLA has actually published two books as well), you're sure to find hours of fun. Each month, they even showcase (and discount) one particular director who has made an impact on the film industry. Now I don't know about you, but I consider any place that devotes an entire month to celebrating the work of John Cassavetes an estimable establishment. Open daily, 10:00 a.m. - 12:00 a.m.

TOWER RECORDS CLEARANCE OUTLET

20 East 4th Street, New York NY 10012. 212/228-7317. **World Wide Web address:** http://www.towerrecords.com. **Description:** Right around the corner from Tower Record's main megaplex, on the corner of Lafayette Street, is their Clearance Outlet. Here they sell closeouts and overstocks in all media -- records, cassettes, CDs, and videotapes -- and all genres from rock to jazz to classical. These are unused, in their original packaging. Most CDs are just $5.99 to $7.99, with LPs and tapes a bit lower. Twelve-inch dance singles are as low as $.49. In the classical section they have the entire Aurophon series of compact discs for $2.99 each, and opera cassettes for $3.99. This extensive section is arranged by composer, with as much to choose from as any full-price store. In the soundtrack area, Mr. C found a two-record set of the complete *Les Miserables* soundtrack for $5.99. Speaking of soundtracks, Tower has tons of pre-viewed VHS movies too; including such titles as *Rain Man*, *E.T.*, and *The Accidental Tourist*. Well-loved lder movie classics (in glorious black and white) are under $10.00. Back in the music section, you can also find an "As Is" final sale display with records and tapes as low as $1.99; along with various music storage racks, like a 15-cassette carrying case for $2.49. Open daily, 9:00 a.m. - 12:00 a.m.

TRITON

247 Bleecker Street (between Avenue of the Americas & Seventh Avenue), New York NY. 212/243-3610. **Description:** Triton deals mainly in CDs, with some good prices on used and unused discs. Most jazz titles and new classical CDs sell for under $10.00. There is also a good selection of used CDs in all categories, mostly $4.99 to $7.99, as well as some new and used cassettes. They also offer a wide selection of laserdisc titles at as much as half the price of other retail outlets. Triton carries a good selection of CD-ROMs as well. If you can't get into the store, call or send for a catalog; Triton does lots of business by mail order. Open Sunday, 12:00 p.m. - 10:00 p.m.; Monday through Thursday, 11:00 a.m. - 11:00 p.m.; Friday, 11:00 a.m. - 12:00 a.m.; Saturday, 11:00 a.m. - 1:00 a.m.

SHOPPING
 Clothing: Children's & Junior's

GOOD-BYES
230 East 78th Street, New York NY 10021. 212/794-2301.
Description: Good-Byes is a children's consignment shop, selling
high-quality clothing and accessories for infants through size 6.
Recent items included lots of coats and snowsuits, for boys and
girls, most in the $10.00 - $15.00 range. Everything has been
cleaned, and it's all in great condition. They even have books and
toys. Considering how soon youngsters outgrow their clothing,
consignment stores are a great way to keep your investments down
as your kids grow up.

KIDS ARE MAGIC
2293 Broadway, New York NY 10024. 212/875-9240. **Description:**
Well, you'll certainly think so when you see what kind of discounts
they can get you on clothing. This large, fun place -- with two
levels of dazzling displays -- sells most major brands of children's
clothing at 40 - 60 percent below retail prices. Sizes range from
infants' clothing, up to boys' size 20 and girls' size 14. It's like a
whole department store. Kids Are Magic has a 12-day return policy
(with receipt) for cash, credit, or exchange; and the salespeople
are quite friendly and helpful. Open daily.

NEW YORK CITY KIDS (NYCK)
495 Seventh Avenue, New York NY 10018. 212/868-NYCK. **World
Wide Web address:** http://www.nyck.net. **Description:** And just
what does it mean to be a New York City Kid? In the case of this
clothing store, it means being on the cutting edge of fashion.
NYCK offers the best names in clothing, shoes, and accessories
for your kids at affordable prices. For your biker baby, you can
pick up a leather Harley Davidson jacket, normally priced at
$80.00, for just $55.00. For the boys, Nautica jeans are a steal at
$19.99 (usually $32.00). NYCK offers girls a variety of pant and
skirt sets to save the aggravation of having to match styles and
colors. Pick up a pair of stylish flare jeans with a cute sweater set
for $35.99 (retails at $45.00). For that upcoming wedding or first
communion, NYCK offers a full line of children's formal wear. A
four-piece suit, which would sell elsewhere for $90.00, was seen
at NYCK for just $69.99. And an adorable pint-sized tuxedo (with
tails) was seen for $49.99. Girls' special occasion dresses, which
would sell for $120.00 or more at any department store, were
selling here for $69.99. Accessories included $4.99 ties and
$19.99 veils. NYCK has a large selection of footwear by many of
the same designers that mom and dad are wearing. All Kenneth
Cole shoes had $5.00 knocked off the price tag (priced around
$50.00 a pair), as did shoes by Donna Karan. You can pick up a
stylish pair of Skechers for around $25.00 - $30.00 a pair, and

Hush Puppies were selling for about $35.00 - $40.00. If you prefer to garb the kids in Italian leather, the prices on Enzo shoes cannot be beat. How about an all-leather zip up boot, originally priced at $90.00, for just $39.99?

RACHEL'S BOUTIQUE
4218 13th Avenue (at 43rd Street), Brooklyn NY 11219. 718/435-6875. **Description:** First of all, Rachel's has kids clothing. Then they have more kids clothing. The old woman who lived in the shoe couldn't begin to make a dent in this stock, as it's truly a vast amount. At Rachel's you can outfit your child completely from head to toe, from underwear to outerwear and everything in between, for very little money. Check out the prices in Rachel's exclusive layette department; or pick up a christening or first communion outfit at discount. Need to find some eveningwear for your little darling? Not a problem, Rachel has got that too. Sizes run infant through size 16 girls, and infant through size 20 boys. The prices here are like those of the Orchard Street shops -- appropriate enough, since this area of Brooklyn has much in common with the Lower East Side. And, like that area, the shops in this Old World neighborhood close up early on Friday and reopen on Sunday. Hours are Sunday through Thursday, 10:00 a.m. - 6:00 p.m. (call for Friday hours).

SHOPPING
👜 Clothing: Consignment/Resale 👜

ALLAN & SUZI
416 Amsterdam Avenue (at 80th Street), New York NY 10024.
212/724-7445. **Description:** This is quite a place. Allan & Suzi
resells dressy women's fashions by the really big designers like
Bob Mackie (you know, the one who barely dresses Cher), John
Paul Gaultier, and Isabelle Allard. One dress, which originally sold
for $3,600.00, was seen here for $1,000.00. If that's still out of
your range, there are even less expensive designs, like a classy
black sequined gown for $80.00. Just about everything in the
store is dramatic; movie stars and the people who costume them
shop here frequently. The store sells a good stock of new clothes
from past seasons too for as much as 70 percent off the original
prices. Allan & Suzi will also work with you to complete the outfit,
perhaps with a pair of $900.00 earrings for just $275.00. If you
want to make a bold statement, or just have a lot of fun, drop into
this Upper West Side boutique.

DOMSEY INTERNATIONAL SALES CORPORATION
431 Kent Avenue, Brooklyn NY 11211. 718/384-6000. **World Wide
Web address:** http://www.domsey.com. **Description:** While
Domsey is not really a consignment shop, it's not really a vintage
shop either. The company operates a warehouse outlet at this site
where you will find Levi's jeans, tuxes, bathrobes, imported
military wear, cosmetics and accessories. Domsey also offers a
wide selection of vintage clothing that has been recycled, and lets
customers purchase clothing-by-the-pound. Open Sunday, 11:00
a.m. - 5:30 p.m.; Monday - Friday, 8:00 a.m. - 5:30 p.m.; Saturday,
8:00 a.m. - 6:30 p.m.

ENCORE
1132 Madison Avenue (at 84th Street), 2nd Floor, New York NY
10028. 212/879-2850. **Description:** Encore, opened in 1954, was
the nation's first resale clothing store. This packed shop sells
barely-used designer clothing at a fraction of their original prices.
An ivory-colored wool sweater by Ungaro (with a $700.00 Saks
price tag still on it) was being sold here for a mere $200.00. New
and unworn clothes are the exception, of course. Other items seen
included an Anne Klein wool dress for $50.00, and splashy cocktail
dresses in various colors by major designers, most from $200.00
to $300.00. Encore is unusual in the resale business in that it has
some men's clothes, too. Mr. C found a navy blue cashmere
overcoat for $90.00, and a Rodier sweater for $45.00. Get on
Encore's mailing list, and they'll notify you of special clearance
sales where you can find even better bargains.

LA BOUTIQUE RESALE
1045 Madison Avenue (at 80th Street), 2nd Floor, New York NY
10021. 212/517-8099. **Description:** If you love designer clothes,

but can't quite afford the designer price tag, the Upper East Side's La Boutique Resale may be just what you are looking for. With more than 2,000 items in stock, La Boutique buys and sells only the most current and pristine-condition clothing. Many of these items arrive with the original price tags still intact, and the rest have only been worn maybe a handful of times. So, just what can you expect to see here? Expect top designer names like Fendi, Dolce & Gabbana, Versace, Donna Karan, Calvin Klein, and Michael Kors; anticipate racks of clothing for both men and women, along with a great selection of shoes and accessories too. But don't expect to pay $10.00 for an Armani suit. Remember, while we are talking *resale*, we're still talking *upscale*! A variety of Chanel suits, in the latest colors and styles, were seen for $600.00 - $700.00. Too rich for your blood? How about a great women's Gucci pantsuit for $350.00? If you can't live without designer clothing and are willing to shell out a little bit more to get them at discount, La Boutique delivers. Open Sunday, 12:00 p.m. - 6:00 p.m.; Monday through Saturday, 11:00 a.m. - 7:00 p.m. (until 8:00 p.m. on Thursday).

RITZ FURS
107 West 57th Street, New York NY 10019. 212/265-4559. **E-mail address:** info@inetny.com. **World Wide Web address:** http;//www.inetny.com. **Description:** For over 50 years, Ritz has been reselling top-quality fur coats at a fraction of their original cost. Actually, they prefer the phrase, "gently pre-owned". Customers come from all over the world to bargain shop here, regularly trading in one style for another. This ensures a large and ever-changing variety of mink, sable, beaver, fox, and more. Ritz also gets new, current-season coats from other furriers. Each item is one of a kind; recently on the racks were a Pierre Cardin raccoon jacket for $295.00, and a Dior mink coat (originally $8,000.00) for $2,900.00. A jet-black rabbit fur jacket by Fendi was selling for $1,000.00. Ritz also has a special collection of cashmere, wool, and microfiber coats that are trimmed and lined with fur (some you can even customize yourself). Service is personal without being high-pressured. Mr. *C*, who does not even come close to looking like a fur coat type, was greeted just as readily as anyone else coming through the door.

TOKIO 7
64 East 7th Street, New York NY 10003. 212/353-8443. **World Wide Web address:** http://tokio7.com. **Description:** If you're looking for fashions that are super-funky, yet appropriate enough for public consumption, then head on over to the East Village's Tokio 7. With the brightest of the brights and the hippest of the hips, you'll find oh-so-funky (but definitely wearable) fashions by the likes of some top name designers like Vivienne Westwood and Helmut Lang. Didn't think they made funky clothing? Check out the selection at Tokio 7 and you'll see that yes, indeed they do. While the prices might be higher than you'd expect to pay at a plain old consignment or resale shop, let's not forget that we are

dealing with top of the line designers here. If that one piece you're admiring is still out of your price range, poke around a bit more... I'm sure you'll find a great an inexpensive piece! Open daily, 12:00 p.m. - 8:30 p.m.

SHOPPING
🏠 Clothing: Men's & Women's 🏠

AARON'S
627 Fifth Avenue (at 17th Street), Brooklyn NY 11215. 718/768-5400. **Toll-free phone:** 888/768-5400. **E-mail address:** info@aarons.com. **World Wide Web address:** http://www.aarons.com. **Description:** Here's one of the biggies: Aaron's is one of those places you have to go outside of Manhattan to find, and it is truly one-of-a-kind. Because they don't have a high midtown rent or advertising costs, Aaron's can save you 20 - 50 percent on women's in-season designer fashions. These are big names, current styles, first quality goods. There are no damaged or irregular items (intentionally) selling here. They carry more than 100 brand names in clothing and accessories. Throughout the year, they offer special promotions like free handbag giveaways. Still, even if you don't walk away with a free gift, you'll definitely walk away with some money in your pocket. Aaron's has even got a comfy waiting area for your not-so-enthusiastic shopping companions complete with coffee, tea, snacks, and reading materials. There are even lots of games and children's books to keep your tiniest companions happy. The store is open late on Thursdays (until 9:00 p.m.), otherwise until 6:00 p.m., and closed Sundays. There's lots of free parking across the street.

BOLTON'S
90 Broad Street, New York NY. 212/785-0513. ◆ 4 East 34th Street, New York NY. 212/684-3750. ◆ 110 West 51st Street, New York NY. 212/245-5227. ◆ 27 West 57th Street, New York NY. 212/935-4431. ◆ 1180 Madison Avenue (at 86th Street), New York NY. 212/722-4419. **Description:** "Flash! Bolton's brandishes big discounts in no-holds-barred battle to be best bargain chain!" Yes, Bolton's continues to expand its empire, as does Labels for Less (see separate listing), and the winner is -- you. Both have plenty of branches scattered about town, and both offer good bargains on designer clothing for ladies. Because of its relationships with the manufacturers, the store prefers not to advertise the names you'll find here; but trust Mr. C, they're top-notch and first-quality. A European-style blazer and skirt set, by a well-known name, was recently seen for just $149.00; a 100 percent silk running suit was $59.99. The clearance racks offer even further discounts, sometimes as much as 50 percent. Then there is the separate room filled with the real high-end names, with plenty of fancy evening wear. Bolton's is also great for accessories, like hats, gloves, scarves, and belts. Call for specific location hours.

BURLINGTON COAT FACTORY
45 Park Place, New York NY 10007. 212/571-2630. ◆ 707 Avenue of the Americas, New York NY. 212/229-1300. **World Wide Web**

address: http://www.coat.com. **Description:** If you're not too familiar with Burlington Coat Factory, don't make the mistake of many first-timers: they offer more than just coats! Since its founding several decades ago, Burlington Coat Factory has grown into one of the nation's largest (and most prolific) brand name discounters. While each store varies in selection, you're bound to find more than just a jacket or a pair of slacks. Everyday discounts of 25 - 60 percent keep customers coming back time and time again. When Burlington Coat Factory says they cater to every member of your family, they mean it! They offer clothing for infants, children, juniors, and grown-ups, and in a range of typically hard-to-fit sizes as well. They've got your fashion week covered with new and trendy looks will keep you looking your best in a board room, bar room, or ballroom. Call for specific location hours.

CANAL JEAN COMPANY

504 Broadway (between Spring & Broome Streets), New York NY 10012. 212/226-1130. **World Wide Web address:** http://www.canaljean.com. **Description:** Four floors and 50,000 square feet of clothing bargains make Canal Jean (yes, it used to be on Canal Street at one point) a must for the latest in hip clothing at low prices. In new clothes, hip always seems to include Levi's jeans; Canal claims to be the largest Levi's outlet in the city. Prices here start as low as $17.99 for the ever-popular 501 button-fly, and $26.99 for the basic zipper. From there it's on to dyed, Silver Tab, baggy, denim jackets, and the rest. First-quality leather fashions from baseball jackets to full-length coats are sold at up to 50 percent off including such makers as Schott, U-2, M. Julian and more. Some even begin at just $40.00. Other outerwear bargains include men's and women's trenchcoats for $30.00 and up. Ladies will love the mezzanine lingerie section, with dancewear, cotton tights at half-price, and some naughtily seductive stylings; not to mention dresses from $5.00 - $10.00 and up. Shoes are here too, including black patent-leather varieties as low as $30.00 to $40.00. It's an experience just to walk around and observe the scene. Downstairs, in the basement, Canal has upped the ante in what it's best known for: "Recycled Clothing" is what they call it. Hey, these days, that's the perfect way to think of these fashions. What they've done, you see, is renovated the basement into 15,000 square feet of new and used clothing bargains -- none of which is priced over $10.00. That's right. Wool overcoats, blazers, sweaters, dresses, skirts, military styles... you name it, they've probably got it, and the highest price you'll see is $10.00 per item. It's really huge, and lots of stuff is still in very good condition. Some of the clothing is new, too; closeouts and irregulars. And this doesn't even include the $.99 bargain bins, filled with accessories, hosiery, T-shirts, sleepwear, and more. The stuff keeps pouring in all the time, so check out the bargains whenever you can! Canal Jean Company is open seven days a week, 365 days a year. Open daily, 10:30 a.m. - 8:00 p.m.

DAFFY'S

111 Fifth Avenue (at 18th Street), New York NY. 212/529-4477. ◆ 1311 Broadway, New York NY. 212/736-4477. ◆ 335 Madison Avenue, New York NY. 212/557-4422. ◆ 125 East 57th Street, New York NY. 212/376-4477. **Description:** There's nothing daffy about shopping here -- unless you think it's crazy to save lots of money on designer clothing. The Fifth Avenue location has two floors of clothing bargains, both fancy and casual, for men, women and children. For the smart-looking exec type, there are lots of imported European suits and jackets. What would you think of paying $140.00 for a $560.00 suit? Mr. C found a Louis Raphael blazer, originally $430.00, selling here for $70.00. Cashmere sweaters were practically flying out the door with a price tag of just $65.00. On the women's side, a blazer by Semplice was reduced from $350.00 to just $50.00. Women will also like wool skirts by various designers starting at just $40.00 (some have retail prices as high as $170.00), and blouses for $6.00 and up. A Max Studio dress, originally retailing for $200.00, was seen here for an affordable $59.99. For the more adventurous type, take home a pair of leather pants (originally priced at $600) for just $119.00. Women's brand names include Anna Sui, Calvin Klein, and Cynthia Rowley. Returning to the guys, there are imported Italian wool sweaters marked down from $120.00 to $36.00; designer jeans reduced from $48.00 to $15.00; silk ties from Saks Fifth Avenue, originally $52.00, now just $14.00; and silk boxer shorts slimmed down from $20.00 to $12.00. Downstairs, along with more women's fashions, you'll find great sections for boys and girls at similar discounts. A young girl's velour party dress was reduced from $120.00 to $50.00, and a boy's fleece pullover from Italy, originally $140.00, was just $30.00. Open Sunday, 12:00 p.m. - 6:00 p.m.; Monday through Saturday, 10:00 a.m. - 9:00 p.m.

DE JANEIRO

420 Lexington Avenue (between 43rd & 44th Streets), New York NY 10170. 212/983-8933. **Description:** Like many of the other women's off-price stores mentioned in this book, the clothes at De Janeiro seem to cater to a more youthful crowd; but that doesn't mean that there's not something for everyone. Newly-arrived skirts, pants, and tops were all priced around $15.00 each. Some career separates were also well-priced; a silk Ann Taylor dress, originally priced at $150.00, was seen here for $50.00. Just in time for winter, leather coats by Colebrook & Co. were 50 percent off their original prices for an affordable $99.00. Upstairs, there's a large selection of shoes. Make your way to the back for the best prices. These racks offer deep discounts on footwear by many of today's most popular designers including DKNY, Steve Madden, Enzo Angiolini, and Nine West. Open Sunday, 11:00 a.m. - 5:00 p.m.; Monday through Friday, 8:00 a.m. - 8:00 p.m.; Saturday, 11:00 a.m. - 5:00 p.m.

EISENBERG & EISENBERG

16 West 17th Street, New York NY 10011. 212/627-1290. **Description:** Up in this great old New York building, the Eisenberg family continues the tradition begun in 1898 of great men's

clothing at great prices. Most of the suits are Eisenberg & Eisenberg's own label, so you can rest assured in knowing that you're buying directly from the manufacturer. These lean toward European, double-breasted styles. They're all priced from $150.00 - $400.00. They compare favorably with suits at twice the price in the uptown department stores. You'll also find designers like Perry Ellis, Ralph Lauren, Tallia, Dior, and Lagerfeld, at up to half off the retail prices; as well as shirts, ties, slacks, raincoats, and accessories. Formal wear is one of the store's biggest draws, with some of the latest fashions. Eisenberg & Eisenberg offers lots of low-key personal attention. You'll want to become a regular and call the place your tailor; alterations are inexpensive and fast. These guys will even beat the prices in other stores' ads, plus 10 percent of the difference, for up to 30 days after you buy a suit!

FISHKIN KNITWEAR
314 Grand Street, New York NY 10002. 212/226-6538. **Description:** Fishkin Knitwear is one of the great finds of the Lower East Side. More like a department store than the area's many no-frills shops, Fishkin Knitwear offers big discounts on women's designer fashions -- all first-quality, current-season styles. On their many racks you may stumble across Eileen Fisher items, in regular and plus sizes, that are always on sale as well as Zanella pants and suits that have undergone some serious markdowns. On my visit, Bedford silk, cashmere, and cotton clothing (in all styles) were 40 - 50 percent off. Gorgeous pashmina shawls, in every shade imaginable, were selling for half-price. Women's shoes, in both styles, fancy and casual, are another specialty here. Again, these are current collections that start at 20 percent below department store prices. A pair of pumps by Nickels, listed at $88.00, sell here for $60.00. End-of-season sales (usually held in late summer and winter) bring further reductions to these already-low prices, like a pair of Justin cowboy boots marked down from $165.00 to $130.00.

FOWAD TRADING COMPANY
2554 Broadway (at 96th Street), New York NY 10025. 212/222-8000. **Description:** Fowad Trading Company is a huge, sprawling clothing store selling good brands and designer labels -- often irregulars -- at big discounts. Chances are you will find men's blazers by Stanley Blacker, Perry Ellis silk ties, and London Fog raincoats all at reduced prices. Fowad Trading Company also carries lesser-known brands of slacks and shirts, sweaters and more; and of course, a similar selection for women.

GABAY'S
225 First Avenue (between 13th & 14th Streets), New York NY 10003. 212/254-3180. **Description:** This is what New York bargain shopping is all about. Gabay's is a small, cramped, storefront that happens to get seconds and irregulars shipped in daily from fancy department stores. You may not find anything today, but come back tomorrow -- or next week -- because people know about this place, and the stock really moves. Most of it sits out on open

tables and bins; better-quality pieces go on the racks along the walls. Mr. C saw a men's wool overcoat by Christian Dior for $50.00 and a leather bomber jacket for $90.00. Barrels of hosiery from Bloomingdale's and Givenchy are $2.00. There are linens here too, like complete sheet sets by Esprit for $20.00 - $50.00 Gabay's also carries designer handbags at rock-bottom prices. Get there as close to the 10:00 a.m. opening as you can for the best selection; and Saturday mornings are apparently the best time for men's stuff. Open Sunday, 10:00 a.m. - 4:00 p.m.; Monday through Saturday, 10:00 a.m. - 5:00 p.m.

GILCREST CLOTHES

900 Broadway, 3rd Floor, New York NY 10003. 212/254-8933. **Description:** You can actually see the "factory" in this factory-direct men's clothing store. Gilcrest Clothes has racks and racks of suits, sport coats, raincoats, tuxedos, and accessories. Another specialty here is Gilcrest's own label of European-style suits, many made in the same factories as Armani and other designers. But instead of paying up to $1,100.00 for these, they go for $269.00 - $599.00 at Gilcrest Clothes. Alterations are made on the premises free of charge; service is a high priority to the folks here, where their slogan is "We cater to our customer." Gilcrest Clothes also provides tuxedo rentals. Open Sunday 10:00 a.m. - 4:00 p.m.; Monday - Friday, 7:30 a.m. - 5:30 p.m., Saturday 8:30 a.m. - 5:00 p.m.

MOE GINSBURG

162 Fifth Avenue (at 21st Street), New York NY 10010. 212/242-3482. **Description:** Most guys know of this longtime institution for discounted dressy clothing. The clothing here is first quality; the discounts come from volume sales. Five -- count 'em, five -- floors of showrooms cover the gamut from suits to outerwear to shoes to accessories. The styles include both classic and Euro-contemporary. A snazzy Perry Ellis suit was recently seen for $230.00, marked down from an original price of $495.00. A Stanley Blacker raincoat was reduced from $295.00 to $180.00, while a Calvin Klein print sweatshirt, originally $85.00, was selling here for only $48.00. There are special sections for Big and Tall and athletic-fit suits. On the third floor, you'll find good deals on tuxedos and formal wear; and the fourth floor has shoes from the comfortable and casual to the shiny and sharp, most at $15.00 - $25.00 off list prices. Be sure not to miss the Red Dot sale areas, where the straggler items sell for as much as 50 percent off. Among the items on the Red Dot table during Mr. C's visit were a pair of Bugle Boy men's pants, originally $38.50, now $19.00. The courteous salesmen know their stuff, and they don't pressure you, which is always a relief. Open Monday through Friday, 9:30 a.m. - 7:00 p.m. (Thursdays until 8:00 p.m.); Saturday and Sunday, 9:30 a.m. - 6:00 p.m.

GORSART CLOTHES

9 Murray Street, 2nd Floor, New York NY 10007. 212/962-0024. **Description:** For over 80 years Gorsart has been quietly selling

the crème de la crème of men's suits and furnishings, all at discount, from a second-floor shop in the Financial District. There is no awning at street level, just the word Gorsart on a door that you can easily miss if you're not looking. Similarly, the store never advertises, doing business simply by word-of-mouth. Current owner Moe Davidson is proud of the prices and service his store offers. Thanks to its low-rent location, Gorsart can sell designer suits as much as 35 percent below retail. Take note, these suits still cost anywhere from $300.00 - $700.00 each, with names such as Hickey-Freeman, Freedberg's of Boston, and the like. But if top names in conservative styles are what you wear, you can save hundreds of dollars by shopping here. The atmosphere is refined and casual, with natural wood floors and comfortable surroundings -- not the common "upstairs warehouse" look. Salesmen help you without pressure. There are even 30 tailors on the premises; this is, in fact, one of the few discount stores offering free alterations. Gorsart also carries everything else you'll need to make that stylish impression, from Robert Talbot neckties to Alden shoes -- the tassled loafers of choice -- at $30.00 - $40.00 below certain well-known midtown clothiers. Mr. C wished he had the budget -- and the wardrobe -- to show off a set of Trafalgar suspenders woven with images of 19th-century baseball players; this limited (numbered!) edition retails for $135.00, but was selling for $99.50 here. Gorsart also sells several designs of formal wear from Lord West and Diamond, as well as Timberland outdoor coats.

INTERMIX

125 Fifth Avenue (between 19th & 20th Streets), New York NY 10003. 212/533-9720. **Description:** Resist the temptation to try on the newly-arrived fashions at the front of the store and you might just find yourself a bargain at Intermix. Along the back wall, you'll find top designer fashions at as much as 50 percent off their regular prices. How about dresses by Tocca, usually hovering right around the $200.00 mark, for as little as $89.00 apiece. Casual khakis for $30.00? Neither the Gap nor J. Crew can do better! Under these same racks, look for reduced accessories that are past-season, but still certainly usable. Mr. C saw a variety of Kate Spade bags, in all different sizes and colors, from $100.00 - $165.00 (retailing anywhere between $150.00 and $250.00). Drop in and see what you can find.

KLEIN'S OF MONTICELLO

105 Orchard Street, New York NY 10002. 212/966-1453. **Description:** Klein's seems very much out of place on the Lower East Side. Mixed in with no-frills wholesalers, the shop seems more like something you'd find on the Upper East Side. It's a true boutique, with natural wood floors, glass display cases, fitting rooms and a quietly chic atmosphere. And yet for over 30 years Klein's has been selling men's and women's tailored clothing for 20 - 40 percent below major store prices. Mind you, because of the high quality, items can still be expensive, even with a discount. But if your style runs to small, specialty European brands, this is the place for you.

L.S. MEN'S CLOTHING

49 West 45th Street, 3rd Floor, New York NY 10036. 212/575-0933. **Description:** Here is another one of the best treasures New York City has to offer for the well-dressed gentleman, with suits at up to 60 percent off retail. It's one of the few shops that offers downtown prices without the taxi ride. While the prices may be cheap, the quality definitely is not. If you want an $800.00 suit for $300.00, this is the place. Indeed, you'll find many classic American designs, all hand-tailored, ranging from $225.00 - $440.00. The retail prices for these same suits can be over $1,000.00 elsewhere. L.S. Men's Clothing can also outfit you in a custom-made suit for $465.00 complete. They will proudly show you the hand-sewn linings, reinforced arm holes, and shoulders that will last and last without stretching out of shape. This is career clothing at its finest, as its likely to last the length of your career. All tailoring is done on the premises; alterations do cost extra, but don't forget how much you're saving in the first place. Open Sunday 10:00 a.m. - 5:00 p.m.; Monday through Thursday, 9:00 a.m. - 7:00 p.m.; Friday 9:00 a.m. - 4:00 p.m.

LABELS FOR LESS

204 Park Avenue South (at 18th Street), New York NY 10003. 212/529-7440. ◆ 130 East 34th Street, New York NY. 212/689-3455. ◆ 1124 Avenue of the Americas (at 43rd Street), New York NY. 212/302-7808. ◆ 130 West 48th Street, New York NY. 212/997-1032. ◆ 800 Third Avenue (at 50th Street), New York NY. 212/752-2443. ◆ 1302 First Avenue (at 68th Street), New York NY. 212/249-4800. ◆ 181 Amsterdam Avenue (at 69th Street), New York NY. 212/787-0850. ◆ 1430 Second Avenue (at 74th Street), New York NY. 212/249-4080. **Description:** Along with Bolton's (see separate listing), Labels for Less has been carving out a big slice of the women's discounting pie all around town. Again, the forte is high-quality designer clothing for the professional woman; again, the names are biggies. The bargains are good ones, and some are terrific. A houndstooth blazer by a famous European designer was recently marked down from $196.00 to $99.75; a big name silk blouse was reduced from $46.00 to $30.00. One recent deal offered wool shaker-style sweaters, normally $30.00, for just $10.00 with any other purchase. You'll also find good prices on accessories like belts and handbags. Call for specific location hours.

LEA'S

119 Orchard Street, New York NY 10002. 212/677-2043. **Description:** Half a flight up from the Lower East Side's famous Fine and Klein (see separate listing), Lea's sells high-fashion women's sportswear at prices about 30 percent lower than in department stores. These include all kinds of blazers, suits, skirts, and slacks by well-known European designers. Whenever the end of a season approaches, slower moving items are further reduced to 50 percent off. What a steal!

NICE PRICE
493 Columbus Avenue (between 83rd & 84th Streets), New York NY 10024. 212/362-1020. **Description:** Nice Price snaps up major brands of contemporary fashions, both first quality and irregulars, and sells them way below retail. Most of the clothing is women's, though there is some men's stuff too -- denim shirts marked way down, sweaters reduced 25 percent, and lots more. Women will love such items as a leather baseball jacket, first quality, half-price or a black lace minidress, slightly imperfect, marked down from $120.00. Nice Price is open seven days but you should try to go on a weekday to beat the crowds!

ORVA
155 East 86th Street (between Lexington & Third Avenues), New York NY 10028. 212/369-3448. **Description:** While they're mostly known for their hosiery, this store stocks a pretty powerful punch when it comes to offering good prices on current fashions. Besides socks and the like (where you can expect to see about $1.00 knocked off the price), Orva carries lots of clothing, jewelry, shoes, and other accessories. Typical savings seem to be in the 30 percent range. They stock name brands too, like Calvin Klein and French Connection. I even spotted some great Deisel handbags and backpacks. While prices between $50.00 and $80.00 for these may not seem like a good buy to everyone, trust me, it is! For the ultra hip and ultra young crowds that frequent the Deisel outlets, they'll be afforded some good savings. There's certainly nothing else like it in this pricey neighborhood. Open Sunday, 10:00 a.m. - 8:00 p.m.; Monday through Saturday, 10:00 a.m. - 9:00 p.m.

PRATO MEN'S WEAR
41 John Street, New York NY 10038. 212/619-9017. ♦ 28 West 34th Street, New York NY. 212/629-4730. ♦ 492 Seventh Avenue (at 36th Street), New York NY 10018. 212/564-9683. **Description:** These small shops -- two in the Nassau Street mall downtown and two in the Garment District -- carry designer sportswear at very good prices. You can pick up a pair of Calvin Klein jeans for $28.00; sweaters by Pierre Cardin for $28.00; and silk shirts for $15.00. They also have lots of Italian, wool-blend suits priced around $150.00; and leather jackets that would retail for over $300.00 elsewhere sell here for $100.00 - $150.00. There is not a huge selection, but it is definitely worth a look.

RAINBOW SHOPS
380 Fifth Avenue, New York NY 10018. 212/947-0837. ♦ 320 West 57th Street, New York NY 10019. 212/333-5490. ♦ 79 Nassau Street, New York NY 10038. 212/964-0756. ♦ 20 Vesey Street, New York NY 10007. 212/406-6044. ♦ 1330 Fifth Avenue, New York NY. 212/987-1323. **World Wide Web address:** http://www.rainbowshops.com. **Description:** Rainbow Shops is a chain of trendy shores that carry a large selection of kids, juniors, and plus-sized apparel (up to size 24). Still, the clothes would probably be more befitting of a teenage daughter than a young-at-heart mom. Chunky-heeled sandals, shoes, and boots retail, on the average, between $10.00 and

$20.00. Mr. C saw a pair of knee-high stretch boots for just $29.99. There was a large selection of more formal dresses priced between $14.99 and $23.00. Junior and plus jeans, in a variety of styles, were priced under $25.00 each. For the kids, character tees were seen for $12.99, and Mr. C spotted a Mickey Mouse top and jean set for just $14.99. Rainbow Shops also carries a variety of equally-well-priced accessories including jewelry, hoisery, bags, and gift items. Get there during clearance time and you can find a range of clothing and accessories for under $5.00.

ROTHMAN'S

200 Park Avenue South (at 17th Street), New York NY 10003. 212/777-7400. **E-mail address:** rothmanus@aol.com. **Description:** Rothman's is one of the classiest and best of the men's suit discounters. The store, located in Union Square, even feels classy, being in a building that was formerly a bank; the top-of-the-line suits are kept in the open vault room downstairs. Owner Ken Giddon has taken over the business that began on the Lower East Side by his grandfather, and he does the old man proud. Suits start at $400.00 and range up to $1000.00 for brand name designers like Hickey-Freeman, Hugo Boss, Calvin Klein, and Joseph Abboud. If you would rather piece the outfit together yourself, sport coats start at $250.00 and a great selection of trousers -- from names like Zanella and Ballin -- are priced from $100.00 - $200.00. But wait, you're not ready to hit the town just yet: dress shirts start at just $45.00 and a great selection of ties can be found for under $20.00. Rothman's shoe department carries only the best in men's footwear including Alden, Paraboot and Kenneth Cole, all at discount prices. For all the fanciness of the clothing, the atmosphere at Rothman's is quite casual, and the service is always polite and friendly. Open Sunday, 12:00 p.m. - 5:00 p.m.; Monday through Friday, 10:00 a.m. - 7:00 p.m.; Saturday, 9:30 a.m. - 6:00 p.m.

S&W

165 West 26th Street, New York NY. 212/924-6656. ✦ 4217 13th Avenue, Brooklyn NY. 718/438-2636. **Description:** For over 30 years, S&W has been a legend in women's designer clothing. They sell current-season styles, all first quality, at 25 - 50 percent below list prices. This rambling store's main branch is wrapped around the corner of Seventh Avenue, with room after room on two levels -- each of which offers a different kind of clothing. Looking for a new coat? S&W has 5,000 in stock. Shearlings, leathers, and wool coats in all styles and lengths are discounted; check the upstairs clearance room for further markdowns of 50 percent off the lowest price. Usually such reductions are made at the end of the season. The boutique department features the collections of Escada, Dior, Lagerfeld, Della Spiga, and many others. They have everything you need to create a full wardrobe including accessories. Again, there is a clearance section with discounts up to 80 percent. Alterations are available on the premises, though there is an extra charge for this service. And don't forget the separate but related shoe store. Here you may

find shoes by Bally, Stuart Weitzman, Ungaro, and Via Spiga at up to 25 percent off retail. Open Sunday, 10:00 a.m. - 6:00 p.m.; Monday through Thursday, 10:00 a.m. - 6:30 p.m.; and Friday, 10:00 a.m. - 3:00 p.m. Closed Saturday.

SSS SAMPLE SALE/NICE PRICE

261 West 36th Street, New York NY 10018. 212/947-8748. **World Wide Web address:** http://www.clothingline.com. **Description:** On any given day, it is easy enough to find a sample sale in the city that many a top designer calls home. But what is not so easy is finding a store that runs sample sales everyday. Nice Price SSS is just such a place. Whether you prefer the classic cuts of Tahari or the hip style of Betsey Johnson, top designer overstocks and samples can be found here everyday at prices that are better than even the best of department store sales. Drop by or call to get on their mailing list so that you'll receive an update on which of your favorite designers will be sending this week's merchandise.

STRAWBERRY

129 East 42nd Street, New York NY 10017. 212/986-7030. ◆ 80 Broad Street, New York NY. 212/425-6627. ◆ 501 Madison Avenue, New York NY. 212/753-5008. ◆ 120 West 49th Street, New York NY. 212/391-8718. ◆ 14 West 34th Street, New York NY. 212/279-8696. ◆ 320 First Avenue, New York NY. 212/505-1291. ◆ 258 Broadway, New York NY. 212/406-2330. ◆ 345 Park Avenue South, New York NY. 212/725-5970. ◆ 38 East 14th Street, New York NY. 212/353-2700. **Description:** While I have just listed numerous locations of this popular chain, you still might want to call to find the location nearest you (there are too many to list, and new locations keep springing up every day). Like Rainbow (see separate listing), Strawberry sells moderately-priced women's apparel including juniors, young missy, and plus size selections. While some of the clothes are your basic department store bargain selection, you'll also find some brand names mixed in at great prices. Mr. C saw lots of cotton tops for $6.99 and dresses for around $19.99 (some more, some less). Strawberry also carries a great line of footwear, like a pair of DKNY sneakers for $29.00. Open Monday, 8:00 a.m. - 8:00 p.m.; Tuesday, 8:00 a.m. - 7:00 p.m.; Wednesday through Friday, 8:00 a.m. - 8:00 p.m.; Saturday and Sunday, 10:00 a.m. - 6:00 p.m.

TATES BOUTIQUE

130 Church Street, New York NY 10007. 212/766-8000. ◆ 1039 Avenue of the Americas (at 39th Street), New York NY. 212/354-7091. **Description:** Most of the clothing here consists of irregulars and second-quality stuff, but you may find perfectly acceptable deals on men's and boys' semi-casual clothing. The walls are lined with tightly filled racks above and below you. Mr. C found lots of nice suits in the $80.00 - $130.00 range; including Polo wool-blend suits. Blazers were under $20.00, while jeans and chinos were available for about $15.00. Tates carries plenty of styles for boys and teens as well.

V.I.M. JEANS

16 West 14th Street, New York NY 10011. 212/255-2262.
Description: For jeans, sneakers, and all of the fashions that go with them, V.I.M. has very good prices. Current-style Levi's start around $25.00; there are even lots of cheap import jeans for as little as $19.99. Along with these are men's casual print shirts for $9.99, women's tops for $5.99, and sweaters for as little as $3.99. The place is great for a lot of outfitting in a hurry. The stores have special clearance sections as well. The other real bargains here are in sneakers for men, women and kids. The vast stock includes current styles at good prices and last year's closeouts at even better prices. Among these are such varieties as Etonic high-tops and running shoes for $19.99; Reeboks for $30.00 and up; and L.A. Gear from $25.00. Children's sneakers may start as low as $15.00, in many of the same brand names. Because these are leftovers, they may not have all sizes for each style; but the big and open displays, with all the shoes in labeled boxes, make it easy for you to rummage through.

VANESSA BOUTIQUE

5 West 42nd Street, New York NY 10036. 212/768-7510.
Description: For more than 10 years, Vanessa Boutique has been offering women great deals on business suits and career separates. Name brand suits (many with original $180.00+ tags still intact) sell here for $69.99 and less. Separately, fully-lined blazers were seen for $35.99, silk blouses for $19.99, and career tops for a penny-saving $6.99. With deals like this, why not drop in and check it out for yourself? Open Monday through Friday, 8:00 a.m. - 7:00 p.m.; Saturday, 10:00 a.m. - 7:00 p.m.

SHOPPING
🏚 Clothing: Vintage Shops 🏚

ALICE UNDERGROUND
481 Broadway (at Broome Street), New York NY 10113.
212/431-9067. **E-mail address:** alice_underground@nyctoday.
com. **World Wide Web address:** http://www.aliceundergroundnyc.
com. **Description:** Definitely among the city's best vintage clothing
stores, Alice Underground has lots and lots of clothing from
Victorian to contemporary, much of it at terrific prices. The SoHo
branch takes its cue from the nearby Canal Jean Company (see
separate listing) and its many competitors on lower Broadway, with
boutique-style displays of clothing, mainly from the 1950s and
1960s. Alice Underground carries lots of jeans, wild shirts, and
cool dresses. A sleeveless minidress, from the sixties but in great
condition, was seen for just $12.00 and well-worn leather jackets
were going for $10.00. The sale bins, which are often placed
outside, are some of the best places to look around. Usually,
you can find lots of great buys from anywhere between $5.00 and
$10.00. On my visit, one of the sale bins featured a huge pile
of leather and suede goods (skirts, shorts, pants, jackets)
for $6.00 each. In the back, there's a room full of linens --
tablecloths, draperies, bedspreads and remnants. The salespeople
know their stuff and will help find specific items. Open daily,
11:00 a.m. - 7:00 p.m.

ANDY'S CHEE-PEES
691 Broadway (between 3rd and 4th Streets), New York NY 10011.
212/420-5980. **E-mail address:** gagink@aol.com. **Description:**
Andy's is crammed with racks and racks of men's and women's
antique clothing. While the prices are not as low as some other
vintage stores, the high-quality clothing and tremendous
selection make it one of the better stores to shop. Handsome
buckskin fringe jackets in clean, brushed suede were seen for
$110.00 each; black velvet cocktail dresses were $55.00; and a
sleeveless dress done up in a rainbow of sequins was $65.00. Men
will find tweed blazers starting at $35.00 and three-quarter-
length winter coats -- when the season demands -- for $55.00.
Upstairs they run frequent sales on their racks and racks of jeans,
T-shirts, and other trendy wear. Downstairs, you'll find their well-
known stash of leather goods and lots of vintage dresses. While
not everything here can be considered a real *chee-pee*, there's
plenty of clothing in everyone's price range. All you need to do is
poke around a bit.

CHEAP JACK'S VINTAGE CLOTHING
841 Broadway (13th Street), New York NY. 212/777-9564.
Description: Cheap Jack's is one of the best-known vintage
clothing stores in town. Two floors allow for a huge selection of
clothing, and while there are bargains to be found here, overall,

prices can lean toward the more expensive side. But don't cross Jack off your list just yet. You can find suede jackets from $20.00 and up; heavy wool military jackets for $19.00; lots and lots of wool overcoats for $50.00 to $75.00; dresses for $25.00 and up; and ties, ties, ties. They also have unusual clothes with an international flair, such as daishiki shirts and Japanese kimonos, all priced under $20.00. Periodic sales can afford better savings, as much as 30 - 50 percent off regular prices. Yet, when it comes to service, Cheap Jack's cannot be beat, offering layaway plans and alterations while you wait.

DARROW VINTAGE CLOTHING AND ANTIQUES
7 West 19th Street, New York NY 10011. 212/255-1550. **E-mail address:** vintagec@aol.com. **World Wide Web address:** http://www.darrowvintage.com. **Description:** Don't be surprised if you see a celebrity or two while browsing the racks at Darrow Vintage. Once you ascend the large storefront staircase and get buzzed into this vintage find, prepare yourself for a glamorous mix of colors, fabrics, and styles. A visit to Darrow is as much an adventure for the eyes as it is for the shopping palate. For those who love to browse, or to snatch up and reconstruct antique clothing, this is probably one of the city's best finds. When Mr. C visited, there was an entire rack of clothing (sweaters, dresses, blazers) that were selling for a mere $10.00 each. Prices throughout the store are consistently good, and the clothes are in fantastic condition.

THE FAMILY JEWELS
832 Avenue of the Americas, 2nd Floor (at 29th Street), New York NY 10001. 212/679-5023. **E-mail address:** familyjewelsNYC@webtv.net. **Description:** The Family Jewels is jammed with racks and racks of men's and women's coats, jeans, formal wear, shoes, and accessories. Bag a fake leopard-skin coat for $59.00, or a Pierre Cardin tweed sport jacket for $29.00. A sleeveless dress of black lace was seen for $39.00; add a pair of strap sandals by Halston for $35.00 more. An array of hats range from $15.00 to $45.00, and there's lots of jewelry, gloves, handbags, and other add-ons. The shop is lots of fun to browse; it's been the backdrop for photo sessions for such fashion magazines as *Mademoiselle* and *Harpers Bazaar. Elle, In Style*, and *Vogue* all named The Family Jewels one of the best vintage stores in the country. Open daily, 11:00 a.m. - 7:00 p.m.

FROM AROUND THE WORLD
209 West 38th Street, Suite 1207, New York NY 10018. 212/343-6536. **E-mail address:** fatwvintag@aol.com. **Description:** More than a vintage shop, From Around The World is a vintage showroom that takes a lot of the guessing out of vintage clothing shopping. No longer will you have to waste time scrounging the racks of a cramped little shop for something that is stylish and in good condition. From Around The World offers a full showroom of only the most high-quality vintage clothing and collectibles, and everything is in excellent condition. The ever-changing

merchandise is comprised mostly of clothing from the 1940s to the 1970s, with an emphasis on the styles of all classes, from working class to the privileged few. And, as the name suggests, the clothing is comprised of international styles, with clothing not only from America, but Japan, Italy, France, Spain, and any other imaginable land. From Around The World carries an enormous selection of merchandise for men, women, and children. Choose your style: Western, Peasant, Hippie, Mod, or Disco. There are lots of finds in the $30.00 - $50.00 range, with rare and new/old vintage apparel starting at around $100.00 Accessories like hosiery, shoes, bags, belts, and jewelry and novelties like housewares and other decorative items start at around $20.00. For even better deals, visit the Flea Market Room where clothing and accessories are priced at $10.00 - $25.00. Open Monday through Friday, 9:30 a.m. - 5:30 p.m. by appointment only.

JANA STARR ANTIQUES

236 East 80th Street, New York NY 10021. 212/861-8256. **Description:** Established nearly 25 years ago, this narrow Upper East Side shop houses an amazing supply of antique clothing, linens, and laces. Starr offers everything for the bride-to-be, from gowns and shoes to hats and jewelry. Items date from the Victorian era onward, and all are one-of-a-kind. So, for that very special outfit, this is the place. Exquisite wedding dresses, often constructed of hand-made laces, can be remodeled for individual tastes with a price to suit everyone's taste: dresses run anywhere between $200.00 and $3,000.00. Ms. Starr takes great pride in helping clients choose the right outfit, and everyone from designers to brides gets ultra-personal attention. "We give our customers a lot of support," says a modest Starr. Like its dresses, the shop itself is one-of-a-kind.

LOVE SAVES THE DAY

119 Second Avenue (at 7th Street), New York NY 10003. 212/228-3802. **Description:** Besides being remembered as the pivotal store in *Desperately Seeking Susan*, Love Saves the Day is one of the East Village's longtime greats for funky clothing and memorabilia. What did Mr. C find? An antique bridal gown from the 1930s for just $45.00, an equally timeless black spaghetti-strap party dress for $15.00; jeans for as low as $12.00; and felt fedora hats for $10.00. Like any vintage store, findings vary each time you go. It's well worth it to Love Saves the Day a regular stop on your personalized shopping itinerary. The shop also has a tremendous collection of period collectibles, from lava lamps ($55.00), to packs of Elvis playing cards ($5.50). Not to mention tons of toys and paraphernalia from all of those keen TV shows from yesteryear. The store and it's merchandise are timeless.

ROSE'S VINTAGE

96 East 7th Street, New York NY 10009. 212/533-8550. **Description:** This East Village shop is crammed from floor to ceiling with great vintage clothing buys. A recent sale featured

stacks and stacks of denim jeans for an incredibly low $12.00 a pair; Mr. C has found few such places with this quantity of jeans in good shape for that price. Rose's also has things like vintage coats, including men's cashmere overcoats from $50.00. Mr. C even saw a woman's 1950s-style leopard-skin coat for $75.00 -- and it was real. Now, that's unusual. Plus, lots of sequined dresses, formal wear, and other fancy stuff.

STAR STRUCK
47 Greenwich Avenue, New York NY 10014. 212/691-5357. **Description:** This Greenwich Village boutique sells very good-quality vintage wear, in styles ranging from the traditional to the outrageous. You can find great black cocktail dresses from $30.00 to $55.00, and men's tweed blazers in the same price range. There are lots of blue jeans from $25.00 and up. The prices are not as low as other vintage stores around town but, again, the merchandise is mostly in good condition and there is a lot to choose from.

SHOPPING
❤ Cosmetics & Perfumes ❤

COSMETIC MARKET
9 East 39th Street, New York NY 10016. 212/725-3625.
Description: In every woman's life, there are three words she longs to hear: "Clinique Bonus Time!" At Cosmetic Market, every day can be bonus time. If you've ever wondered what happens to the sample perfumes, makeup, lotions, and nail polishes when a cosmetic promotion is over, here's your answer. Tons of top brand cosmetic samples are all here, with a tiny price to match their tiny size. Besides Clinique, choose from names such as Lancôme, Chanel, Max Factor, L'Oreal, and Revlon. Mr. C spotted lots of Clinique eyeliners and eye shadows for just $4.00 each. And how about Chanel nail polish, in a variety of colors, for just $5.50 a bottle (retails at about $16.00)? Like any good pharmacy, Cosmetic Market also stocks a range of bath and beauty products at fantastic prices, like L'Oreal Feria hair coloring for $1.00, or John Freida hair care necessities for $2.50. Have you ever seen a curling iron for under $5.00? Mr. C found a Salon Selectives curling iron for just $4.99. But, unlike your typical pharmacy or drugstore, Cosmetic Market has a wide selection of stylish handbags, from $6.00 to $8.00. But don't worry guys, there's plenty of stuff for you here too, like fragrances by the likes of Ralph Lauren, all at unbeatable prices. To keep the kids happy, let them browse along the back wall, where toys from the latest Disney movies will probably make their way into your bag. And why shouldn't they at these prices?

COSMETICS PLUS
516 Fifth Avenue (at 43rd Street), New York NY 10036. 212/221-6560. ◆ 1320 Avenue of the Americas (at 53rd Street), New York NY. 212/247-0444. ◆ 1431 Broadway (at 40th Street), New York NY. 212/293-6604. ◆ 1601 Broadway (at 48th Street), New York NY. 212/757-3122. ◆ 171 West 57th Street (at Seventh Avenue), New York NY. 212/399-9783. ◆ 1201 Third Avenue (at 70th Street), New York NY. 212/628-5600. **Description:** Just as often as you see a Starbucks or a Gap in the Big Apple, you're bound to see one of the many locations of Cosmetics Plus. The "Plus" signifies the store's one-stop shopping mentality, where you can pick up all your health and beauty needs in one fell swoop, and usually at a darn good price. While they carry all your everyday essentials (shampoos and conditioners, soaps, makeup), your best bet for a good bargain is with their large assortment of designer perfumes and colognes, like a bottle of Ralph Lauren's Polo cologne for $29.99. Whatever your favorite scent, you'll most likely be able to find it here (while saving a few bucks in the process).

JAY'S PERFUME BAR

14 East 17th Street, Ground Floor, New York NY 10003. 212/243-7743. **Description:** This block of 17th Street, between Fifth Avenue and Broadway, is another one of those New York shopping miracles: The Enclave. Here, several perfume discounters work both sides of the street, allowing you, the consumer, to easily find the best deals. Jay's is one of the better shops of the group. The difficulty in both getting to the counter and getting some service, proves its popularity. Meanwhile, you'll find great discounts on all your favorites: Halston Z-14 men's cologne, list price $40.00, here $15.00; Calvin Klein's Eternity for women lists at $55.00 and sells here for $39.00; and Gucci Envy for men, which is priced at $55.00 sells for $36.00. Jay's also carries a large selection of Estee Lauder and Clinique cosmetics.

PERFUME PALACE

233 Fifth Avenue (at 27th Street), New York NY 10016. 212/481-1942. **Description:** You don't have to be royalty to save up to 75 percent on your favorite designer fragrances. At Perfume Palace, everyone is treated like a king or queen with prices that are hard to beat. A 1.7 ounce bottle of eau de parfum by Anne Klein would cost you around $50.00 anywhere else, here it is just $32.50. Or, a 1.7 ounce bottle of Krazy Krizia (retailing at $35.00) is a steal at just $25.00. Men are also invited to save, with a $39.00 bottle of Grey Flannel selling here for just $29.00. Pierre Cardin, Nautica, Halston, and Lagerfeld are just some of the other names that can be found, all at great discounts. If you're looking for a gift for that hard-to-buy-for-friend, send them a designer gift set of their favorite fragrance: Eternity, Safari, Obsession. All the names are here and gift sets start at just $15.00 each. Perfume Palace can help you fill up your makeup bag as well, they sell a number of designer lipsticks by Elizabeth Arden, Clinique, Ralph Lauren and more for just $5.00 each.

RICKY'S

44 East 8th Street, New York NY. 212/254-5247. ◆ 590 Broadway, New York NY. 212/226-5552. ◆ 1675 Third Avenue, New York NY 10128. 212/348-7400. ◆ 718 Broadway, New York NY 10003. 212/979-5232. **Description:** Ricky's has everything for your cosmetic needs at low prices. For the more daring, the store carries flashy wigs and temporary tattoos, as well as makeup and accessories from the Manic Panic line (the first to bring punk rock style to New York in the 1970s).

SALLY BEAUTY SUPPLY

2129 Ralph Avenue (between K & L Streets), Brooklyn NY. 718/968-2502. ◆ 2128 Bartow Avenue, Bronx NY. 718/862-9162. **Toll-free phone:** 800/275-7255. **World Wide Web address:** http://www.sallybeauty.com. **Description:** What a great discovery! For those of you who would like to get the professional styling products and supplies they use on you at the salon -- without spending a fortune -- stop in to Sally Beauty Supply. This nationwide chain of over 2,000 stores stocks everything you could want. Bargain prices can be found on hair brushes and combs; skin products; shampoos and conditioners; and nail polish galore. Some locations even carry more high-end items like barber chairs and industrial sized hair dryers. You're guaranteed to get blown away by the prices.

SHOPPING
🏠 Discount Department Stores 🏠

BLOOMINGDALE'S
1000 Third Avenue (at 59th Street), New York NY 10022.
212/705-2000. **World Wide Web address:** http://www.
bloomingdales.com. **Description:** If you're thinking that this listing
is a mistake under the "*Discount* Department Stores" chapter,
read on. While it is well known that Bloomingdale's is a department
store, it is perhaps lesser known that they offer some of the
better bargains to be had in the city. Let me explain... as one of
New York's largest department stores, there is an unbelievable
amount of merchandise that comes into this store each week.
Subsequently, there needs to be an equally enormous amount of
merchandise leaving the store every week. And just how do they
do it? By offering fantastic savings on some of the latest fashions
by top designers. For example, at the time of Mr. C's visit,
Bloomingdale's was having a huge sale on men's dress shirts and
ties. Ties by Armani, Calvin Klein, Versace, and Joseph Abboud
were all priced between $25.00 and $48.00, 50 percent off the
price tags. Tons of Giorgio Armani dress shirts, in all styles, sizes,
and colors were selling for just $55.00 each. The bargains
continued well into the women's section with $15.00 French
Connection tanks and $25.00 Max Studio tops. An always popular
little black dress by Vivienne Tam was just $29.00. The outerwear
department at Bloomingdale's offered some of the deepest
discounts on leather and wool coats (completely in-season, no less).
Mr. C saw an Anne Klein raincoat, originally $400.00, for just
$125.00; a long wool Calvin Klein coat, with a price tag of $450.00,
for $165.00; and a short wool coat, also by Calvin Klein, reduced
from $275.00 to just $105.00. So, don't let the big name (or the
big size) intimidate you. Whatever your price range and whatever
your style, Bloomingdale's has got an awfully big selection to
choose from. And hey, if you can't find it here for less today, try
again next week. Open Sunday, 11:00 a.m. - 7:00 p.m.; Monday
through Wednesday, 10:00 a.m. - 8:00 p.m.; Thursday and Friday,
10:00 a.m. - 10:00 p.m.; Saturday, 10:00 a.m. - 7:00 p.m.

BONDY EXPORT CORPORATION
40 Canal Street, New York NY 10002. 212/925-7785. **Description:**
For more than 45 years, this shop on the eastern fringes of
Chinatown has been offering tremendous prices on all kinds of
merchandise. Bondy Export carries a wide range of small
appliances and electronics including cordless telephones, answering
machines, cameras, and personal stereos. If you are planning a trip
abroad, Bondy specializes in appliances for overseas usage, with a
vast knowledge of the different voltage requirements for
different countries. They also carry a great selection of personal
accessories like luggage, watches, and sunglasses. Mr. C saw a

Samsonite Silhouette E-Z cart, with a list price of $330.00, for just $145.00. The cramped, no-frills store stocks as much merchandise as it can; but anything you don't see, from almost any manufacturer, can be ordered at the same great prices. With so many similar stores in the area, it can be confusing to pick the right one. But you can rest assured in knowing that Bondy is among the only ones approved by the Better Business Bureau.

CENTURY 21 DEPARTMENT STORE

22 Cortlandt Street, New York NY. 212/227-9092. ♦ 472 86th Street, Brooklyn NY. 718/748-3266. **E-mail address:** customer_service@century21deptstores.com. **World Wide Web address:** http://www.c21stores.com. **Description:** Century 21 may be unique in New York: it's a complete department store in which everything is discounted. Not only do they carry well-known brands, but lots of designer clothing at bargain prices. Among these, men can find soft-leather Italian loafers by Caporicci reduced from $145.00 to $60.00. Sport shirts by Bill Blass sell for $29.00, well below the retail price of $55.00; and for the stylish, a Versace raincoat marked down from $780.00 to $250.00. Women may go for cashmere sweaters, half-price at $99.00; and they'll love the designer samples section, where exotic fashions are sold below half-price. Of course, these can still run you over $1,000.00, even on clearance. But aren't all bargains relative? Century 21 also sells an extensive section of cosmetics: it's a good place to stock up on the basics. Nearby, you'll find counters lined with jewelry and watches for men and women, along with gloves, handbags, and other accessories. And then there are sections of toys, seasonal gifts, and miscellaneous clearance items. Century 21 is a huge store for the Mr. (or Ms.) Cheap in all of us. The downtown store is open Sunday, 11:00 a.m. - 6:00 p.m.; Monday through Wednesday, 7:45 a.m. - 8:00 p.m.; Thursday, 7:45 a.m. - 8:30 p.m.; Friday, 7:45 a.m. - 8:00 p.m.; Saturday, 10:00 a.m. - 7:30 p.m. The Brooklyn store is open Sunday, 11:00 a.m. - 7:00 p.m.; Monday through Wednesday, 10:00 a.m. - 8:00 p.m.; Thursday, 10:00 a.m. - 9:00 p.m.; Friday, 10:00 a.m. - 8:00 p.m.; Saturday, 10:00 a.m. - 9:30 p.m.

CONWAY STORES

11 West 34th Street (between Fifth Avenue & Avenue of the Americas), New York NY. 212/967-1370. ♦ 49 West 34th Street (between Fifth Avenue & Avenue of the Americas), New York NY. 212/967-6454. ♦ 1333 Broadway (between 35th & 36th Streets), New York NY. 212/967-3460. ♦ 201 East 42nd Street (at Third Avenue), New York NY. 212/922-5030. ♦ 45 Broad Street, New York NY. 212/943-8900. ♦ 160 Jamaica Avenue (between 160th & 161st Streets), Queens NY. 718/526-7640. ♦ 505 Fulton Street, Brooklyn NY. 718/522-9200. **World Wide Web address:** http://www.conwaystores.com. **Description:** Conway is a clothing and housewares department store that is in the midst of a major expansion, capturing a big share of the discount market. For many it has become *the* place to stock up on health and beauty aids, linens, toys, and clothing basics. The stores are big and well-stocked with first-quality merchandise. Regular weekly specials make for further savings on such items as White Rain shampoo,

Arm & Hammer laundry detergent, Revlon cosmetics, Fruit of the Loom underwear, and Kodak film, as well as small appliances by Hamilton Beach and Proctor Silex, Barbie and Sesame Street toys, and Fieldcrest towels. Suede bottom backpacks were seen here for just $4.99. A variety of styles and colors of bed and bath linens including towels, carpets, and pillow shams were priced right at $2.99. They also have inexpensive sportswear fashions, like men's sweaters for $15.99 and women's dress blazers for $39.00 - $49.00. For the kids, pick up Hanes tops and bottoms for just $3.99 each, girls skirts and tops for under $6.00, and boys jeans and baseball tops for under $9.00 each. One extra note: With so many stores concentrated in the midtown area, not all branches have every department. Women's larger-size clothing, for example, is a specialty at certain locations. With an ever-growing number of locations, it is best to call and check the one closest to you.

DEE & DEE
97 Chambers Street, New York NY 10007. 212/233-3830. ♦ 39 West 14th Street, New York NY. 212/243-5620. **Description:** Another of the closeout specialists. There's a lot of junk here -- though you can find name brands among the various bins. The store mainly sells clothing, with lots of cheap jeans and underwear. It can be a good place to stock up on the basics. You may find Lee Riders jeans (irregulars) for $12.00, or Fruit of the Loom sweat pants for $7.99. Also check out cheap things for the home, such as draperies, bathroom accessories, and linens.

FILENE'S BASEMENT
2222 Broadway (at West 79th Street), New York NY. 212/873-8000. ♦ 620 Avenue of the Americas (between 18th & 19th Streets), New York NY 10011. 212/620-3100. **Description:** Throughout the country, Filene's Basement is widely known as a bargain treasure trove. All you need to do is plunge in and find yourself a deal or two. The stock comes from many quality stores and manufacturers-overstocks, leftovers, irregulars, things from last season. Not everything is super-cheap, but you never know what may turn up. That's why Basement veterans try to cruise through on a regular basis. And of course, every few weeks, prices on unsold items are marked down further. Of course, there is more here than just clothing. Many shoppers never even venture into the housewares, linens, home decorations, children's items, and toy sections.

MACY'S
151 West 34th Street, New York NY 10001. 212/695-4400. **World Wide Web address:** http://www.macys.com. **Description:** While it has long been known as a Big Apple institution (think Macy's Thanksgiving Day Parade), people rarely think of Macy's when they think discount shopping in New York. But I've got news for you: of all the many department stores (big and small), Macy's is one of the most generous when it comes to giving customers a break in price. Even the cheapest of the city's discount stores cannot and

do not offer bargains like you'll find at Macy's. And the place is so big, you're bound to find exactly what you're looking for. And if you're of the mentality that if you've seen one Macy's, you've seen them all, you are dead wrong. This is not the same Macy's that you'd find in the local mall of any suburb. If you thought purchasing a set of sheets for under $10.00 was beyond the realm of possibility, think again. Mr. C saw sheets by Di Lewis for Revman at $3.50 apiece. For the kids, pick out a fully-lined Adidas running suit for just $35.00 (selling elsewhere for $50.00). Mr. C saw a dressy short-sleeved Donna Karan sweater for just $17.50 (originally $115.00), a gauze-like Ralph Lauren sweater for $40.00 (originally $115.00), and a sporty Polo running jacket for just $41.00 (originally priced well over $150.00). Similar bargains were found in the men's store, with major discounts on all top designer duds like Polo, Tommy Hilfiger, and Calvin Klein. If it's accessories you're after, the ground floor is the place to be. A leather DKNY handbag (selling just a month before at $75.00) was reduced to an entirely affordable $18.00. So, before you head out to the nearest discount shop, hoping to find something that *resembles* this season's hottest fashions, meet me in Herald Square.

NYC LIQUIDATORS

158 West 27th Street, New York NY 10001. 212/675-7400. **Toll-free phone:** 888/248-1500. **Description:** If you enjoy browsing through aisles and aisles of, well, stuff -- the flotsam and jetsam left over from what seems to be every store in the city -- you'll love NYC Liquidators. They've got so much more, with much less space, than many of the other job lot stores. What do you need? An oil-filled electric space heater, half-price at $35.00; silk ties by Ralph Lauren (can it be true?), originally $60.00, here $10.00; a quartz wall clock by Westclox for $8.00; a box of one dozen magic markers for $1.50. For kids, there are plenty of toys and games, most at half their original prices. Mr. C noticed an HO scale Silver Shadow four-car train set for $30.00. Other brands include Fisher-Price, Playskool, and Milton Bradley. Music is big here. NYC has lots of unopened classical and jazz compact discs, by the likes of Andre Previn or Fats Waller, for $3.98; or rock & roll, like the Pretenders, for $6.98. Cassettes are priced from $.50 to $4.50; most fall somewhere in between. And the record section, at the other end of the store, is a vast treasure trove of cutouts and overstocks in all categories, from rap singles to Broadway shows. Most of these, unused, are just $1.00 each -- making this a popular stop for disc jockeys who want to fill out their collections cheaply or replace worn-out albums. There are tons of videos, from half-hour cartoons ($1.50) to previously-viewed movies like *Sophie's Choice* and *Drugstore Cowboy* ($3.98). And then there's the rest of the odds and ends -- paper supplies, cosmetics, handbags, holiday decorations, and more. The store is a mix of new, used, and slightly imperfect merchandise; but if you're dissatisfied with any purchase, you can bring it back for an exchange. The folks in here are friendly and helpful. And it sure is cheap!

NATIONAL WHOLESALE LIQUIDATORS

632 Broadway (between Bleecker & Houston Streets), New York NY 10012. 212/979-2400. **Description:** This is perhaps Mr. C's favorite among New York's many closeout specialists. The selection is vast and, more importantly, it includes lots of well-known names; not just junk and copycat brands. I found a Dirt Devil vacuum cleaner marked down from $70.00 to $50.00; a 20-piece Corelle dinnerware set, $15.00 off at $34.00; women's sweaters from The Limited, half-price at $26.00; and more. The cosmetics section alone features everything from Paul Mitchell conditioner, reduced from $11.00 to $7.00; colognes and perfumes by Ralph Lauren, Elizabeth Taylor, and Calvin Klein, at bargain-basement prices; and every vitamin from A to Z. Plus housewares, hardware, toys, candy, videos, and anything else you can conjure up. For a store that relies on getting its stuff from manufacturers' overstocks and seconds, they maintain almost as good a variety as a real department store -- for a lot less money.

ODD JOB TRADING CORP.

36 East 14th Street, New York NY. 212/741-9944. ◆ 465 Lexington Avenue, New York NY. 212/949-7401. ◆ 149 West 32nd Street, New York NY. 212/564-7370. ◆ 390 Fifth Avenue, New York NY. 212/239-3336. **Description:** One of the big boys in the closeout business, Odd-Job's stores boast savings on just about anything and everything imaginable. You'll find chino pants marked down from $45.00 to $15.00; Franklin baseball mitts reduced from $80.00 to $30.00; acrylic sweaters for just $3.99; a Profile fan-resist exercise bicycle for $100.00, a third of its original price; $60.00 Regal deep-pile bathroom rugs for $18.00; a one-ounce bottle of Chaps Musk aftershave, reduced from $10.00 to $2.99; a microwave for $85.00; a four-piece, silverplated tea serving set for $16.99; a set of four Mikasa glasses for $19.99; and timeless Star Wars character mugs for $2.99 -- plus toys and games, hardware, gardening tools and shovels, kitchen gadgets and major cookware. You can even find a box of thirty Christmas cards marked down from $12.00 to $2.99 -- and that's before Christmas!

RALPH'S DISCOUNT CITY

72 Nassau Street, New York NY 10078. 212/964-9386. **World Wide Web address:** http://ralphscity.com. **Description:** Located one level from the street, Ralph's Discount City is in the perfect location to offer bargain-basement prices, and it does. You can pick up many of your everyday needs including a 3-pack of Palmolive Soap or an 18-ounce bottle of Joy dishwashing detergent for $.99 each. How about a Gillette Sensor razor for $2.99? There was a Hamilton Beach juice machine for $29.99, and a Black & Decker Cup-At-A-Time coffee maker was seen for a mere $9.99. Brew your own coffee for a week, and it has paid for itself. Open Monday through Friday, 7:30 a.m. - 6:00 p.m.

WEBERS CLOSEOUT CENTERS

132 Church Street, New York NY. 212/571-3283. ◆ 475 Fifth Avenue (at 41st Street), New York NY. 212/251-0613. ◆ 45 West

45th Street, New York NY. 212/819-9780. ◆ 2064 Broadway (at 72nd Street), New York NY. 212/787-1644. **World Wide Web address:** http://www.webersonline.com. **Description:** Webers is one of the biggest of the job-lot sellers, specializing in designer names wherever possible. Here, among the floors of manufacturers' closeouts, you may find a pair of ladies' casual shoes by Perry Ellis, originally priced at $45.00, selling for $14.99 -- or a pair of Converse hi-top sneakers for $9.99. During Mr. C's visit, he also saw: men's dress shirts by Botany 500, reduced from $30.00 to $9.99; down vests for $19.99; leather portfolios for $30.00, Pierre Cardin tweed-sided luggage marked down from $105.00 to $30.00, a selection of compact discs for $4.99; gold-plated monogram flatware for 99¢ per piece, plus colognes, cosmetics, teas and jams, woven baskets, kitchen gadgets, tools, books, and toys. Many clothing items are irregulars; check carefully to see if these meet with your approval. All sales are final. Due to such high demand, Webers now offers the same great deals online. On Mr. C's most recent virtual visit, this superstore had such diverse offerings as a 6-outlet surge protector for $3.99 (originally $12.00), a tasteful mahogany humidor for $19.99 (originally $75.00), and a variety of suitcases ranging in price from $17.99 to $39.99 (originally listed from $53.00 to $120.00).

SHOPPING
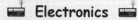 Electronics

---

ALKIT CAMERA
222 Park Avenue South (at 18th Street), New York NY 10003.
212/674-1515. ✦ 820 Third Avenue (at 52nd Street), New York
NY. 212/832-2101. **Description:** Alkit has been around for over 50
years, with competitive prices on all kinds of cameras and related
equipment. These large stores are well stocked with all the big
brands in 35mm cameras, instamatics, video camcorders, TVs,
VCRs, binoculars, and accessories. They also have good discounts
on film and blank audio and video tapes. A Nikon N5005 semi-
automatic, with built-in flash, was recently on sale; while the fully-
automatic Minolta Freedom Zoom 70c was selling for under
$200.00. Panasonic VCRs start under $200.00. Alkit also rents
equipment and accepts trade-ins on purchases -- another great
way to save cash. The sales staff is very helpful; the atmosphere
is pleasant and professional. Open Monday through Saturday. Call
for specific location hours.

B&H PHOTO-VIDEO-PRO AUDIO
420 Ninth Avenue (between 33rd & 34th Streets), New York NY
10001. 212/444-6600. **Toll-free phone:** 800/947-9950. **World
Wide Web address:** http://www.bhphotovideo.com. **Description:**
For all your camera, video, and pro audio equipment needs, B&H
Photo-Video has got what you're looking for. With more than
130,000 items in stock, they're almost guaranteed to have what
you're looking for. The prices are good, and frequent specials and
promotions make these prices even better. A lot of the equipment
is high-end, and it is no surprise that many professional
photographers and/or cameramen outfit their businesses here. If
you know exactly what you are looking for, this is a great place to
come and compare prices. How about an Olympus IS-20 Q-D 35mm
camera for $299.95? Or an Olympus 1.4 mega pixel digital camera
for $499.95? For those more traditional photo-takers, try the
Polaroid One Step Express camera for $39.95. B&H also has all
the necessities to complement your new camera: bags and carrying
cases (starting at just $13.95), tripods and supports, paper, film,
and darkroom equipment. A large selection of video cameras are
available, and video tapes start at just $1.70. B&H also carries a
range of used photographic and video equipment, so rare parts and
equipment can also be found here. With more than 25 years
experience, it is no wonder that B&H has attracted so many
customers. Whether you are in the market for some new or used
equipment, or just want to have a look at America's largest
(35,000 square-feet to be precise) photo-video superstore, go in
and take a peek. Call ahead for hours.

BROADWAY COMPUTER & VIDEO
1623 Broadway (between 49th & 50th Streets), New York NY
10019. 212/307-6260. **Toll-free phone:** 800/406-0768. **E-mail**

address: bcv@ix.netcom.com. **World Wide Web address:** http://www.broadwaycomputer.com. **Description:** Theater isn't the only thing Broadway is good for; at Broadway Computer & Video, you can find excellent deals on all sorts of computer, electronic, and video equipment. For you photographers out there, Broadway has got digital cameras and camcorders by big name makers like JVC and Panasonic. How about a digital camera by Casio for just $179.00? Broadway also carries a large selection of computers including desktops, laptops, and palmtops. A fully-loaded Compaq notebook computer was seen for just $949.00. If you're looking for accessories for your computer, they've got those too; Epson Stylus color printers start around $129.00, or pay the same price for a brand-new iomega Zip drive. With a convenient location and convenient hours, there's no reason not to stop by. All this and free delivery too! Open Sunday, 10:00 a.m. - 10:00 p.m.; Monday through Saturday, 8:00 a.m. - 12:00 a.m.

CANAL HI-FI
319 Canal Street, New York NY. 212/925-6575. **Description:** Of Canal Street's many stereo shops, Canal Hi-Fi has one of the best selections of quality audio components at competitive prices. They actually specialize in professional sound equipment, the stuff used by disc jockeys and recording studios. Toward the back, a separate room has lots of speakers, tape decks, and compact disc players for home use. Usually there are a couple of models of each on sale, stacked in the center of the room.

CROCODILE COMPUTERS
360 Amsterdam Avenue (between 77th & 78th Street), New York NY 10023. 212/769-3400. **World Wide Web address:** http://www.crocs.com. **Description:** Crocodile Computers offers an interesting option for saving money on computers: buy one used. Not unlike the used-car market, used computers -- starting off as such a big-ticket purchase -- have become a whole new field. You never know what they'll have, but Crocodile always maintains a good stock of various models, both IBM and Macs. All computers carry a warranty, with repairs done in the store. If you're looking to get into the computer game and don't have a lot of cash to spend, this is definitely the way to go. It's an especially good idea for parents who want an inexpensive starter setup for their kids, or for students looking for something basic for writing. Crocodile also carries a full-line of music keyboards and recording equipment.

DATAVISION
445 Fifth Avenue (between 39th & 40th Streets), New York NY 10016. 212/689-1111. **Toll-free phone:** 888/888-2087. **World Wide Web address:** http://www.datavis.com. **Description:** They call themselves The Intelligent Superstore, and the nickname is right in line with the smart shoppers they attract. DataVision is brimming with all of your electronic and computer needs, and at some of the city's best prices. The fact that they are New York's second largest computer and video retailer should tell you

something! At the time of my visit, there was an amazing storewide clearance where I saw an IBM Thinkpad for an unbelievable $399.00, computer monitors for as low as $49.00, software for under $1.00, cellular phones for next to nothing ($24.99), digital cameras from $99.00 and up, and camcorders at a remarkable $299.00. Mr. C also saw a variety of home entertainment necessities (televisions, VCRs, DVDs, and stereos) at rock bottom prices. For great deals year-round, check out DataVision's supply of close-outs and refurbished equipment (all with guarantees), like a Hitachi M-120 notebook computer for just $699.00, or a new IBM MM50 monitor for $149.00. When you're all done shopping and are ready to relax, head to The Cyber Bar, DataVision's free Internet-access lounge.

OLDEN CAMERA & LENS COMPANY
1265 Broadway (at 32nd Street), 2nd Floor, New York NY. 212/725-1234. **Description:** For more than 60 years, Olden Camera & Lens Company has been offering great values on top name cameras like Leica, Nikon, Canon, Pentax, Hasselblad, and Sinar. Olden carries a large selection of both new and used cameras so, whatever your price range, chances are they'll have something to fit your needs. Open daily.

SOUNDCITY
58 West 45th Street (between Fifth Avenue & Avenue of the Americas), New York NY 10036. 212/575-1060. **Toll-free phone:** 800/326-1677. **World Wide Web address:** http://www.soundcity. baweb.com. **Description:** The folks at SoundCity urge you to "discover something you never thought possible", and rightfully so. If you didn't think it was possible to get great discounts on all major brand audio equipment, think again. A helpful staff member will be more than happy to lead you to your favorite name including Sony, Yamaha, Bose, JVC, Onkyo, and Technics. For your listening pleasure, recent bargains included a Panasonic Discman for $59.95, a set of JBL wireless speakers for $199.95, and a pack of 10 Sony minidiscs for $29.95. Video buffs will love a JVC VHS-C camcorder for $349.95, a JVC digital camcorder for $799.95, or a pack of five Sony VHS tapes for just $7.95. Open Monday through Friday, 8:30 a.m. - 7:00 p.m.; Saturday, 9:00 a.m. - 6:00 p.m.

STEREO EXCHANGE
627 Broadway (between Bleecker & Houston Streets), New York NY 10012. 212/505-1111. **World Wide Web address:** http://www. stereoexchange.com. **Description:** If your tastes in high-fidelity sound equipment run to the exotic, but your bank account does not, this may be the place for you. Stereo Exchange, as the name implies, repairs and sells used components from the very best high-end brands at a fraction of their original costs. Thus, you may find things like a Teac compact disc player, selling here for about half the regular price. A pair of Bose 901 speakers, the classic directional design, was seen for well below the original price. These all carry a 30-day store warranty covering parts and labor. But you'll realize once you go in that this is a store for the serious audiophile, not just some resale joint; and the people in here know what they're doing. Hours are Monday through Friday, 11:00 a.m. -

7:30 p.m.; Saturday 10:30 a.m. - 7:00 p.m.; and Sunday 12:00 p.m. - 7:00 p.m.

VICMARR STEREO AND TV

88 Delancey Street, New York NY 10002. 212/505-0380. **Description:** Way down on the Lower East Side, Vicmarr Stereo and TV sells sound and video systems for the home and car at very competitive prices. Among these, Mr. C found a Kenwood dual-cassette recorder, with auto-reverse and other nice features, on sale for under $200.00. Some items are floor samples on sale, such as a Sony 13-inch color TV. In addition to new items in most major brands, the store also sells factory-refurbished units at further discounts like a JVC four-head VCR, reduced from $299.00. Open daily, 10:00 a.m. - 7:00 p.m.

WILLOUGHBY'S

136 West 32nd Street (between Avenue of the Americas & 7th Avenue), New York NY. 212/564-1600. **Description:** Willoughby's, founded in 1898, is New York City's oldest camera store. Megavolume is the style here, which means it's best if you check out their prices after you already know exactly which model you want. Cameras come in every size, shape, brand, and price range. You can find a fully-automatic Konica Point for $19.99. Willoughby's also takes trade-ins to help you save more money; which means that they have lots of used cameras for sale. In the video department, you'll find competitive prices on camcorders, televisions, and VCRs. A JVC camcorder with pop out screen was recently on sale for $349.00. And we haven't even gotten to video games, telephones, stereo, fax machines, electronic organizers, and all the rest. Plus, look for the frequent free film giveaways: customers can buy a three pack of Konica film for $3.00, and then mail in the $3.00 rebate. Needless to say, there's a lot to plow through here, so know what you want and you shouldn't get swamped.

SHOPPING
🎒 Flea Markets 🎒

ANNEX ANTIQUE FAIR & FLEA MARKET

Avenue of the Americas (from 24th to 27th Streets), New York NY. 212/463-0200. **Description:** Annex Antique Fair & Flea Market has become a weekend institution for many in the area. Each weekend, more than 600 dealers line both sides of the Avenue formerly known as Sixth to sell their goods. Many of the dealers here are selling furniture and decorative items for the home. So if you'd like to find a full-size brass bed frame, a dining table and chair set, lamps, or more unusual items (Say, honey, isn't a four-foot-tall African conga drum just the thing for our living room?), you'll have lots to look at here. Also look for some of the city's best deals on clothing, jewelry, and art work. The enormous popularity of the Annex Flea Market (it is estimated that more than 10,000 people visit each weekend) has spawned another market across town (run by the same folks): The Garage Antique Show (see separate listing). Open weekends from approximately 9:00 a.m. - 5:00 p.m. and admission is just $1.00!

GARAGE ANTIQUE SHOW

112 West 25th Street (between Avenue of the Americas & Seventh Avenue), New York NY 10001. 212/647-0707. **Description:** Garages all over the city have been transformed into bargain hunter paradises and the Garage Antique Show is no exception. Just remember that the term "antique" is used as an adjective here, and not as a noun. So, those expecting to strictly find artifacts recently hauled from grandma's attic are in for a pleasant surprise. The Garage Antique Show is more than 20,000 square feet of antique clothing, art, and jewelry. Vintage clothing fiends will find much to salivate at here, as will lovers of jewelry and furniture, both new and old. Consequently, this place can get pretty crowded. That's just a friendly warning and word of preparation, not at all a determent, as I love this place! Open Saturday and Sunday, 7:00 a.m. - 5:00 p.m.

GREENFLEA MARKET EASTSIDE

East 67th Street (between First & York Avenues), New York NY 10021. 212/721-0900. **Description:** Greenflea Incorporated is the company that runs not only the Greenflea Market Eastside, but its sister market on the opposite side of town, Greenflea Market Westside (see separate listing). Greenflea Eastside houses both indoor and outdoor booths; a collection of vendors offering wares that run the gamut from prepared foods to jewelry to produce (Hence the name *Green*flea). While true flea marketers may rejoice in the joy of having yet another market to attend to, those looking for a fun-filled bargain or two might be better suited to the West Side location. Open Saturday, 6:00 a.m. - 6:00 p.m.

GREENFLEA MARKET WESTSIDE

Columbus Avenue (between 76th & 77th Streets), New York NY 10023. 212/721-0900. **Description:** Operating in conjunction with the Eastside flea market, Greenflea Market Westside is a bit more popular. Because the Westside market is larger, it allows for more vendors and a larger variety of merchandise. From food to flowers, clothing to jewelry, and records to literature, Greenflea Westside is a virtual smorgasbord of flea market and green market delights. Open Sunday, 10:00 a.m. - 6:00 p.m.

SoHo ANTIQUES FAIR

Corner of Broadway & Grand Streets, New York NY. 212/682-2000. **Description:** One of the better outdoor markets in New York City, shoppers can find a wide variety of items to browse through at SoHo Antiques Fair. There are approximately 100 vendors displaying their wares on any given weekend; offering antiques and collectibles from the eclectic to the mundane. Selections include furniture, jewelry, clothes, books, and a whole lot more. Open every Saturday and Sunday, 9:00 a.m. - 5:00 p.m.

SHOPPING
Flowers & Plants

FLOWERS BY EAST 81ST
450 East 81st Street (between York & First Avenues), New York NY 10028-5865. 212/628-5793. **Toll-free phone:** 800/542-4142. **E-mail address:** florist81@aol.com. **World Wide Web address:** http://www.ftd.com/flowersbye81st. **Description:** Looking for Upper East Side style without the Upper East Side prices? Flowers By East 81st delivers. Whatever your fancy -- flowers, green plants, flowering plants, balloons, fruit, gourmet treats, stuffed animals -- Flowers By East 81st has got it for an unexpectedly low price. All-occasion bouquets start at just $29.99. They've also got a large inventory of gorgeous roses, and they'd be more than happy to let someone know you've been thinking of them for under $20.00. What's more, they'll deliver around the corner, or around the world with 100 percent satisfaction guaranteed. If you're planning a wedding or any other event that calls for flowers, they've got an expert design staff. Stop by or give them a call and let them help find a gift that is right for you. And, for some added savings, don't forget to mention that you saw them in *Mr. Cheap's New York*! Open Monday through Saturday, 9:00 a.m. - 6:00 p.m. (and Sundays in December).

MOSTLY ROSES
599 Lexington Avenue (at 52nd Street), New York NY 10022. 212/758-7673. **Toll-free phone:** 800/760-9123. **World Wide Web address:** http://www.mostlyrosesny.com. **Description:** Looking for a special way to show someone you care? Flowers will usually do the trick, but they'll cost you a fortune, right? Wrong! At Mostly Roses, you can send a dozen roses for under $30.00. Mostly Roses boasts a large selection of the city's most beautiful flowers, imported daily from Holland and South America. While roses are the bud of choice, they also carry an assortment of flower bouquets. When they say that they offer "The Most Beautiful Roses for 1/3 the Normal Price", they're not kidding around.

NEW YORK FLOWERS & PLANT SHED
209 West 96th Street, New York 10025. 212/662-4400. **Description:** Just a few steps east of Broadway, this Upper West Side shop is more than a shed; they call themselves 'your house plant supermarket,' and that seems more appropriate. Wandering up and down the lush green aisles, you'll find anything from cute little cacti, $2.99 each, to a big, strapping, yucca plant in a ten-inch pot for $14.99. Leafy, green scheflera plants for $9.99 will add a healthy look to your apartment; same price for pretty cyclamens, with bright pink and red blossoms; throw in a woven

basket planter for just $1.99 more. Open Sunday, 10:00 a.m. to 6:00 p.m.; Monday through Saturday, 9:00 a.m. to 8:00 p.m.

ROSE VALLEY
140 Montague Street, Brooklyn NY 11201. 718/625-7673. **Description:** Half a flight down from the sidewalk, along this pleasant row of shops, Rose Valley specializes in bouquets of roses fresh from the farm. These start at just $8.00 for a dozen roses with 16-inch stems. The prices range slightly upward through five more sizes; $9.00 for 20-inch stems on up to a top price of $20.00 for 32-inch stems. These are fine-quality flowers at prices that are only slightly higher than at your corner grocery. The shop is clean and attractive, with a relaxed atmosphere and careful personal attention.

ROSES ONLY
1040 Avenue of the Americas (at 39th Street), New York NY 10018. 212/869-7673. ◆ 803 Lexington Avenue (at 62nd Street), New York NY. 212/751-7673. ◆ 1467 Third Avenue (at 83rd Street), New York NY 10021. 212/360-7673. **Description:** They specialize in just one thing here, and thus they can do it cheaply. A bouquet of roses starts at just $9.00 a dozen for flowers with 12-inch stems. The menu ranges up to $30.00 for extra-long, 32-inch stems. The quality, meanwhile, is better than what you might expect at these prices. Oh, and don't ask them for anything else -- it really is "roses only."

TONY'S GREENERY
542 Third Avenue (at 36th Street), New York NY 10016. 212/689-9600. ◆ 1200 Third Avenue (between 69th & 70th Streets), New York NY 10021. 212/439-0040. ◆ 66-48 80th Street, Queens NY 11379. 718/326-9146. **World Wide Web address:** http://www.tonysgreenery.baweb.com. **Description:** If your house needs a certain touch of green, but grocery-store-bought-hanging-plants aren't cutting it, give Tony a call. Tony's Greenery has got it all when it comes to both indoor and outdoor plants. For nearly 20 years, Tony has been the one to call when you are in need of a strange or exotic plant. Still, if you prefer to stick to an everyday fern, he's got those too. Tony's Greenery also carries a large selection of garden and greenery supplies, all at great prices.

SHOPPING
🏺 Home Furnishings 🏺

BROADWAY PANHANDLER
477 Broome Street, New York NY 10013. 212/966-3434.
Description: For anything and everything to do with the kitchen, Broadway Panhandler will allow you to create delectable works of culinary art on any budget. From the simplest paring knife to entire sets of designer pots and pans, the selection here is immense, and it's all at discount. Stainless steel cookware by All Clad, for example, includes things like a three-quart casserole dish with lid, list price $120.00, here $101.95. A 13-inch paella pan sells not for $158.00, but for $127.50. Mr. C also saw a five-quart oval French oven by Le Creuset, in that famous speckled orange finish, reduced from $195.00 to just $124.95. And the same discounts apply to the appliances. A Kitchen Aid 300-watt mixer, with stainless steel bowls and beaters and a retail price of $324.95, sells here for $210.00; a Krups four-cup coffeemaker was marked down from $30.00 to $25.95. You get the idea. It's rare, even in New York, to find such discounted prices in what is essentially a specialty store.

CARPET FACTORY OUTLET
1492 First Avenue (79th Street), New York NY. 212/988-5326.
Description: Carpet Factory Outlet has a substantial selection for a tiny storefront. A bound 9' x 12' remnant in grey wool was seen here for $500.00. The same size in tight-weave industrial/office remnants start at $169.00. They also have some orientals including runners as well as tile and linoleum by the foot.

CERAMICA GIFT GALLERY
1009 Avenue of the Americas (between 37th & 38th Street), New York NY 10018. 212/354-9216. **Toll-free phone:** 800/666-9956. **E-mail address:** ceramicagg@aol.com. **World Wide Web address:** http://www.ceramicagifts.com. **Description:** If you're looking for fine china, crystal, or silverware at an even finer price, Ceramica Gift Gallery is hard to beat. Since 1976, Ceramica Gift Gallery has been offering the finest names in high-quality ceramic gifts. It is not surprising that Ceramica Gift Gallery has been a leading choice for bridal registries, after all, who doesn't want to get more for less? With hundreds of patterns on display, simple and elaborate tastes alike will not be disappointed. Some notable items. dinnerware by Villeroy & Boch and Rosenthal; flatware by Ralph Lauren and George Jensen; stemware by Baccarat, Lenox, and Waterford; and a variety of figurines, plates, and collectibles by Armani, Wedgwood, and Hummel.

DIRECT FURNITURE DISCOUNTERS
470 Seventh Avenue (between 35th & 36th Streets),12th Floor, New York NY 10018. 212/947-3283. **Description:** For furnishing

your home on a budget, look to Direct Furniture Discounters. With more than 400 manufacturers to choose from, Direct Furniture Discounters is bound to have your favorite. Lexington, Hickory, Sealy, Rowe, and Broyhill are just a few of the names you will find in this furniture paradise.

EASTSIDE CHINA
5002 Twelfth Avenue (at 50th Street), Brooklyn NY 11219. 718/633-8672. **Description:** In the New Utrecht Avenue area of Brooklyn, a district identical to Manhattan's Lower East Side, is another east side -- this china shop. Like its downtown counterparts, Eastside China offers discounts of 25 percent and more on hundreds of patterns in china and crystal from Noritake, Wedgewood, Spode, Royal Doulton, Lenox, and many others. They'll spruce up the decor of your home, but the decor in the shop itself is minimal. Some patterns are on display, but if you don't see what you're after, they have all the catalogs and can order just about anything at the same low prices. Eastside China is open Sunday through Friday. The store is closed on Saturday.

FISHS EDDY
889 Broadway (at 19th Street), New York NY 10003. 212/420-9020. • 2176 Broadway (at 77th Street), New York NY 10023. 212/873-8819. **Description:** Fishs Eddy specializes in china, glassware, and food-related accessories that are collected from stores, manufacturers, restaurants, and other industrial institutions around the country. This enables you to acquire a coffee mug emblazoned with the logo of Krispy Kreme Donuts, found somewhere deep in the nation's heartland, for your own cupboard. Lots of all-American diners are represented here, some of their coffee mugs going for as little as $.95. Country clubs and snooty restaurants too, though these are more expensive; sugar bowl and creamer sets, ashtrays, beer mugs, and shot glasses in the shape of cowboy boots ($1.95) are just some of the ever-changing repertoire to be discovered here. Fishs Eddy also sells industrial china by such restaurant mainstays as Fiesta and Fire King. They even offer a bridal registry, and will ship orders of $50.00 and up to anywhere in the country. Don't laugh, people do it! Fishs Eddy has raised salvage to an art form, as evidenced by such visitors as Spike Lee and Donna Karan. The Broadway store is the main location; the West Village shop is tiny, so be careful as you walk through. Open Sunday, 11:00 a.m. - 8:00 p.m.; Monday through Saturday, 10:00 a.m. - 9:00 p.m.

GARLEN CARPET CORP.
1412 Remsen Avenue, Brooklyn NY 11236. 718/444-9140. **World Wide Web address:** http://www.garlencarpetcorp.baweb.com. **Description:** For more than 30 years, Garlen Carpet has been offering everyday low prices on wall-to-wall carpeting, and commercial and vinyl tiles. What's more, they are not stingy when it comes to using Mr. C's favorite word: FREE! Free estimates, free measuring, free delivery, and free installation are just a few more of the reasons to drop by and visit.

HARRIS LEVY

278 Grand Street, New York NY 10002. 212/226-3102. **Description:** Here's another of the Lower East Side's great stores for bargains on all kinds of domestic items. Harris Levy boasts one of the largest selections in the country, and does mail-order business far and wide. Even the most expensive of tastes can save money here; many of the fabrics are imported from Europe and the Far East, but sell for 20 - 60 percent off list prices. Thus, a complete set of bed linens from Italy, which would retail uptown for as much as $700.00, are discounted to $500.00 here. Among the names found here are Laura Ashley, Bill Blass, and Adrienne Vittadini. Of course, with a selection ranging from the fancy to the everyday, there is plenty to choose from at far more reasonable prices too. And the folks at Harris Levy don't stop at the bedroom -- there are big savings on kitchen towels and pot holders, bathroom rugs, shower curtains, and laundry hampers. The store is spacious and comfortable, with display areas that make it more boutiquey than most in the area; service is relaxed and shopper-friendly.

JONAS DEPARTMENT STORE

40 West 14th Street, New York NY 10011. 212/242-8253. **Description:** Along the parade of junk stores for which 14th Street is famous, you'll find several stores like Jonas Department Store -- filled with inexpensive housewares of varying quality. They have lots of domestics, kitchen gadgets, and the like. If you need simple stuff for your apartment, these may do: Hand towels for $.99, tweed-style luggage at $18.99 (half its original price), touch-activated table lamps for $19.99, and more. There are some name brands mixed in, so it's worth a look. You may see a Proctor-Silex two-slice toaster for $13.99, or a cast-iron Dutch oven with a glass top for $19.99. It's easy to buy cheap in New York as long as you know where to look.

KALFAIAN & SON

475 Atlantic Avenue, Brooklyn NY 11217. 718/875-2222. **World Wide Web address:** http://www.kalfaian.com. **Description:** Here's a great American story: this huge operation began around the turn of the century as a rug cleaning service in a backyard. It's now one of New York's largest dealers of rugs and carpeting, yet it's still in the same family. Current owners George and Cliff Kalfaian keep that family atmosphere going today, offering great prices and full service. The store has recently expanded to three floors of orientals, residential and commercial broadloom, and remnants. The warehouse building is nevertheless bright and comfortable inside. On the main floor, you'll find all-wool berber rugs at up to half the cost of many other stores; a 12' x 19' rug, list price $920.00, sells here for $459.00. Wool blends and synthetics are much lower still, as little as $14.00 per square yard including padding and installation. They also have such new innovations as Kangaback carpeting, which has the padding sewn in underneath; Mr. C saw a 12' x 9' rug for $99.00. Tightly woven commercial broadloom, suitable for offices, starts around $12.00 a

square yard installed; remnants are as low as $8.00 to $10.00 a yard. Upstairs showrooms include the orientals and country-style rugs, also well-priced. They even have oriental runners. A 2' x 8' size will make your hallway dazzling for just $49.00. Every item is clearly marked. Kalfaian claims to be the first major store in New York, way back when, to display each piece, tagged with the size, style and price. The name brands show that these guys have nothing to hide; personal attention is their watchword here. Open daily, 10:00 a.m. to 5:00 p.m.

KAUFMAN ELECTRICAL APPLIANCES
365 Grand Street, New York NY 10002. 212/475-8313. **Description:** This tiny shop on the Lower East Side serves up some of the city's best deals on china, silver, and kitchen appliances. You can get fine place settings and stainless steel flatware by some of the world's best manufacturers including Noritake, Yamazaki, and Mikasa, at just above wholesale prices. With many flatware designs plated in 24-karat gold, you can live like royalty without mortgaging the castle. Kaufman's also sells small appliances by Sunbeam, Regal, and Farberware, as well as larger items like Frigidaire refrigerators and Hotpoint ranges -- again, at substantial discounts. They will also make free deliveries to anywhere in the five boroughs. What could be easier? Remember, all stores in this area close at 2:00 p.m. on Friday, and all day Saturday.

LAMP WAREHOUSE
3824 Fort Hamilton Parkway, Brooklyn NY 11218. 718/436-2207. **Description:** If you're hoping to see the light, you'll probably find it in one of Lamp Warehouse's six big showrooms. What's more, you'll find it for 10 - 50 percent less than at most other stores. LW claims to be New York's biggest; Mr. C wasn't about to start counting, but it's certainly right up there. They've got it all -- halogen lamps, track lighting, crystal chandeliers, ceiling fan/lights, wall sconces -- and, of course, bulbs for all. Some of these bargains are closeouts; and some are copies of famous brands that LW makes in its own factory -- another great way to save. Repairs and restoration can also be done in the store. Open every day but Wednesday.

LEE'S STUDIO
1755 Broadway (56th Street), New York NY 10019. 212/581-4400. ✦ 1069 Third Avenue (at 63rd Street), New York NY. 212/371-1122. **Description:** Lee's Studio discounts many famous brands of contemporary and designer lighting. You'll find track and recessed lighting, halogen lamps, and outdoor landscape fixtures by such names as Koch & Lowy, Juno, Halo, Luxo, and lots more. There are plenty of bulbs, dimmers, and spare parts, too. They offer installation and repair services as well as rentals. Call for specific location hours.

LIGHTING BY GREGORY
158 Bowery, New York NY 10012. 212/226-1276. **Toll-free phone:** 800/796-1965. **Description:** Just off of Delancey Street, Lighting By Gregory is actually four stores in one location. What goes on in

this bustling complex is nothing less than the sale of 126 lines of lighting -- in stock -- at contractor prices. LBG is the largest in-stock distributor of Lightolier and Halo in the eastern United States. And if there's a brand you want that they've somehow missed, they can literally get it for you wholesale. They have Tizio lamps, considered the "grandaddy of halogens," Casablanca ceiling fans, Stiffel and Lenox traditional lamps, and ultra-contemporary designs by Artemide, George Kovacs, and Flos. Stained-glass lamps can be custom-made to order. They even have theatrical stage lighting. The helpful salespeople will consult with you and figure out just what you need. Open daily, 8:30 a.m. - 5:30 p.m.

PORTICO OUTLET
233 Tenth Avenue (at 24th Street), New York NY 10011. 212/807-8807. **World Wide Web address:** http://www. porticonewyork.com. **Description:** If you've ever fantasized about owning a Portico furnishing, but scoffed at the price ($2,650.00 bed frames, $225.00 sheets, $60.00 pillowcases, $50.00 towels), the Portico Outlet may be able to make that dream a reality. Portico Outlet offers the same high-end furnishings found in the SoHo store (as well as stores throughout the country) at a discount. If you've had your eye on one of their modern steel-framed or iron beds but can't quite foot the bill, this place is definitely worth checking out. I'm not promising you'll find the same bed frame for $100.00, but I can promise you substantial discounts from the retail store prices. Open Monday through Friday, 11:00 a.m. - 7:00 p.m.; Saturday, 10:00 a.m. - 7:00 p.m.; Sunday, 12:00 p.m. - 6:00 p.m.

THE RUG WAREHOUSE
220 West 80th Street, 2nd Floor, New York NY 10024. 212/787-6665. **Description:** Just around the corner from Broadway on the Upper West Side, The Rug Warehouse is one of Manhattan's largest dealers of area rugs with over 1,000 on display. Unlike many stores, which run special sales, Rug Warehouse calls itself a year-round discounter, keeping prices as low as possible on Orientals, Persians, Dhurries, hook rugs, and contemporary designs. These are all about 20 - 25 percent below prices in many other stores. They even run an annual three-week anniversary sale, when prices are reduced by a further 10 - 15 percent. All-wool rugs start as low as $199.00, with a wide range of 8' x 11' and 9' x 12' rugs from $500.00 to $800.00. Rug Warehouse also sells used rugs -- mainly Persians -- as well as copies of expensive hand-made rugs. Every rug is clearly labeled with its price, age, and country of origin, making it easy for you to browse without heavy pressure from salespeople. They even offer a seven-day return policy -- clearly a reputable operation.

STRAIGHT FROM THE CRATE
344 West 57th Street, New York NY 10019. 212/541-4350. ♦ 261 Madison Avenue (at 38th Street), New York NY. 212/867-4050. ♦ 1251 Lexington Avenue (between 84th & 85th Streets), New York NY. 212/717-4227. ♦ 161 West 72nd Street, New York NY. 212/579-6494. **World Wide Web address:** http://www.straightfromthecrate.com **Description:** This shop

offers good prices on furniture, appliances, and decorative items for the home. A 500-watt halogen torch lamp, in a black enamel finish, goes for $59.99; you can also get a regular-bulb version for $35.00. A five-foot-tall Scandinavian white dresser with eight drawers was seen for $140.00. You'll also find things like coffee makers and food processors at decent prices, along with glassware and china and decorative items for the kitchen and bathroom. At some locations, you'll find even more furniture -- like a twin-size futon that folds up into a chair for $159.00. Mr. C also saw several handsome coffee tables including one with a round glass top for $69.00. Open Sunday, 12:00 p.m. - 6:00 p.m.; Monday through Friday, 10:00 a.m. - 8:00 p.m.; Saturday, 10:00 a.m. - 7:00 p.m.

TUDOR ELECTRICAL SUPPLY
222 East 46th Street, New York NY. 212/867-7550. **Description:** Surprisingly enough on the East Side of midtown, Tudor Electric offers good prices -- if not rock bottom -- on lots of classic and modern lighting fixtures and lamps. The tiny showroom is jam-packed with displays of floor lamps, desk lamps, halogen lighting, track lighting, ceiling fixtures, and more. The rear half of the store is given over to bulbs of seemingly every size and shape, as well as other hardware and accessories.

SHOPPING
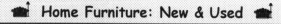
Home Furniture: New & Used

ALBEE BABY CARRIAGE COMPANY
715 Amsterdam Avenue (at West 95th Street), New York NY 10025. 212/662-5740. **Description:** "We supply everything but the baby" is more than just Albee's slogan, it's a fact. If you're expecting a child, this is a great place to start the preparations. Albee offers top name brand car seats, cribs, strollers, high chairs, dressing tables, and carriages at discount prices. Morigeau, Carters, Aprica, Fisher Price, Snugli, Graco, Evenflo, Baby Björn -- you name it, they've got it. They even carry juvenile furniture, for when your little darling isn't so little (and perhaps not so darling) anymore. But Albee is more than just a furniture store, they carry a full line of toys and even have a complete layette department chock full of matching quilts, bumpers, and accessories. Open Monday through Saturday, 9:00 a.m. - 5:30 p.m.; Thursday 9:00 a.m. - 7:30 p.m.

BAMBI'S BABY CENTER
2150 Third Avenue, New York NY 10035. 212/828-8878. **Toll-free phone:** 877/88-BAMBI. **World Wide Web address:** http://www.elbambi.com. **Description:** If you're expecting a little bambino, Bambi's Baby Center is a great place to start your journey into parenthood. Since 1976, Bambi's Baby Center has been a leading discounter of baby and juvenile furniture and accessories including cribs, playpens, car seats, strollers, high chairs, changing tables, dressers, and bunk beds. Items seen included Maclaren strollers for $149.99, Century car seats for just over $60.00, Graco high chairs for $79.99, and Angel Line cribs for under $250.00. They also carry lots of accessories (otherwise known as necessities), such as bottles for under $5.00.

COUCH POTATO
5113 New Utrecht Avenue, Brooklyn NY 11219. 718/972-7632. **Description:** Underneath the elevated train along the northern end of New Utrecht Avenue there is a whole district of bargain shops much like Manhattan's Lower East Side. Many are owned by orthodox Jews, meaning two things: Good prices and odd hours. They close on Friday afternoons and reopen all day Sunday, in observance of the Sabbath. This store specializes in sofas of all kinds, from loveseats to modular sets to recliners and convertible beds. They sell between 30 - 50 percent below list prices. There are good names to be found here including Sealy, Lane, Berkline, and Flexsteel. Basic models start around $299.00; sleep sofas start about $100.00 higher. All mattresses, by the way, are proper inner-spring mattresses, not foam rubber. The prices are cheap, not the quality.

FREDERICK FURNITURE

107 East 31st Street (between Park & Lexington Avenues), New York NY 10016. 212/683-8322. **Toll-free phone:** 800/FREDDYS. **Description:** This place probably should be known as Frederick Bedding. From A to Z, Frederick has got you covered in the bedding market: bunks, trundles, lofts, adjustables, electrics, platforms, Murphy beds, sofa beds, day beds, futons, you-name-it, they're all here and priced to move. Frederick Furniture also carries a wide selection of bedding accessories including headboards and canopies. If you're frequently on the move, pick up one of their many air mattresses. With three floors of showroom space, chances are, if you sleep on it, Frederick sells it.

FUTON WAREHOUSE

113 University Place (at 13th Street & Union Square), New York NY 10003. 212/473-4400. **Description:** Here's another store that you can only imagine must be littered with financially-strapped college students. After all, they are selling a student's favorite piece of furniture--the futon. Yet, in addition to futons, the 6,500 square-foot Futon Warehouse also carries a large selection of frames, covers, and pillows; tables and chairs; and shelving. Pick up a twin loft bed for just $199.00, or upgrade yourself to a full or queen for just $239.00 or $299.00, respectively. All furniture is warranteed. Open Monday through Friday, 10:00 a.m. - 8:00 p.m.; Saturday, 10:00 a.m. - 6:00 p.m.; Sunday, 12:00 p.m. - 6:00 p.m.

GOTHIC CABINET CRAFT

1655 Second Avenue, New York NY 10028. 212/288-2999. ♦ 1601 Second Avenue (at 83rd Street), New York NY. 212/472-7359. ♦ 2543 Broadway (at 95th Street), New York NY. 212/749-2020. ♦ 27-50 First Street, Queens NY. 718/626-1480. ♦ 36-48 Main Street, Queens NY. 718/762-6246. ♦ 31 Smith Street (at Fulton Street), Brooklyn NY. 718/625-2333. ♦ 6929 Fifth Avenue (at Ovington Street), Brooklyn NY. 718/745-0715. ♦ 2163 White Plains Road, Bronx NY. 718/863-7440. ♦ 2366 University Avenue, Bronx NY. 718/365-9333. **Description:** Unfinished furniture is one great way to save money. Gothic Cabinet Craft makes a wide variety of functional pieces for every room in the house, with plenty of styles and solid woods to choose from. A colonial-style hardwood rocking chair can cost as little as $39.00, and a four-drawer writing desk is just $189.00. Contemporary styles include solid-pine platform beds from just $99.00; or choose a birch model that includes headboard, drawers, and nightstands complete for $399.00. They can complete the outfit for you with discount prices on mattress sets by Serta and Sealy, as well as futons. There are also butcher-block tables, loft beds, computer desks, entertainment centers, bookcases, and much more.

LONG'S BEDDING & INTERIORS, INC.

121 West 72nd Street (between Columbus & Broadway), New York NY 10023. 212/873-1752. **World Wide Web address:**

http://www.longsbedding.com. **Description:** Need a mattress on the cheap and on the double? Long's Bedding & Interiors has got one of the city's largest selections of mattresses (sofa, platform, electric, horsehair, foam, non-allergenic) at great prices. And you haven't even heard the best part -- they offer three-hour delivery. So, if you're in a fix or on a budget, doesn't it make sense to go to Long's? The rest of New York has been going since 1911.

MB DISCOUNT FURNITURE

2311 Avenue U (between 23rd & 24th Streets), Brooklyn NY 11229. 718/332-1500. **World Wide Web address:** http://www.mbchildrensfurniture.baweb.com. **Description:** MB is a large operation that offers substantial discounts on children's furniture. They have everything you'll need for infants to teenagers; from cribs and high chairs to bunk beds, traditional-style desks and dressers, and ultra-modern indestructible stuff. Service is a big part of their approach; they offer layaway plans, delivery, and even free consultations on the design of your kids' room. They know what they're talking about -- they've been at it a good, long time.

MIKE'S FURNITURE STORE

566 Columbus Avenue (between 87th & 88th Streets), New York NY. 212/873-1336. ◆ 520 Amsterdam Avenue, New York NY. 212/875-9403. ◆ 254 West 88th Street, New York NY. 212/787-6661. **World Wide Web address:** http://www. mikeslumber.baweb.com. **Description:** You know, Mike's must be the kind of place that is a Godsend for students in the Big Apple. Mike's Furniture offers substantial discounts on both finished and unfinished cabinets, bookcases, beds, entertainment centers, and wall units. And, to ensure that those same students are reading Shakespeare more often than they are *TV Guide*, Mike's Furniture will discount all pine bookcases an extra 10 percent when you present a valid student ID. For the frugal homeowner, they also offer great deals on shutters, kitchen tables, and chairs. For the Bob Vila in all of us, Mike's Furniture is also happy to offer cut-to-size lumber. Stop by one of Mike's three Upper West Side locations and check the deals out for yourself.

THE SMALL FURNITURE STORE

363 Lafayette Street, New York NY 10012. 212/475-4396. **Description:** Yes, it's small, and it's barely a store. Someone set up shop on a busy street corner in the East Village and began refinishing old furniture. He knew that if he built it they would come, and they did. Folks wander in and out of this shack and canvas tent looking at pieces such as a maple-frame mirror for $35.00, or a four-drawer pine dresser for $165.00, as well as chairs, tables, bookshelves, and whatever else the crew happens to be working on. There are also some proper antiques priced somewhat higher. The store stays open well into the evening, with flood lights that make it resemble a used car lot more than a furniture shop, but don't be fooled.

TOWN BEDDING
205 Eighth Avenue (between 20th & 21st Street), 1st Floor, New York NY 10011. 212/243-0426. ◆ 1014 Second Avenue (between 53rd & 54th Streets), New York, NY 10022. **Toll-free phone:** 800/706-2699. **Description:** A small, no-frills store, Town Bedding is able to offer great prices on all mattresses, sofa beds, and futons. Find a Sealy Posturepedic or Serta Perfect Sleeper mattress and box spring for $800.00 in queen size, which ain't bad; and you can save even more with smaller, independent brands, which Town ensures are made to the same standards as the big names, or better. A similar queen set by Sleep Aid, for example, sells for just $400.00. Mattresses by these independent makers start as low as $59.00 for a twin-size and $78.00 full-size. Town Bedding will deliver anywhere in the metro area including Long Island and New Jersey. There is no charge for delivery of name-brand sets, and only a small fee for budget models.

WEISSMAN FURNITURE WHOLESALERS, INC.
115 East 29th Street, New York NY 10016. 212/673-2880. **Description:** Forty is the only number you need to know at this great store. Larry Weissman sells residential and commercial furniture and bedding, with big-brand names like Hooker, Lane, Rowe, Sealy, Stanley, Lexington, and many others -- at about 40 percent below the prices in major department stores. Anyone, whether in business or the general public, can walk in and get the same great deals. The store does not advertise; word-of-mouth, and lots of regular customers, are what keep the prices so low. A recent sale featured a complete bedroom set in solid oak; a triple dresser, two night tables, mirror, chest, and queen-size headboard, with a value of $3,400.00 -- selling for $1,900.00. There are lots of sofa beds, starting from $699.00, with real inner-spring mattresses -- none of that cheap, back-aching foam rubber! Excellent prices on mattress sets by Simmons and Sleep-Aid. They'll ship and install anywhere in the tri-state area; personal service is a big plus here.

SHOPPING
🏠 Jewelry 🏠

ALL BY HAND
7810 Third Avenue (78th Street), Brooklyn NY. 718/745-8904.
Description: This lovely shop specializes in handmade jewelry of all kinds, as well as crafts from candlesticks to pottery to stained glass. Each one is a unique piece, created by a gallery of artists. Prices are very reasonable; many items are in the $5.00 - $10.00 range, including lots of little knickknacks, like artsy refrigerator magnets. The store is open seven days a week.

IDEAL DIAMOND COMPANY
7 West 47th Street, New York NY 10036-3302. 212/221-0050.
Description: For more than 20 years, Ideal Diamond Company has been getting shoppers some of the best deals on some of the best quality diamonds. If you're in the market for diamonds, whether it be a ring, a necklace, or a bracelet, this store is an Ideal place to start. Because they manufacture and import their own diamonds, Ideal Diamond Company is able to offer high-quality diamonds to you at wholesale prices. Diamond stud earrings, tennis bracelets, and solitaire necklaces are just a few of the items that can be found here at fantastic prices. All jewelry is guaranteed and comes with a lifetime upgrade policy.

LEEKAN DESIGNS
93 Mercer Street (between Broome & Spring Streets), New York NY 10012. 212/226-7226. **Description:** This large, beautiful SoHo shop specializes in Asian folk art, but also carries such treasures as enameled porcelain bracelets from $8.00 - $12.00, jade earrings from $16.00, and myriad tiny cases and decorative boxes ranging from $8.00 - $16.00. Or look at all the little handmade toys, from Japanese tin pins for $.50 to a Noh character hand puppet for $12.00. These are all gifts that should certainly make a unique impression on anyone.

MAX NASS JEWELRY
118 East 28th Street, New York NY 10016. 212/679-8154.
Description: There may not be too many jewelry shops as distinctive (and affordable) as this one. Perry Shah, who took over from founder Nass, keeps this narrow shop filled with trinkets of every conceivable kind, old and new. He can repair jewelry or make items new again by putting old pieces onto new chains or settings. These stones may be your own, or something from his collection of turquoise, onyx, ivory, coral, and more. There is a large collection of antique jewelry pieces, many of which are genuine gold and silver, at low prices: silver rings for $6.00, $7.50, $10.00, and up, earrings from $5.00, and 14-karat gold earrings from $30.00. Some have semiprecious stones; some

are plain. If they are faded and tarnished, you may have them restored, or kept as is. The options are nearly endless! Shah also buys up closeouts from department stores, like splashy decorated watches that once sold for $30.00 - $200.00, all sold here for $20.00 and up. And, twice a year, everything in the place goes on extra sale: 25 percent off all prices for two weeks in July, and 33 percent off for three weeks in January.

SHOPPING
Liquor & Beverages

B&E QUALITY BEVERAGE
511 West 23rd Street (between Tenth & Eleventh Avenues), New York NY 10011. 212/243-6559. **Description:** Just off Tenth Avenue, B&E's location looks industrial and foreboding, but this warehouse-style operation is open to the public. They have some of the best prices around on beers from all over the world, mineral water, soda, and fruit juices; yet you can shop here as though it were your corner liquor store or supermarket. A 12-pack of Michelob goes for just $6.99, and 12-packs of Molson bottles are $8.99. Heineken cans are $21.99 per case. You can also buy by the keg at great prices. San Pellegrino mineral water is $1.39 for a 25-ounce bottle; but you can get a case of 12 for $13.95. They also have mixer-sized bottles of orange, cranberry, and grapefruit juices. Bruce, the B of B&E, is a friendly guy, and he makes sure that his staff is just as friendly and very helpful. If you find this kind of shopping at all intimidating, you're in for a pleasant surprise here.

BEST CELLARS
1291 Lexington Avenue (at 87th Street), New York NY 10128. 212/426-4200. **World Wide Web address:** http://www.best-cellars.com. **Description:** Your days of wandering the liquor store, in a desperate search for the perfect wine are over! Consider Best Cellars help for the hopeless. This is a truly unique place. All the wines here are organized according to a simple system. Wines are broken down by color and flavor; you simply search in the section that best suits your taste. Looking for something fruity? Try the Juicy Light Bodied Red Wines. Want something more powerful? Select a Big Full-Bodied Red Wine. Are bubbles more your style? Celebrate with a Fizzy Sparkling Wine. Oh, have I mentioned that every bottle in the store in priced under $10.00? You can't do better than this. Open Monday through Thursday, 10:00 a.m. - 9:00 p.m.; Friday & Saturday, 10:00 a.m. - 10:00 p.m.

CROSSROADS
55 West 14th Street, New York NY 10011. 212/924-3060. **Description:** Many folks swear by this Greenwich Village shop, which is usually crowded with both bottles and buyers. But Crossroads is filled with interesting wines from all over the world, and has lots of good values tucked away on its racks. If you're confident about wines (and know what's good and not so good), you'll be able to find yourself a genuine bargain or two.

GARNET WINES & LIQUORS
929 Lexington Avenue (at 68th Street), New York NY 10021. 212/772-3211. **Toll-free phone:** 800/USA-VINO. **Description:**

Conveniently located near Hunter College and the 6 train, Garnet is a large and bustling shop offering what many shoppers consider the best wine prices in the city. There is an outstanding selection of wines and liquors from around the world, but be warned, the quality of their service can sometimes be as low as the prices. But hey, look at it this way, the discounts are well worth the aggravation, and you can relax once you get home with a great bottle of wine.

McADAM'S LIQUOR CORP.
398 Third Avenue (between 28th & 29th Streets), New York NY 10016. 212/679-1224. **World Wide Web address:** http://www. mcadam-buyrite.com. **Description:** To have a true New York experience, you have to think New York, talk New York, and drink New York. As the world's largest purveyor of Long Island wines, Thomas J. McAdam is nice enough to bring them to you, and at incredible discounts. Try a bottle of 1995 Bedell Reserve Chardonnay for just $13.99, or a Pellegrini East End Chardonnay for $9.99. If dinner calls for red, an $11.99 bottle of 1996 Hargrave Merlot Lattice should match your taste and budget. After dinner, try one of their many dessert wines, reasonably priced between $6.99 and $24.99 a bottle. And for those special occasions, McAdam's is happy to offer a wide range of sparkling wines, like a Pugliese pinot noir champagne for just $14.99. For added convenience, you can order online.

NANCY'S WINES FOR FOOD
313 Columbus Avenue (at 75th Street), New York NY 10023. 212/877-4040. **World Wide Web address:** http://www. nancyswine.com. **Description:** A hidden treasure for food lovers and wine connoisseurs alike, Nancy's is New York's only wine shop devoted to the art of matching food and wine. Nancy's boasts an eclectic and exciting assortment, including over 150 good -- *really* good -- bottles under $10.00, and a staggering collection of German Rieslings. The friendly, experienced staff tastes every wine, so you can't go wrong asking for help here. And yes Virginia, there really *is* a Nancy.

NEW YORK BEVERAGE
428 East 91st Street (between York & 1st Streets), New York NY. 212/831-4000. **E-mail address:** info@newyorkbeverage.com. **World Wide Web address:** http://www.newyorkbeverage.com. **Description:** If you're looking to entertain (on a budget), then you're looking for New York Beverage. Throughout Manhattan, New York Beverage delivers an impressive list of beer, hard cider, water, juice, and soda. Hundreds of imports and microbrews from around the world (Israel, Japan, Poland, Trinidad, Panama, Vietnam...you get the picture) allow you to traverse the world of beer without stepping foot outside your front door. Celebrate Cinco de Mayo with a case of Dos Equis ($25.29) or Modelo Especial ($22.79); savor some Singha with your Thai food ($25.99/case); or paint yourself green and bring in St. Patrick's Day with your good friend Murphy ($23.29 - $32.99/case). For

the less adventurous, you can always opt for a case of Bud ($16.99) or Coors (17.49). New York Beverage is also happy to deliver a variety of sodas, waters, and juices. Cases of 1-liter Pellegrino bottles ($16.99), 32-ounce Snapple bottles ($16.99), half gallon Tropicana juices ($19.99), and 2-liter Coca-Cola products ($6.99) can also be had.

THRIFTY BEVERAGE CENTER
256 Court Street (at Butler Street), Brooklyn NY. 718/875-0226. **World Wide Web address:** http://www.americanthriftybeverage. baweb.com. **Description:** This supermarket plus offers one of the city's best selections of beer, soda, juice, water, and all else that is drinkable. Choose from hundreds of beers including domestics, imports, and U.S. microbrews; all sorts of non-alcoholic beverages are available too, at equally great prices. Open Sunday, 12:00 p.m. - 6:00 p.m.; Monday, 2:00 p.m. - 7:00 p.m.; Tuesday through Thursday, 11:00 a.m. - 7:00 p.m.; Friday, 11:00 a.m. - 8:00 p.m.; Saturday, 10:30 a.m. - 6:00 p.m.

WAREHOUSE WINES & SPIRITS
735 Broadway (between Waverly Place & 8th Street), New York NY 10011. 212/982-7770. **Description:** Warehouse Wines & Spirits offers great values, low prices, an incredible selection, and a huge inventory. Their warehouse image is backed up by their warehouse prices. Warehouse Wines & Spirits also works to take a lot of the guesswork out of wine shopping, listing their "Top Twenty Everyday Whites." They have beverages to meet all tastes and budgets, with an enormous selection of wines for under $10.00 and bargain liquor prices. Hours are Monday through Thursday, 9:00 a.m. - 8:45 p.m.; Friday and Saturday, 9:00 a.m. - 9:45 p.m.

SHOPPING
✈ Luggage ✈

ALTMAN LUGGAGE
135 Orchard Street, New York NY 10002. 212/254-7275.
Toll-free phone: 1-800-372-3377. **Description:** The Lower
East Side's luggage discounter, Altman carries all major brands
(American Tourister, Perry Ellis, Le Sportsac) at 30 - 50 percent
off list prices. How do they do it? Volume! The aisles are
packed with suitcases, briefcases, garment bags, overnight totes,
army duffels, backpacks -- and shoppers. The salespeople are
hard to get to sometimes, so be patient. Be sure to check for
clearance markdowns; anything that hasn't sold after a few
months is sold at cost, to keep the stock moving. Altman also sells
all kinds of supplies for the business person, such as pens by Cross
and Parker. Open Monday through Thursday, 9:00 a.m. - 6:30 p.m.;
Friday, 9:00 a.m. - 5:00 p.m.; Sunday, 9:00 a.m. - 6:00 p.m.; closed
Saturday.

AMBASSADOR LUGGAGE
371 Madison Avenue (between 45th & 46th Streets), New York
NY. 212/972-0965. **Description:** Unlikely as it seems on the
east side of midtown, Ambassador Luggage sells fine brand-name
bags at discounts of up to 40 percent below list prices. Of
course, as Mr. C often notes, "list price" can sometimes be a
fictitious number that no one ever really pays. Nevertheless,
with such a substantial discount, you can be sure that the prices
are good even with a little padding. Speaking of which, the high-
quality names you'll find here include Hartman, Lark, Delsey, and
Andiamo.

JOBSON'S LUGGAGE
666 Lexington Avenue (between 55th & 56th Streets), New York
NY 10022. 212/355-6846. **Toll-free phone:** 800/221-5238.
Description: Since 1949, Jobson's has been offering the best
names in luggage at the best prices. Jobson's has everything for
the traveler including famous names like Andiamo, Halliburton,
American Tourister, Lark, and Ciao. How about snagging a rolling
Samsonite suitcase, originally priced at $300.00, for just
$149.00? They also have a complete selection of business needs,
like portfolios and briefcases.

LEXINGTON LUGGAGE LIMITED
793 Lexington Avenue (between 61st & 62nd Streets), New York
NY 10021. 212/223-0698. **Toll-free phone:** 800/822-0404.
E-mail address: lexingtonluggage@juno.com. **Description:**
Lexington Luggage Limited makes this area something of a luggage
district. Like Jobson's (see separate listing), they offer a vast
array of suitcases, garment bags, and attaches; plus business

accessories like pens, day planners, wallets, and more. The brands, again, include all the big boys (American Tourister, Boyt, Infinity, Kenneth Cole, Timberland, and Tumi), and the store claims it will not be undersold. Take them up on the offer: compare the two dealers and see how well you can do.

SHOPPING
♪ Musical Instruments ♪

SAM ASH
155 West 48th Street, New York NY 10036. 212/719-2625.
Description: With its empire based in the heart of the midtown Manhattan music district, just above Times Square, Sam Ash is the undisputed king of musical instruments and related products. Four different storefronts are spread out around the block, selling everything you've ever heard tooted or strummed (and several things you may not have heard of). Almost all items are new, sold at discount, though there are occasionally some deals on used instruments. The company is perhaps best known for guitars, most of which sell for 30 - 40 percent below list price; you can get a new Fender Stratocaster for $199.00. But they also sell brass, woodwinds, drums, and all the accessories. You can find a set of D'Addario guitar strings here for $3.75, about half the price of other stores. Across the street from the guitar shop is their electronics branch, where they have all manner of keyboards and MIDI computers. A Kawai electric piano was recently on sale for $430.00, reduced from $650.00; and a Macintosh Mac Classic II, complete with keyboard, monitor, and mouse, was on sale for $990.00. This same branch also sells stereo equipment, like a set of JBL oak cabinet speakers, marked down from $360.00 to just $199.00 for the pair. The mega-store continues to expand and rearrange its empire, so the various departments may have played musical chairs since this was written; but the bargains will always make you the winner.

FIRST FLIGHT MUSIC
174 First Avenue (between 10th & 11th Streets), New York NY 10009. 212/539-1383. **World Wide Web address:** http://www.firstflightmusic.com. **Description:** Whether you're Miles Davis or Herbie Hancock, First Flight Music has got your instrument of choice. From percussion to woodwind, First Flight Music houses a great stock of all instrument families. Ampeg, Boss, and Gibson are just a few of the names that you will find here, and all at great prices. Ask about close-outs for additional savings. Open Monday through Friday, 11:00 a.m. - 8:00 p.m.; Saturday, 12:00 p.m. - 8:00 p.m.; Sunday, 12:00 p.m. - 6:00 p.m.

KING JAMES MUSIC
2352 Flatbush Avenue, Brooklyn NY 11234. 718/377-8532.
Description: Not far from Kings Plaza, King James is one of the city's longtime landmarks in the guitar biz, although they also offer discount prices on a few lines of keyboards, drums, and recording equipment. Student-model guitars start at just $50.00; name brands, like Ibanez and Epiphone, are around $135.00 and up. Other makes of guitars and basses here include Gibson, Fender, Ovation, Music Man, and all the biggies. Amplifiers too, by Crate, Ampeg, and more. Servicing is done in the shop, under full

manufacturers' warranties. Open Monday through Saturday, 10:00 a.m. - 6:00 p.m. (until 8:00 p.m. on Mondays and Thursdays).

ROYAL MUSIC CENTER
1966 Rockaway Parkway, Brooklyn NY 11236. 718/241-3330.
Description: For more than thirty years, Royal Music Center has been offering very competitive prices on a full range of band instruments, keyboards, guitars, and drums. They carry the big brand names, like Peavey amplifiers, Rickenbacker guitars, Selmer woodwinds, Ludwig drums, and much more. And service is a big emphasis here, too. For further bargains, ask whether any used instruments are currently available.

30TH STREET GUITARS
236 West 30th Street, New York NY 10001. 212/868-2660.
World Wide Web address: http://www.30thstreetguitars.com.
Description: As New York's biggest guitar store, 30th Street Guitars has the luxury of being the most forgiving when it comes to pricing. With a huge inventory and lots of used guitars and amplifiers, you can find something in almost any price range. From acoustic to electric to vintage, 30th Street Guitars has got the instrument you've been looking for at the right price.

SHOPPING
🗄 Office Furniture 🗄

ACE OFFICE FURNITURE
229 42nd Street, Brooklyn NY 11232. 718/965-8457.
E-mail address: ace@highclass.net. **World Wide Web address:**
http://www.aceofficefurniture.baweb.com. **Description:** When
you're looking to refurnish or build an office, Ace Office
Furniture is worth the trip. Ace stocks a large inventory of both
new and used furniture, at prices that are usually discounted 35
percent or better. And, while some of the furniture may be used,
it is by no means worn. Try finding a Steelcase four-drawer lateral
filing cabinet anywhere else for just $200.00. Mr. C also spotted
an adjustable multi-task steno chair for just $145.00, and a double
pedestal desk for just $295.00. If you're looking for name brands,
have no fear, as Ace carries top names like Hon, Virco, Herman
Miller, and Global.

DAVID'S OFFICE EQUIPMENT
327 Canal Street, New York NY 10013. 212/966-5418.
Description: David's sells office furniture from a tiny storefront;
in fact, you can't miss him, since his merchandise spills out
onto the sidewalk. Most of the stuff he deals in is used, like
the drafting tables Mr. C saw for $125.00, or the four-drawer file
cabinets for $85.00 and up. He does carry several lines of
catalog merchandise, which he can order for you; and, there are
the occasional closeout deals, like some unused computer system
tables for $99.00. Open Monday through Saturday, 9:00 a.m. -
6:00 p.m.

DISCOUNT OFFICE FURNITURE
132 West 24th Street, New York NY 10011. 212/691-5625. **E-mail
address:** info@NYDOF.com. **World Wide Web address:**
http://www.NYDOF.com. **Description:** Whether you're buying a
single chair or outfitting an office of 50, the folks at Discount
Office Furniture will have what you need. Specializing in high-end
manufacturers like Herman Miller, Steelcase, and Knoll, you can
find great quality items at budget prices. Herman Miller Ergon
chairs, listed at $675.00 new, can be had for under $200.00 used.
The small storefront serves as a showroom for a large and ever-
growing warehouse inventory. On the main level, you'll find
refinished vintage wood desks tucked in between conference
tables and assorted chairs. Downstairs are the files, such as a
Steelcase five-drawer lateral file for only $375.00 used (retails
at over $1,100.00 new). Most of the items are in excellent
condition, and Discount Office Furniture guarantees all items to
be 100 percent operational. If you'd prefer to save yourself a trip,
you can check out pictures of what is available at the Discount
Office Furniture Website. With a good network around the

country, Discount Office Furniture can get you almost anything you need, even if they don't have it in stock today. And if you're buying in bulk, they're also willing to negotiate even deeper discounts. And hey, while you're in the market to redecorate your office, don't forget that Discount Office Furniture may be more than willing to buy your used furniture as well.

FILEWORKS, LLC

333 Hudson Street, 7th Floor, New York NY 10013. 212/989-5687. **Description:** Charlie Kessler runs a very impressive one-man operation catering to the needs of artists, architects, photographers, and anyone else who needs to furnish an office inexpensively. He scavenges a huge stock of top-quality brands from offices around town and resells them, by his estimate, at about half the price of the city's best discounters. He specializes in drafting furniture, concentrating on flat storage systems for paper and artwork and offers new, used, factory second, and vintage flatfiles and drafting tables. Used flatfiles are often priced in the $200.00 range, with high-end drafting tables at even lower prices. He also offers top-of-the-line vertical and lateral filing systems, as well as posture chairs by some of the most notable manufacturers around including Steelcase, Herman Miller, and Knoll. Many of these files, which retail for about $200.00 per drawer, can be had for a fraction of the price through Charlie. And all those nifty office chairs, sensors, concentrix, ergons, equas, diffrients, what-have-you that are normally priced between $500.00 and $800.00 can be purchased for as low as $150.00. Even if you can't find exactly what you're looking for, Mr. Kessler would be more than happy to put you on his computerized waiting list and keep a sharp lookout for you...at no charge or obligation to buy! That's right, Charlie knows the benefit of good customer service and repeat business. How else would he stay in business for 20 years? Hours are flexible, but by appointment only.

FRANK EASTERN COMPANY

599 Broadway (at Houston Street), 6th Floor, New York NY 10012. 212/219-0007. **World Wide Web address:** http://www.belowcost.com. **Description:** This is a major downtown showroom offering brand names in new office furniture at discount. Save as much as 50 percent off list prices on chairs for everyone from secretaries to the president. These start as low as $89.95, with further discounts through quantities of three or more. Leather executives' chairs start around $189.00. Frank Eastern also has a wide variety of computer workstations for every application and amount of space. Many of these are made of inexpensive wood with veneer finishes; assembly required. However, you can get a genuine oak executive desk for $499.00 -- a smart executive decision. And there are filing cabinets aplenty in wood and in steel, from such companies as Oxford and Hamilton. These are all very well-priced, and again, offer quantity discounts. Open Monday through Friday, 9:00 a.m. - 5:00 p.m. (April through October the Frank Eastern Company is also open Saturday, 11:00 a.m. - 3:30 p.m.)

OFFICE FURNITURE HEAVEN

22 West 19th Street, 7th Floor, New York NY 10011. 212/989-8600. **Description:** You may well believe you've gone to heaven when you enter this store -- that is, if you need to furnish any kind of office on a budget. The 16,000 square foot showroom is filled with first-quality contemporary and traditional pieces, all selling at hundreds of dollars off. The stuff is gorgeous; this looks more like a fancy regular full-price store. One recent item seen was an executive's desk made of cherry wood, which originally retailed for $2,300.00; it was on sale here for $775.00. These are manufacturer's closeouts and discontinued items, never used. As soon as they come into the store, they are instantly marked down to 50 percent below retail price. Many go down further until they sell. All the big names are here -- Steelcase, Knoll, Herman Miller, Gaiger, and more -- in conference tables, chairs, bookcases, file cabinets, and work stations. They specialize in quality used furniture and work stations; the work stations are sold either "as-is" or completely done to your specifications; wood furniture is completely refurbished. The sales staff is friendly and laid-back; they know, as you will see, that they've got a good thing going.

SECURITY OFFICE FURNITURE COMPANY

31 East 28th Street (between Park & Madison Avenues), New York NY 10016. 212/696-2020. **E-mail address:** info@securityofficefurn.com. **World Wide Web address:** http://www.securityofficefurn.com. **Description:** Security Office Furniture offers working professionals substantial discounts on not only new office furniture, but design, purchasing, delivery, and setup services as well. Choose from an enormous selection of desks, chairs, storage equipment, shelves, bookcases, and safes. Some of the bargains that I happened upon included a pneumatic chair for just $599.99, a leather high-back chair for $249.99, and a low-back pneumatic for $119.99. A four-drawer letter-sized vertical filing cabinet, which lists at $250.00, was selling for just $139.99. Look for a large inventory of desks at unbelievable prices as well. How about a double pedestal desk for under $400.00? Or a U-group workstation that elsewhere would sell for $1,690.00, for under $900.00? For some of the city's best values in furniture, whether redecorating the conference room or building a home office, you can feel secure in shopping here.

TWO JAKES USED OFFICE FURNITURE WAREHOUSE

320 Wythe Avenue, Brooklyn NY 11211. 718/782-7780. **E-mail address:** jake@usedofficefurniture.com. **World Wide Web address:** http://usedofficefurniture.com/twojakes. **Description:** These Two Jakes are nowhere near *Chinatown*. Deep in the heart of Brooklyn, Two Jakes is in the business of discounts. Look for top-quality used office furniture by Herman Miller, Steelcase, Knoll, Berhardt, Kimbal, and Goodform. Designer furniture from Ero Saarinen, Hans Wegner, Otto Zapf, Charles & Ray Eames, and Jens Rison is also in abundance. From desks, tables, chairs, and sofas to filing and storage cabinets, Two Jakes offers a large

selection of whatever it is your office is in need of. If all you need it a little bit of color, Two Jakes even sells used artwork to prettify your walls. Two Jakes also offers reupholstering and custom finishing of furniture, as well as a full line of stripped metal desks, files, and cabinets. And, true to Cheapster form, all furniture and services are offered at more than reasonable prices. Open Wednesday through Sunday, 11:00 a.m. - 7:00 p.m.

SHOPPING
🐈 Pets & Supplies 🐈

AMERICAN SOCIETY FOR THE PREVENTION OF CRUELTY TO ANIMALS (ASPCA)
424 East 92nd Street, New York NY 10128-6804. 212/876-7700.
World Wide Web address: http://www.aspca.org. **Description:** Established in 1866, the ASPCA is America's oldest humane society. When you apply for adoption, you'll be scrutinized almost as much as the pets they show you. You may even be turned down. Of course, there's a reason for such a careful process; the ASPCA is dedicated to quality matchups that work out for both pet and owner. The fee they charge is lower than the prices you'd pay at stores: $50.00 for a dog or a cat (and senior citizens may even be exempt). The animals have had all the required initial shots and have been spayed or neutered. They also have a Behavior Help Line you can call if it's having trouble adjusting to your home. The society is truly committed to the happiness of both you and your pet and currently has over 475,000 members and donors.

THE BEASTLY BITE
140 Court Street (between Atlantic & Pacific Avenues), Brooklyn NY 11201. 718/522-5133. **Description:** It was a very friendly New Yorker who told Mr. C that he must check out "that pet food store in Cobble Hill." She didn't even remember the name of it, but she said it had the best prices in New York. In spite of its name, the prices at Beastly Bite are indeed remarkably tame. They stock one of the largest varieties of dog and cat food that Mr. C has found, from the ordinary to the gourmet. Beastly Bite offers good prices on individual packages, and even better prices by the case. You and your cat will sing over a case of Figaro, 48 six-ounce cans for $16.25. You'll also find Science Diet, Pro-Plan, Old Mother Hubbard, Eukanuba, Neura, Max, Mighty Dog, and lots more. Not to mention cat litter, scented clay, cedar chips and all the accessories. Beastly Bite prints a flyer regularly detailing whatever is new in the store, as well as products whose prices have increased or decreased lately. They also make deliveries for a small charge in the local Brooklyn areas, as well as Lower Manhattan for a slightly higher charge. The store is open seven days a week into the early evening.

LITTLE CREATURES
126 St. Mark's Place, 1st Floor, New York NY 10009. 212/473-2857. ◆ 770 Amsterdam Avenue (at 97th Street), New York NY; 212/932-8610. **Description:** Here's a pair of small but well-stocked neighborhood pet supply stores that'll make it easy for you to keep Fido fed. High-volume buying makes it possible for Little Creatures to keep prices low on a good selection of dog and cat foods -- in such quality brands as Iams, Cornucopia and Science Diet. If you like to buy in volume yourself, you can do very well; a recent example seen was Lick Your Chops cat food, a case of 24

tins, for just $17.79. They also have a good variety of accessories, from dog leashes to cat condos. The stores are open into the early evening seven days a week, and they even offer free delivery.

PETLAND DISCOUNTS

404 Third Avenue, New York NY 10016. 212/447-0739. ◆ 312 West 23rd Street, New York NY 10011. 212/366-0512. ◆ 2708 Broadway, New York NY 10025. 212/222-8851. **E-mail address:** info@petlanddiscounts.com. **World Wide Web address:** http://www.petlanddiscounts.com. **Description:** Petland Discounts is a huge chain whose volume sales allow them to keep prices very low. Shopping around for an eight-pound bag of Eukanuba dog food or a four-pound bag of Iams cat food? You will find everything you need to keep your pet happy at competitive prices. And they have plenty of snack treats, rawhide bones and accessories for dogs and cats. They also have full lines of aquariums and fish, birds and cages, and other things for small animals. Here's an insider tip for all you pet owners; check out the Website. It has monthly discount coupons you can print out and bring to the store for added savings.

SHOPPING
✂ Sewing & Fabrics ✂

HERSH BUTTON
1000 Avenue of the Americas (at 37th Street), New York NY
10018. 212/391-6615. **Description:** Button fell off? No problem.
Zipper stuck? No problem. Hole in your knee? No problem. Not too
much money to spend? No problem. More than just buttons, Hersh
carries an exhaustive array of zippers, patches, and everything
else you could possible need to spruce up your wardrobe. Just
don't forget the thread and needle. Hersh carries all the tools of
the trade. The staff is friendly and ready to help, so if you're
feeling overwhelmed, just find the nearest salesperson for some
much needed succor.

LONG ISLAND FABRIC
406 Broadway (off Canal Street), New York NY. 212/925-4488.
Description: Yard-after-yard of affordable fabrics are what you
will find at Long Island Fabric. They stock everything from
feather boas (starting at $6.00) to silks galore (from $8.00/yard
up). Open daily, 9:00 a.m. - 6:00 p.m.

M&J FABRICS
1008 Avenue of the Americas, New York NY. 212/391-9072.
Description: If you are looking for the perfect finishing touch for
a dress, coat, etc. give M&J a try. Chances are you will find
something that suits both your budget and your tastes. Tons of
ribbons, buttons, and beads at reasonable prices.

P&S FABRICS
355 Broadway (between Franklin & Leonard Streets),
New York NY. 212/226-1534. **World Wide Web address:**
http://www.psfabrics.baweb.com. **Description:** P&S Fabrics is your
source for sewing, quilting, and craft supplies. At P&S Fabrics,
you'll find a wide selection of fabrics, trimmings, yarn, ribbons, and
more all at more than reasonable prices. P&S offers two floors of
everyday values, with weekly discounts making the prices even
better. P&S Fabrics also sells specialty fabrics, imports, and
remnants; and a large selection of sewing and knitting books. P&S
Fabrics offers sewing machine sales and repair services, and is an
authorized Baby Lock® dealer. You never know what you'll find on
sale at P&S Fabrics, so drop in whenever you're in the downtown
area.

PARON FABRICS
206 West 40th Street, New York NY 10018. 212/768-3266. ◆ 56
West 57th Street, New York NY 10019. 212/247-6451.
Description: Paron Fabrics sells a good variety of linens, wools,
imported silk and other clothing fabrics, wholesale and retail.
While their prices are good, you should check out their clearance
center on the second floor of the 57th Street location. Here,

everything is reduced to 50 percent of its original retail price, and you can still find some nice stuff. The other shop is the fabric area of the Garment District, just below the Port Authority.

RAE HOME
452 Broadway, New York NY. 212/966-1414. **Toll-free phone:** 888/966-1414. **World Wide Web address:** http://raetrading.com. **Description:** An enormous home fabric and decorating outlet (encompassing an entire city block), open to the public and offering wholesale prices. As a direct importer of fabrics, Rae Home sells Rae Trading Corporation's stock of major domestic brand home furnishings at low costs. The outlet also has a staff of decorators to assist you with services such as re-upholstery and window treatments.

HARRY ZARIN COMPANY
318 Grand Street, New York NY 10002. 212/925-6112. **Description:** This may be the best place for discount fabrics in town. Harry Zarin has become a legend as a wholesale source for upholsterers; about 20 years ago they decided to sell to the public as well, so now you can benefit from their vast selection and buying power. The main storefront, on Grand Street, offers complete upholstery services; but you don't have to use them to shop in the upstairs warehouse, around the corner at 72 Allen Street (212/226-3492). Upstairs you'll find a vast universe of fabrics, all first-quality current designs, most at about one-third the price you'd pay for the same materials at retail upholstery shops. Not only that, but everything is right there; no need to place an order from a book and wait a month. The stock moves quickly, new patterns are coming in all the time -- and you can buy any amount, large or small. One of the best values is Zarin's collection of woven tapestries in ornate patterns. While these can cost up to $100.00 a square yard elsewhere, here they go for just $25.00 - $35.00 a yard for the very same fabric. Occasionally you'll also find some closeouts and overruns, reduced even further. And there's another location across the street selling all the accessories -- rods and other trimmings -- to create your own draperies, slipcovers, bedspreads, etc., if you wish. The main store is open six days a week, but the warehouse is open daily, from 9:00 a.m. - 5:30 p.m.

SHOPPING
🏰 Shoes & Sneakers 🏰

BENEDETTI CUSTOM SHOES
225 West 34th Street (between 7th & 8th Streets), New York NY 10122. 212/594-6033. ◆ 530 Seventh Avenue (at 38th Street), New York NY. 212/719-5075. **Description:** With two small stores in the Garment District, Benedetti specializes in men's dress shoes. They discount such brands as Dexter, Aiden, Bostonian, Edmonds, Ecco, Nunn-Bush, Timberland, and others. Save about $15.00 - $20.00 on Rockport casual shoes and $40.00 - $70.00 on tassled loafers from Bally. They also have some athletic shoes, like Reeboks at about $10.00 - $20.00 below retail.

EITAN'S BOOTERY
23 East 33rd Street, New York NY 10016. 212/725-6240. **Description:** Just off Madison Avenue, Eitan's Bootery offers ladies footwear in all styles (dressy pumps, casual loafers, sandals, and boots) priced to go ($9.99 - $29.99). A pair of leather MIA boots were seen for $14.99, with many other styles priced at under $10.00. Brand names included Nine West, Steve Madden, and Skechers.

FRANKEL'S DISCOUNT STORE
3924 Third Avenue (at 39th Street), Brooklyn NY 11232. 718/768-9788. **Description:** For discount prices on the ever-popular Timberland hiking boots, New Balance running shoes, and more, check out this Brooklyn institution located in the shadow of the BQE. Looking for a pair of Red Wing work shoes? Frankel's carries the largest selection anywhere. Frankel's specializes in large size shoes, with footwear running all the way up to size 20! Frankel's offers discounts of 25 percent and up on closeouts and surplus of these very desirable brands. Frankel's also sells designer sunglasses at a discount. Closed Sundays and Mondays.

MOSHELL'S
87 Nassau Street, New York NY 10038. 212/349-6630. ◆ 2459 Broadway (at 91st Street), New York NY. 212/712-9146. **Description:** These stores feature a mix of shoes and handbags, all at discount prices. Shoes are the main deal, where you'll find brands from Steve Madden to Aerosoles to Nine West, in both dressy and casual styles. Let a salesperson help you find the right size.

TRAINING CAMP
25 West 45th Street (between Fifth Avenue & Avenue of the Americas), New York NY. 212/840-7842. ◆ 1079 Avenue of the Americas, New York NY 10018. 212/921-4430. **Description:** Sports enthusiasts and fitness mavens alike will love the discounts they can find at Training Camp. The latest styles in sports apparel and

footwear and the biggest names are all here, with great price tags attached. If you've recently been to Foot Locker and ogled a pair of $100.00 sneakers, drop by your nearest Training Camp for a little comparative shopping. Chances are you'll find the same shoes at a better price. Team shirts and running suits are just a few of the clothing items you will find here at equally good prices.

SHOPPING
🚲 Sporting Goods 🚲

DARTS ON CUE
108 Fourth Avenue (between 11th & 12th Streets), New York NY
10003. 212/375-1540. **Toll-free phone:** 888/970-1100.
World Wide Web address: http://www.dartsoncue.baweb.com.
Description: If you've always wanted to build a game room, but
didn't think you could afford the necessary toys, think again.
Darts on Cue is all about helping you afford the adult playroom you
have always dreamed of. And we're not talking just darts, dart
boards, and related accessories. Pool tables, cue sticks, foosball,
air hockey, ping pong, card tables, games, and puzzles can also be
found here at affordable prices. And while you're constructing
this game room, doesn't it make sense to build a bar? Darts on Cue
sells bars and bar stools. Hey, they've even got gumball machines!
So, if you're looking to redecorate and put a little fun in your life,
drop by their Fourth Avenue showroom.

LARRY & JEFF'S BICYCLES PLUS
1400 Third Avenue (between 79th & 80th Streets), New York NY
10021. 212/794-2929. **E-mail address:** bicyclespl@aol.com.
World Wide Web address: http://www.bicyclesnyc.com.
Description: For over 20 years, Larry & Jeff have been offering
cycling enthusiasts some of the city's best discounts on bikes,
clothing, and accessories. For the fitness enthusiast, they also
offer a line of stationary and spinning bikes. All the top names are
here as well: Shimano, Campagnolo, Manitou, Oakley, Thuley, BMX,
Cannondale, and Mongoose just to name a few. So, whether your
looking for a new bike or just a helmet, Larry & Jeff's Bicycles
Plus (the "Plus" being the key) can help you find it at an affordable
price.

MODELL'S SPORTING GOODS
498 7th Avenue, 20th Floor, New York NY 10018-6701. 212/964-
4007. ◆ 280 Broadway (at Chambers Street), New York NY.
212/267-2882. ◆ A&S Plaza, Avenue of the Americas (at 33rd
Street), New York NY. 212/594-1830. ◆ 109 East 42nd Street,
New York NY. 212/661-5966. ◆ 243 West 42nd Street, New York
NY. 212/575-8111. ◆ 39-12 Main Street, Queens, NY. 718/539-
6100. ◆ 163-40 Jamaica Avenue, Queens NY. 718/297-4402. ◆ 30-
88 Steinway Street, Queens, NY. 718/956-4526. Starrbrook
Plaza, 1000 Penn Avenue, Brooklyn NY. 718/345-9300. ◆ 360
Fulton Street, Brooklyn NY. 718/855-1921. ◆ 31 East Fordham
Road, Bronx NY. 212/295-7800. ◆ 2929 Third Avenue, Bronx NY.
212/993-1844. **Description:** From humble beginnings in 1889 as a
small family-run shop, Modell's Sporting Goods has become one of
the city's largest retailers of sports gear and clothing. Just about
everything is sold at very good prices. Find good deals on in-line

skates by Bauer, Rollerblade, and California Pro. They have lots of exercise equipment; a monorail Ski-Master by Weider was recently seen for $129.00, along with weightlifting sets, stair climbers, and everything else to get you in shape before you go to the gym. Sneakers are another great reason to shop at Modell's, with high-tops, running shoes and walkers by Champion, Reebok, Etonic, Pony, and more at low prices. Nylon warm-up suits by Spalding and Pony start as low as $40.00, and women's lycra activewear separates as low as $10.00. Lots of stuff for kids, too, like football jerseys, sweats, and sneakers. You'll also find hiking boots, parkas, and plenty of camping and fishing gear. Modell's really covers all the bases.

NEW YORK GOLF CENTER, INC.

131 West 35th Street (between Seventh Avenue & Broadway), New York NY. 212/564-2255. **World Wide Web address:** http://www.nygolfcenter.com. **Description:** Tee off here for all your golfing needs. It's not a discount store, but their prices are well under par. Save on clubs, bags, shoes, balls, and accessories. Looking to suit up for the course? New York Golf Center is your place for clothing as well. With business as good as it is, New York Golf Center is now doing business on the Internet. If 35th Street is out of your way, log onto their Website and see what they have to offer you. If golf is your game, this place will hit a hole-in-one.

PARAGON SPORTING GOODS

876 Broadway (at 18th Street), New York NY 10003. 212/255-8036. **Description:** Founded in 1908, Paragon has long been the crowned champ of sporting goods stores in New York. Recent expansions have created three full floors of departments covering every sport imaginable. While this is not, strictly speaking, a discount store, Paragon's prices are as competitive as any gridiron match. Frequent sales afford you the chance of even better savings. Mr. C found a pair of Avia men's walking shoes, a pair of Rossignol Advantage AR skis, a Head Atlantis large-size tennis racquet, and Wilson footballs all at amazingly low prices. Clearance racks and off-season equipment offer further bargains. In any department you may find things like wood or aluminum baseball bats at 40 percent off their original prices, or Nike windbreakers at 50 percent off. Mr. C also saw ladies' Nordica ski jackets, reduced from $180.00 to $144.00. On their top floor, Paragon Sporting Goods also has an extensive selection of outdoor wear and equipment. You can find anything from a bow and arrow to binoculars, as well as down vests, hiking boots, sunglasses, and sailing gear.

TRIANGLE SPORTS

182 Flatbush Avenue, Brooklyn NY 11217. 718/638-5300. **Description:** This packed store seems to take its name from the traffic formation that makes the store appear to be sitting out in the middle of the road. Once you get inside, though, you'll see that they definitely take the low road when it comes to prices on sporting goods and athletic wear. They have terrific discounts on

shoes by Nike, Reebok, Adidas, and more; as well as Timberland hiking boots and other outdoor gear, all kinds of team sports equipment, swimming and tennis stuff, and exercise machines. With such a huge stock, Triangle can usually offer even better deals on last year's leftover models; be sure to check these out.

SHOPPING
✍ Stationery, Office, & Art Supplies ✍

ART STATION
144 West 27th Street, New York NY. 212/807-8000. **World Wide
Web address:** http://www.artstationltd.com. **Description:** Art
Station offers good prices on just about anything an artist or
crafter may need: paint, paper, tools, canvas, sewing supplies, and
more. Recently advertised items have included see-through
storage cases ($7.39); 50 acrylic pom poms in assorted colors
($3.24); and portfolio folders for under $2.00 each. Lamps, light
tables, and framing services are just a few of Art Station's other
offerings. Open Monday through Friday, 8:30 a.m. - 6:30 p.m.;
Saturday, 10:00 a.m. - 5:00 p.m.

THE ART STORE
1-5 Bond Street (between Broadway & Lafayette), New York
NY 10012. 212/533-2444. **World Wide Web address:**
http://www.artstore.com. **Description:** The name says it all, this is
The Art Store. Everyday discounts from 20 - 50 percent off list
prices are just one of the reasons why this store is so popular.
Even without these deep discounts, those looking for art supplies
might still come in just for the helpful staff. More than
salespeople, The Art Store staff is like a team of problem-solvers,
ready with a quick and insightful answer to all your art questions
and needs. With over 30,000 items to choose from, there's
probably nothing they don't have in stock. Oil and acrylic paints by
Winsor Newton, Gamblin, Liquitex, and Golden; artist brushes by
Robert Simmons and Grumbacher; drawing and decorative papers
from Canson and Fabriano; and ergonomically-sound and pneumatic
chairs from Alvin and Mayline are just a small sampling of the
products you'll find at The Art Store. They even have their own
brand of oil, acrylic, and tempera paints; excellent pre-stretched
canvas; and gesso and artists brushes that are guaranteed to be
the best value for your money.

CIRO OFFICE SUPPLIES
123 Fulton Street, New York NY 10038. 212/406-7256.
Description: This small shop is crammed from floor to ceiling with
every kind of paper and stationery supply imaginable. You may find
a 500-sheet ream of blank white three-hole paper, reduced from
$8.95 to just $2.99; or a box of 10 floppy disks, marked down
from $25.00 to a mere $5.00. Other accessories spotted included
a plastic printer stand, $10.00 off at $19.95.

JAM PAPER & ENVELOPE
111 Third Avenue (between 13th & 14th Streets), New York NY
10003. 212/473-6666. ✦ 611 Avenue of the Americas, New York
NY 10011. 212/255-4593. **Description:** Jam is the undisputed king
of discount paper supplies. From business to artsy, Jam carries all
sorts of paper overstocks. Find a 500-sheet ream of high-quality

business stationery, in a variety of colors and thickness, marked down from $54.00 to $35.00. They also sell envelopes, note cards, invitations, gift wrapping, notepads, and loose note stationery. The selection is vast, with everything out on display. The helpful staff will find you what you need, or the next-best thing. Jam does carry new stock as well, also at discount. Open Monday through Friday, 8:30 a.m. - 7:00 p.m.; Saturday and Sunday, 10:00 a.m. - 6:00 p.m.

LEE'S ART SHOP
220 West 57th Street (between Seventh Avenue & Broadway), New York NY 10019. 212/247-0110. **World Wide Web address:** http://www.leesartshop.baweb.com. **Description:** Got a question or an art supply need? Bring it to Lee! From pens and paper to filofaxes and drafting tables, Lee's Art Shop takes pride in their reputation as the "Department Store for the Artist." Even better, they're really a *discount* department store, offering great prices everyday. Open Sunday, 12:00 p.m. - 5:30 p.m.; Monday through Friday, 9:00 a.m. - 7:00 p.m.; Saturday, 9:30 a.m. - 6:30 p.m.

MASTER TONER PRODUCTS, INC.
454 Bedford Avenue, Brooklyn NY 11211. 718/218-9353. **Toll-free phone:** 800/287-3177. **World Wide Web address:** http://www.tonercartridges.baweb.com. **Description:** Come on, we've all been there: you've procrastinated long enough on finishing a particular project, and just as you hit the "print" button (with less than five minutes to spare), you get the message that there is no ink left in your printer. What can you do in times like this? Call Master Toner Products for an emergency delivery. As toner cartridges are one of the most vital components to a computer, they are also one of the most costly. Lessen the cost by buying your toners through Master Toner. Master Toner offers new and remanufactured toners, cartridges, fusers, drums, and developers for all brands of faxes, copiers, and printers. But don't let the word "remanufactured" scare you; toner cartridges are one of the few recyclable products that we don't advocate reusing. Plus, all products are guaranteed and put through a rigorous post-testing process. Same day and emergency deliveries are available throughout Manhattan and Brooklyn. So, before you find yourself in a jam, stock up with Master Toner Products. Open Monday through Thursday, 9:00 a.m. - 7:00 p.m.; Friday, 9:00 a.m. - 3:00 p.m.

NEW YORK CENTRAL ART SUPPLY
62 Third Avenue (at 11th Street), New York NY 10003. 212/477-0400. **Toll-free phone:** 800/950-6111. **E-mail address:** sales@nycentralart.com. **World Wide Web address:** http://www.nycentralart.com. **Description:** Since 1905, New York Central Art Supply has been offering some of the best deals on supplies and services to artists at every experience level. From paper, paints, and brushes to canvases, easels, and furniture, New York Central Art Supply has got it all. What's more, their extremely knowledgeable staff can help you try and figure out exactly what

materials would best suit your needs. For those who prefer to stretch the constraints of typical art, New York Central Art Supply will be more than happy to stretch them with you...along with your canvas. Custom stretching and priming are just a taste of the services they are more than happy to offer you. Open Monday through Saturday, 8:30 a.m. - 6:30 p.m.; Sunday, 11:00 a.m. - 5:00 p.m.

OAS (OFFICE AUTOMATION SYSTEMS)

132 West 31st Street (between Avenue of the Americas & Seventh Avenue), New York NY 10001. 212/714-2233. **Toll-free phone:** 800/454-COPY. **Description:** Whether you're the president of a major corporation, or you count your family and pets among your employees, OAS has got the business systems, supplies, and services to help you furnish your home and office. Come in and find one of the city's best deals on office equipment including copiers, faxes, and laser printers. Monthly specials (including deals on equipment rentals and leasing) make OAS prices even better. Call today or drop by to see if they have what you're looking for. Open Monday through Friday, 9:00 a.m. - 5:00 p.m.; Saturday, 10:00 a.m. - 3:00 p.m.

PEARL PAINT

308 Canal Street, New York NY 10013. 212/431-7932. **Toll-free phone:** 800/221-6845. **World Wide Web address:** http://www.pearlpaint.com. **Description:** Pearl is a sort of art supply department store. Five floors offer complete lines of paints, paper, portfolios, easels, canvas, tools, tables, lamps, chairs, storage systems, computer desks, and pretty much everything for the studio or office. They've even spread to a second store a block away on Lispenard Street, as well as national chain outposts. Among the many sale items recently spotted (Pearl's everyday prices are great, but there are always special promotions for even better deals) included an HP-B Pro-Pak airbrush kit, listed at $185.00, here for $100.00; leather briefcases for under $50.00; a 60-piece Rembrandt soft pastel set for half-price; a mosaic mercantile tile kit listed at $30.00, here it's just $24.00; and the comprehensive *Artist's Handbook*, with information on the latest techniques and technologies, reduced from a cover price of $30.00 to $19.99. Pearl offers lots of package deals too, so grab a flyer when you come in the front door. Open Monday through Saturday, 9:00 a.m. - 6:00 p.m.; Sunday, 10:00 a.m. - 5:30 p.m.

STAPLES

699 Avenue of the Americas, New York NY 10010. 212/675-5698. ◆ 217 Broadway, New York NY. 212/346-9624. ◆ 9 Union Square West, New York NY. 212/929-6323. ◆ 345 Park Avenue, New York NY. 212/683-2959. ◆ 205 East 42nd Street, New York NY. 212/697-1591. **World Wide Web address:** http://www.staples.com. **Description:** This national chain calls itself "The Office Superstore," and it's easy to see why. They've brought the mega-warehouse approach to office supplies. They stock thousands of items, making them pretty hard to beat. Now, while I usually try to avoid discussing big-name stores like this one,

Staples has too many deals to ignore. Especially if you run an office -- home or *Fortune* 500 -- which needs lots of supplies on a regular basis. Many of the best bargains are available in large quantities. You can get a 6-pack of Bellwether fax paper, for just $12.88, example, a savings of 70 percent off retail; a dozen bottles of Liquid Paper correction fluid for $7.89; or a dozen pads of Post-It Notes for as low as $2.99. Staples offers some great deals on business supplies and equipment, like copying and fax machines from $399.00, personal computers at competitive (if ever-changing) prices, workstations on which to put those computers from about $100.00, and filing cabinets for as low as $85.00. But remember, even megastores can't carry everything. For basic stuff, though, Staples is pretty darn good. And popular. New branches keep popping up all over the city.

UTRECHT ART SUPPLY

111 Fourth Avenue (between 11th & 12th Streets), New York NY 10003. 212/777-5353. ◆ 215 Lexington Avenue, New York NY. 212/683-8822. **Toll-free phone:** 800/223-9132. **World Wide Web address:** http://www. utrechtart.com. **Description:** From its base in New York, Utrecht has become one of the country's largest art supply houses, even manufacturing its own line of paint, canvas and related products. The store boasts over 20,000 items, all at discount. Save money on Rembrandt oils and pastel sticks, Chartpak lettering, Pelikan inks, Neilsen frames, Rapidograph pens, and a variety of guide books. In addition to their regular low prices, Utrecht has periodic sales offering discounts of up to 60 percent on many items. The staff is friendly and very professional as well, making a trip to Utrecht an enjoyable experience. Open Monday through Friday, 8:00 a.m. - 9:00 p.m.; Saturday, 9:00 a.m. - 5:00 p.m.

SHOPPING
🛍 Thrift Stores 🛍

CALVARY/ST. GEORGE'S THRIFT SHOP
209 East 16th Street (at Third Avenue), New York NY 10010.
212/475-5510. **Description:** Calvary/St. George's easily wins the
prize for most dramatic thrift store. Tucked into the basement of
a marvelous old brownstone church, the exposed stone walls and
stone steps give the shop an almost medieval atmosphere. The
prices are almost as old-fashioned. The clothing styles, however,
are quite current. Mr. C found an Italian-style blazer from Brooks
Brothers for $10.00, and a girl's down jacket for $15.00. Wool
overcoats for men and women are $10.00 - $25.00; there are
racks of dresses for just $5.00 each; and sweaters for all at
$2.00 and $3.50. Open Tuesday through Saturday, 11:00 a.m. -
5:30 p.m.

CANCER CARE THRIFT SHOP
1480 Third Avenue (between 83rd & 84th Streets), New York NY
10028. 212/879-9868. **Description:** Yes, it may sound ironic, but
one of the best places to do some thrift shopping in New York City
is on the posh Upper East Side. Right along Third Avenue, there
are a number of great places to find high-quality goods that have
been tossed aside by the area's many affluent locals. Cancer Care
Thrift Shop is no exception. Step inside and you'll find all the
usual thrift suspects: clothing, furniture, jewelry and other
accessories. Again, because of its location, much of the
merchandise is barely used... and of impeccable quality and taste.
A lot of the items found here have even been donated by the
manufacturers themselves. Best of all, you can shop guilt-free: all
proceeds benefit cancer patients. Open Sunday, 12:00 p.m. - 5:00
p.m.; Monday through Friday, 11:00 a.m. - 6:00 p.m. (until 7:00 p.m.
on Wednesday and Thursday); Saturday, 10:00 a.m. - 4:00 p.m.

GODMOTHERS' LEAGUE THRIFT SHOP
1459 Third Avenue (between 82nd & 83rd Streets), New York NY
10028. 212/988-2858. **Description:** This narrow and cluttered
thrift shop is a bit more of what you'd expect from a thrift shop.
Clothing is hung on racks and piled on top of them; it's not all in
the best of shape, but if you rummage through you may find a
diamond in the rough. Mr. C came up with a Ralph Lauren tweed
suit; at $250.00 it's still a bargain even if it is much more
expensive than anything else in the store. Other discoveries
included a brightly colored ski jacket for $35.00 and a Scottish
wool sweater for $10.00. If you're brave and can find the back
steps, there is a basement area stacked with dusty old furniture.
But again, there may be something buried down here that you can
use. This charity benefits The West End Day School, an
elementary school for children with special needs. Open Monday
through Saturday, 10:30 a.m. - 6:00 p.m.

GOODWILL THRIFT SHOP

217 West 79th Street, New York NY 10024. 212/874-5050. **Description:** One of the more nicely kept thrift stores of this type, Goodwill is just off of Broadway on this popular stretch of the Upper West Side. You'll probably find some nice things among the racks of men's dress shirts for $4.00, jeans for $8.00, suits for $20.00, skirts for $8.00, and shoes for $6.00. Each day, tickets of a particular color will be half-price. There is also some small furniture here, along with lots of books and records. It's worth a look.

HELP LINE THRIFT SHOP

382 Third Avenue (between 27th & 28th Streets), New York NY 10016. 212/532-5136. **Description:** Help Line Thrift Shop is just a step or so above the Salvation Army variety, but you can find some nice things here, like a Christian Dior women's blazer, in good shape for $12.00; men's tweed jackets from $10.00 - $20.00, and winter overcoats from $15.00. Sales benefit a 24 hour counseling hotline, that was founded in 1969 by Norman Vincent Peale.

HOUSING WORKS THRIFT SHOP

143 West 17th Street (between Avenue of the Americas & Seventh Avenue), New York NY 10011. 212/366-0820. ◆ 306 Columbus Avenue (between 74th & 75th Streets), New York NY 10023. 212/759-7566. ◆ 202 East 77th Street (between Second & Third Avenues), New York NY 10021. 212/772-8461. **Description:** Maybe it's because of the area it lies in (the Chelsea location), but this place is undoubtedly the hippest thrift shop I've ever seen. First of all, everything about the store is beautiful, clean, and organized; just how I like it. The store is run by Housing Works, a nonprofit agency that provides health care, housing, job training, and support services to people living with AIDS. If you're looking for affordable, used furniture that's also high-quality, this is your place. Furniture is donated to the shop on a daily basis, so it's worth revisiting if you don't find something on your first visit. Mr. C saw a leather couch for just $185.00. How about a piano for $950.00? Videos and CDs, both old and new, make up their own section in the back corner. Classic comic books (wrapped carefully in plastic) are just $5.00 each. Mr. C watched on as an elegantly-clad businessman rifled through the store's rack of suits, casual pants, and khakis (starting at $15.00), and wondered if he had bought his current attire here as well. For women, Charles David and Calvin Klein shoes graced the shelves of shoes at rock-bottom prices. How about a Gap cargo skirt for just $5.00? Or a cotton J. Crew dress for just a few dollars more? I especially like the way that Housing Works keeps their customers coming back. All around the store, already purchased artwork and furniture remain to be gazed at by those that were too late (thus assuring them that there are definitely some finds here); while other items sit about with the promise that they will be "On Sale Tomorrow. No Holds." Hours at the Chelsea and Upper East Side locations are Monday through Saturday, 10:00 a.m. - 6:00 p.m.; Sunday, 12:00 p.m. - 4:00 p.m. Upper West Side hours are Monday through Friday, 11:00 a.m. - 7:00 p.m.; Saturday, 10:00 a.m. - 7:00 p.m.; and Sunday, 1:00 p.m. - 5:00 p.m.

IRVINGTON INSTITUTE THRIFT SHOP
1534 Second Avenue (at 80th Street), New York NY 10021. 212/879-4555. **Description:** You'll hardly think you're in a thrift shop when you walk into this place. It's large and comfortable, with neatly displayed clothing that includes a lot of designer names. Well, this is the Upper East Side, dahling. You may find a grey pinstripe blazer and skirt by Anne Taylor for a mere $50.00, or a men's Perry Ellis raincoat for $20.00. Rummage through racks and racks of shirts and blouses, for $2.00, $5.00 and $10.00; plus jewelry, neckties, and other accessories.

MEMORIAL SLOAN-KETTERING THRIFT STORE
1440 Third Avenue (at 81st Street), New York NY 10028. 212/535-1250. **Description:** Part of the Upper East Side thrift shop district, this store has lots of high-quality fashions for men and women. Mr. C found a Brooks Brothers classic blue pinstripe suit for $25.00. Same price for a woman's houndstooth blazer and skirt set by Jones New York. Another find in the women's section was a black rain poncho from Bergdorf Goodman for $75.00. And women will like the shoe section, where they may find a pair of alligator heels for $25.00. The store also has lots of books, as well as housewares and some furniture. Proceeds benefit the Memorial Sloan-Kettering Cancer Center.

OUT OF THE CLOSET THRIFT SHOP
220 East 81st Street (between Second & Third Avenues), New York NY 10028. 212/472-3573. **Description:** Yes, the name is a pun. Out Of The Closet distributes 100 percent of its proceeds to community organizations and institutions fighting AIDS, and is fully staffed by volunteers. This packed store goes on and on with great fashions, small appliances, antiques and collectibles. The front of the store features women's clothes, like a black and red print top by Donald Brooks for Lord & Taylor, just $20.00. A red knit dress from Victoria's Secret was seen for $10.00, and there is a big selection of women's shoes. For men's clothing you actually go out the back of the store to a separate building, which is even larger. Here, you'll see suits for $45.00, and racks of shirts and trousers for $10.00. This area is also lined with bookshelves featuring hundreds of fiction and nonfiction titles. Also check out the linens, rugs, and appliances found back here. Open Tuesday through Saturday, 10:15 a.m. - 5:00 p.m.

REPEAT PERFORMANCE
222 East 23rd Street, New York NY 10010. 212/684-5344. **Description:** This thrift store benefits the New York City Opera; one visit will have you singing its praises. Find lots of good-quality clothing, like a Jacqueline de Ribes evening dress in black silk with rhinestone buttons for $75.00, or a brushed suede skirt for $40.00. Men can find lots of classic looks, like a Nino Cerruti corduroy blazer for $20.00. Lots of shoes, too; a pair of high heels in gold lame, like new, were seen for $30.00. Upstairs there is furniture, artwork, books, and all kinds of things for the home.

Among the recent booty were a great-looking sofa bed upholstered in grey and white striped cloth for $350.00 and a framed poster from *A Chorus Line* for $30.00. Speaking of music, you will, of course, find records here, many for $1.00 each; same price for a library full of used books. Items marked with a red dot are on sale for half-price.

THE SALVATION ARMY THRIFT STORES

112 Fourth Avenue (between 11th & 12th Streets), New York NY 10003. 212/673-2741. ♦ 535 West 46th Street, New York NY. 212/757-2311. ♦ 268 West 96th Street, New York NY. 212/663-2258. ♦ 69 Spring Street (between Broadway & Lafayette), New York NY. 212/925-1909. ♦ 208 Eighth Avenue (between 20th & 21st Streets), New York NY. 212/929-5214. ♦ 115 Allen Street (at Delancey Street), New York NY. 212/254-2916. ♦ 220 East 23rd Street (between Second & Third Avenues), New York NY. 212/532-8115. ♦ 41 West 8th Street (between Fifth Avenue & Avenue of the Americas), New York NY. 212/995-5384. **Description:** You hardly need Mr. C to describe the scene at the Salvation Army. Suffice it to say, they're everywhere, and tend to have a decent selection of clothing at rock-bottom prices. Men's sport coats for $15.00, women's for $10.00, jeans for $5.00, T-shirts for $2.00. And you never know what labels may turn up; at one location Mr. C even spotted a Ralph Lauren dress shirt for $3.99. Oh sure, most of this clothing has seen better days, but then, who hasn't? For bulk buying, you can't beat these prices (or the work your few dollars will help support).

SPENCE-CHAPIN THRIFT SHOP

1473 Third Avenue (between 83rd & 84th Streets), New York NY 10028. 212/737-8448. **Description:** Spence-Chapin is a most impressive thrift store, more typical of its posh East Side environs than the rock-bottom prices found inside. Their two floors of clothing and accessories resemble like a fancy boutique. Right up in the front window, in fact, is a rack of fur coats selling for a fraction of their original prices. Next to them is a separate designer room, with women's dressy fashions like a Nina Ricci blue and black knit dress for $125.00. An Adolfo blazer and skirt, like new, in a black and red print was seen for $250.00. Elsewhere in the store, women will find lots of shoes by Ferragamo, Charles Jourdan, and Kenneth Cole. A pair of Bandolino heels for just $20.00? Plus lots of handbags, jewelry, and other accessories. Men may find a London Fog raincoat or a Jaguar herringbone blazer, each for $45.00. And we haven't even gotten downstairs to the basement, where everything is either $5.00 or $10.00. These clearance racks include shirts, pants, sweaters, dresses, coats, and more. This area also has furniture and housewares. The proceeds benefit Spence-Chapin's Adoption Resource Center. Open Sunday, 12:00 p.m. - 5:00 p.m.; Monday through Friday, 10:00 a.m. - 7:00 p.m.; Saturday 10:00 a.m. - 5:00 p.m.

SHOPPING
🎎 Toys, Games, & Hobbies 🎎

ABRACADABRA SUPERSTORE
19 West 21st Street (between Fifth Avenue & Avenue of the Americas), New York NY. 212/627-5745. **Description:** In addition to selling all kinds of professional magician's supplies, Abracadabra has enough wacky costumes and gag gifts to make lots of fun appear in your life. They have all the novelty items you've ever groaned at, like the ever-popular dribble glass and the shocking cigarette. Abracadabra is fully prepared to meet all your Groucho glasses needs. If more elaborate get-ups are your style, they have wigs, mustaches, and theatrical makeup as well as full costumes and accessories for sale or for rentals. On the weekends they even host magic shows. Open Sunday, 12:00 p.m. - 5:00 p.m.; Monday through Saturday, 11:00 a.m. - 7:00 p.m.

BROOKLYN WOMEN'S EXCHANGE
55 Pierrepont Street, Brooklyn NY 11201. 718/624-3435. **Description:** Not far from the popular shops of Montague Street, this beautiful store sells all sorts of lovely handmade clothing, toys, and things for the home, much of it in classic American and country styles. Find all sorts of soaps and candles, stationery, educational toys and clothing for children and infants, and hand-knit scarves and afghan blankets. Not everything is particularly cheap, but many items are quite reasonable, and all proceeds benefit this nonprofit organization, which was begun in the 19th century as an outlet for women who were unable to find work. The Women's Exchange, the oldest in the United States, has played a major role in much of our nation's history. The women made warm garments for the soldiers of the Civil War, the Spanish-American War, and World War I. At the time of Lincoln's assassination, the women bound together to create a commemorative flag that can now be viewed at the Brooklyn Historical Society. In 1867 and again in 1876, the women of the exchange won medals for "Fine Sewing" at the Paris Exposition and the Philadelphia Centennial, respectively. That celebrated work continues today. The store is open Tuesday through Saturday, 10:00 a.m. - 4:30 p.m. (open until 7:00 p.m. on Thursday).

CTA SOUND, INC.
401 Fifth Avenue (between 36th & 37th Streets), New York NY 10016. 212/679-0728. **Description:** If you've ever felt the compulsion to order one of those late-night infomercial knickknacks (i.e. Oxi Clean GS27, or The Eurosealer), then this is the place for you. The huge "As Seen On TV" sign that graces the front of the store and their business card is no lie...if you've seen it on TV at some point in the past decade, it can be found at CTA Sound. At CTA Sound, instant gratification is yours, and the prices are usually a few bucks better than what you would spend on

television. So, if you've been dying to order a pair of Ambervision sunglasses, but you can't find the phone number, give CTA Sound a try.

STAR MAGIC
1256 Lexington Avenue (at 85th Street), New York NY 10028. 212/988-0300. ✦ 745 Broadway, New York NY. 212/228-7770. **E-mail address:** star@starmagic.com. **World Wide Web address:** http://www.starmagic.com. **Description:** With its glistening gems and minerals, space-age music, and dramatic lighting, Star Magic truly is a magical store to browse in. They also specialize in the latest way-out toys and trinkets, not all of which are as expensive as they may look. Digital watches with hologram faces -- one has an eye that seems to look back at you -- are just $15.00. There are lots of hologram stickers too, just $1.95 each. Official NASA shoulder patches from various space missions are $5.00 each, and there is a bewildering array of cube, maze, and puzzle toys and doodads, most between $3.00 and $10.00.

TOYS 'R US
1293 Broadway (at 34th Street), New York NY 10001. 212/594-8697. ✦ 2432 Union Square East, New York NY 10003. 212/674-8697. **World Wide Web address:** http://www.toysrus.com. **Description:** Perhaps the country's biggest retail toy chain, Toys 'R Us is also the premier discounter on aisle after aisle of toys, games, bikes, kids' clothing -- and even diapers. The place is huge, and the prices are likely to be the lowest in town for the latest in toys. They even offer to match the advertised prices from any other store. They've got Barbie, they've got roller skates, they've got radio-powered cars. If your game boys and girls are screaming for the very latest Nintendo technology, get it here. But do yourself a favor -- go on a weekday if you can, and leave the kiddies at home. That way, you're sure to spend less money. Open daily, 9:00 a.m. - 9:00 p.m.

VILLAGE CHESS SHOP
230 Thompson Street (at 3rd Street), New York NY 10012. 212/475-9580. **World Wide Web address:** http://www.chess-shop.com. **Description:** Since 1972, Village Chess Shop has been helping the Bobby Fischers of the world master their craft. Aside from being a retail shop where you can find chess sets and boards of just about any material, from wood to marble to metal to bone, the Chess Shop is the site of many a fierce competition. Aficionados from all over delight in the store's 365-day schedule, and the late hours that they keep. If, at the midnight hour, you're still raring to go, take a set home with you. In addition to sets and boards, Village Chess Shop sells clocks, books, computers, and video games. You can also find lots of Go, Backgammon, and Dominoes accessories. For those of you yearning to learn the game, Village Chess Shop offers instruction from beginner to expert levels. Open every day, 12:00 p.m. - 12:00 a.m.

WEST SIDE KIDS
498 Amsterdam Avenue (at 84th Street), New York NY. 212/496-7282. **Description:** An all-purpose store for young children with

books and educational toys, West Side Kids has a fun section up front with bins and bins of tiny, colorful, cheap toys. They range in price from 25¢ to about $3.00, and include the always-popular Silly Putty, super balls, wind-up robots, kazoos, and much more. Take a kid with you, so you won't look too foolish while you're playing. Open Sunday, 12:00 p.m. - 6:00 p.m.; Monday through Saturday, 10:00 a.m. - 7:00 p.m.

FOOD
🌶 Bakeries 🌶

ADDEO'S BAKERY
2372 Hughes Avenue, Bronx NY 10458. 718/367-8316.
Description: This tiny bakery in the old-world Italian section of the Bronx doesn't offer much in the way of variety, but what they *do* sell is sure to please. For $1.00, you can grab a hot loaf of the "pane di casa" (the house bread). While they only offer about four different kinds of bread, it might not be worth your while to make an excursion specifically to go to Addeo's Bakery. But, if you're in the area, they're definitely worth stopping by.

THE BREAD MARKET
485 Fifth Avenue (between 41st & 42nd Streets), New York NY 10017. 212/370-7356. ◆ 1290 Avenue of the Americas (at Fifth Avenue), New York NY 10036. 212/957-5677. ◆ 180 Madison Avenue (at 34th Street), New York NY 10016. 212/981-1140. **World Wide Web address:** http://www.breadmarket.com. **Description:** Whether you're looking to sit down and enjoy a snack or bring it home with you, The Bread Market is the place to go for top-quality baked goods and great prices. While you can grab a quick bite to eat here, I highly recommend taking something home with you, so that you may savor such quality eats. Pick a bread, any bread; from white, wheat, french, and rye to corn rye, egg twist, and challah. If you can name a bread, chances are they make it. Loaves are priced between $1.99 and $3.50. But bread isn't the only thing you'll find here, how about huge muffins (chocolate chip, banana walnut, lemon poppy, low-fat triple berry) for just $1.75; danish (cinnamon raisin, fruit, cheese) for $1.60; or a variety of other pastries (buns, scones, tarts, strudels) for $1.75 or less? And let's not forget the coffee at The Bread Market, where plain old cups of Joe ($.85 - $1.10) meet specialty drinks like cappuccino and cafe au lait ($1.25 - $2.95). But the menu doesn't stop there, try one of The Bread Market's salads, like a Cajun Mediterranean Salad (Cajun chicken strips over roasted peppers, avocado, and mixed greens) for just $3.95, or a Chicken Cilantro Salad (cilantro-grilled chicken over lettuce, tomatoes, cucumbers, carrots, and sprouts) for the same price. A tossed salad bar was recently added. You can pick your greens -- mesclun, romaine, or spinach -- then choose your toppings (no charge for croutons). They also offer a variety of sandwiches and wraps from $4.25 to $6.25, as well as soup and pasta dishes. The casual atmosphere only adds to the relaxed aura of this place. So, if you're having some guests for dinner but don't have time to do all the cooking, let the cooks at The Bread Market slave over the stove for you.

MIO PANE, MIO DOLCE
77 Irving Place (between 18th & 19th Streets), New York NY. 212/677-1627. **World Wide Web address:** http://www.salanthonys.com. **Description:** And yet, another one of Sal

Anthony's food ventures finds its way into Mr. Cheap's little book. Mio Pane, Mio Dolce translates into "My Bread, My Sweets," and that pretty much sets the scene for this bakery. Among the fresh baked breads and fantastic pastries and desserts, you'll find great prices as well. A large variety of breads consists of semolina ($1.65), tomato focaccia ($1.90), and sliced bruschetta ($1.75). For tonight's dinner, surprise your family with a ricotta cheese cake ($10.00), a black and white chocolate cake ($10.00), or an apricot layer cake ($12.00). And what would an Italian market be without fresh pasta and sauces. Pick up a pound of papardelle or fettucine pasta ($3.50) with your choice of sauce including marinara, vodka, and pesto ($3.75 - $6.00) and enjoy the taste of Sal Anthony's restaurants in your very own kitchen. They even offer free delivery. Open daily, 7:00 a.m. - 11:00 p.m.

MOISHE'S HOMEMADE KOSHER BAKERY
199 Orchard Street, New York NY 10002. 212/475-9624. **Description:** Yuppies and artsy types mingle freely with the remainders of the old-world life that started here and refuses to leave. Such a business is Moishe's, offering wonderful loaves of rye, pumpernickel, and challah breads, along with rugelach and other pastries. The prices are no more modern than the setting. Closed on Friday afternoons and all day Saturday.

A. ZITO AND SONS
259 Bleecker Street, New York NY. 212/929-6139. **Description:** Of the many bakeries along this bustling Greenwich Village strip, Zito's is perhaps the best -- in both quality and value. Try a loaf of their fresh, crusty Italian bread; or a loaf filled with layers of prosciutto and provolone cheese. See for yourself why they've outlasted everyone on the block.

FOOD
🌰 Candy & Nuts 🌰

BAZZINI IMPORTERS
339 Greenwich Street, New York NY 10013. 212/334-1280.
Description: Since 1885, Bazzini has been at the top of the New York heap in peanuts, dried fruits, and candies. This bustling shop looks like an oasis of gourmet treats. Once inside, you'll be amazed at how fancy it is -- and yet, the prices can't be beat. A wholesaler that sells to the public as well, this is your chance to shop where the buyers for Dean & Deluca get their stuff. Would you believe honey-roasted peanuts for $2.30 a pound? Get five pounds or more, and the price drops to an amazing $1.80. How about salted cashews for $5.60 a pound, or a five-pound bag of pistachios for $20.00...plus all kinds of mixed assortments and gift baskets. Dried jumbo apricots from Turkey are $12.00 for a five-pound bag, while Bing cherries are just $9.50 per pound. Bazzini also has candy jars in a palette of colors, along with imported specialties, condiments, and cookies. Open weeknights until 7:00 p.m.

ECONOMY CANDY
108 Rivington Street, New York NY 10002. 212/254-1531.
Toll-free phone: 800/352-4544. **World Wide Web address:** http://www.economycandy.com. **Description:** The old-time shops of the Lower East Side aren't just for clothing bargains. Economy Candy takes the same approach to sweets and snacks, selling a wide variety of items -- at near wholesale prices. As a result, this place can be just as jammed with customers as it is with treats from around the world. They're stacked in the aisles, packed into glass counters, and shelved up to the ceiling. From Baby Ruths to Baci, if it's sweet, you'll find it here somewhere. Fresh halvah, cut to order in several flavors, is just $2.99 a pound. Chocolates of every conceivable kind, also sold by the pound, are delectable and cheap. There are dried apricots, pears, and other fruits; cashews; peanuts, and the rest. Boxes of Perugina assortments are here at good prices, as well as store-made gift baskets for that basket-case of a sweet tooth. And for the sweet tooth who can't or shouldn't, there are sugar-free varieties too. There are also loose teas and fresh-ground coffees from around the world. Speaking of which, owners Jerry and Ilene Cohen will ship gifts -- or personal reserves -- anywhere you want. Open Sunday through Friday, 8:30 a.m. - 5:30 p.m.; Saturday, 10:00 a.m. - 5:00 p.m.

JUSTMIM CANDY
37 Seventh Avenue (at 13th Street), New York NY. 212/727-3304. **Description:** Justmim Candy offers a wide variety of sweets and goodies, all at discount prices. Offerings include sumptuous hand made truffles, imported chocolates, and various sugar-free candies.

J. WOLSK'S GOURMET CONFECTIONS
81 Ludlow Street, New York NY 10002. 212/475-0704.
Description: Not far from Economy Candy is Wolsk's, a similar operation with yet another vast assortment of sweets. Fresh chocolate candies, dried apricots and other fruits, halvah, and nuts are just a few of the treats you'll find here. The prices are comparable to those at Economy. And why not send something home to your loved ones? Whether you are an NYC-native or an out-of-towner, Wolsk's offers delivery throughout Manhattan and nationwide. Management encourages you to design a gift basket "perfect for any Monday and occasion." These folks, too, close up on Friday afternoon and Saturday.

FOOD
🖙 Cheese 🖙

EAST VILLAGE CHEESE STORE
34 Third Avenue (at 10th Street), New York NY. 212/477-2601.
Description: It is a generic enough name and you can barely see into the place through all the window signs listing the weekly specials, but the East Village Cheese Store is one place you don't want to miss. Each week, over a dozen varieties of cheese are designated "Superspecials," selling for just $2.99 per pound. Double Gloucester and smoked gouda were among the tasty comestibles on this list during Mr. C's visit. But there's so much more here -- a veritable smorgasbord of culinary delights. Pâtés, such as green peppercorn with cognac, or duck liver mousse, sell for $6.99 a pound; that same price will also get you a 34-ounce container of extra-virgin olive oil; or try a pound of French Roast coffee for just $5.99. They have fresh-baked breads and imported goods, too. Open Monday through Friday, 8:30 a.m. - 6:30 p.m.; Saturday and Sunday, 8:30 a.m. - 6:00 p.m.

IDEAL CHEESE SHOP LTD.
1205 Third Avenue (between 63rd & 64th Streets), New York NY 10021. 212/688-7549. **Toll-free phone:** 800/382-0109. **World Wide Web address:** http://www.idealcheese.com. **Description:** The name of this shop is somewhat of a double entendre: on the one hand, it's *ideal* because of the unparalleled variety; on the other hand, with prices like these for such high-quality goods, it's the *ideal* place to prepare for your next gourmet endeavor. No matter what your dairy diet palate, Ideal Cheese is the place to shop. With an astounding variety of all cheeses imaginable, you can't go wrong at Ideal. From Australia to Cyprus to Denmark to France, Ideal Cheese imports and ages cheeses from all over. And don't fret, your favorite French and Italian varieties are well-represented too. Pick up a pound of smoked mozzarella for $7.98, a pound of brie for $6.98, or a pound of asiago for $8.98. If you're partial to the domestics, a pound of Vermont cheddar is just $5.98. For those who are into gourmandism, try a pound of aged Mimolette (much like a gouda) for a pricier (but still fair) $13.00. If, after all you're browsing, you're still overwhelmed, ask one of the salespeople for help. They have all been well-schooled in the fine art of cheese under the tutelage of owner Ed Edelman. Besides authoring the *Ideal Cheese Book*, Edelman has contributed to a number of respected gourmet magazines, and has appeared (on more than one occasion) on TV's Food Network. So, basically, he knows what he's talking about, and so do his employees. Open Monday through Friday, 9:00 a.m. - 6:30 p.m.; Saturday, 9:00 a.m. - 6:00 p.m. *$Cash Only$*

JOE'S DAIRY
156 Sullivan Street (between Houston & Prince Streets), New York NY 10012. 212/677-8780. **Description:** While the original

namesake, Joe Aiello, has long since left the shop, his expertise in fine cheese-making can still be tasted in every delicious bite. Homemade mozzarella cheese, which can be mixed with a variety of ingredients -- from peppers to prosciutto -- are sold at prices that will please. You can pick up a variety of imported cheeses as well, but I don't think your trip would be complete without tasting the mozzarella. Joe's offers a small selection of other grocery items as well, all at good prices. Open Tuesday through Friday, 9:00 a.m. - 6:00 p.m.; Saturday, 8:00 a.m. - 6:00 p.m. *$Cash Only$*

MURRAY'S CHEESE SHOP

257 Bleecker Street, New York NY 10014. 212/243-3289. **E-mail address:** murrays_cheese@msn.com. **World Wide Web address:** http://www.murrayscheese.com. **Description:** With the East Village so well represented in this category, Mr. C had to find you something comparable in Greenwich Village -- and this is it. A Village institution since 1940, Murray's Cheese Shop features the largest selection of international and domestic cheeses at everyday low prices. Even New York's leading restaurants, including Daniel, Jean George, and Le Bernadin, get their cheese from Murray's. What makes this store even more unique is their huge array of antipasto, charcuterie, breads, oils, vinegars, and specialty groceries. Even if you can't get to Murray's, their catalog makes mail order easy. Drop by Murray's Cheese Shop and see why *The New York Times*, *The Village Voice*, and *New York Magazine* unanimously agree that Murray's is New York's "Best Cheese Shop."

NINTH AVENUE CHEESE MARKET

615 Ninth Avenue (between 33rd & 34th Streets), New York NY 10036. 212/397-4700. **Description:** Mr. C's cooking expert calls this one of his favorite shops. Among the gourmet foods from around the world, at very good prices, you'll find such cheeses as Swiss Emmenthal, and a sharp Iberico from Spain. A handful of these are always on special sale, and you can surely sample a taste of something exotic before committing to a purchase. They also have such items as duck mousse pâté for as little as $9.95 a pound. You can even pick up your favorite flavored coffee for $3.95 a pound (decafs $4.95), including flavors like maple walnut and peaches and cream.

FOOD
🖋 Coffee & Tea 🖋

EMPIRE COFFEE & TEA
592 Ninth Avenue (at 42nd Street), New York NY. 212/586-1717.
Toll-free phone: 800/262-5908. **Description:** This shop offers
over 70 types of coffees and teas, as well as accessories like
coffee grinders and tea pots. If you'd like to test the waters
before diving into a purchase, grab a cup of coffee or tea at their
bar. They've been around since 1908, and it shows. Open Monday
through Friday, 8:00 a.m. - 7:00 p.m.; Saturday, 9:00 a.m. - 6:30
p.m.; Sunday, 11:00 a.m. - 5:30 p.m.

McNULTY'S TEA & COFFEE
109 Christopher Street (between Bleecker & Hudson Streets),
New York NY. 212/242-5351. **Description:** McNulty's began selling
tea and coffee over 100 years ago, and is still going strong today.
Expect to find close to 100 blends in this Greenwich Village shop,
ranging from the affordable to the extremely expensive.
McNulty's also carries a large selection of teas with nearly 100 to
choose from. Coffees come from as far away as Africa, Arabia,
the Caribbean, and South America. Teas include oolongs from
China and Taiwan, black teas from Russia and Sri Lanka, and green
teas from China and Japan. This is certainly the place for the well-
traveled tea and coffee connoisseur. Open Sunday, 1:00 p.m. - 7:00
p.m.; Monday through Saturday, 10:00 a.m. - 9:00 p.m.

OREN'S DAILY ROAST
33 East 58th Street (between Madison & Park Avenues), New
York NY 10022. 212/838-3345. ♦ 1574 First Avenue (between
81st & 82nd Streets), New York NY 10028. 212/737-2690. ♦ 434
Third Avenue (between 30th & 31st Streets), New York NY 10016.
212/779-1241. ♦ 985 Lexington Avenue (at 71st Street), New York
NY 10021. 212/717-3907. ♦ 1144 Lexington Avenue (between 79th
& 80th Streets), New York NY 10021. 212/472-6830. ♦ 31
Waverly Place (between University Place & Greene Street), New
York NY 10003. 212/420-5958. **World Wide Web address:**
http://www.orensdailyroast.com. **Description:** While the costly
temptation of a Starbucks espresso, macchiato, etc. looms around
every corner of New York, the sight of an Oren's Daily Roast is
one of the few places that should cajole you otherwise. After all,
the "Daily" in their name is no myth. Since 1986, Oren's has been
scrounging the earth to bring you the finest coffees from around
the world; America, Africa, and Indonesia are just a few of the
places where these beans originate. But what Oren's does
differently (and spectacularly) is roasts their beans daily.
Somewhere in the far off land of Jersey City, NJ. Oren's owns a
facility that's sole purpose is to roast the beans. Beans are
roasted in seven pound batches so that they are always fresh, and
it is because of this ingenious (and inexpensive) roasting method
that you won't have to skip lunch in order to buy a cup (or

mortgage your house if you're in the market for a whole pound). Oren's also sells a variety of teas, and both coffee and tea accessories to complete your purchase. Due to the self-contained nature of the operation, beans are sold at extremely reasonable prices and are, indubitably, some of the best in the city. Try a pound of Colombian Supremo or Brazilian Cerrado for just $8.99. Or purchase one of your favorite flavored coffees (most available in decaf as well). If you want to host a dinner party that is remembered for its great coffee, stop on by your nearest Oren's location.

PORTO RICO IMPORTING COMPANY

201 Bleecker Street, New York NY 10012. 212/477-5421. **Toll-free phone:** 800/453-5908. **World Wide Web address:** http://www.portorico.com. **Description:** Walk into this shop and pause. Take a deep breath. Sure, it'll probably put caffeine into your veins simply by osmosis, but if you're part of the coffee generation, it's pure heaven. For more than three generations, the Longo family has been serving up delicious, caffeinated imports at many a New York breakfast table. Porto Rico's floor is dominated by sacks and sacks of beans: dozens of flavors from around the world. Brazil, Costa Rica, Venezuela, Santo Domingo...all of these tropical places have contributed beans that you can buy here for just about $5.99 a pound. The folks at Porto Rico will, of course, grind these for you. A handful of blends are usually on special sale; when Mr. C wafted through, it was French roast from Costa Rica for $4.99 a pound. During special sales, the price can go down to $3.99. Porto Rico also sells loose teas from India, Russia, and the Far East. Huge glass jars of these line the walls, most selling for around $7.50 per pound. But again, look for flavors that are on sale, like English Breakfast or Earl Grey for just $5.00. You can even pick up a box of filters: a 100-count box of Melitta filters sells for just over $1.00. They also have exotic spices, as well as gourmet chocolate-covered espresso beans, honeys, jams, syrups, and other condiments to enjoy with your beverages.

TEN REN TEA & GINSENG COMPANY

75 Mott Street, New York NY 10013. 212/349-2286. ◆ 35-18 Roosevelt Avenue, Queens NY. 718/461-9305. ◆ 5817 Eighth Avenue, Brooklyn NY 11220. 718/853-0660. **Description:** If you enjoy not only great teas but the entire culture surrounding tea, you should pay a visit to Chinatown's Ten Ren Tea and Ginseng Company. They grow their own tea in Asia and import it directly to these three outlets, where you can select from a bewildering array of teas, both loose and in bags. The friendly folks here will be happy to explain what each variety is like, and you can even sample their exotic brew of the day. In fact, Ten Ren holds a traditional tea service daily, held at an ornate mahogany table in the store. Stop in to find out the schedule; there is no charge to participate. While some teas can be as exotically-priced as $116.00 for a ten-ounce canister of loose tea leaves, most are as inexpensive as any old box of Lipton. A basic box of black tea, with twenty bags, is just $2.10; dozens of other varieties sell between $2.00 to $5.00

a box -- including lemon, oolong, jasmine, plum, and ginger. Each kind of tea sold is touted for various health benefits, which they have carefully researched. For example, one kind of tea is made specifically to relax you; another is good for dieters. The staff will be happy to explain these benefits to you. Whether or not you believe them is another matter. Still, the world of tea is a pleasant one to explore.

FOOD
✒ General Markets ✒

EAGLE PROVISIONS
628 Fifth Avenue (at 18th Street), Brooklyn NY. 718/499-0026.
Description: Working your way along Brooklyn's Fifth Avenue, toward the Greenwood Cemetery area, in the midst of a largely Hispanic neighborhood, you suddenly come across a pocket of Polish restaurants and businesses. And they all shop at Eagle Provisions, a rambling food store where the shelves are packed with both the familiar and the unfamiliar -- at least, to American shoppers. A full supermarket, with deli, butcher and bakery counters, Eagle specializes in European delicacies like kielbasa, fresh-baked hearty breads, and Polski jelly doughnuts. Yet you may also find Middle Eastern foods, coffees and teas or polenta and other Italian ingredients. They even sell newspapers from these various corners of the world. Packaged foods are often imported, without a word of English to tell you what they are. The delightful aspect of all this is that, here, the exotic is also inexpensive. Be open-minded and daring!

THE FOOD EMPORIUM
10 Union Square (at 14th Street), New York NY. 212/353-3841.
♦ 1175 Third Avenue (at 68th Street), New York NY 10021. 212/249-6778. ♦ 1660 Second Avenue (at 86th Street), New York NY 10021. 212/410-3208. ♦ 1450 Third Avenue (at 82nd Street), New York NY 10028. 212/628-1125. ♦ 452 West 43rd Street (at Tenth Avenue), New York NY 10036. 212/714-1414. ♦ 200 East 32nd Street (at Third Avenue), New York NY 10016. 212/686-0260. **World Wide Web address:** http://www.thefoodemporium. com. **Description:** While Mr. C normally tries to avoid big-name supermarkets (especially ones that inhabit the tri-state area), The Food Emporium is different in that it maintains the essence of a corner store, while operating more than 30 locations. Known for the unparalleled freshness of its foods (in fact, it's guaranteed to be fresh or else it's free), this grocery store chain takes pride in its wide variety of foods for good prices. You'll find everything here -- fruits and vegetables, produce, meats, seafood, and lots more. At the bakery, you can pick up your favorite kind of bagel for just $.55 each, butter croissants for $1.19, or fruit turnovers for $.99. The Food Emporium deli carries more than 275 varieties of cheese from all over the world. Coffee beans are another of The Food Emporium's better deals, with nearly 50 varieties in stock. Lots of specialty foods can also be had here, like fresh caviar, from Beluga to Sevruga. In addition, the store is inundated with choice organic foods. Yet, while The Food Emporium treats each location like a small market, they offer you all the perks of a big grocery store. Like weekly coupons and a free Bonus Savings Card, which will afford you additional savings off their already low prices. Visit their Website to find the location nearest you.

GOURMET GARAGE

453 Broome Street (at Mercer Street), New York NY 10013. 212/941-5850. ◆ 301 East 64th Street (between First & Second Avenues), New York NY 10021. 212/535-6271. ◆ 2567 Broadway (at 96th Street), New York NY 10025. 212/663-0656. ◆ 117 Seventh Avenue South (at 10th Street), New York NY. 212/699-5980. **Description:** Boy, SoHo doesn't have too many bargains like this. Gourmet Garage looks expensive, with whitewashed walls and an espresso bar up front; but in fact, the fancy food they sell can cost as much as half that of nearby produce markets. That's because these guys had been wholesaling to New York's best restaurants for over 10 years when they decided to spend part of their day selling to the general public. So, once the morning rounds have been done, about noon or so, they open up and offer you the same tremendous prices, like shiitake mushrooms for $6.00 a pound, or $7.00 for a liter of extra virgin olive oil; plus meats and fish, like smoked salmon for just $17.00 a pound (compare it to deli prices of $35.00 or more). And you'll find similar savings on free-range chicken, venison, fennel, several varieties of tomatoes, white asparagus, and other delicacies; plus cheeses, prepared salads, and breads. Deals like a five-pound bag of Colombian, decaf, or espresso coffee beans for $14.00 (just $2.80 per pound!) can't be beaten anywhere in Mr. C's travels. Everything is displayed as beautifully as in any market, and the coffee bar (hot espresso for $1.00) makes shopping all the more pleasurable. And since these folks are wholesalers in the food business, they really know their stuff. Open daily, 12:00 p.m. - 6:00 p.m.

ITALIAN FOOD CENTER

186 Grand Street, New York NY 10013. 212/925-2954. **Description:** File this one under the category of "Insider's Discovery". Tucked away in the heart of Little Italy, the Italian Food Center is heaven for fans of Italian cooking. Stock up on your supplies of extra-virgin olive oil, imported tomato paste, dried pastas, freshly stuffed sausages and other meats, breads, and all the rest. At these prices, you can afford to do it easily. The store also makes fresh, wonderful sandwiches, as well as cooked specialties you can heat up at home. Take a friend along, and brag that you know the authentic places to shop in this hyped-up area.

MERCATO PICCOLO

55 Irving Place (between 17th & 18th Streets), New York NY. 212/228-0994. **E-mail address:** salanthon@aol.com. **World Wide Web address:** http://www.salanthonys.com/mercato.htm. **Description:** As part of the Sal Anthony's group of food establishments, Mercato Piccolo sells only the freshest and highest-quality fish, meats, and prepared foods. And the prices are entirely reasonable; like a pound of pork chops for $11.70, a pound of aged steak for $12.95, or a pound of stew meat for $3.50. Mercato Piccolo offers a wide variety of fresh seafood as well, like trout, live lobster, salmon, catfish, and swordfish. Deli meats and cheeses are also offered at good prices (a pound of roast beef for $4.75, a pound of fresh mozzarella for $4.25). And hey, if cooking is not your thing, they've got tons of prepared foods, like a whole stone oven pizza Margherita for $10.95, whole

roasted chickens for $7.00, and delicious homemade soups that average $2.75 each. And don't forget the delicious bakery, where you can pick up delicious cakes, pastries, and breads. I don't know where else you could find mini panini for just $.25. For those of you who work late or like to take a late night stroll, drop by Mercato Piccolo after 9:00 p.m. and you can find a huge selection of items for 50 percent off. Now if that's not a guarantee that their food is fresh, I don't know what is. Open daily, 9:00 a.m. - 10:00 p.m.

PARK SLOPE FOOD COOP
782 Union Street, Brooklyn NY 11215. 718/622-0560. **Description:** Though probably more convenient for those who live in or near the Park Slope neighborhood (since you do have to become a member to shop here), Park Slope Food Coop has enticed residents from all over NYC and even out-of-state to join with the incredible bargains they offer. Mr. C was so impressed with this unique opportunity to save money on everyday groceries that he wanted to pass it along to anyone who might be interested in joining. The Coop offers everything you'd find in an ordinary supermarket, along with many specialty items, at a markup of only 16 percent above wholesale cost. By shopping at Park Slope Food Coop, you can save yourself hundreds of dollars a year on groceries. You'll find fresh-baked breads, organically grown produce (a three-pound bag of Macintosh apples for $.95!), and lots of grains, nuts, dried fruits, and spices. So you have to work for your savings, right? Sure -- all of three hours per month. That, plus a one-time $25.00 joining fee, gets you in. There is also a $100.00 member investment, which you can pay over time and which is returned if you cancel your membership. Considering the amount of food they have (much of it health-oriented), and the amount of money you're going to save overall, it's still quite a bargain. Stop in for membership info and a look around.

SAHADI IMPORTS
187 Atlantic Avenue, Brooklyn NY 11201. 718/624-4550. **Description:** Larger and more elaborately laid-out than its Manhattan counterparts, Sahadi Imports has an excellent stock of imported meats, cheeses, baked goods, prepared foods, candies, and the rest -- mostly, but not exclusively, with a Middle Eastern touch. At the take-out counter you can get a falafel sandwich for $2.50; in the bakery area, grab a French baguette for $1.35, or an onion baguette for $1.75. Plus a cook's encyclopedia of spices, oils, dried beans, coffees, loose teas... the list goes on and on. Wind your way through; it's like a reasonably-priced Balducci's!

TEITEL BROTHERS
2372 Arthur Avenue, Bronx NY 10458. 718/733-9400. **World Wide Web address:** http://www.teitelbros.com. **Description:** How guys with this name found their way into this predominantly Italian neighborhood is of little consequence. They know what they're doing, and if you know what's good for you, you'll shop here for all your cooking needs. Get a gallon of extra-

virgin olive oil, imported from the old country (that would be Italy, of course) for just $13.99. They also have cheeses, sliced meats, fresh and bottled olives, and all the other delicacies for your most special recipes.

WESTERN BEEF
403 West 14th Street, New York NY 10014. 212/989-6572. **World Wide Web address:** http://www.westernbeef.com. **Description:** Despite its name, Western Beef is like a complete discount supermarket. To be sure, this is a great place to buy all kinds of meats, especially if you can buy in quantity. That's where you'll get the best deals. Sirloin steaks, for example, may cost as little as $1.98 a pound -- if you can buy 10 pounds at a time (they will cut them for you). Beef spare ribs may be as low as $.98 a pound. Or, you may find whole Perdue chickens for just $.58 a pound, in a bag of two. Everything's super fresh; this Manhattan location is side-by-side with the many meat wholesalers near the river on 14th Street. This is one of the few places along that strip, in fact, which sells to the public and you generally get the same wholesale prices. Meanwhile, Western Beef also has bargains on all kinds of other supermarket items. It's a no-frills setting, and probably not as convenient as the corner store, but it's definitely worth the trip for savings. Western Beef operates more than 20 supermarkets in the New York City area.

ZABAR'S
2245 Broadway (at 80th Street), New York NY 10024. 212/787-2000. **World Wide Web address:** http://www.zabars.com. **Description:** Though perhaps not as inexpensive as they once were -- success breeds excess -- Zabar's is still *the* New York food market to many. For sheer selection, of course, they're hard to beat. And when they have specials, they're really special -- like their sales on cheeses from around the world. One recent feature included French aged Emmenthaler for just $3.98 a pound, and Old Amsterdam cheese, reduced from $8.98 a pound to $5.98. Coffee beans, chocolates, caviar, smoked whitefish, fresh-baked loaves of bread, and other delicacies are all here at quite reasonable prices. Open daily, including evenings -- and no matter when you go, be prepared for the crowds.

FOOD
🌶 Health Food & Vitamins 🌶

BELL BATES NATURAL FOODS
97 Reade Street, New York NY 10013. 212/267-4300. **World Wide Web address:** http://www.bellbates.com. **Description:** A health and gourmet food store with even more: coffees, herb teas, spices, dried fruits, nuts, and some of the lowest-priced vitamins around! Some of the items Mr. C came across included loose Earl Grey tea for $6.75 a pound; B-complex vitamins, almost $6.00 below retail price; a four-ounce package of catnip for only $3.49; and 32-ounce bottles ofAfter the Fall fruit juices for $1.89. For those who seek healthy alternatives for an insatiable sweet tooth, Bell Bates has fat-free chocolate, as well as oatmeal-raisin cookies (made with whole-wheat flour and no refined sugar) at about $.50 below the supermarket prices (if you can find them there at all). Other bargains seen included organic peanut butter, marked down from $5.49 to $3.29; Nasoya tofu at $.50 off; and Ener-G brown rice bread for $2.59 a loaf. The Internet-savvy Mr. C recommends checking out Bell Bates online. The store offers an online coupon that can be used for 5 percent off a purchase of $25.00 or more. Also be sure to pick up one of the monthly sales flyers. Open Monday through Friday, 9:00 a.m. - 8:00 p.m.; Saturday, 10:00 a.m. - 6:00 p.m.

FREEDA PHARMACY
36 East 41st Street, New York NY 10017. 212/685-4980. **Toll-free phone:** 800/777-3737. **E-mail address:** FreedaVits@aol.com. **World Wide Web address:** http://www.imall.com/stores/freeda. **Description:** Since 1928, the Freeda family has been manufacturing and selling over 250 vitamins and related items at affordable prices. Expectant moms can expect to save with a bottle of 100 KPN tablets for just $8.85; help strengthen your immune system with a bottle of Oceanic Selenium for just $9.95. Save on everyday vitamins from A-to-Z, like a 100-count bottle of Vitamin A for just $5.90, some B6 vitamins for just $6.45, 250 chewable C tablets for $5.95, or a 100-count bottle of D3 for just $5.75. If nutriceuticals are your bag, Freeda is your place. Pick up a bottle of garlic tablets (with parsley, if you wish) for just $4.65, or skip the veggies and have a broccoli pill instead (100-count bottle for $7.95).

THE HEALTH NUTS
835 Second Avenue (at 45th Street), New York NY 10017. 212/490-2979. ◆ 1208 Second Avenue (at 63rd Street), New York NY. 212/593-0116. ◆ 2141 Broadway (at 75th Street), New York NY. 212/724-1972. ◆ 2611 Broadway (at 99th Street), New York NY. 212/678-0054. ◆ Bay Terrace Shopping Center, Queens NY. 718/225-8164. **Description:** There's nothing nuts about this store. The Health Nuts offers good prices on organic foods (with discounts on everything from muesli to mozzarella), dietary

supplements, and personal care products. If you partake of Super Enzymall Tabs, Mr. C found them on sale here for well below the retail price; and Milk Creek Natural Elastin Creme for almost half-price. The stores also carry the Traditional Medicinal line of products whose discounts and product names (Throat Coat, Nighty Night Tea, Eater's Digest Tea, Smooth Move Laxative Tea) are sure to make you smile. You can also get lots of books and printed information about health products, vitamins, and alternative medicine. The Health Nuts stores stay open late, call for hours.

HEALTHY PLEASURES
489 Broome Street, New York NY 10003. 212/431-7434. ✦ 93 University Place (between 11th & 12th Streets), New York NY. 212/353-3663. **E-mail address:** healthypleasure1@aol.com. **Description:** If you're one of the many Americans who is trying to live a holistic lifestyle, Healthy Pleasures is the place to go. And if you're one of the many Americans who dismisses health food as "tasteless" or "bland", Healthy Pleasures just might change your mind. Healthy Pleasures is a full-service grocery store specializing in all-natural and organic foods. All produce is organic; all meat, fish, and poultry are free-range; and all prices are great! Everyday discounts of 15 percent on the more than 1,000 items in stock are the norm at Healthy Pleasures. For additional discounts, pick up a Healthy Pleasures discount card. Healthy Pleasures also sells a wide range of vitamins and herbs that are always 20 - 50 percent off. Buy in bulk and save even more. To obtain natural beauty, visit their health and beauty aid section, where you can guarantee that no harsh chemicals will damage your skin. Now, back to the food! Pick up a pound of organic banana chips for just $5.99 (regularly $12.99), or some Washington nectarines for just $9.99 a pound (usually $12.99). Balance Bars, usually priced at $1.79 and above, were seen here for just $1.29 each. And, for you Paul Newman fans out there, turn on *The Hustler* and snack away on a bag of his organic pretzels for just $1.49 (cost of movie additional). Got a sweet tooth? Pick up a bag of licorice bites (priced elsewhere at $1.75) for just $1.19, or some Speakeasy mints for just $.75 a box. The Healthy Pleasures deli offers unbelievable discounts on all of their free-range and natural meats and poultry. Pick up a pound of hot or sweet Italian sausage for just $2.99, or a pound of 93 percent lean organic beef for just under $4.00. Healthy Pleasures guarantees that there are no antibiotics, no growth hormones, and no unsatisfied customers. The seafood department offers the city's freshest farm-raised delicacies like extra large shrimp ($11.99/lb.), fresh sea scallops ($11.99/lb.), and salmon steaks ($6.39/lb.). If you still don't think Health Pleasures is *Cheap*-worthy, do a bit of research. If you can find a better price elsewhere, Healthy Pleasures will meet it and deduct an additional 10 percent. Now that's what I call confidence!

MR. M DISCOUNT CENTER
192 Seventh Avenue South, New York NY 10014. 212/741-2225. **Description:** In this case the "M" must stand for "muscles", as Mr. M is all about health food and vitamins. Besides other assorted

discounts, Mr. M. Discount Center offers health enthusiasts fantastic prices on vitamins and dietary supplements. Everyday discounts include 25 percent off all Muscletech products, 50 percent off all Cybergenics merchandise, and 40 percent off all Nature's Way vitamins. Mr. M carries a large selection of health foods including Power Bars for $1.09 each, Natural Always soup for $.89, and After the Fall juices $1.99. Open Monday through Friday, 8:00 a.m. - 10:00 p.m.; Saturday, 9:00 a.m. - 10:00 p.m.; Sunday, 9:00 a.m. - 9:00 p.m.

THE VITAMIN SHOPPE

375 Avenue of the Americas, New York NY 10011. 212/929-6553. • 459 Lexington Avenue, New York NY. 212/818-0633. • 666 Lexington (between 55th & 56th Streets), New York NY. 212/421-0250. • 139 East 57th Street, New York NY. 212/371-3850. • 2841 Broadway, New York NY. 212/316-4681. • 210 East 86th Street, New York NY. 212/585-3091. **World Wide Web address:** http://www.vitaminshoppe.com. **Description:** Bigger may not always mean better, but in the case of the Vitamin Shoppe, it does indeed mean better prices. Save up to 20 percent on hundreds of national brands, and as much as 40 percent on selected "Super Savers" throughout the store. The Vitamin Shoppe also markets its own line of vitamins at very low prices. Also save on herbs, from aloe to yucca; body-building supplements; homeopathic medicines; and thousands of personal care items like natural hair colors and shampoos, skin masques, natural dental floss, blood pressure monitors, massagers and back pillows. Best of all, if you're not satisfied with any product, you can return the unused portion within two months for a refund. It's too much to take in, really, but don't worry -- The Vitamin Shoppe has a 110-page catalog, from which you can also order by mail. It's very informative, with articles and descriptions carefully explaining the benefits of each item; this is clearly a company that cares about its customers. They even have a Vitamin Shopper Plus program, which rewards loyal catalog customers with discount coupons for future purchases. If you just can't get enough of The Vitamin Shoppe, visit their factory outlet across the river in North Bergen, New Jersey for further bargains (It's only open on Saturdays). Call for specific store hours.

FOOD
← Meat & Fish →

BALDWIN FISH MARKET
1584 First Avenue (between 82nd & 83rd Streets), New York NY
10028. 212/737-4100. **Description:** When Upper East Siders are
looking for fresh fish at great prices, they go to Baldwin Fish.
With free delivery and low everyday prices, Baldwin Fish is hard to
beat for value. Pick up a pound of fresh cod for just $5.99, salmon
for $8.99, or a pound of live lobster for $8.99. Open Monday
through Saturday, 8:30 a.m. - 8:00 p.m.

CENTER MEAT MARKET
514 Third Avenue (between 34th & 35th Streets), New York NY
10016. 212/689-5090. **Description:** Since 1935, the quality and
the prices at Center Meat Market have been in strong
disagreement with one another. Center Meat Market offers the
best in top quality meats and poultry, with prices that seem too
good to be true. Center Meat Market also offers a standard (but
good) fresh produce selection. It's no wonder why they've been in
business so long. Open Monday through Saturday, 7:00 a.m. - 6:30
p.m.

CENTRAL FISH COMPANY
527 Ninth Avenue (between 39th & 40th Streets), New York NY
10018. 212/279-2317. **Description:** While Mr. C hates to
distribute superlatives, I must say that Central Fish Company is
definitely in the top tier of New York City fish markets. Ask any
native and I'm sure they'll tell you the same. What makes this
market so great is the enormous variety of fresh and delicious
seafood, combined with some of the lowest prices you will
anywhere. From shrimp and scallops to salmon and snapper, Central
Fish Company is like the Noah's Ark of fish markets. It would be
apocalyptic to find that Central Fish Company did not stock your
item of choice. Be warned, however, that the crowds can get kind
of intense. Yet, instead of foregoing these seafaring delights and
opting for the local grocery store, immerse yourself in the chaos
and authenticity of this fish market and I promise you won't be
disappointed. All I ask is that you resist the urge to throw a fish
or two. Open Monday through Friday, 7:00 a.m. - 6:30 p.m.;
Saturday, 7:00 a.m. - 5:30 p.m.

FLORENCE PRIME MEAT MARKET
5 Jones Street (between Bleecker & 4th Streets), New York NY
10014. 212/242-6531. **Description:** For more than 60 years, this
Greenwich Village landmark has been pleasing the palates of more
than just the local neighborhood (though they are regulars here
too). With glowing accolades from *The New York Times* and other
finicky Big Apple gourmets, I hope it's not too late for me to jump
in with applause for their prices. The same steaks that have been
voted the city's best, easily meriting an escalation in their prices,

remain at under $10.00 a pound. A pound of prime aged sirloin sells for roughly $6.50, while Newport steak (the house specialty) retails at $5.50 a pound. One visit to this charmingly nostalgic market and I guarantee you'll be hooked. Open Tuesday through Saturday, 8:00 a.m. - 6:00 p.m.

LEONARDS' SEAFOOD & PRIME MEATS

1385 Third Avenue, New York NY 10021. 212/744-2600. **Description:** For nearly a century, the Leonard family has been offering New Yorkers an affordable option to top quality meats and seafood. Aged meats and the freshest seafood are just two of the reasons that keep people coming back to this Third Avenue landmark. The great prices are an added bonus. At Leonards' you can pick up a pound of prime boneless sirloin for $5.95, or a pound of Gulf shrimp for just $7.95. All orders can be custom cut and/or prepared to your specifications by the Leonards' friendly team. Free delivery is just another great service they provide. Stop in today and see for yourself why, since 1910, the Leonard family has been a preeminent name in quality meats and seafood. Open Monday through Friday, 8:00 a.m. - 7:00 p.m.; Saturday, 8:00 a.m. - 6:00 p.m.; Sunday, 11:00 a.m. - 6:00 p.m.

THE LOBSTER PLACE

75 Ninth Avenue (between 15th & 16th Streets), New York NY 10011. 212/255-5872. **World Wide Web address:** http://www.lobsterplace.com. **Description:** Located at the Chelsea Market, The Lobster Place offers more than the name implies. From clambakes to salmon cakes, you will find everything your seafood-loving heart desires. Here is a sampling of delicacies: lobster ($7.95/lb.); bluefish fillets ($5.50/lb.); mahi-mahi ($8.95/lb.); red snapper ($12.50/lb.); steamer clams ($3.99/lb.); sea scallops ($13.50/lb.). The Lobster Place is open Monday - Saturday, 9:00 a.m. - 8:00 p.m. and Sunday, 10:00 a.m. - 6:00 p.m.

RANDAZZO'S FISH MARKET

2327 Arthur Avenue, Bronx NY 10458. 718/367-4139. **Description:** Randazzo's is a crazy carnival of a seafood shop, bustling with shoppers and brimming with fish. After 80 years across the street, they recently moved into more spacious, attractive quarters at their present address. "We wanted to be on the sunny side of the street," says the cheerful, talkative owner. But you'll go, of course, for the fish. Whether you want live lobster, or their other specialties of clams, mussels, and crabs, you'll get excellent prices. They also carry baccala, that salt-dried cod that's considered a delicacy in these parts. Buy a whole fish or just the center cut, the choice is yours.

SEA BREEZE SEAFOOD

541 Ninth Avenue (at 40th Street), New York NY 10018. 212/563-7537. **Description:** Of the many wholesale/retail food shops along Midtown's Ninth Avenue, Sea Breeze Seafood is unique in that it has that real "just off the boat" feel to it with live lobsters roaming around in bubbling tanks. Recent specials offered one-

pound lobsters for $9.99; swordfish for $6.50 a pound; and whole, large salmon for $3.99 a pound. Of course, prices are seasonal, rising in winter and falling in the summertime, when the fishing is easy. But you'll definitely find bargains here anytime.

YOUNGS FISH MARKET
141 First Avenue, New York NY 10003. 212/254-9147.
Description: For a great selection and great prices, Youngs Fish Market is one of the best in the city. If you know your seafood prices and have some time to compare, Youngs is definitely worth a visit. Here, fresh seafood is often priced lower than the stuff you'd find in your local supermarket, and the difference in taste is undeniable. Pick up a pound of cod for $4.99, a pound of haddock for $5.98, or a pound of salmon for $8.99. If you've got $6.98 to spare, choose between a pound of red snapper or a pound of lobster. A pound of tuna or a pound of swordfish can also be had for $9.98 apiece. Yet, while they skimp on price, Youngs does not skimp on selection. While it may be difficult to find fresh mahi-mahi in other seafood shops throughout the city, Youngs will sell you a pound for under $10.00. These are some unbelievable deals.

FOOD
🌶 Pasta 🌶

BORGATTI'S RAVIOLI EGG NOODLES
632 East 187th Street, Bronx NY 10458. 718/367-3799.
Description: One of the many gems in the Arthur Avenue area,
Borgatti's is a bustling shop selling homemade pasta to an eager
throng of customers. The line frequently runs out the door of this
tiny store. Fresh, soft, pasta noodles are literally cut to order;
just name your thickness. Choose from a variety of noodles
including spinach, carrot, tomato, whole wheat, no yolk, and
semolina. Among the other items on their menu are fresh ravioli,
filled with your choice of spinach, meat, or ricotta cheese.
Whichever you choose, it'll cost just $9.00 for a box of 100
ravioli. Can you beat it?

BRUNO'S PASTA
653 Ninth Avenue (between 45th & 46th Streets), New York NY
10036. 212/246-8456. ◆ 2204 Broadway (between 78th & 79th
Streets), 212/580-8150. ◆ 249 Eighth Avenue (between 22nd &
23rd Streets), 212/627-0767. ◆ 387 Second Avenue (between
22nd & 23rd Streets). **Description:** The King of Ravioli, they
proclaim, and Bruno's has been at the top since 1905. This shop
uses all natural ingredients for its fresh pastas and sauces; and
they're so concerned about your enjoyment of their goods that
they'll happily offer up some emphatically precise cooking
instructions to garner you the best results. Health-conscious
diners will be happy to find that many pastas are made without
eggs. One portion of 12 ravioli costs just $5.25, and varieties
include beef, chicken, and cheese. But, Bruno's doesn't stop there;
they also have manicotti with basic and exotic fillings ($4.29 -
$6.99), tortellini ($5.25), gnocchi, fresh pasta noodles, and all
kinds of sauces to go on top of these. Try a pint of spicy fradiavlo
sauce for $3.99. You can even get complete dinners to take home,
from $4.99 per pound. And they have all the imported fixings to
help you whip up a festive meal or party. The midtown branch is
closed on Sundays; the others are open seven days a week.

THE RAVIOLI STORE
75 Sullivan Street, New York NY 10012. 212/925-1737.
Description: If you find yourself in the middle of a ravioli
emergency, there's no place to go but The Ravioli Store. For more
than 10 years, The Ravioli Store has been customizing ravioli to
the size and ingredient specifications of its many loyal customers.
Whether the ravioli you're seeking is as big as a bread box or as
small as a pea, the folks at The Ravioli Store will work with you to
make sure that you are happy with the result. If you're not in a
creative mood, The Ravioli Store offers a number of inventive,
ready-made ravioli dishes in combinations you'd never dream of.

You'll have to stop by to see what I'm talking about. Even if ravioli is not your thing (still, I urge you to try some), The Ravioli Store sells fresh pasta in your favorite shapes and sizes. Pick up some fresh penne, spaghetti, linguine, or fettucine for just under $2.00 a pound. Or, for just a dime more, you can try a pound of their delicious gnocchi. One visit and you won't want to go anywhere else.

FOOD
🖋 Produce 🖋

FAIRWAY FRUITS & VEGETABLES
2127 Broadway (at 74th Street), New York NY 10023. 212/595-1888. **Description:** Along with Zabar's up the street, Fairway Fruits & Vegetables is the supermarket of choice for good food, good prices, and shoving crowds. Look at it this way: it's not just food shopping, it's an adventure. Fairway Fruits & Vegetables has great values in fresh foods, like breads and cheeses. West Side residents also swear by the prices and vast selection of fruits and vegetables, brought in daily from metro-area farms. And you can grind your own coffee beans, starting at just $2.99 a pound, with enough varieties to keep you busy for more than a month.

GUSS PICKLES
35 Essex Street (between Grand & Hester Streets), New York NY. 212/254-4477. **Description:** Many New Yorkers consider Guss' (also known as Essex Street Pickles) the premier pickle place. Every type of pickle is represented, from sour to dill. But don't stop with what you know; make sure to try the sauerkraut, watermelon rinds, and other pickled items.

STILES FARMER'S MARKET
472 Ninth Avenue (at 41st Street), New York NY 10018. 212/967-4918. **Description:** The zillions of bargain food shops running down Ninth Avenue from the Port Authority don't end with the station itself. Just on the other side, in the shadow of the bus ramps, is Stiles Farmer's Market. Despite its carnival-tent architecture, Stiles is a year-round operation, doing a brisk business in all kinds of fruits and vegetables. Buying in quantity makes for the best bargains; recent specials included two pounds of fresh green beans, three pounds of carrots, or three pounds of bananas for just $1.00. Gourmet coffee beans are sold here too, starting at $3.49 a pound for French roast, decaf, or the house blend.

ENTERTAINMENT
🏛 Art Galleries 🏛

AMERICAS SOCIETY ART GALLERY
680 Park Avenue, New York NY 10021. 212/249-8950. **E-mail address:** webmaster@americas-society.org. **World Wide Web address:** http://www.americas-society.org. **Description:** An art gallery run by the Americas Society, a nonprofit organization that fosters understanding of the cultural heritage as well as political, social, and economic issues facing Latin America, the Caribbean, and Canada. The gallery hosts a variety of exhibitions that feature pieces such as Mexican ceramic art. Many events are free of charge; call or visit the Website for details and exhibition schedules. Open Tuesday through Sunday, 10:00 a.m. - 6:00 p.m.

ARTISTS SPACE
38 Greene Street, 3rd Floor, New York NY 10013. 212/226-3970. **E-mail address:** artspace@artistsspace.org. **World Wide Web address:** http://www.artistsspace.org. **Description:** This SoHo gallery combines the latest in multimedia art environments with performance by such avant-garde artists as Ping Chong. The organization promotes diversity and experimentation in the arts. They even have fun participatory art -- like a recent exhibit of miniature golf, with each hole created by a different artist. Admission is free. Open Tuesday through Saturday, 11:00 a.m. - 6:00 p.m.

ASIAN AMERICAN ARTS CENTRE (AAAC)
26 Bowery, New York NY 10013. 212/233-2154. **E-mail address:** AAArts@aol.com. **World Wide Web address:** http://aac.sunysb.edu. **Description:** Near Canal Street in Chinatown, AAAC specializes in works of contemporary Asian American arts and artists. The Centre is host to approximately five exhibitions per year, with recent shows including a folk art exhibition and festival, three special exhibitions by Robert Lee and other artists, and a juried exhibition selected from works by emerging artists.

BENEDETTI GALLERY
52 Prince Street (between Mulberry & Lafayette Streets), New York NY 10012. 212/226-2238. **E-mail address:** fineart@benedetti.com. **World Wide Web address:** http://www.benedetti.com. **Description:** Focusing primarily on 20th century European art, this SoHo gallery has an especially large collection of sculptures by Erte as well as works by Falai, Anthony Quinn, Wilkinson, Murakami, Robazza, and others. Open daily, 11:00 a.m. - 6:00 p.m.

CDS GALLERY
76 East 79th Street, New York NY. 212/772-9555. **Description:** CDS primarily presents the work of Latin American and North American artists with exhibitions encompassing paintings,

sculpture, drawings, and more. Exhibited artists have included Pierre Bonnard, Joaquin Torres-Garcia, and Melvin Edwards. Open Tuesday through Saturday, 10:00 a.m. - 5:00 p.m.

CHINA INSTITUTE GALLERY
125 East 65th Street, New York NY 10021. 212/744-8181. **Description:** Each year the China Institute Gallery hosts two major exhibits which focus on the unique aspects of Chinese art. Popular among museum-goers is the annual Folk Art Exhibition, which offers a special look at art relating to the Chinese New Year as well as more traditional arts and crafts. Admission is $3.00 for adults, $2.00 for students and seniors. Open Monday through Friday, 9:00 a.m. - 5:00 p.m. When an exhibit is open, the gallery also opens on Saturday (10:00 a.m. - 5:00 p.m.) and Sunday (1:00 p.m. - 5:00 p.m.). Call ahead to be sure.

FISCHBACH GALLERY
24 West 57th Street, Suite 806, New York NY 10019. 212/759-2345. **E-mail address:** fishbachgallery@msn.com. **Description:** An art gallery specializing in American contemporary representation, paintings, sculpture, and drawings.

FOCAL POINT GALLERY
321 City Island Avenue, Bronx NY 10464. 718/885-1403. **World Wide Web address:** http://www.focalpointgallery.com. **Description:** An art gallery focusing on photographic and other visual arts. Admission is free. Open Tuesday through Sunday, 12:00 p.m. - 7:30 p.m.; Friday and Saturday, 7:30 p.m. - 9:00 p.m.; closed Monday.

BARRY FRIEDMAN GALLERY
32 East 67th Street, New York NY 10021. 212/794-8950. **Description:** This gallery is known for its fine exhibits of early 20th-century, avant-garde artists. Open Monday through Friday, 10:00 a.m. - 6:00 p.m.; Saturday, 10:00 a.m. - 5:00 p.m.

GALERIE ST. ETIENNE
24 West 57th Street, New York NY 10019. 212/245-6734. **Description:** This gallery specializes in Austrian and German Expressionism and Outsider/Folk art. Open Tuesday through Saturday, 11:00 a.m. - 5:00 p.m.

MARIAN GOODMAN GALLERY
24 West 57th Street, New York NY 10019. 212/977-7160. **E-mail address:** goodman@mariangoodman.com. **Description:** A mixed media art gallery featuring a variety of international artists and styles. Open Monday through Saturday, 10:00 a.m. - 6:00 p.m.

GREENWICH HOUSE POTTERY
16 Jones Street, New York NY 10014. 212/242-4106. **Description:** Located in the heart of the Village, Greenwich House Pottery has been a major center for ceramics since 1909. Besides offering quality instruction in studio classes, the Pottery's Jane Hartsook

Gallery maintains an ongoing exhibition series. Greenwich House Pottery, in conjunction with the Office Gallery, is committed to supporting ceramics artists, and sharing the diversity of historical and contemporary ceramics with the community.

GREY ART GALLERY

New York University, 100 Washington Square East, New York NY 10003. 212/998-6780. **World Wide Web address:** http://www.nyu.edu. **Description:** Located in historic Washington Square Park, New York University's Grey Art Gallery is focused on interpreting and exhibiting art with considerable historical, cultural, and sociological significance. The Grey Art Gallery exhibits artifacts in a variety of visual art mediums including paintings, sculptures, photographs, decorative arts, videos, films, and live performances. Exhibitions have included the works of John Singer Sargeant, Shiro Kuramata furniture, and Krizia fashions. Admission is a suggested $2.50 donation. Open Tuesday, Thursday & Friday, 11:00 a.m. - 6:00 p.m.; Wednesday, 11:00 a.m. - 8:00 p.m.; Saturday, 11:00 a.m. - 5:00 p.m.

HIRSCHL & ADLER GALLERIES

21 East 70th Street, New York NY 10021. 212/535-8810. **World Wide Web address:** http://www.hirschlandadler.com. **Description:** Located in an Upper East Side townhouse, Hirschl & Adler Galleries exhibits the works of American and European artists. The works can be as diverse as the periods at Hirschl & Adler: 18th-century paintings, 19th-century decorative arts, 20th-century drawings, and contemporary art from the Post-War period onward can all be found here. The gallery also hosts more than 10 special exhibitions each year, paying homage to particular artists or historical themes.

JANE KAHAN GALLERY

1020 Madison Avenue (at 78th Street), 5th Floor, New York NY 10021. 212/744-1490. **World Wide Web address:** http://www.janekahan.com. **Description:** Founded in 1973, Jane Kahan Gallery has been representing European and American masters of the 19th and 20th centuries. Featured artists have included Picasso, Arp, Chagall, and Miro. As a member of the International Fine Print Dealers Association, Jane Kahan Gallery is able to offer museum quality prints, paintings, tapestries, and other artwork in a variety of price ranges. Throughout the year, Jane Kahan presents a number of special exhibitions. To hear a list of upcoming shows, give them a call.

KENNEDY GALLERIES

730 Fifth Avenue, 2nd Floor, New York NY 10019. 212/541-9600. **E-mail address:** kennedygal@aol.com. **World Wide Web address:** http://www.kgny.com **Description:** Since 1874, Kennedy Galleries is one of the most recognizable and respected names in American art. Their collection -- which consists of paintings, sculptures, drawings, and watercolors of 18th, 19th, and 20th century masters -- has included the works of Edward Hopper and Georgia O'Keeffe.

Throughout the year, they showcase these artists in a number of exhibitions that are open to the public. For a listing of upcoming exhibitions, call or visit their Website. Open Tuesday through Saturday, 9:30 a.m. - 5:30 p.m. during the winter; Monday through Friday, 9:30 a.m. - 5:30 p.m. during the summer.

JAN KRUGIER GALLERY
41 East 57th Street, New York NY 10022. 212/755-7288. **Description:** An art gallery specializing in the paintings, sculptures, and drawings of the masters of the 19th and 20th centuries. The Jan Krugier Gallery is the exclusive agent for the Marina Picasso collection of works by Pablo Picasso.

LITTLEJOHN CONTEMPORARY ART
41 East 57th Street, Suite 702, New York NY 10022. 212/980-2323. **Description:** A contemporary art gallery. Littlejohn Contemporary Art's past exhibitions have featured an eclectic and always-interesting mix of figurative and abstract paintings, sculptures, frescoes, mosaics, and prints. Open Tuesday through Saturday, 10:00 a.m. - 5:30 p.m.

MARLBOROUGH GALLERY
40 West 57th Street, 2nd Floor, New York NY 10019. 212/541-4900. **E-mail address:** mny@marlboroughgallery.com. **World Wide Web address:** http://www.marlboroughgallery. com. **Description:** Founded in London by Frank Lloyd and Harry Fischer, Marlborough Gallery has locations worldwide including Argentina, Chile, Japan, and Madrid. The Marlborough Gallery represents and presents major retrospectives of such established artists as Richard Estes and Larry Rivers. Open Monday through Saturday, 10:00 a.m. - 5:30 p.m.

JASON McCOY GALLERY
41 East 57th Street, New York NY 10022. 212/319-1996. **E-mail address:** jmg@dti.net. **Description:** Jason McCoy Gallery presents works of contemporary, modern, and abstract art. Exhibitions have included the photographs of Anoushka Fisz, stained glass decorative arts by Louis Comfort Tiffany, and newfound works by Jackson Pollock. Open Tuesday through Saturday, 10:00 a.m. - 5:30 p.m.

METRO PICTURES
519 West 24th Street, New York NY 10011. 212/206-7100. **World Wide Web address:** http://www.metro-pictures.com. **Description:** Cute name for a serious SoHo gallery. Featured artists have included Cindy Sherman, John Miller, and Tony Oursler. Open Tuesday through Saturday, 10:00 a.m. - 6:00 p.m.

ROBERT MILLER GALLERY
526 West 26th Street, New York NY. 212/980-5454. **Description:** The Robert Miller Gallery has featured the works of many modern artists, including the notorious SAMO graffiti artist and Warhol protégé, Jean-Michel Basquiat. Open Tuesday through Saturday, 10:00 a.m. - 6:00 p.m.

NoHo GALLERY
168 Mercer Street, New York NY 10012. 212/219-2210.
Description: Though it originated in NoHo, when much of the SoHo art scene began spreading north of Houston Street, the NoHo Gallery is now smack dab in the middle of SoHo. This gallery shows a variety of works by current New York artists, similar to the galleries on the other side of the street. Open Tuesday through Sunday, 11:00 a.m. - 6:00 p.m.

NOLAN/ECKMAN GALLERY
560 Broadway (at Prince Street), New York NY 10012. 212/925-6190. **E-mail address:** nolan.eckman@prodigy.net. **Description:** A contemporary art gallery offering exhibitions from noted artists like Salvador Dali. Open Tuesday through Friday, 10:00 a.m. - 6:00 p.m.; Saturday, 11:00 a.m. - 6:00 p.m.

PACEWILDENSTEIN GALLERY
142 Greene Street, New York NY 10012. 212/431-9224. ♦ 32 East 57th Street, New York NY 10022. 212/421-3292. **Description:** Here's another gallery hitting both the uptown and downtown scenes. Each gallery runs separate exhibitions, focusing on works by major artists like Robert Rauschenberg, Kiki Smith, and the estates of Picasso and Calder. The uptown branch also has a print gallery, which has been known to exhibit such rare pieces as a set of lithographs by Matisse. The Greene Street location is open Tuesday through Saturday, 10:00 a.m. - 6:00 p.m.; 57th Street location is open Tuesday through Friday, 9:30 a.m. - 6:00 p.m., and Saturday, 10:00 a.m. - 6:00 p.m.

REECE GALLERIES
24 West 57th Street, Suite 304, New York NY 10019. 212/333-5830. **World Wide Web address:** http://www.reecegalleries.com. **Description:** For more than 20 years, this art gallery has featured contemporary abstract paintings by Ricardo Benaim, Michael Dillon, Bruce Dorfman, and Sica. The gallery also houses works by some contemporary master stone sculptors from Zimbabwe. Open Monday through Saturday, 10:00 a.m. - 5:30 p.m.

SCHMIDT-BINGHAM GALLERY
41 East 57th Street, 5th Floor, New York NY. 212/888-1122. **World Wide Web address:** http://www.schmidtbingham.com. **Description:** A contemporary art gallery showcasing various American artists. Open Tuesday through Friday, 10:00 a.m. - 5:00 p.m.; Saturday, 1:00 p.m. - 6:00 p.m. (closed on Saturday during summer months).

SoHo PHOTO GALLERY
15 White Street, New York NY 10013. 212/226-8571. **Description:** The name says it all -- but then, a picture's worth a thousand words, so you should absolutely go and see for yourself. SoHo Photo Gallery is the Big Apple's oldest gallery run exclusively by artists. Be sure to go with an open mind and expect the non-traditional. After all, this *is* the place that hosted the first national Krappy Kamera Competition.

303 GALLERY
525 West 22nd Street, New York NY 10011. 212/255-1121.
Description: Young and upcoming artists like Doug Aitken, Thomas Demand, Kristin Oppenheim, and Sue Williams have made names for themselves at 303 Gallery. If you're in the neighborhood stop in -- it's free. Open Tuesday through Saturday, 10:00 a.m. - 6:00 p.m.

JOAN T. WASHBURN GALLERY
20 West 57th Street, New York NY 10019. 212/397-6780.
Description: With an innate artistic sense, Joan Washburn has rightfully earned her title as one of New York City's preeminent art dealers. Her gallery has showcased the works of many of the most celebrated artists (think Jackson Pollock) and is nondiscriminatory when it comes to style. Come in and see for yourself why Ms. Washburn's discerning eye has deified her amongst art connoisseurs. Open Tuesday through Saturday, 10:00 a.m. - 6:00 p.m.

ENTERTAINMENT
 Arts & Cultural Centers

CENTERFOLD
263 West 86th Street, New York NY 10024. 212/866-4454.
Description: Centerfold offers poetry readings, concerts, and theatrical performances in a beautiful setting at The Church of St. Paul and St. Andrew. But don't let the pious atmosphere scare you into thinking that Centerfold is not a lot of fun. Readings are open to comics, singers, and songwriters; theater performances have encompassed everything from William Shakespeare to Steve Allen; and concerts can be anything from classical to jazz to folk. Call for a schedule of upcoming events.

CLEMENTE SOTO VELEZ CULTURAL CENTER (CSV)
107 Suffolk Street, New York NY 10002. 212/260-4080. **World Wide Web address:** http://www.csvcenter.org. **Description:** Named after the late avant-garde poet, this Lower East Side cultural center helps to develop new and emerging art talent. CSV is home to four theater companies: LA TEA Theater promotes Latino culture and heritage through the arts. LA TEA produces three plays each year that focus on existing social problems. LA TEA also offers exhibit space for local and international artists, folk music concerts, and lectures; Los Kabayitos Puppet Theater provides entertaining shows for both children and adults. Call to get on their mailing list; Como Coco Cafe is a multidisciplinary performance space that is home to the Milagro Theater Company; and Flamboyan Theater presents a variety of traveling performances. Call or visit CSV's Website for the most up-to-date offerings and prices.

CULTURAL SERVICES OF THE FRENCH EMBASSY
972 Fifth Avenue (at 79th Street), New York NY 10021. 212/439-1400. **E-mail address:** new-york.culture@diplomatie.fr. **Description:** You should expect to see more than harried travelers at The French Embassy. In the entrance hall, stands The Marble Boy. While the origination of this statue is not certain, experts believe this fragmented nude is an early work of Michaelangelo. After failing to sell at a Christie's auction, the piece was purchased by architect Stanford White and installed in the home of the Payne Whitney family (the former tenants). Drop by and join in the controversy: is it Michealangelo's or not? Admission is free, and the statue can be viewed Monday through Friday, 9:30 a.m. - 5:00 p.m. Another site to behold is the Venetian Room, one of White's loveliest and last creations. Enter this former reception room behold the mirrored interior and neoclassical ornamentation. As the dying wish of Helen Hay Whitney, the Venetian Room was fully restored and opened for public viewing (free of charge), on Fridays from 12:30 p.m. - 2:30 p.m.

DIA CENTER FOR THE ARTS

548 West 22nd Street, New York NY. 212/989-5566. **World Wide Web address:** http://www.diacenter.org. **Description:** Dia Center for the Arts has long been dedicated to preserving the history and development of the nation's artistic and poetic heritage. Through exhibitions and educational programs, Dia has been able to successfully involve the public in continuing this mission. Collected works include the art work of Joseph Beuys, Blinky Palermo, and Andy Warhol. Dia Center also presents a widely-respected *Readings in Contemporary Poetry* series. Readings are $6.00 for adults, $3.00 for students and seniors, and free to members. For a listing of upcoming events and exhibitions, call or visit their Website.

GOETHE-INSTITUT

1014 Fifth Avenue (at 82nd Street), New York NY. 212/439-8700. **World Wide Web address:** http://www.goethe.de. **Description:** Many cities around the world host a Goethe-Institut, set up by the Republic of Germany to present its art and culture to interested parties. Touring exhibitions include photography and paintings, classic and contemporary films, lectures, concerts, and more. Admission is free to all events. Goethe-Institut also houses an enormous library with books written in both German and English, along with several German magazines and newspapers, CDs, CD-ROMs, and videos. All materials are available for three-week loans. Gallery hours are Tuesday and Thursday, 10:00 a.m. - 7:00 p.m.; Wednesday and Friday, 10:00 a.m. - 5:00 p.m.; Saturday, 12:00 p.m. - 5:00 p.m. Library hours are Tuesday and Thursday, 12:00 p.m. - 7:00 p.m.; Wednesday and Saturday, 12:00 p.m. - 5:00 p.m.

HERE

145 Avenue of the Americas (between Spring & Dominic Streets), New York NY 10013. 212/647-0202. **World Wide Web address:** http://www.here.org. **Description:** An award-winning performance and art center. On the "performance" end, Here offers a variety of staged performances, usually daily ticket prices range from $0.00 - $15.00. Some shows even have student rates as low as $5.00. For "art", Here offers the MAINGallery, open Tuesday through Sunday, 2:00 p.m. - 10:00 p.m.; and the DOWNUnder gallery, open Tuesday through Sunday, 2:00 p.m. - 10:00 p.m. When you're done browsing, drop by the HERECafe for a quick drink, open Monday through Friday, 10:00 a.m. - 12:00 a.m.; Saturday, 12:00 p.m. - 12:00 a.m.; Sunday, 12:00 p.m. - 10:00 p.m.

THE MUNICIPAL ART SOCIETY OF NEW YORK

457 Madison Avenue (at 50th Street), New York NY 10022. 212/935-3960. **Description:** The Municipal Art Society of New York is a membership organization that champions excellence in urban design and planning, and the preservation of the city's past. In keeping with this mission, the society hosts a full calendar of walking tours, lectures, exhibits, and educational programs. Each Wednesday at 12:30 p.m., The Municipal Society offers a free tour of Grand Central Station. The society also offers a variety of specialty tours that are announced every other month. For

information on upcoming events, exhibits, and classes, give them a call.

SNUG HARBOR CULTURAL CENTER
1000 Richmond Terrace, Staten Island NY 10301. 718/448-2500. **Description:** If you're taking a cruise around the outer boroughs, take a walk through more than 100 years of American architectural history, talk with working artists about their exhibitions, strike up the band -- music from classic jazz to folk songs of Hawaii --, or just kick back and relax with a little guitar music. All of these events and more take place at various locations around the 86 acres and 29 historic buildings that comprise Snug Harbor, a former retirement home for merchant sailors that was converted into a "snug harbor" for the arts. Throughout the year, Snug Harbor offers a variety of concerts, art exhibitions, and hands-on educational programs. The Center is also home to the Staten Island Botanical Gardens and its New York Chinese Scholar's Garden, the Staten Island Children's Museum, and the maritime art of the John A. Noble collection. Call for information on upcoming events.

WORLD FINANCIAL CENTER
West Street (between Liberty and Vesey Streets), New York NY. 212/945-0505. **World Wide Web address:** http://www. worldfinancialcenter.com. **Description:** Since its inception in 1988, millions of people have enjoyed the free performances and exhibits presented by the World Financial Center's Arts & Events Program. Rising and established artists alike have been lucky enough to show their stuff at the World Financial Center, a building that is occupied by more than 60,000 people each day. While housing the world headquarters of many prominent financial companies (hence the name) like American Express, Dow Jones, and Merrill Lynch, the WFC also houses more than 45 restaurants and retail shops including Barneys New York and Ann Taylor (okay, so they're not cheap, but you can look, right?). Even if you don't plan on attending any of the festivities, the building itself is a sight to behold. The WFC has a grove of 50-foot palm trees inside the Winter Garden. The WFC is also home to The Plaza, the Hudson River's first waterfront piazza. Open seven days a week. Call or visit their Website for a schedule of upcoming events.

ENTERTAINMENT
☿ Bars/Nightclubs ☿

BMW BAR
199 Seventh Avenue (between 21st & 22nd Streets), New York NY 10011. 212/229-1807. **Description:** No, you won't be able to find any luxury cars, but you will find lots of B(eer), W(ine), M(usic), food, and good fun. This tiny little cafe and cigar bar features live music and artwork, and serves up a mean cup of coffee at one of the best prices in the city. If caffeine is not the delicacy you are seeking, BMW also serves a full menu of beer and wine. Stop in for Happy Hour (2:00 p.m. - 8:00 p.m. daily) for $3.00 drafts. Every day, BMW Bar offers live music from 5:00 p.m. - 2:00 a.m. You can even test out your own vocal chords on a live audience at the open-mike, Saturdays from 5:00 p.m. - 8:00 p.m. And, if neither of these options sounds too appealing to you, BMW lets you bring your own tapes and CDs with you. Prices are great, and the neighborhood feeling you'll receive from your visit is worth any claustrophobia you may experience. Open daily, 2:00 p.m. - 4:00 a.m.

BAKTUN
418 West 14th Street (between Ninth Avenue & Washington Street), New York NY 10014. 212/206-1590. **World Wide Web address:** http://www.baktun.com. **Description:** For the latest in trip-hop and deep house music, devotees make many a pilgrimage to this multimedia lounge in the Meatpacking District. Besides live instrumental and electronic entertainment, Baktun indulges their audience with video performances. Many an evening you can dance the night away to the happening sounds of some of the club's regular and guest DJs. On the first Friday of every month, house-lovers can Bang the Party with a night full of music. Still, as hip and happening as this place is, you never feel overcrowded and squished. What's more, the bar menu is more than reasonably priced, and cover charges are usually in the $5.00 to $10.00 range.

BOXERS
190 West 4th Street (between Avenue of the Americas & Seventh Avenue), New York NY 10014. 212/633-2275. ♦ 1152 First Avenue (at 63rd Street), New York NY 10012; 212/688-9663. **Description:** While they'll be more than happy to cook you up a burger or some other typical pub food, Boxers is more of a bar than a fancy restaurant with which to impress your date. Drinks are well-priced, with a bottled beers running from $4.00 - $5.00, and drafts from $3.00 - $3.50. Get there early for Happy Hour (Monday through Friday, 5:00 p.m. - 7:00 p.m.) and take advantage of the 2-for-1 special. Open daily, 11:30 a.m. - 4:00 a.m.

THE COOLER
416 West 14th Street (between Ninth Avenue & Washington Street), New York NY 10014. 212/229-0785. **Description:** For a

truly Gotham City experience, take a trip to New York's Meatpacking District and step inside The Cooler. But be warned, The Cooler is not just this place's name, it also describes the club's sometimes frigid climate. No matter, the club's eclectic soundtrack and alternative atmosphere draw a hip crowd that can be seen dancing and drinking until the wee hours of the morning. The part that impresses Mr. C is that cover charges can range anywhere from $0.00 to $12.00, and there is no drink minimum. It doesn't get much cooler than that. Open Monday through Saturday, 8:00 p.m. - 4:00 a.m.

CULTURE CLUB
179 Varick Street (between King & Charlton Streets), New York NY 10014. 212/243-1999. **Description:** If you're up for a cheesy good time, step into the eighties time warp that is Culture Club. For all 1980s revival enthusiasts, this club delivers. You'll hear the DJs spinning tunes from the likes of Madonna, Devo, Van Halen, Milli Vanilli, etc. Television sets mounted on the walls run faves such as *The Breakfast Club* and *St. Elmo's Fire*, while murals of pop icons fill the club's walls. On the main floor, the focus is on dance and pop music, while upstairs features new wave, techno, old school hip-hop, and big-hair bands. Throw on some jelly shoes and legwarmers and have a blast! Bottled beers cost $5.00, and the club offers $2.00 shot specials all night. Open Thursday - Sunday, 9:00 p.m. - 5:00 a.m.

McSORLEY'S OLD ALE HOUSE
15 East Seventh Street (between Second & Third Avenues), New York NY 10003. 212/473-9148. **Description:** As one of the oldest bars in the city, McSorley's has become legendary and draws massive crowds on the weekends. Historic photos line the walls, and the two house ales, McSorley's Dark and McSorley's Light (the only beers offered), are unrivaled. Pints cost only $2.75. Open Monday through Saturday, 11:00 a.m. - 1:00 a.m.; Sunday, 1:00 p.m. - 1:00 a.m. *$Cash Only$*

RESERVOIR
70 University Place, New York NY 10003. 212/598-0055. **Description:** Cheap beer and sports -- the perfect combination. Nightly beer specials, late-night hours, simple grub, and Direct TV are just a few of the things that make this place so popular. If you've got the munchies, they've got all your pub standards: wings ($4.95 - $6.95); skins ($4.95); chicken fingers ($6.95); jalapeño poppers ($5.95); and a large sandwich menu including grilled chicken, a turkey club, and burgers. On Saturday and Sunday, cool down with $2.00 Bud pints; on Sunday and Monday, heat things up with $.20 wings; spend your Tuesday night in the company of a $3.00 pint; on Wednesday, indulge yourself with $2.00 pints of Black Star Lager; and on Thursday, meet up with some friends and share an $8.00 pitcher of Molson Ice. When you've had enough of their continual televised sports, strike up a game of darts or pool. And if you're just in the mood to relax, lie back and listen to the Sunday night acoustical jam. Open daily, 11:30 a.m. - 4:00 a.m.

THE RODEO GRILL

375 Third Avenue (at 27th Street), New York NY. 212/683-6500.
Description: A Tex-Mex bar and club that offers live music every
night -- never a cover!! Bands cover all the bases from rock and roll
to country. Call for a schedule.

vOID

16 Mercer Street, New York NY 10013. 212/941-6492. **E-mail
address:** void@escape.com. **World Wide Web address:**
http://www.escape.com/~void. **Description:** Have you ever been to
an "electronic lounge"? Well, that's exactly what vOID describes
itself as and, take it from Mr. C, it's definitely worth checking
out. For discerning film critics and cult enthusiasts alike, Film in
vOID (Wednesdays at 8:00 p.m.) is not to be missed. The films
encompass many of the New Hollywood "conspiracy" films of the
seventies such as Alan Pakula's *The Parallax View*, as well as cult
classics like *Repo Man* and *Altered States*. If movies aren't your
thing, don't fret. vOID also offers experimental music
performances, Internet connectivity, and a range of CD-ROM
games. Every Thursday night at 10:30 p.m. is Null at vOID, where
DJs spin a variety of electronic and experimental tunes. Admission
is usually free, but be sure to have a drink or two (they've got
bills to pay, you know). For a list of upcoming events, visit the
vOID Website or give them a call. Open Tuesday through
Thursday, 8:00 p.m. - 2:00 a.m.; Friday and Saturday, 8:00 p.m. -
3:00 a.m.

ENTERTAINMENT
👪 Children's Activities 👪

BOOKS OF WONDER
16 West 18th Street (between Fifth Avenue & Avenue of the Americas), New York NY 10011. 212/989-3270. **E-mail address:** BooksWonder@earthlink.net. **World Wide Web address:** http://www.booksofwonder.com. **Description:** There is perhaps no greater "wonder" (or joy) than the excitement that literature can bring to a child. Yet, in this Information Age, the excitement and education of literature is often pushed aside for the flashing lights of the newest CD-ROM or video game. So, to you loyal readers, I bring you Books of Wonder. As one of the city's oldest and largest children's bookstores, Books of Wonder truly brings back the excitement of children's literature (to both kids and adults alike). Besides being a bookstore, Books of Wonder is also a publisher. They re-publish and re-cover many of the children's classics that are hard to find or out of print. While you browse and relive the tales of your youth, kids can play at tables set up along the store's left wall. Books of Wonder also offers a variety of (often free) programs and performances for kids (storytelling and the like). It's a great place to take kids when there's some sort of engagement going on, and still a great place when all that's there is you and the books. Call ahead for a schedule of events.

BROOKLYN ACADEMY OF MUSIC
30 Lafayette Avenue, Brooklyn NY 11217. 718/636-4100. **World Wide Web address:** www.bam.org. **Description:** This is one of the oldest operating performing arts centers in the country. BAMfamily is a series of shows specially geared toward children and families, and is held during the spring. These are fully professional shows, and are at aimed exposing children to theatrical innovation and art forms they're probably unfamiliar with. Recent performances have included an American jazz musician, and a Dutch theater ensemble. Tickets are $10.00. Most BAMfamily performances are held at the Harvey Theater, 651 Fulton Street. Other activities at include BAM Rose Cinemas which offers first-run independent and foreign films. Tickets are $8.50 ($5.00 for seniors, BAM Cinema Club members, children under 12 and students with valid I.D.). Call 718/623-2770 or 718/363-4157 for ticket information. BAMcafé offers jazz, pop, funk, world/folk, cabaret, and spoken word performances, There is no cover charge, but there is a $10.00 food/drink minimum. They also have a Happy Hour Tuesday through Friday, from 4:00 p.m. - 6:00 p.m.; dinner service from 5:00 p.m. - 10:00 p.m., Tuesday through Saturday; Sunday brunch from 12:00 p.m. - 4:00 p.m.; and a concession menu from 4:00 p.m. - 10:00 p.m. (Tuesday through Thursday), 12:00 p.m. - 11:00 p.m. (Friday and Saturday), and 12:00 p.m. - 9:00 p.m. on Sundays. Call 718/636-4139 for more information on BAMcafé.

BROOKLYN CHILDREN'S MUSEUM

145 Brooklyn Avenue (at St. Mark's Avenue), Brooklyn NY 11213. 718/735-4400. **Description:** Tucked away in the heart of Brooklyn, this is one of the nation's first and foremost children's museums. Yes, it's in Crown Heights, but it's a large, safe location in Brower Park and the museum even takes racial issues as a point of departure for many of its exhibits. Kids can learn about the many cultures of people in the city, and perhaps gain a better understanding through participation in hands-on workshops and play areas. It's a modern facility, in which an old-fashioned subway entrance leads into neon-lit tunnels; the history of the city in symbols. Special programs (free with admission) focus on plant life, animal survival, or even body movement workshops. Admission is a suggested $4.00 donation. Open Wednesday through Friday, 2:00 p.m. - 5:00 p.m.; Saturday and Sunday, 10:00 a.m. - 5:00 p.m.; closed Monday and Tuesday.

CENTRAL PARK CAROUSEL

Central Park at 64th Street, New York NY 10019. 212/879-0244. **Description:** Features some of the nation's largest, antique, hand-carved horses. Only $.90 per ride. Open Monday through Sunday, 10:30 a.m. - 6:00 p.m.

CHILDREN'S MUSEUM OF THE ARTS

182 Lafayette Street (Broome & Grand Streets), New York NY 10013. 212/274-0986. **Description:** Families who enjoy browsing SoHo art galleries can get their kids right into the scene without leaving the neighborhood. This museum/learning center offers exhibits and encourages active participation from children; it's recommended for toddlers of 18 months up to kids of about 10 years old. Among their programs are afterschool art classes and weekend workshops, in which children can really express themselves and just have fun. Admission is $5.00, and free to anyone under one year or over 65 years. Wednesday nights, from 5:00 p.m. - 7:00 p.m., it's "Pay What You Wish." Family memberships are also available, reducing the costs for regular visitors. Open Wednesday, 12:00 p.m. - 7:00 p.m.; Thursday through Sunday, 12:00 p.m. - 5:00 p.m.

CHILDREN'S MUSEUM OF MANHATTAN (CMOM)

212 West 83rd Street (Broadway and Amsterdam), New York NY 10024. 212/721-1234. **World Wide Web address:** http://www.cmom.org. **Description:** CMOM is a hands-on haven for youngsters -- big, bright, and lively. Everything is geared toward activities that make learning painless and just plain fun. What else would you expect from a gallery called the Brainatarium, or the Urban Tree House? There's a media laboratory where kids can make their own effects-laden videos, and lots of workshops in which they can design flags or stamps, musical instruments, or pottery. Add live music and theater performances, and you've got what amounts to an indoor carnival. Great, creative toys in the gift shop, too. Admission is $6.00; $3.00 for senior citizens; kids under one and members get in free. There may be a $1.00 or $2.00 additional fee for workshops and performances. Open Wednesday through Sunday, 10:00 a.m. - 5:00 p.m.

INTREPID SEA-AIR-SPACE MUSEUM

Pier 86, West 46th Street & Twelfth Avenue, New York NY 10036. 212/245-0072. **World Wide Web address:** http://www.intrepidmuseum.org. **Description:** This nonprofit museum hosts a variety of exhibits on aviation, deep sea, and space exploration. Events include live demonstrations by the Navy SEALS, the New York City Police Department, and the Coast Guard. The Annual Intrepid Tugboat Festival is held in September and features tugboat races and a line-throwing competition. And in the spirit of Popeye, there's even a spinach eating contest. Call or visit the museum's Website for specific events and times. Admission is $12.00 for adults; Veterans/U.S. Reservists, $9.00; seniors/college students, $9.00; students (ages 12 - 17), $9.00; children (ages 6 - 11), $6.00; children (ages 2 - 5), $2.00. Admission is free for children under 2 years, active duty U.S. military, and museum members. Wheelchair patrons pay half price. Discounts are available for groups.

LAZER PARK

163 West 46th Street, New York NY 10036. 212/398-3060. **World Wide Web address:** http://www.lazerpark.com. **Description:** Suit the family up for combat and head to Times Square for one of the most physically exciting (or, if you like, demanding) challenges New York has to offer. No, we're not talking about dodging taxis or getting tickets to the hottest play on Broadway, we're talking about a game of laser tag. Lazer Park houses the East Coast's largest and most technologically-advanced laser tag arena, weighing in at 5,000 square-feet. Laser tag missions are divided into two categories: Capture the Flag (the team game) or Manhunt. With high-tech special effects and sounds, all participants will feel transported to another time and place. And don't worry, there will be no cheating. All hits and shots are monitored by the Lazer Park computer. When it's all over, a encyclopedic score sheet will let you know your strengths and weaknesses so that, when you're ready to play again, you'll have already devised the perfect strategy. Families can work together as a group, or compete against one another. In addition to laser tag, Lazer Park offers a variety of virtual reality games like Battle Tech® and Red Planet®, and more modernized video games like Time Crisis II and Star Wars. Kids can try their hand at simulated skiing, motorcycle driving, drag racing, and jet skiing. Besides a great snack bar with such amusement park standards as pizza slices ($1.90), hot dogs ($2.25), nachos ($3.75), and pretzels ($1.75), Lazer Park houses a variety of arcade classics like pinball and skeeball. And yes, high-scorers will experience the joy of seeing the machines spit out a chain of tickets that can later be redeemed for a number of great prizes (gag gifts, bubble gum, etc.). Admission to Lazer Park is free. A single game of laser tag or Battle Tech® is $8.95 per person, a double play (or a combination of the two) is $15.95 per person. Video games cost $.25 to $2.00. Only kids ages seven and up will be allowed on the "battlefield." Open Sunday through Thursday, 11:00 a.m. - 12:00 a.m.; Friday and Saturday, 11:00 a.m. - 2:00 a.m.

THE NEW VICTORY THEATER
209 West 42nd Street, New York NY 10036. 212/239-6200. **World Wide Web address:** http://www.newvictory.org. **Description:** It's like Broadway Junior. The New Victory Theater is the premier name in family theater in New York City. Offering drama, dance, music, circuses, puppet shows, and films, The New Victory Theater's productions are both professional fun, teaching kids the value of culturing themselves at a young age. Kids will even love the performance titles like *The Flying Fruit Fly Circus*, *The Flaming Idiots*, and *Frogs, Lizards, Orbs, and Slinkys*. And the surroundings aren't bad either; New Victory Theater performances take place in the city's oldest active theater. So, while you're teaching your kid about the arts, you can throw a little history lesson in as well. Tickets generally run between $10.00 and $25.00, depending on the performance. Call or visit their Website for the upcoming season schedule.

THE PUPPETWORKS, INC.
338 Sixth Avenue (at 4th Street), Brooklyn NY 11215. 718/965-3391. **E-mail address:** puppetworks@worldnet.att.net. **World Wide Web address:** http://www.puppetworks.org. **Description:** Though they perform all over the city, this cozy theater is the home base for one of New York's longtime, popular puppetry troupes. These folks make their own marionettes, presenting them in 45-minute shows every Saturday and Sunday afternoon. Fairy tales and other children's stories make up most of the repertoire, good especially for the younger kiddies. Tickets are $7.00 for adults and $5.00 for children.

SONY WONDER TECHNOLOGY LAB
550 Madison Avenue (at 56th Street), New York NY 10022. 212/833-8100. **World Wide Web address:** http://www. sonywondertechlab.com. **Description:** Sony really does a lot for the kids in this city. Their latest offering is the Sony Wonder Technology Lab, a science and technology museum that is aimed at teaching kids the importance of multimedia communication in their everyday lives. The Lab is a fun and exciting way for kids to learn the history of communication and media technology, while interacting with it as well. Kids are invited to join in an occupational simulation experiment where they can become a robotics engineer, camera operator, or video game designer for a day. Four floors of all this fun and, best of all, it's always free. Open Tuesday through Saturday, 10:00 a.m. - 6:00 p.m. (until 8:00 p.m. on Thursday); Sunday, 12:00 p.m. - 6:00 p.m.

STATEN ISLAND CHILDREN'S MUSEUM
Snug Harbor Cultural Center, 1000 Richmond Terrace, Staten Island NY 10301. 718/273-2060. **Description:** It may not be huge, but this museum is a goldmine for active children with lots of hands-on exhibits and special activities. Taking a cue from the most famous thing about Staten Island, for example, there is a large workshop area where kids can pretend to build their own ferry boat (complete with passing skyline) or work on any other

project of their choice. Visiting one of the museum's bridge exhibits might be a good idea as, in order to get on or off Staten Island, you need to use one of their five bridges. The museum also offers a variety of exhibits on some of the subjects kids are most interested in, like bugs! A five-minute ride on the S40 bus takes you from the ferry (the real one, that is) to the museum. Admission is just $4.00 per person (children under two are free). Open Tuesday through Sunday, 12:00 p.m. - 5:00 p.m.; closed Monday.

TADA! THEATER
120 West 28th Street, 2nd Floor, New York NY 10001. 212/627-1732. **World Wide Web address:** http://www.tadatheater.com. **Description:** Now, we all know that kids are dramatic, but is your kid good enough to translate that behavior to the stage? If you think your child has what it takes to make it on Broadway or in Hollywood, TADA! Theater may be their ticket to stardom. On the other hand, if your child's acting ability is limited to in-home temper tantrums, then it might be better to just attend a performance. Since 1984, TADA! Theater has been giving kids the chance to take the stage, and families the opportunity to watch them perform. TADA! presents original musicals and plays year-round with a cast of New York City kids aged 8 - 17. Since its founding, TADA! has produced more than 50 plays with close to 1,000 performances. Audiences have included not only parade-goers at the Macy's Thanksgiving Day Parade, but the big guy himself, the President of the United States. In addition to their regular performance schedule, TADA! offers free staged readings. Performance tickets are $12.00 for adults and $6.00 for children. Call today or visit their Website for this season's schedule.

THE WEST END
2911 Broadway (at 113th Street), New York NY 10025. 212/662-8830. **Description:** The West End has been there for Columbia students for more than 80 years now. During the school year, they offer a variety of entertainment activities with low or no cover charge, and a big and diverse menu of resonably-priced meals. But what interests Mr. C most about The West End is the entertainment that takes place every weekend. The restaurant offers children's theater every Saturday at 1:00 p.m. (recommended age range is three to nine). Performers include real circus clowns, magicians, and ventriloquists, as well as musicians, comedians and everything in between. The restaurant even serves up a specially priced children's lunch before and after the show. Tickets for most performances are $7.00, with discounts for groups of seven or more. Call or drop in any time for the season's lineup.

ENTERTAINMENT
 ## College Performing Arts

BROOKLYN CENTER FOR THE PERFORMING ARTS
WHITMAN HALL
Campus Road & Hillel Place, Brooklyn NY 11210. 718/951-4500.
World Wide Web address: http://www.brooklyncenter.com.
Description: Opera in Flatbush? Sure. Take in an aria by the
Brooklyn College Opera Theater, at BC's Walt Whitman Hall.
Tickets are usually around $10.00 ($7.00 for students, senior
citizens, and children). Crave a bit of comedy instead? Actor Frank
Ferrante recently brought his off-Broadway rendition of *Groucho*
to the Whitman, with tickets just $10.00. Write to get on the
mailing list for Brooklyn Center's free brochure, packed with
events, prices, and addresses: P.O. Box 100163, Brooklyn NY 11210.

COLUMBIA UNIVERSITY
KATHRYN BACHE MILLER THEATRE
Dodge Hall, 2960 Broadway at 116th Street, New York NY 10025.
212/854-7799. **World Wide Web address:** http://www.columbia.
edu/cu/arts/miller/. **Description:** Columbia's Miller Theatre hosts
over 60 different performances from October through April. The
past year was host to the Barnard Dance Spring Showcase
featuring student dancers from Barnard and Columbia. Ticket
prices were $10.00. Tickets to Enrico Labayen Dance, modern
dance influenced by Asian movement and the martial arts were
$15.00. The season also includes jazz, from the likes of Mose
Allison, Jimmy Heath, and Windham Hill pianist Billy Childs.
Literary Evenings may consist of readings by anyone from Susan
Sontag to Irish poet Seamus Heaney -- tickets $8.00, students
$5.00. Columbia's theater department also offers an ongoing
series of student-written and -directed plays, also for $5.00 per
ticket (the department chair is the award-winning playwright
Romulus Linney).

FORDHAM UNIVERSITY THEATRE COMPANY
Lincoln Center Campus, 113 West 60th Street, New York NY
10023. 212/636-6000. **World Wide Web address:**
http://www.fordham.edu. **Description:** Fordham's theater
department presents plays several times a year; productions have
included the ambitious *Our Country's Good*, a recent Broadway hit.
These generally take place at the Lincoln Center location. At Rose
Hill's Collins Auditorium, you can hear music from the likes of the
Bronx Arts Ensemble Chamber Orchestra (see listing under Live
Music: Classical); tickets to concerts are often free, or around
$5.00.

THE JUILLIARD SCHOOL
60 Lincoln Center Plaza, New York NY 10023. 212/799-5000.
World Wide Web address: http://www.juilliard.com. **Description:**
Juilliard can't be beat for inexpensive, high-quality classical music

-- as well as dance and theater. Juilliard being one of the top arts schools anywhere, it's a fair bet that some of these young musicians will soon be playing concert halls around the world; likewise for the dancers, and the actors can practically write their own tickets to Broadway stages. Performances take place from late September through May, and best of all, most of them are free! Located at the northern edge of Lincoln Center, Juilliard has several locations in which performances take place. Alice Tully Hall is the main site, hosting everything from informal lunchtime concerts to the Juilliard Symphony. But in the Juilliard building there is Paul Hall, a cozy and handsome three-hundred-seat recital hall with good sightlines and acoustics; and the Juilliard Theater, an intimate thrust-stage auditorium for drama and opera. There are so many kinds of shows to see here. Tuesday and Friday evenings at 8:00 p.m., hear the Symphony or one of the many chamber ensembles in Alice Tully Hall, all for free. Same place for "Wednesdays at One," with freebies like "Music for Winds, Harp and Guitar" or "Arias and Scenes." In Paul Hall you can check out the finalists of the Vaughn Williams Violin Competition, again free. Juilliard Theater offers operas twice a year, as well as fall and spring drama and dance repertories. Tickets for each of these are $10.00. And at the impressive Avery Fisher Hall, major concerts by the Juilliard Orchestra are given four times a year, tickets $5.00 and $10.00. Tickets are available through the box office for just a few weeks in advance; even most free concerts do require tickets. One exception is "Wednesdays at One," for which you simply show up at Tully Hall from 12:30 on. Needless to say, the major series are extremely hot tickets; to take full advantage of this treasure trove, Mr. C recommends getting on the mailing list for Juilliard's monthly calendar of all events.

LEHMAN COLLEGE/LEHMAN CENTER
250 Bedford Park Boulevard West, Bronx NY 10468. 718/960-8000. **Description:** Like Manhattan's Central Park, the Bronx has a "SummerStage" series of its own on the campus of this CUNY branch. You'll find theater, children's activities, concerts, and much more. Other places where you may find free performances around the Bronx include Pelham Bay Park and Van Cortland Park.

MANHATTAN SCHOOL OF MUSIC
Broadway & 122nd Streets, New York NY 10027. 212/749-2802x 428. **Description:** Near the Riverside Church, Manhattan School of Music is one of the city's foremost training schools for classical and jazz musicians. Four different halls -- from 100 seats to a 1,000 -- present the Manhattan School of Music Symphony Orchestras, the Jazz Orchestra, myriad chamber ensembles, opera, and more. Many of the concerts free; who can complain about that? The program choices offer a nice mix of traditional warhorses and modern challenges. The students, meanwhile, are known for their dedication and budding talent.

MARYMOUNT MANHATTAN THEATRE
221 East 71st Street, New York NY 10021. 212/774-0760. **World Wide Web address:** http://www.marymount.mmm.edu. **Description:** This Upper East Side college space is, in fact,

frequently rented by small professional companies. Most of these are "homeless" dance troupes -- those without a theater of their own. So you can often see innovative modern dance performances here; drop by to sort through the flyers advertising upcoming events. Ticket prices vary, depending on the company, but they're sure to be cheap. Marymount also has an art gallery, with shows of paintings, murals and multimedia works. These change over once or twice a month; admission is free.

SCHOOL OF VISUAL ARTS

209 East 23rd Street, New York NY 10010. 212/592-2000. **Description:** This downtown school may be small, but it's one of the city's most vibrant for artists. They run two main galleries, showing work by students and professionals. The Visual Arts Museum, at the above address, presents exhibitions of graphics, crafts, photography, video installations and more, mostly by professional artists. Once a year, their "Masters Series" highlights the work of major stars in these fields. The Visual Arts Gallery, at 137 Wooster Street in SoHo (212/598-0221), shows the school's best thesis work in fine arts. Both galleries are open year-round and are free. There are also smaller student galleries in the 23rd Street building.

ENTERTAINMENT
🗣 Comedy Clubs 🗣

BOSTON COMEDY CLUB
82 West Third Street (between Thompson & Sullivan Streets), New York NY 10003. 212/477-1000. **Description:** A jewel of a club, this establishment offers comedy seven nights a week. Monday is "New Talent Night" with shows at 8:00 p.m. ($8.00 cover, two-drink minimum); Tuesday through Thursday standup comedy is featured at 9:30 p.m. ($8.00 cover, one-drink minimum); Friday and Saturday showcase "All-Star Comedy," with various comedians from Comedy Central, HBO, and Late Night with David Letterman. Shows are at 8:00 p.m., 10:00 p.m., and 12:15 a.m. ($12.00 cover, two-drink minimum); and Sunday night standup comedy is at 9:00 p.m. ($7.00 cover, two-drink minimum).

CHICAGO CITY LIMITS
1105 First Avenue, New York NY 10021. **World Wide Web address:** http://www.chicagocitylimits.com. **Description:** New York's longest running comedy review, has been thrilling audiences for over 20 years with its unique blend of improvised comedy and political satire. Top prices here are $20.00; but again, you can save dough by going on Monday nights. That's when "CCL Unlimited," the touring version of this fast-moving show, performs for just $10.00. The rest of the week they're working at corporate seminars and colleges throughout the region. One of the earliest groups to present this kind of humor in New York, at the beginning of the comedy wave, Chicago City Limits is consistently funny and innovative. It's also worth noting that this is the only top-line comedy show in town at which no alcohol is served. This makes a great alternative for teens, or anyone who prefers to avoid the drinking scene at other comedy clubs. Shows are Wednesday and Thursday at 8:30 p.m., Friday and Saturday at 8:00 p.m. and 10:30 p.m., and Sunday at 3:00 p.m. Tickets are $20.00 ($10.00 with a valid student ID).

COMEDY CELLAR
117 McDougal Street (between 3rd & Bleecker Streets), New York NY 10012. 212/254-3480. **World Wide Web address:** http://www.comedycellar.com. **Description:** Yes, this really *is* a cellar! But don't let that deter you, as Comedy Cellar is widely considered one of the best places in the city to really yuck it up. The small space makes for an intimate evening... just you, your friends, the comedians, and tons of other people who want to crowd in and watch the act. There's definitely some big acts that like to play here, and the more regular comics are the funny men and women who write hilarious dialogue and sketches for *Saturday Night Live*, MTV, and Comedy Central. If you're looking for a comedy bargain (and less of a crowd), it is best to go during the

week. Best of all, it's the bigger names that actually prefer to perform during the week. Drop in Sunday through Thursday (9:00 p.m. - 2:00 a.m.) and you'll pay just a $7.00 cover charge plus a two-drink minimum. For a list of upcoming appearances, call or visit their Website.

COMIC STRIP LIVE

1568 Second Avenue (between 81st & 82nd Streets), New York NY 10028. 212/861-9386. **World Wide Web address:** http://www.comicstriplive.com. **Description:** Comic Strip Live is acclaimed as the club where many successful comedians got their start including Eddie Murphy, Jerry Seinfeld, Carol Leifer, and Adam Sandler. If you purchase tickets 48 hours in advance, you can laugh it up for only $10.00 per ticket, and one ticket admits two people. Call between noon and 7:00 p.m. Reservations are required for all shows. Two-drink minimum. Showtimes: Monday - Thursday, 8:30 p.m.; Friday, 8:30 p.m., 10:30 p.m., and 12:30 a.m.; Saturday, 8:00 p.m., 10:15 p.m., and 12:30 a.m.; Sunday, 8:00 p.m.

DANGERFIELD'S

1118 First Avenue (between 61st & 62nd Streets), New York NY 10021. 212/593-1650. **Description:** A staple to the New York comedy scene since its opening in 1969, it was Mr. Rodney Dangerfield himself who opened this always-happening club. From Sunday through Thursday, the laughing starts at 8:45 p.m. with continuous acts running until the wee hours. Admission is $12.50. Friday shows are at 9:00 p.m. and 11:15 p.m.; Saturday shows are at 8:00 p.m., 10:30 p.m., & 12:30 a.m. Weekend admission is just $15.00 ($20.00 for the 10:30 p.m. show on Saturday). One of Mr. C's favorite things about this club is that there is no food or drink minimum (a money-saving rarity in this town)!

GOTHAM CITY IMPROV

158 West 23rd Street, #2, New York NY 10011. 212/367-8222. **World Wide Web address:** http://www.gothamcityimprov.com. **Description:** Gotham City Improv has a new theater located in Chelsea. It is the home of this madcap troupe, which performs a mix of written sketches and improvisation on the spot. They've also been a training ground for many famous comics and actors performing on Broadway, commercials, TV, and movies. They perform every Wednesday night at 10:00 p.m., and Friday and Saturday nights at 8:00. Tickets are only $5.00. It's a comedy bargain in this hopping part of the city.

NEW YORK COMEDY CLUB

241 East 24th Street, New York NY 10010. 212/696-5233. **World Wide Web address:** http://members.aol.com/nycomclub. **Description:** As one of New York's premier comedy clubs, New York Comedy Club has seen the likes of some of today's top performers. Do the names Chris Rock, Damon Wayans, or Rodney Dangerfield ring a bell? Though, unlike Rodney Dangerfield, New York Comedy Club does get respect; it is lauded not only for its great comedy, but for its tremendous prices as well. Sunday

through Thursday, club-goers will be smiling about the $5.00 admission price (plus a two-drink minimum); on Friday and Saturday night, pay only $10.00 (and be sure to imbibe another two drinks). Call or visit their Website for the most up-to-date scheduling information.

STAND-UP NEW YORK
236 West 78th Street, New York NY 10024. 212/595-0850. **Description:** Stand-Up New York is one of the preeminent comedy clubs in the New York area. Giving a boost to the careers of many of today's most successful comics, Stand-Up New York is often a stopping point for several well-known comedians who are looking to try out some new material. Robin Williams, Jerry Seinfeld, and Brett Butler are just a few of the names I'll drop. Show schedule is Sunday through Thursday, 7:00 p.m. and 9:00 p.m.; Friday, 7:00 p.m., 9:00 p.m., and 11:30 p.m.; Saturday, 8:00 p.m., 10:00 p.m., and 12:00 a.m. Cover is usually between $7.00 and $12.00, depending on the show. Call for a listing of upcoming performances.

ENTERTAINMENT
Dance Theater

CHEN & DANCERS
70 Mulberry Street, 2nd Floor, New York NY 10013. 212/349-0126. **Description:** Located on the border (if there really is one anymore) of Chinatown and Little Italy, this theater specializes in Asian-American dance performances of all kinds. These often include children's shows as well. Ticket prices range from $4.00 to $10.00 -- leaving enough cash for the inevitable dinner nearby.

MERCE CUNNINGHAM STUDIO
55 Bethune Street, 11th Floor, New York NY 10014. 212/255-8240. **World Wide Web address:** http://www.merce.org. **Description:** Considered the elder statesman of modern dance, Merce Cunningham runs his company from these West Village studios, part of the vibrant Westbeth Artists' Complex. Eleven stories up, looking out over the Hudson River, the Cunningham loft space seats 125 and is host to workshops by this world-famous troupe as well as performances by other companies that rent the space out. Tickets are usually in the $10.00 range. Call for current information.

DANCE SPACE
451 Broadway, 2nd Floor, New York NY 10012. 212/625-8369. **World Wide Web address:** http://www.dancespace.com, **Description:** Another one of New York's many informal, inexpensive studios in which you can see a variety of local dance (and theater) troupes performing on a regular basis. Dance Space, in fact, has two different flexible spaces, both with limited seating -- which means you'll see everything up close and personal. Tickets are generally around $15.00. DS is also known for its monthly showcases featuring short works by several choreographers, a sort of Whitman sampler of modern dance. Call for schedules.

DANCE THEATER WORKSHOP
BESSIE SCHONBERG THEATER
219 West 19th Street, 2nd Floor, New York NY 10011. 212/924-0077. **World Wide Web address:** http://www.dtw.org. **Description:** One of New York's most renowned avant-garde performance spaces for over 30 years, Dance Theater Workshop has been a "birthplace" for such current celebs as Mark Morris, Bill T. Jones, Bill Irwin, and Whoopi Goldberg. This organization also sponsors the "Bessie" Awards, dance's version of the Tonys. Discover the stars of tomorrow for yourself, before their ticket prices become as big as their names. The packed schedule features performers from all over the country, developing serious works in dance, music, and performance art. These have recently

included choreographer John Malashock, formerly a dancer with Twyla Tharp; Douglas Dunn & Dancers, accompanied in person by jazz musician Steve Lacy; and award-winning performance artist Linda Mancini, whose "Economy Tires Theater" blends words, music, movement, sound effects, and visual imagery. All of the artists presented at DTW are in some way funded by its many supportive programs, making this a sort of farm club for the major leagues of performance art. Tickets to most shows are $20.00 or less; Dance Theater Workshop also offers "Cheap$eats," a design-your-own subscription: There are dozens to choose from.

NEW YORK CITY BALLET
New York State Theater, 20 Lincoln Center, New York NY 10023. 212/870-5660. **World Wide Web address:** http://www.nycballet.com. **Description:** New York City Ballet presents an affordable option for balletomanes at Lincoln Center's New York State Theater. New York City Ballet ticket prices start at just $16.00 for the topmost circle. A related option is the "Fourth Ring Society." Join this group for $10.00, and then you can purchase tickets in the fourth ring for $25.00 - $35.00 each. Go as often as you like, and buy in advance for any performance. Membership also includes access to pre-show lectures by the company, a free cup of cappuccino, discount coupons for area restaurants, and a NYCB T-shirt. Talk about friends in high places.

ENTERTAINMENT
🎬 Movies 🎬

ANTHOLOGY FILM ARCHIVES
32 Second Avenue (at 2nd Street), New York NY 10003.
212/505-5110. **World Wide Web address:** http://www.
anthologyfilmarchives.org. **Description:** This Lower East Side film
archive and movie theater is well-known for its dedication to
preservation of classic, and new independent, and avant-garde
cinema. While several entertainment entities have recently taken
it upon themselves to help in the preservation of films, Anthology
Film Archives has been a leader in this mission since 1970. The
Anthology Film Archives library houses one of the world's most
important collections of historical and theoretical books,
periodicals, stills, posters, and manuscripts. Whether you're
looking for a fictional cinematic journey, or a true-grit
documentary, Anthology Film Archives presents year-round
screenings, retrospectives, and special events. Often, after the
presentation of a film, the audience is invited to listen and
participate in a panel discussion with critics, filmmakers, actors,
and experts. Admission is $8.00 for adults; $5.00 for students
and seniors; and $1.00 for children. For even better savings, you
can become a member of Anthology Film Archives. For as little as
$50.00 (or as little as $30.00 if you're a student or senior
citizen), become a member and enjoy member privileges, including
$5.00 admission to all films, free admission to all Essential Cinema
and Members-Only programs, and 20 percent off all Anthology
Film Archives publications. If you and your spouse, sibling, or
roommate join together, the cost for a dual membership (with all
previously-mentioned benefits) is only $75.00. You can save
yourself some money while doing some good for the filmmaking
community, now that's what I call a true philanthropist. Call or
visit their Website for a listing of upcoming events.

BROOKLYN HEIGHTS CINEMA
70 Henry Street, Brooklyn NY 11201. 718/596-7070. **Description:**
If you want to avoid the long lines and high prices of commercial
movies nowadays, you pretty much have to avoid Manhattan
altogether. In Brooklyn Heights, however, this renovated
moviehouse shows current Hollywood hits at decent prices. Regular
admission is $7.50 -- cheaper than others in the city. Better still,
catch the first show of the day (usually a matinee) and pay just
$4.00. They also offer "Bargain Days" all day on Mondays and
Tuesdays, when tickets are $4.00 (that includes holidays on those
days). Call to find out what's playing.

CINEMA CLASSICS
332 East 11th Street (between First & Second Avenues),
New York NY 10003. 212/971-1015. **World Wide Web address:**
http://cinemaclassics.com. **Description:** While those expecting to
screen a Hepburn-Tracy romance or one of The Duke's westerns

might be surprised by this cinema's definition of "classic," those that have grown up in the age of MTV know these films as nothing but "classics." Who *wouldn't* consider Quentin Tarantino's *Reservoir Dogs* an exemplar of modern cinema? Cinema Classics presents a wonderful mix of films that defined the latter three decades of the 20th century. With the 1967 release of Arthur Penn's *Bonnie and Clyde*, the history of cinema took a turn toward the "independent"; Cinema Classics celebrates this turning point. From French New Wave to New Hollywood to the sometimes campy cult classics of the seventies and eighties, Cinema Classics does not discriminate in its screening choices. For those who delight in international cinema, Cinema Classics presents movies from just about every country, from Japan's *In the Realm of the Senses* and France's *Breathless* to Spain's *Women on the Verge of a Nervous Breakdown* and Italy's *Fellini Satyricon*. Sci-fi classics like *Blade Runner* and the Kubrick masterpiece *2001* are always a welcome diversion. And speaking of *A Space Odyssey*, check out Mr. Ziggy Stardust himself in *The Man Who Fell to Earth*. The traditional and always-exciting midnight movies span a variety of genres; *The Long Goodbye*, *Jason and the Argonauts*, and *James and the Giant Peach* have all at one point had a midnight showing. But enough about the movies, let's get to the prices: $5.00 at all times. You can't beat it!

COBBLE HILL CINEMA

265 Court Street, Brooklyn NY 11201. 718/596-9113. **Description:** Another fine old neighborhood moviehouse, showing five current hits at a time. Tickets are regularly $8.50, but the first showing of the day is just $5.50 -- on all five screens, every day of the week. These showtimes are usually around 1:00 p.m. - 1:30 p.m., but be sure to call so you don't miss out on the bargains.

FILM FORUM

209 West Houston Street (West of Avenue of the Americas), New York NY 10014. 212/727-8110. **World Wide Web address:** http://www.filmforum.com. **Description:** It is difficult to see a movie for under $10.00 in New York City, much less a worthwhile one. But at SoHo's Film Forum, you are invited to screen the newest and the best in classic, foreign, and independent cinema for just $9.00 a ticket ($5.00 for children at all times, and $5.00 senior citizen weekday matinees). From unique retrospectives to director premieres, the movies at Film Forum represent the best filmmaking (as an art form rather than a merchandising vehicle) has to offer. Be the first to see the new Jarmusch flick, or scare yourself silly with an old Hitchcock classic. For real film buffs (I'm talking the weekly or biweekly theater-goers), the real discount lies in becoming a Film Forum member. For as little as $45.00 a year, you can enjoy member benefits which -- above all else -- will allow you to enter the theater at any time for just $5.00. Think about it, if you go to the movies even only once a month, the membership has paid for itself. Plus, while coworkers are sitting around the water cooler discussing the latest blockbuster or special-effects-laden-bad-acting-action-film, you can rest easy in the fact that you have seen all the Oscar nominees for Best Foreign Film. Find out what's playing today by

calling the box office at the number listed above. To be put on the Film Forum mailing list or to get more information on becoming a member, visit their Website or call at 212/627-2035.

FLORENCE GOULD HALL

55 East 59th Street (between Park & Madison Avenues), New York NY 10022. 212/355-6160. **Description:** As part of New York's French Institute Alliance Française, Florence Gould Hall presents a weekly film series each Tuesday at 12:30 p.m., 3:30 p.m., 6:30 p.m., and 9:30 p.m. With seating for 400, you should have no problem getting a ticket to see your favorite French films by all the greatest directors (Jean-Luc Godard, François Truffaut, Jean Cocteau, etc.). Call ahead for an upcoming schedule. Tickets are $8.00 each.

PLAZA TWIN CINEMA

314 Flatbush Avenue, Brooklyn NY 11238. 718/636-0170. **Description:** Plaza Twin Cinema offers regular movie tickets for $7.00, and matinees for $4.00. Like the Brooklyn Heights Cinema, the Plaza offers "Bargain Days" (in this case, Tuesdays and Wednesdays), when tickets are $4.00 all day, both days. Between these two cinemas, it looks like you've got half your week covered for movie bargains.

QUAD CINEMA

34 West 13th Street (between Fifth Avenue & Avenue of the Americas), New York NY 10011. 212/255-8800. **World Wide Web address:** http://www.quadcinema.com. **Description:** Film buffs rejoice at the Quad Cinema, a cutting-edge, family-owned theater known for showing the best in independent and foreign films. With a loyal audience of regular movie-goers, this Greenwich Village theater has become somewhat of a fixture. Admission for adults is $8.50, and $5.50 for children and seniors. Children under 5 years are not admitted.

WALTER READE THEATER

165 West 65th Street (between Broadway & Amsterdam Avenue), New York NY 10023. 212/875-5600. **World Wide Web address:** http://www.filmlinc.com. **Description:** Though, if you're not from New York City, $9.00 for a movie could seem normal if not a bit pricey, the Walter Reade Theater is worth a visit. If you've ever wondered which Big Apple theater has the prestigious honor of being home to the New York Film Festival, this is the place. As the screening room for The Film Society of Lincoln Center (those brilliant cineastes who bring you *Film Comment* magazine), Walter Reade schedules a variety of classic, new, independent, and foreign films that (if at all) can only be seen on video or television. The theater presents a number of mini-festivals and themed schedules, like a week of Danish New Wave. The immaculate theater is extremely comfortable, and there are *no* bad seats (no, even the ones up front separate you from the screen with a small stage). When the movie lets out, take a walk around the rest of Lincoln Center. Have a seat along the benches of the reflecting

pool and fountain, stare at the enormous pigeon-topped statue in the middle of the pool, or listen to the passing Juilliard School students as they recite lines or belt out a tune from their latest musical. Admission is $9.00 for adults, $5.00 for members, $4.50 for seniors during weekday matinees only, and $2.00 for children. Bring back the culture and meaning that used to exist in film with a visit to the Walter Reade Theater. Call of visit their Website to get on the mailing list and learn about upcoming events and films.

THE SCREENING ROOM

54 Varick Street (just below Canal Street), New York NY 10013. 212/334-2100. **World Wide Web address:** http://www. thescreeningroom.com. **Description:** While the "dinner and a movie" date has long been a staple of the American singles scene, never has it been made so easy. The Screening Room is a restaurant/bar/movie theater. While this may seem like an overwhelming concept, the result is fantastic. Drop in for a quick bite to eat, then step inside one of The Screening Room's two 1940s-inspired theaters. Now, you may be wondering how expensive this could be. Well, actually, prices at The Screening Room can and *do* go well over Mr. C's limit, but that doesn't mean you have to spend a fortune to enjoy this inventive establishment. While chef Mark Spangenthal's first-class dinner menu, with offerings such as cornmeal-crusted trout ($19.00) and grilled and braised duck ($21.00), is definitely going to cost you, why not grab a light bite before heading out, and instead choose a salad ($6.00 - $9.00); or opt for the "Dinner and a Movie" special, which includes soup or salad, entree, dessert, and a movie ticket, all for $30.00. While it still may be a bit pricey, do you think you make out any better in a plain old movie theater? With the price you pay for popcorn and a soda nowadays, you may as well order the osetra caviar ($26.00)! Check out The Screening Room's lounge menu (salmon, shrimp cocktail, barbecued spare ribs, burgers), with prices rarely reaching beyond $10.00. The lunch menu has sandwiches looming in the $9.00 - $10.00 range, while brunch entrees start at only $8.00. The Screening Room's Sunday brunch is well known throughout the city; people pack in to grab a bite to eat and see the ultimate New York classic, *Breakfast at Tiffany's* (ticket is only $5.00 with brunch). What more could a lazy Sunday morning ask for? Still, all food aside, even if you just want to see a movie, The Screening Room is still a great place to go. With movie tickets reaching more than $10.00 and $11.00 (especially if you're ordering by phone), The Screening Room tickets are a modest $8.50 (modest for New York anyway). And what can you expect to see there? Anything and everything, from the newest documentary, to favorite screen classics and everything in between. And, if you're still not ready to go home after the movie (though they do have midnight showings), you can always pop back into the restaurant for a nightcap or some dessert! If only all entertainment were so convenient. Call or visit their Website for the latest schedule and to be put on The Screening Room's mailing list.

SONY THEATRES LINCOLN SQUARE/SONY IMAX THEATRE
1998 Broadway (at 68th Street), New York NY 10023. 212/336-5000. **World Wide Web address:** http://www.enjoytheshow.com.
Description: If you're just looking to see a regular movie, Sony Theatres Lincoln Square offers 12 state-of-the-art auditoriums boasting digital sound, rocker seats, and huge movie screens. However, if you are looking for a truly unparalleled 3D and 2D cinematic experience, the Sony IMAX Theatre is just what you are looking for. If you've never been to an IMAX theater, it is definitely worth the trip. A sky-high, eight-story screen, projecting both two and three dimensional images, is certain to be the largest and most exciting movie screen you've ever seen. IMAX films are educational as well as entertaining, with titles such as *Across the Sea of Time*. Better still, all Sony IMAX films offers a unique experience that the whole family can enjoy. Tickets are $9.50 for adults, $6.00 for children 12 and under. Call 212/50-LOEWS for today's showtimes or to purchase advance tickets with a credit card.

ENTERTAINMENT
🏛 Museums 🏛

AMERICAN CRAFT MUSEUM
40 West 53rd Street (between Fifth Avenue & Avenue of the Americas), New York NY 10019. 212/956-3535. **Description:** Showcasing crafts of the 20th century, ordinary objects such as teapots and chairs become extraordinary at the American Craft Museum. Recent exhibitions have included "Spirits of the Cloth: Contemporary Quilts by African American Artists" and "Brooching it Diplomatically: A Tribute to Madeleine K. Albright." The museum also offers lots of creative and educational workshops. Admission is $5.00 for adults, $2.50 for students and seniors, and free to kids under 12. Open Tuesday through Sunday, 10:00 a.m. - 6:00 p.m.; Thursday, 10:00 a.m. - 8:00 p.m.

AMERICAN MUSEUM OF THE MOVING IMAGE
35th Avenue (at 36th Street), Queens NY 11106. 718/784-0077. **E-mail address:** info@ammi.org. **World Wide Web address:** http://www.ammi.org. **Description:** Originally built by Paramount in 1920, Astoria Studios (where the Marx Brothers made their first movies) has been converted into this wonderful museum dedicated to the moving image in all its forms: film, television, and digital media. For the price of admission, you can see classic films from the United States and all around the world. Film series here cover all time periods and genres, from silent German Expressionism to a Blake Edwards retrospective. The films may be old, but the theater is state-of-the-art; ready for both silent nitrate films, and the latest Dolby widescreen spectaculars. The museum also features Tut's Fever Movie Palace, a reproduction of an ornate roaring twenties movie theater, showing newsreels and Saturday afternoon cliffhanger serials. There's a small screening room too, showing the latest in experimental videos. And let's not forget the exhibits themselves (this *is* a museum after all); three floors of exhibition space contain lots of genuine Hollywood props, costumes, and sets. For those of you who like a hands-on experience, you'll be happy to learn that many of the exhibits are interactive. So, while your dreams of being the next Martin Scorsese may be delusions of grandeur, at least you can pretend. If you're a movie and/or television buff, you'll love this place! Admission is $8.50 for adults, $5.50 for seniors and students, $4.50 for children, and free to museum members. Open Tuesday through Friday, 12:00 p.m. - 5:00 p.m.; Saturday and Sunday, 11:00 a.m. - 6:00 p.m.

AMERICAN MUSEUM OF NATURAL HISTORY
Central Park West at 79th Street, New York NY 10024. 212/769-5000. **World Wide Web address:** http://www.amnh.org. **Description:** American Museum of Natural History houses room after room of science and nature exhibits -- and, of course, all those dinosaur bones. The museum also offers dance performances

of groups from the United States and around the world in four separate auditoriums of varying sizes (from 1,000 seats to under 100). Many of these are traditional folk dance troupes. Tickets are usually around $10.00, but some shows are free -- with many geared toward children. Call to see what's coming up! Open Sunday through Thursday, 10:00 a.m. - 5:45 p.m.; Friday and Saturday, 10:00 a.m. - 8:45 p.m.

BARTOW-PELL MANSION MUSEUM AND GARDENS

895 Shore Road, Bronx NY 10464. 718/885-1461. **Description:** Bartow-Pell Mansion is a national landmark with a wonderful collection of 19th-century decorative arts and beautiful gardens. Self-guided tours of the mansion can be taken Wednesday, Saturday, and Sunday, from 12:00 p.m. - 4:00 p.m. Admission is a mere $2.50 for adults, $1.50 for seniors, and free to kids under 12. Admission to the gardens is free and hours are Tuesday through Sunday, 8:30 a.m. - 4:30 p.m.

BRONX MUSEUM OF THE ARTS

1040 Grand Concourse (at 165th Street), Bronx NY 10464. 718/681-6000. **Description:** Not far from Yankee Stadium, you'll find this small but impressive museum. Along with its permanent collection, the Bronx Museum of the Arts usually has one or two special exhibits focusing on contemporary artists. Suggested admission is just $3.00 for adults; $2.00 for students and seniors; free children under 12 and members. On Wednesdays, the admission fee is waived for all. Open Wednesday, 3:00 p.m. - 9:00 p.m.; Thursday and Friday, 10:00 a.m. - 5:00 p.m.; Saturday and Sunday, 12:00 p.m. - 6:00 p.m.

BROOKLYN MUSEUM OF ART

200 Eastern Parkway, Brooklyn NY 11238. 718/638-5000. **E-mail address:** bklynmus@echonyc.com. **World Wide Web address:** http://www.brooklynart.org. **Description:** As the nation's second largest art museum, the Brooklyn Museum of Art is a sight to behold; even the building itself is a NYC icon. The more than 1.5 million artifacts are comprised of multi-ethnic arts, costumes, textiles, paintings, sculptures, prints, and photographs. If you're going to be in the area in the early part of the month, be sure to check out "First Saturdays" at the museum (held, obviously, the first Saturday of each month). Not only are "First Saturdays" fun, but they're free after 5:00 p.m. "First Saturdays" are chock full of lively music, intelligent conversation, classic film screenings, and, well, art! Admission is $4.00 for adults, $2.00 for students (have your I.D. ready, they'll check), and $1.50 for seniors. Members and children under 12 are free. Open Wednesday through Friday, 10:00 a.m. - 5:00 p.m.; Saturday and Sunday, 11:00 a.m. - 6:00 p.m. On First Saturdays, the Brooklyn Museum of Art is open from 11:00 a.m. - 11:00 p.m.

THE CLOISTERS MUSEUM

Fort Tryon Park, New York NY. 212/923-3700. **Description:** An outpost of the Metropolitan Museum of Art, the Cloisters is located *wayyyyyyy* up at the top of Manhattan Island -- above the George Washington Bridge, looking out over the Hudson River. It's a trek, but a grand one, with its collected sections of various European monasteries all put together into a peaceful museum and park. Some parts of the collection date as far back as the 11th century -- needless to say, these are among the very oldest structures you can see on this or any other continent. Visit the stained-glass gallery, the famous Unicorn Tapestries, and the outdoor garden. Suggested donation is $10.00 for adults, $5.00 for seniors and students. Kids under 12 and Metropolitan Museum members are free. Open daily (except Mondays), 9:30 a.m. - 5:15 p.m.

COOPER-HEWITT NATIONAL DESIGN MUSEUM

2 East 91st Street, New York NY 10001. 212/849-8400. **World Wide Web address:** http://www.si.edu/ndm. **Description:** Owned by the Smithsonian Institute, this 64-room marvel of Georgian architecture (formerly owned by Andrew Carnegie) has become a museum dedicated to -- architecture. Appropriate enough? Its galleries display permanent design collections and special exhibits. Past exhibits have included "The Architecture of Reassurance: Designing the Disney Theme Parks," "The Huguenot Legacy: English Silver, 1680 - 1760," and "El Nuevo Mundo: The Landscape of Latino Los Angeles." Admission is $8.00 for adults, $5.00 for students and seniors. From 5:00 p.m. - 9:00 p.m. on Tuesdays, there is no admission charge. Open Sunday through Friday, 10:00 a.m. - 5:00 p.m. (until 9:00 p.m. on Tuesday); Saturday, 12:00 p.m. - 5:00 p.m.

EL MUSEO DEL BARRIO

1230 Fifth Avenue (at 104th Street), New York NY 10029. 212/831-7272. **E-mail address:** elmuseo@aol.com. **World Wide Web address:** http://www.elmuseo.org. **Description:** For 30 years, this museum had been celebrating the art and culture of Latin America. Recent exhibitions have included "Pressing the Point: Parallel Expressions in the Graphic Arts of the Chicano and Puerto Rican Movements," "Viva La Muerta: Artwork Inspired by the Day of the Dead Celebration," and "A Tribute to En Foco: 25 Years of Making Photographic History." There are also a wide range of permanent collections including pre-Colombian, traditional arts, works on paper, paintings, sculptures, installations, photography, and films. Suggested contributions are $4.00 for adults, $2.00 for students and seniors. Open Wednesday through Sunday, 11:00 a.m. - 5:00 p.m.

FORBES MAGAZINE GALLERIES

62 Fifth Avenue (at 12th Street), New York NY 10011. 212/206-5548. **Description:** This brownstone showcases the impressive collections of the late millionaire, Malcolm Forbes. Foremost in the collection are the bejeweled Faberge eggs. Forbes, who was also a military fan, owned lots of intricate model ships and toy soldiers; and he amassed a considerable catalogue of presidential memorabilia. Considering his vast wealth, it's fitting that you can see it all for free. Open Tuesday through Saturday, 10:00 a.m. - 4:00 p.m.

FRAUNCES TAVERN MUSEUM

54 Pearl Street, New York NY 10004-2429. 212/425-1778.
Description: This isn't the actual tavern in which George
Washington raised a farewell glass with his men. It's actually a
replica on the same site, but it's still pretty neat. How can you not
be curious about an exhibit entitled "Washington in Glory: America
in Tears"? Or what about a correlation between Washington and
Wall Street? The museum also gives lectures on a regular basis,
relating to all sorts of 18th-century topics. These are free with
museum admission, which is $2.50 for adults and $1.00 for
students and senior citizens. Got a whole gaggle of people? Guided
tours cost $40.00 for groups of up to 35 people. Open Monday
through Friday, 10:00 a.m. - 4:45 p.m.; Saturday, 12:00 p.m. - 4:00
p.m.

FRICK COLLECTION

One East 70th Street, New York NY 10021. 212/288-0700. **World
Wide Web address:** http://www.frick.org. **Description:** One of
the foremost private art holdings in the world, The Frick
Collection is yet another result of a late millionaire whose vaults
have been opened for all to behold. The paintings featured are
predominantly European; room after room is filled with major
works by the like of Turner, Fragonard, Boucher, and Vermeer.
Sculptures and period French furniture are also among the
highlights. And there is a delightful interior courtyard, with
flowery landscaping and a large fountain. This fabulous art museum
also presents free chamber music concerts on Sunday afternoons.
During the warm-weather months, these take place by the
fountain in the glass-topped Garden Court; otherwise, they're
given in the Music Room. Either way, the concerts are high quality,
high class, and as low-priced as any can be. The schedule can be
irregular, so call ahead to find out what's going on. Admission is
$7.00 for adults, $5.00 for students and seniors. Open Tuesday
through Saturday, 10:00 a.m. - 6:00 p.m.; Sunday, 1:00 p.m. - 6:00
p.m.; closed Monday and major holidays.

GUGGENHEIM MUSEUM

1071 Fifth Avenue (at 89th Street), New York NY 10128.
212/423-3500. **World Wide Web address:** http://www.
guggenheim.org. **Description:** This famous Frank Lloyd Wright
design, with its spiral shape, is probably one of New York's most
recognizable buildings. The building is meant to be walked from
the top down -- you'll be less tired that way! The modern art
inside is one of the world's premier collections. In addition to the
works of pioneers, from Impressionism on through to the artists
of today, you can see ever-changing and always-exciting special
exhibits. Adult admission is $12.00, students and seniors are
$7.00; kids under 12 and members are free. Open Sunday through
Wednesday, 9:00 a.m. - 6:00 p.m.; Friday and Saturday, 9:00 a.m. -
8:00 p.m. (closed Thursday).

GUGGENHEIM MUSEUM/SoHo

575 Broadway, New York NY 10012. 212/423-3500. **World Wide
Web address:** http://www.guggenheim.org. **Description:** Built in
1992, this is the newest branch of the Guggenheim Museum. The

building itself (a six-story, red brick treasure) is representative of the historical cast-iron district the museum inhabits. Admission is free. Open Thursday through Monday, 11:00 a.m. - 6:00 p.m. (closed on Tuesday and Wednesday).

HARBOR DEFENSE MUSEUM OF FORT HAMILTON

Building 230, Fort Hamilton Military Community, Brooklyn NY 11252-5101. 718/630-4349. **Description:** Fort Hamilton is a place where history continues to happen! Harbor Defense Museum of Fort Hamilton is dedicated to highlighting the importance of the U.S. Army to the New York area -- past and present. The on-site museum houses a number of artifacts and exhibits that further demonstrate the importance of the fort when it comes to defending New York from invaders. You'll find everything from uniforms and weapons to models and dioramas. The museum is fairly easy to locate; it's adjacent to the base of the Verrazano Bridge. Admission is free, though donations are always happily accepted. Open Monday through Friday, 10:00 a.m. - 4:00 p.m. and the second Saturday of every month. If you'd like a guided tour of the area, you must call and schedule an appointment.

HISTORIC RICHMOND TOWN
STATEN ISLAND HISTORICAL SOCIETY

441 Clarke Avenue, Staten Island NY 10306. 718/351-1617. **Description:** This is a museum only in the broadest sense; it's really a living, working re-creation of one of New York's original settlements. Just like Plymouth, Massachusetts or Williamsburg, Virginia, actors and historians in full costume wander around the 27-building complex and demonstrate the crafts and daily tasks of colonial settlers. Several periods are represented, including the Civil War era. See a one-room school, buy something in the general store, and even drink at the local tavern where, on weekend evenings, singers perform sea chanteys and other folk music. Admission is $4.00 for adults, $2.50 for children six to 18 and senior citizens. Hours change seasonally, so call ahead to be sure they're open.

INTERNATIONAL CENTER OF PHOTOGRAPHY/MIDTOWN

1133 Avenue of the Americas (at 43rd Street), New York NY 10036. 212/768-4682. **World Wide Web address:** http://www.icp.org. **Description:** Looking for an exciting lunch-hour activity *besides* eating? Try the International Center of Photography's Midtown location. Opened in 1989, ICP/Midtown houses a permanent collection of award-winning photos, printed up into large displays; there are also temporary traveling exhibits, as in any museum. ICP/Midtown also sponsors a lecture series and a variety of special events. Admission is $6.00 for adults, $4.00 for seniors and students, and $1.00 for kids under 12. Open Tuesday through Thursday, 10:00 a.m. - 5:00 p.m.; Friday and Saturday, 10:00 a.m. - 6:00 p.m. (with 5:00 p.m. - 8:00 p.m. accepting "voluntary contributions" instead of admission).

INTERNATIONAL CENTER OF PHOTOGRAPHY/UPTOWN

1130 Fifth Avenue (at 94th Street), New York NY 10128. 212/860-1777. **E-mail address:** info@icp.org. **World Wide Web**

address: http://www.icp.org. **Description:** While there are many museums to behold along the Museum Mile (hence the name), there might be none so dedicated to its particular craft than the International Center of Photography. For more than 25 years, ICP has been devoted the to exhibition, preservation, and study of all that is photography. Exhibitions encompass the amateur photographer to the masters, and the basic portrait to the avant-garde. Since their inception, ICP/Uptown has featured the work of more than 2,000 artists including such notables as Harry Callahan, Henri Cartier-Bresson, Man Ray, Ansel Adams, and Annie Leibovitz. But even that is not dedication enough for ICP. The center offers the largest full-time and continuing education photography programs in the world. Frequent lectures are taught not only by notable photographers, but critics, art historians, designers, publishers, and anyone else who might know a thing or two about an f-stop. Community outreach programs inform the community, both young and old, about the history of photography, and what we can do to preserve it. Not a bad goal, and one that ICP (with both its locations) has been instrumental in achieving.

THE JEWISH MUSEUM
1109 Fifth Avenue (at 92nd Street), New York NY. 212/423-3200. **World Wide Web address:** http://www.thejewishmuseum.org. **Description:** For more than 50 years, the Warburg Mansion on Fifth Avenue has been home to NYC's Jewish Museum. Founded with less than 30 artifacts, The Jewish Museum has grown to include a library, gallery, auditorium, and educational facilities. The museum plays host to a variety of entertainment events including lectures, plays, live poetry, and music. The Jewish Museum offers an especially large number of programs for children including arts and crafts, music, storytelling, and sing-alongs. But don't worry, these programs are educational as well as fun; let the kids decorate and practice their shofars, create a unique wimple message, or hang a mezzuzah. And kids aren't the only ones allowed to have fun, The Jewish Museum's "SummerNights" series allows adults to enjoy an exciting mix of exhibitions, various music, and...television? That's right, Tuesday nights (5:00 p.m. - 9:00 p.m.) in the summer months are a time to kick back and relax while watching some of your favorite television shows that are held in the museum's National Jewish Archive of Broadcasting. Screened programs include *The Twilight Zone, All in the Family, Rhoda,* and *Bonanza.* SummerNights events include free admission (and free popcorn and soda if you're vegging out in the auditorium). Admission is $8.00 for adults, $5.50 for seniors and students, and free for children under 12. Tuesday nights, from 5:00 p.m. - 8:00 p.m., it's "Pay What You Wish." Open Sunday through Thursday, 11:00 a.m. - 5:45 p.m. (open until 8:00 p.m. on Tuesday); closed, Friday, Saturday, and all major Jewish holidays.

LOWER EAST SIDE TENEMENT MUSEUM
90 Orchard Street, New York NY. 212/431-0233. **World Wide Web address:** http://www.tenement.org. **Description:** And you thought Orchard Street was only good for shopping! This museum

preserves the culture of New York City's 19th-century merchant class, a perfect complement to Ellis Island. The building itself is a genuine tenement, built in 1863. Its exhibits display artifacts and re-created storefronts, tracing the experience of the Jews, Italians, Irish, African-Americans and Asians who successively found this neighborhood a "Gateway to America." Films, photographs, and live performances by the museum's own theatrical troupe bring it all to life. The museum also sponsors walking tours through the actual neighborhoods themselves. The museum is open to visitors by guided tour only. Tour admission prices are $9.00 for adults, and $7.00 for students and seniors. Tours run Tuesday through Friday, every half hour from 1:00 p.m. to 4:00 p.m.; and Saturday and Sunday, every half hour from 11:00 a.m. to 4:30 p.m.

MUSEUM FOR AFRICAN ART
593 Broadway (between Houston & Prince Streets), New York NY 10012. 212/966-1313. **E-mail address:** museum@africanart.org. **World Wide Web address:** http://www.africanart.org. **Description:** The Museum for African Art is dedicated to increasing the public's understanding and appreciation of African art and culture. Recent exhibitions have included "A Congo Chronicle: Patrice Lumumba in Urban Art" and "Liberated Voices: Contemporary Art from South Africa," featuring over 65 paintings, sculptures, installations, photographs, and videos made since the end of Apartheid in 1984. Admission is $5.00 for adults, $2.50 for seniors, students, and children. Open Tuesday through Friday, 10:30 a.m. - 6:30 p.m.; Saturday and Sunday, 12:00 p.m. - 6:00 p.m.

MUSEUM OF AMERICAN FINANCIAL HISTORY
28 Broadway, New York NY 10014. 212/908-4110. **World Wide Web address:** http://www.financialhistory.org. **Description:** It's all about money here, but not out of your own pocket. As a museum dedicated solely to the role of finance in American history, the collections and exhibits you'll see here are truly unique. Permanent collections include antique stocks, bonds, and currency; and a multitude of exhibits feature greats like John D. Rockefeller. You can also take a walking tour, like "World of Finance," where you'll visit the New York Stock Exchange's trading floor. Exhibit and tour prices average $15.00 for adults, $10.00 for seniors and students. Prices *can* vary, so call for specifics. A donation of $2.00 is suggested for admission to the gallery. Open Tuesday through Saturday, 10:00 a.m. - 4:00 p.m.

MUSEUM OF AMERICAN FOLK ART
2 Lincoln Square (Columbus Avenue & 66th Street), New York NY 10023. 212/595-9533. **Description:** This charming gallery focuses on the diversity of America's rich cultural heritage. Exhibitions such as "Millennial Dreams: Vision and Prophecy in American Folk Art" explore the keen observances and eloquent recordings of American life that can be documented though works of art. Paintings, sculptures, textiles, and various decorative arts all help

to comprise the museum's extensive collection. Museum of American Folk Art also offers free educational programs for children, such as Sunday workshops and weekend storytelling and puppet shows. Admission is free. Open Tuesday through Sunday, 11:30 a.m. - 7:30 p.m.

MUSEUM OF THE CITY OF NEW YORK

1220 Fifth Avenue, New York NY. 212/534-1672. **Description:** If you could really fit the entire city into one building, this might be it. Five floors of more than 1.5 million artifacts house everything from actual rooms of the first Rockefeller mansion to furniture by NYC's own Duncan Phyfe. A fast-moving multimedia show gives the entire history of the city in 20 minutes. Galleries host both changing and permanent exhibits. Admission is free, although a contribution of $5.00 is suggested. Open Wednesday through Saturday, 10:00 a.m. - 5:00 p.m.; Sunday, 12:00 p.m. - 5:00 p.m.

MUSEUM OF JEWISH HERITAGE-A LIVING MEMORIAL TO THE HOLOCAUST

18 First Place, Battery Park City NY 10004-1484. 212/509-6130. **World Wide Web address:** http://www.mjhnyc.org. **Description:** The Museum of Jewish Heritage-A Living Memorial to the Holocaust is dedicated to telling the stories and tragedies of the 20th-century Jewish experience before, during, and after the Holocaust. The museum is an educational institution for visitors of all ages and backgrounds. Through photographs, artifacts, films, and educational programs, the museum provides people with an entertaining as well as enlightening visit. The museum is arranged chronologically by floor. The three themes are "Jewish Life a Century Ago," "The War Against the Jews," and "Jewish Renewal." If you'd like an in-depth tour, let Meryl Streep or Itzhak Perlman guide you; audio tours are available for an additional $5.00. Visitors are invited to experience the museum's various activities including musical performances, walking tours, films, and educational workshops. The museum presents its annual Film and Discussion series, sponsored by the Bess Myerson Film and Video Collection. These tickets are free to the public, though tickets are distributed on a first-come first-serve basis. Films are screened at Florence Gould Hall (55 East 59th Street) and begin at 7:00 p.m. Museum admission is $7.00 for adults, and $5.00 for students and seniors. Open Sunday through Wednesday, 9:00 a.m. - 5:00 p.m.; Thursday, 9:00 a.m. - 8:00 p.m.; Friday, 9:00 a.m. - 3:00 p.m. The museum is closed on Saturday and all Jewish holidays.

MUSEUM OF MODERN ART

11 West 53rd Street, New York NY 10019. 212/708-9400. **World Wide Web address:** http://www.moma.org. **Description:** Well, you probably don't need Mr. C to tell you about this landmark on the artistic map of New York (and the world). Anyone who tried to get tickets to the Pollock exhibit knows how hot this place can get -- and how expensive. But don't be deterred, it's not always so difficult to get into. MOMA also offers free "Summergarden" concerts in its famous sculpture garden behind the museum. These

take place on Friday and Saturday evenings at 7:30 p.m. during July and August. Admission is $10.00 for adults, $6.50 for students and seniors, and free for children under 16 (when accompanied by a parent). On Fridays, from 4:30 p.m. - 8:15 p.m., you may "Pay What You Wish" to enter the museum. Open daily (except Wednesdays), 10:30 a.m. - 5:45 p.m. (until 8:15 p.m. on Friday).

THE MUSEUM OF TELEVISION AND RADIO

25 West 52nd Street (between Fifth Avenue & Avenue of the Americas), New York NY. 212/621-6600. **World Wide Web address:** http://www.mtr.org. **Description:** The Museum of Television and Radio was the first place to begin preserving the sounds and moving images of the 20th century, and it seems that entertainers and entertainment companies alike have come out in full force to support the cause. The Museum of Television and Radio teaches the history of these mediums through visual and audio presentations. Your journey starts out on the ground floor where, in the Steven Spielberg Room, you'll view tons of television posters. Move on upstairs for some interactive fun. The modern, cozy screening room presents television classics from the museum's archives. You may see comedy ranging from Lenny Bruce to *Saturday Night Live*, or live dramas from the golden age of TV. They've even been known to screen a bunch of Hanna-Barbera classics, like *The Flinstones, The Jetsons, Scooby Doo,* and *The Banana Splits*. These can be lots of fun on a screen that's measured in feet instead of inches, and viewed with a crowd of fellow fans. The Guild Radio listening rooms has special feature exhibits (sometimes in conjunction with the visual screenings), or you can choose what you want to listen to from the museum's extensive library of tapes. Admission is $6.00 for adults, $4.00 for students with valid ID, and $3.00 for kids under 13. Open Tuesday and Wednesday, 12:00 p.m. - 6:00 p.m.; Thursday, 12:00 p.m. - 8:00 p.m.; Friday, 12:00 p.m. - 9:00 p.m.; Saturday and Sunday, 12:00 p.m. - 6:00 p.m.

NATIONAL ACADEMY OF DESIGN

1083 Fifth Avenue (at 90th Street), New York NY 10128. 212/369-4880. **World Wide Web address:** http://www. nationalacademy.org. **Description:** The National Academy of Design is perhaps one of the lesser-known stops along the Museum Mile, but no less respected -- and well worth a visit. Dedicated to the preservation and instruction of fine art, the Academy features special exhibits that often focus on lesser-known subjects themselves. The National Academy of Design also hosts the nation's oldest juried art show, presenting works by contemporary artists. Saturday is "Family Fun Day" at the National Academy of Design; after a tour of the current exhibition, kids and their families are invited to engage in some interactive fun and games. Family Fun can be had for just $8.00 per person. A final note about the museum: if architecture is your thing, you definitely want to make this place a stop. The museum is housed inside the Beaux-Arts townhouse, one of the few Fifth Avenue mansions that remains open to the public. Just walking inside the home is a breathtaking experience. All-marble floors surround the Diana sculpture in the main lobby. Admission is $8.00 for adults, and $5.00 for children and seniors. Open Wednesday through Sunday, 12:00 p.m. - 5:00 p.m.; closed Monday and Tuesday.

NEW MUSEUM OF CONTEMPORARY ART
583 Broadway (between Houston & Prince Streets), New York NY 10012. 212/219-1222. **World Wide Web address:** http://www. newmuseum.org. **Description:** Founded in 1977, SoHo's New Museum may not be so *new* anymore, but it's definitely built itself a reputation as one of the world's grandest places to view the best in contemporary art. Yet, the New Museum is about more than just art, it is also about social change and awareness. Through art, the New Museum's "Visible Knowledge" program deals with such omnipresent social themes as racism, ageism, and sexism. This mixed media extravaganza gives visitors the opportunity not only to view art in its three galleries and mezzanine, but to interact with the art as well. Take an "Insider's Tour" and discuss the art with other visitors. Go "Downstairs" in the New Museum (which is always free and open to the public) for a truly interactive experience: watch a performance or two, study an interactive art piece, read a book, or browse in the museum bookstore. The New Museum also presents a number of film screenings that are followed up with a discussion by the filmmaker. So if you like art and you like to talk (let's face it, there's lots of talking going on here), the New Museum of Contemporary Art is the place for you! Call of visit the museum's Website for a list of upcoming events. Admission is $6.00 for adults; $3.00 for seniors, students, and artists; and free to those who are 18 and under. While these prices are definitely something to sing about, the New Museum makes them even better by waiving the admission fee from 6:00 p.m. - 8:00 p.m. on Thursdays. Open Sunday and Wednesday, 12:00 p.m. - 6:00 p.m.; Thursday through Saturday, 12:00 p.m. - 8:00 p.m.; closed Monday and Tuesday.

NEW YORK AQUARIUM
Surf Avenue (West 8th Street), Brooklyn NY. 718/265-3474. **World Wide Web address:** http://www.wcs.org. **Description:** Given its location on the Coney Island boardwalk, the New York Aquarium is a rather odd blend of wildlife conservation center (its true mission) and Sea World. Daily dolphin and sea lion shows are mixed in with exhibits and demonstrations about life at the bottom of the sea. The Discovery Cove, New York Aquarium's environmental display area, features recreations of coastal tidepools and habitats for a variety of fish, reptiles, and other animals. And don't miss the shark feeding sessions, which are always a tensile event. Admission is $8.75 for adults, $4.50 for seniors and kids aged two to 12, and free for ages two and under. Open daily, 10:00 a.m. - 4:30 p.m. Because the hours can change from season to season, it is best to give them a call first and verify what hours they'll be open the day you go.

NEW YORK CITY FIRE MUSEUM

278 Spring Street, New York NY 10013. 212/691-1303.
Description: Just how hot does New York City get? For the
thousands of individuals who have risked their lives as firefighters
in the past 100 years, the heat can be pretty intense. The New
York City Fire Museum salutes these brave men and women, and
preserves their occupational tradition through exhibits and
displays dating back to Colonial times. The museum boasts one of
the country's finest collections of fire memorabilia, and the
museum itself is situated in a renovated firehouse. In addition to
an array of artifacts, including several fire engines, the museum
takes an active role in teaching today's youngsters about what to
do in the case of a fire. Families will enjoy this nostalgic peek at
one of the world's most respected and time-honored occupations.
Adult admission is a mere $4.00, with kids costing only $1.00.

NEW YORK TRANSIT MUSEUM

Boerum Place & Schermerhorn Street, Brooklyn NY. 718/243-
8601. **Description:** The New York Transit Museum is home to over
100 years of transit lore and memorabilia. Housed in an actual
subway station (dating back to the 1930s), the museum is chock
full of authentic subway remembrances including vintage subway
and elevated cars, antique turnstiles, and a working signal tower.
New York Transit Museum offers a variety of educational
programs including special exhibitions, lectures, and workshops. If
you can't make it out to Brooklyn while you're in town, drop by the
museum's gallery annex and store at Grand Central Terminal, or
their store and travel information center in Times Square.
Admission is $3.00 for adults, $1.50 for children and seniors.
Senior citizens can enjoy an added discount on Wednesday
afternoons when, from 12:00 p.m. until 4:00 p.m., the admission
fee is waived. Open Tuesday through Friday, 10:00 a.m. - 4:00 p.m.;
Saturday and Sunday, 12:00 p.m. - 5:00 p.m.

NEW YORK CITY POLICE MUSEUM

25 Broadway, New York NY 10004. 212/301-4440. **World Wide
Web address:** http://www.nycpolicemuseum.org. **Description:** No,
you won't find any mummified or waxen officers. You will find a
variety of educational and historical police and crime-related
memorabilia., and you may even qualify to shoot in the Fire Arms
Training Simulator! Open Monday through Friday, 10:00 a.m. - 6:00
p.m.; Saturday and Sunday, 10:00 a.m. - 4:00 p.m.

NEW YORK HALL OF SCIENCE

47-01 111th Street, Flushing Meadows Corona Park, Queens NY
11368. 718/699-0005. **World Wide Web address:** http://www.
nyhallsci.org. **Description:** With over 200 exhibits, the New York
Hall of Science is hailed as one of America's best science
museums. Just a few of the museum's regular features include a
"Technology Gallery," "Hidden Kingdoms -- The World of
Microbes," and a "Science Playground." Admission is $7.50 for
adults, $5.00 for children and seniors, and free to members.
Museum hours are as follows: fall/winter/spring: Monday through

Wednesday, 9:30 a.m. - 2:00 p.m.; Thursday through Sunday, 9:30 a.m. - 5:00 p.m. Summer: Monday 9:30 a.m. - 2:00 p.m.; Thursday through Sunday, 9:30 a.m. 5:00 p.m.

OLD MERCHANT'S HOUSE
29 East 4th Street (between Bowery & Lafayette Streets), New York NY 10003. 212/777-1089. **Description:** Many consider this mansion one of the finest examples of Greek Revival architecture in the country, and who are we to disagree? Built in 1832 by a wealthy haberdasher-turned-real-estate-magnate, the museum offers a chance to experience a hint of days long past. Admission is $3.00 for adults, $2.00 for seniors and students. Open Sunday through Thursday, 1:00 p.m. - 4:00 p.m.

P.S. 1 CONTEMPORARY ART CENTER
22-25 Jackson Avenue (at 46th Street), Long Island City NY 11101. 718/784-2084. **E-mail address:** mail@ps1.org. **World Wide Web address:** http://www.ps1.org. **Description:** If you get a chance to make it Long Island City (only seven minutes from midtown Manhattan), be sure and drop by P.S. 1 Contemporary Art Center, a noncollecting institution that houses a variety of exhibits in its 125,000 square feet of gallery space. P.S. 1 has long championed the innovative and the avant-garde, presenting experimental national and international artists. Come bask in the many video, sound, digital, sculptural, and multimedia environments P.S. 1 has to offer. During the summer, P.S. 1 presents an early evening series of electronic and live musical performances in the outdoor courtyard. Admission to the museum is a suggested $4.00 donation for adults, and $2.00 for students and seniors. Open Wednesday through Sunday, 12:00 p.m. - 6:00 p.m. The museum is closed on Monday and Tuesday.

PIERPONT MORGAN LIBRARY AND ANNEX
29-33 East 36th Street, New York NY 10016. 212/685-0008. **Description:** The Pierpont Morgan Library and Annex is another turn-of-the-century millionaire's home. Except this one wasn't even built for ol' J.P. himself, it was built for his books! Based on ancient Roman architecture, the Pierpont Morgan Library is now a public museum dedicated to literature and design. You'll be entranced by its domed entrance hall, done up in marble and murals. Exhibits range from stately landscape drawings to collections of rare manuscripts. "Requested Contributions" are $7.00 for adults, $5.00 for students and seniors, and free for children under 12. Open Tuesday through Thursday, 10:30 a.m. - 5:00 p.m.; Friday, 10:30 a.m. - 8:00 p.m., Saturday, 10:30 a.m. - 6:00 p.m.; Sunday, 12:00 p.m. - 6:00 p.m. The library is closed on Mondays and holidays.

QUEENS MUSEUM OF ART
New York City Building, Flushing Meadows Corona Park, Queens NY. 718/592-9700. **Description:** This museum is about *making* art as much as it is *viewing* it; they give you the chance to do both. Enjoy the ever-changing array of exhibits, usually leaning toward

the work of contemporary artists. On Sundays during the fall and spring, let your kids join a "Drop-In Workshop" ($3.00 per child), where they can try their hand at something inspired by the shows. These take place between 1:00 p.m. and 4:00 p.m. The museum is located near the Grand Central Parkway, part of the original 1939 World's Fair grounds. The World's Fair theme continues within the museum: Queens Museum of Art houses the incredible Panorama of the City of New York, a scale model of all NYC built for the 1964 World's Fair. Admission is $4.00 for adults; $2.00 for students, seniors, and children over age five; free for kids under five. Open Tuesday through Friday, 10:00 a.m. - 5:00 p.m.; Saturday and Sunday, 12:00 p.m. - 5:00 p.m.

ABIGAIL ADAMS SMITH MUSEUM
421 East 61st Street, New York NY 10021. 212/838-6878. **Description:** Another one for you architecture and history fans: built in 1799 as a carriage house, this building has led a varied and illustrious life. It was in 1975 that Abigail Adams Smith (daughter of President John Adams) and her husband designed an estate on the banks of the East River. They never occupied it; before it was finished they sold it off. This stone carriage house later became The Mount Vernon Hotel in 1826, an elegant country resort for upper-middle class New Yorkers seeking to escape the dust, noise, and crime of the rapidly-expanding city. The museum's nine period rooms reflect this era of New York City history. How much to see all of this? $4.00 for adults, $3.00 for students and seniors, and children under 12 are free. Open Tuesday through Sunday, 11:00 a.m. - 4:00 p.m.

SOUTH STREET SEAPORT MUSEUM
207 Front Street, New York NY 10038. 212/748-8600. **World Wide Web address:** http://www.southstseaport.org. **Description:** Founded in 1967, the South Street Seaport Museum is dedicated to preserving the history and tradition of the Port of New York City. Galleries, exhibits, and educational programs are just a few of the ways in which this history is preserved. The museum even boasts the nation's largest collection of historic vessels. After touring the museum, drop by the nation's largest fish market, which also occupies part of this 11-square-block district. Admission is $6.00 for adults, $5.00 for seniors, $4.00 for students, $3.00 for children, and free to members. Spring/summer hours are daily, 10:00 a.m. - 6:00 p.m.; fall/winter hours are daily (except Tuesdays), 10:00 a.m. - 5:00 p.m.

STATUE OF LIBERTY NATIONAL MONUMENT & ELLIS ISLAND
Liberty Island, New York NY 10004. 212/363-3200. **World Wide Web address:** http://www.nps.gov/stli. **Description:** It goes without saying that every American should visit these landmarks. Not only are they of historic importance, but they make great, inexpensive outdoor activities as well. For starters, of course, you have to get there by ferry. On a sunny day, this is a worthwhile outing in itself. Ferries depart from Battery Park (at the southernmost tip of Manhattan), affording you dramatic views of

the Financial District skyline. Don't forget your camera because there are some great photo opportunities here. The ferry boats head for the Statue first, then on to Ellis Island. Climb up to Lady Liberty's crown, all 350 steps of it; or just walk around the quiet island haven. At Ellis Island, the building which probably processed someone in your family, you'll find a fascinating museum. Find out, in the flash of a computer, which states now have the highest concentration of your nationality. See actual artifacts from immigrants of all ethnic origins, films about the experience, and the stately Great Hall itself. With frequent sailings, you can get on and off and spend as much time as you wish at each destination. For ferry schedule and information, call 212/269-5755. Round-trip fares are just $7.00 for adults, $6.00 for seniors, $3.00 for children under seventeen. And since there are no admission fees at the monuments, these prices can be your only expenses for the whole day. Want to save even more money? Pack a lunch. Both islands have picnic areas. While both islands are a must-see, be warned that waiting times can be lengthy in the spring and summer months, with it sometimes taking between one and two hours to reach the top of Lady Liberty's crown. Also, with so many people milling around, the heat can be intense. Crown access is limited to the first ferry *only* during the summer months. Make sure to dress appropriately and expect all weather extremes.

THEODORE ROOSEVELT BIRTHPLACE

28 East 20th Street (between Broadway & Park Avenue), New York NY 10003. 212/260-1616. **World Wide Web address:** http://www.nps.gov/thrb. **Description:** On September 14, 1901, Theodore Roosevelt took the reigns as President of the United States after the unexpected assassination of William McKinley. Yet, our 26th President was not always the outspoken stalwart he is remembered as. Roosevelt spent the first 14 years of his life in this home (actually, a reconstruction of his real home, built in 1923), many of which were spent suffering from debilitating asthma. Learn how the sickly boy became one of our most beloved Presidents. Tour the five period rooms and two exhibit galleries, complete with much of the furniture from the original home. General admission is $2.00; seniors and children under 17 are free. Tours run every hour on the hour, Wednesday through Sunday, 9:00 a.m. - 4:00 p.m.

UKRAINIAN MUSEUM

203 Second Avenue (between 12th & 13th Streets), New York NY 10003. 212/228-0110. **Description:** This museum focuses on the culture and history of American Ukrainians over the past 100 years. Exhibits include decorative ceramics, jewelry, and a magnificent collection of 900 hand-painted Easter eggs called *pysanky*. Admission is $1.00 for adults, $.50 for seniors and students. Open Wednesday through Sunday, 1:00 p.m. - 5:00 p.m.

WHITNEY MUSEUM OF AMERICAN ART

945 Madison Avenue (at 75th Street), New York NY 10021. 212/570-3676. **World Wide Web address:** http://www.

whitney.org. **Description:** One of the city's great art museums, Whitney Museum of American Art's popularity is due not only to its estimable collections, but to its manageable size as well. You can see the entire place in just one afternoon. The exhibits are 20th-century; the sculptor Alexander Calder has long been associated with the Whitney Museum, and his delightful mobiles are evident throughout the building and courtyard. The museum's many exhibit halls change over regularly, showing the work of important modern American artists, past and present. If you don't get the chance to make it to the Madison Avenue location, The Whitney Museum operates a branch location at the Philip Morris Companies headquarters. While admission is $12.50 for adults ($17.50 for audio tour) and $10.50 for students and seniors ($15.50 for audio tour), the museum offers a "Pay What You Wish" admission price on the first Thursday of every month, from 6:00 to 8:00 p.m. Members and children under 12 are always admitted free. For even better deals, visit the Whitney's Website, where you can sometimes download special tour coupons. Open Tuesday and Wednesday, 11:00 a.m. - 6:00 p.m.; Thursday, 1:00 p.m. - 8:00 p.m.; Friday through Sunday, 11:00 a.m. - 6:00 p.m.

WHITNEY MUSEUM OF AMERICAN ART AT PHILIP MORRIS 120 Park Avenue (at 42nd Street), New York NY 10017. 917/663-2453. **World Wide Web address:** http://www.whitney.org. **Description:** Located within the international headquarters of Philip Morris Companies, this branch of the Whitney Museum of American Art offers just as much culture, at a much better price -- free! The gallery's exhibitions focus on contemporary living artists. In addition to a 900-square-foot gallery, the Whitney at Philip Morris houses an unbelievable Sculpture Court. Aside from the visual art, the museum also offers "Performances on 42nd," a free series of music, theater, dance, and performance art. Sip an espresso and let the culture sink in. Tours of the gallery are offered on Wednesday and Friday at 1:00 p.m. sharp. The gallery is open for self-guided tours Monday through Friday, 11:00 a.m. - 6:00 p.m. (on Thursday, the gallery stays open until 7:30 p.m.). Maneuver your way through the Sculpture Court Monday through Saturday, 7:30 a.m. - 9:30 p.m.; or on Sunday, 11:00 a.m. - 7:00 p.m.

ENTERTAINMENT
♬ Music: Classical ♬

AMATO OPERA THEATRE
319 Bowery, New York NY 10003. 212/228-8200. **E-mail address:** info@amato.org. **World Wide Web address:** http://www. amato.org. **Description:** Opera has to be big, right? Big theater, big sets, big prices. Not true! For over 50 years now the Amato Opera has been producing operas that are up-close-and-personal. This tiny East Village auditorium only holds about 100 people, and the neighborhood has seen better days; but oh, do they flock here. (Crowds in fur coats, mingling along the Bowery before going in, is quite a sight only in New York!) The atmosphere inside is very homey, presided over by Anthony Amato and his wife Sally. He directs the cast, conducts the orchestra, and makes the fundraising curtain speech. Given his name, it's no surprise that the repertoire leans toward the Italians: Rossini's *Barber of Seville*, Verdi's *Otello*. Yet their season of half a dozen productions may also yield a Mozart, or an unusual work rarely heard at all. Many of the operas are sung in English. Since New York is the center of the American opera world, you can rest assured that the singers are well qualified indeed. You may catch the occasional weak voice, but these are all serious professionals, and they've got the reviews to prove it. Talented too are the set designers and costumers, who seem to create just as much spectacle as the Met with a fraction of the space -- and budget. Speaking of which, how much does all this cost? A mere $25.00 per ticket ($20.00 for seniors).

BARGEMUSIC
Fulton Ferry Landing, Brooklyn NY. 718/624-2083. **Description:** Great, inexpensive music in New York is often going on right under your nose -- or, in this case, right under the Brooklyn Bridge. Begun by Olga Bloom, a concert violinist who still runs the program, this is a chamber music series that actually takes place in an old barge, converted into an informal concert hall. The performers include soloists from the international circuit, working in intimate ensembles -- or larger groupings, when the program (Bach's Brandenburg Concerti, for example) requires it. Concerts are presented throughout the year, on Thursday evenings at 7:30 and Sunday afternoons at 4:00. Tickets are $23.00 for adults, $20.00 for seniors, and $15.00 for students; further discounts are available with subscriptions. It's one of the city's great and unique bargains.

BRONX ARTS ENSEMBLE INC. (BAE)
Golf House, Van Cortlandt Park, Bronx NY 10471. 718/601-7399. **Description:** The Bronx's fully professional resident company, BAE presents a wide variety of concerts in an equally wide variety of settings from outdoor orchestral shows in parks around the

borough to chamber ensembles performing in private homes. They are frequently found at the Rose Hill Campus of Fordham University, the Riverdale YMCA, the Bronx Zoo, and other such places. To best keep up with this lively company, write to the address above and get on their mailing list. Tickets for these concerts are usually in the $10.00 range, with discounts for students and senior citizens. Many summer family performances are free.

BRONX SYMPHONY ORCHESTRA
2141 Muliner Avenue, Bronx NY 10462. 718/601-9151. **E-mail address:** BxSym@yahoo.com. **World Wide Web address:** http://www.bronxsymphony.org. **Description:** For more than 50 years the Bronx Symphony Orchestra has been presenting concerts of traditional symphonic fare. The orchestra blends serious nonprofessional musicians with professional players. Don't go in expecting the New York Philharmonic, and you'll enjoy yourself -- especially when you consider the price. These concerts are free and open to all.

NEW YORK GRAND OPERA
154 West 57th Street, New York NY 10019. 212/235-8837. **World Wide Web address:** http://www.csis.pace.edu/newyorkgrandopera. **Description:** What is more grand about these opera performances -- the music or the price? For more than 25 years, founder Vincent La Selva has presented more than 150 fully-staged performances, to an estimated 2 million onlookers, at no charge! Beginning in 1974 and lasting well into the new millennium, La Selva (who also directs the NYGO) has paid the ultimate tribute to master Giuseppe Verdi by presenting all 28 of his operas in chronological order. Performances take place under the stars on the "SummerStage" in the center of Central Park. Call for details about this season's schedule.

NEW YORK PHILHARMONIC ORCHESTRA
AVERY FISHER HALL
10 Lincoln Center Plaza, New York NY 10023. 212/875-5000. **World Wide Web address:** http://www.newyorkphilharmonic.org. **Description:** Avery Fisher Hall is home to one of the nation's oldest symphony orchestras, the New York Philharmonic. As might be expected, ticket prices can soar well into the $300.00 range when attending the hall of such a masterful orchestra. Fortunately for you, Mr. C knows a few shortcuts. Attending a Friday matinee show *can* reduce the cost to about $25.00; Saturday matinees will also allow you savings off the regular ticket prices. For $25.00 each, orchestra seats may be available if purchased the same day of the concert. Students, seniors, and disabled individuals may be eligible to receive $10.00 for certain shows as well (excluding Friday matinees and Saturday night performances). If you plan on an extended stay in the Big Apple and you just can't get enough of these Avery Fisher Hall performances, it might be a wise investment to join the Ticket Buyers Club. While tickets will still

cost you around $50.00 each, this can still be a pretty good savings from what you would pay to buy each ticket individually. For more info on these Mr. C short cuts, call Audience Services at 212/875-5656.

PEOPLE'S SYMPHONY CONCERTS
201 West 54th Street, Suite 4C, New York NY 10019. 212/586-4680. **Description:** This may be the ultimate in low-priced classical music -- apart from summer freebies, of course. The People's Symphony is dedicated to providing music to those who can't afford tickets to the big concert halls, yet who don't want to miss out on high-quality delights. It was founded at the turn of the century by just such a person; a poor music student who vowed to make things better for future generations of students and other music lovers. The top price is usually -- get ready -- a mere $10.50. Most tickets, in fact, are in the $5.00 to $8.50 range. And with a subscription, you can actually pay as little as $3.00 per concert to hear some of the city's top musicians! Concerts take place at the Washington Irving High School Auditorium (40 Irving Place, at 16th Street), and at Town Hall (see separate listing), both in Manhattan. Call for more details.

REGINA OPERA COMPANY
1251 Tabor Court, Brooklyn NY 11219. 718/232-3555. **World Wide Web address:** http://www.reginaopera.org. **Description:** Founded in 1970, Regina Opera Company has been presenting such renowned operas as *Carmen, Madame Butterfly,* and *La Traviata,* fully-staged with a 35 to 40 piece orchestra, for more than three decades. These operatic performances take place at 7:00 p.m. on Saturday, and 4:00 p.m. on Sunday. Saturday admission prices are $12.00 for adults, $8.00 for seniors and college students, $5.00 for high school and middle school students, and free to children under 12. Operatic and popular music Sunday matinee concerts start at 4:00 p.m. Sunday admission prices are $6.00 for adults, $5.00 for high school and middle school students, and are free to children under 12.

ST. PAUL'S CHAPEL
211 Broadway (at Fulton Street), New York NY 10007. 212/602-0874. **Description:** One of New York's oldest churches is also the site for wonderful, free, lunchtime concerts every Monday at noon. Chamber groups, chorales, and soloists are among the delightful performers heard here. While catching an earful of music, take a peek at the pew where, in 1789 (when NYC served as the nation's capital), George Washington worshipped on his inauguration day. St. Paul's is related to another historic church, Trinity Church (see separate listing under Walks & Tours), which holds its own series of lunchtime concerts on Thursdays. Times and places may be subject to change, but the concerts take place year-round.

SYMPHONY SPACE
2537 Broadway (at 95th Street), New York NY 10025. 212/864-5400. **Description:** This large Upper West Side hall is a musical

landmark for New York City. A nonprofit institution, they offer a full schedule of concerts, theater, spoken word, and children's performances at reasonable ticket prices. Take in some Indian music (both American and Asian), Irish theater, or the New York Gilbert and Sullivan Players. There are also free concerts by such groups as the Mannes College Orchestra. The "Selected Shorts" series of short stories, read by Broadway and Hollywood actors, is recorded here for future broadcasts on NPR and WNYC radio. And then there are the free marathons, all-day presentations focusing on one composer or author. Very few events are priced above $15.00 or $20.00, and many shows start under $10.00. Become a member for as little as $35.00 a year, and among other benefits, you'll save $3.00 to $5.00 on most tickets.

TOWN HALL
123 West 43rd Street (between Avenue of the Americas & Seventh Avenue), New York NY 10001. 212/840-2824. **Description:** Built during the 1920s, Town Hall has fallen somewhat into disrepair but is still regarded as one of the city's finest concert halls. With 1,500 seats and excellent acoustics, the auditorium hosts classical, jazz, and popular music concerts at very reasonable prices. You can hear piano soloists and string quartets, big bands and experimental modern jazz, rock stars and international sounds from Africa or Brazil. Ticket prices vary, but many start as low as $10.00 -- and they have discount books of tickets that can bring prices even lower. Call for details.

ENTERTAINMENT
♫ Music: Jazz & Blues ♫

BIRDLAND
315 West 44th Street, New York NY 10036. 212/581-3080.
Description: While the original Birdland was located on Broadway between 52nd and 53rd Streets, it's current location is in the heart of Times Square. Some of the jazz world's top names have come to New York just to play to Birdland's appreciative and discerning audience. Pat Metheny, Michael Brecker, Tito Puente, Freddie Hubbard, The Count Basie Orchestra, and Stanley Turrentine have all graced the stage at the new Birdland. Live music is featured seven nights a week with ticket prices ranging from $15.00 - $25.00, depending on the day of the week. Not a bad deal considering some of the many jazz legends who have played here. Birdland also offers a Southern cuisine menu with entree prices ranging from $8.00 to $18.00. Now, though the $18.00 range is a bit out of Mr. C's budget, you may want to make a night of it and splurge. Otherwise, the area is crawling with good, cheap eats.

BLUE NOTE
131 West 3rd Street, New York NY 10012. 212/475-8592. **E-mail address:** bluenote@interjazz.com. **World Wide Web address:** http://www.bluenote.net. **Description:** One of the most famous jazz spots in the country, Blue Note is also one of the city's more expensive night clubs. Considering the top-name stars who shine here, it's no wonder. But wait -- there are ways around this! If you're a night owl, drop in after hours -- from 2:00 a.m. - 4:00 a.m., when the players hang out and jam. You never know who, after "working" for the evening, may drop in to wail just for fun. There's only a $5.00 cover charge, less than half the prime-time rates, and no minimum. For an inexpensive option at more "normal" hours, try the weekend brunches, where you get live music, a variety of breakfasts, and one drink -- all for $14.50 per person. These take place every Saturday and Sunday from 12:00 p.m. - 6:00 p.m., with sets at 1:00 p.m. and 3:30 p.m. You may catch headliners like Houston Person and Etta Jones -- in what finer fashion to while away a lazy afternoon?

DETOUR
349 East 13th Street (between First & Second Avenues), New York NY 10003. 212/533-6212. **Description:** This comfortable East Village jazz lounge showcases some of the city's hottest up-and-comers. With a comfortable setting, late hours, and no cover charge policy, this is one place where jazz aficionados should definitely make a detour stop. Drop in for Happy Hour (Monday through Friday, 4:00 p.m. - 7:00 p.m.), when Detour offers two-for-one drink specials at their art deco bar. Music starts at 9:00 p.m. on weeknights and at 9:30 p.m. Friday and Saturday. Until

then, have fun with the Detour jukebox, offering a variety of artists to suit every taste. Open Sunday through Thursday, 4:00 p.m. - 2:00 a.m.; Friday and Saturday, 4:00 p.m. - 4:00 a.m.

DON'T TELL MAMA

343 West 46th Street (between 8th & 9th Avenues), New York NY. 212/757-0788. **World Wide Web address:** http://www.donttellmama.com. **Description:** The piano bar at this very popular Theater District hangout features singing waiters and waitresses, waiting, of course, for that big break to land them at a Broadway theater. Customers are invited to join in as well -- many of whom turn out to be aspiring actors too. That just gives you high-quality entertainment for the cost of a couple of, well, high-priced drinks. Still works out to be quite inexpensive overall. The music starts at 9:30 p.m. every night, with no cover charge or drink minimum.

ROSE'S TURN

55 Grove Street, New York NY 10014. 212/366-5438. **Description:** Longtime fans of the cabaret scene may still think of this Greenwich Village club as the Duplex (which moved to 61 Christopher Street). Meanwhile, the current operation looks exactly the same as it always has. The downstairs piano bar is a popular hangout for lovers of show tunes and ribald comedy songs, sung by a parade of waiters, waitresses, bartenders (all aspiring singers and actors), and even patrons who want to get in on the act. The pianist seems to know every song ever written, and many that were not; the audience sings along in a truly campy fashion. All the entertainment is free, with no cover or minimum; "But we do expect you to drink heavily," says the bartender. Well, don't overdo it but there certainly is a merry atmosphere. Get there early if you can, because the place really packs 'em in. Music starts at 9:00 p.m. every night of the week and plays on into the wee hours. If you've ever wanted to sing in front of a crowd, squeeze your way in and take a turn at Rose's. *$Cash Only$*

SOUTH STREET SEAPORT, PIER 17

South Street (at Fulton Street), New York NY. 212/SEA-PORT. **World Wide Web address:** http://www.southstreetseaport.com. **Description:** Upstairs in the atrium of these popular food and shopping halls, South Street Seaport sponsors free concerts each spring and fall. These midweek shows generally take place during the dinner hours. Jazz in all its forms is the mainstay, and some major names pass through.

WORLD MUSIC INSTITUTE

49 West 27th Street, Suite 930, New York NY 10001. 212/545-7536. **E-mail address:** wmi@interport.net. **World Wide Web address:** http://www.heartheworld.org. **Description:** This organization puts together a busy schedule of great concerts at various halls around town. You may hear "Celtic Fiddles" at Symphony Space, avant-garde jazzman Anthony Braxton at the

Merkin Concert Hall, or a Caribbean festival at Brooklyn College. Tickets to most events are under $30.00; become a member up and you'll save 15 - 30 percent on two tickets to each WMI event. Their monthly calendar is not only an interesting read, but it also lists lots of non-WMI concerts around town.

ENTERTAINMENT
♫ Music: Rock & Pop ♫

ARLENE GROCERY
95 Stanton Street (between Ludlow & Orchard Streets), New York NY 10002. 212/358-1633. **World Wide Web address:** http://www.arlene-grocery.com. **Description:** This tiny little club on the Lower East Side offers great music in a truly intimate setting. The philosophy at Arlene Grocery is a unique one: wannabe rock stars with lots of talent (and hopefully some fans) play here for free in the hopes that they will be scouted by some big wig music executive. To make this idea work, however, music lovers must be willing to flock to the place and keep it financially-sound enough to remain open. But just what can a club owner do to ensure that the club will be packed every night of the week? Offering no cover charge is a start! Arlene Grocery showcases lots of local talent (talent being the key word here) and let's the cheap beer selection take care of the finances. It's a great way to operate; it benefits those struggling musicians and Cheapsters like us! And, if after the show, you're looking to unwind with a quiet cocktail, head on over to The Butcher Bar (owned by the same smart folks) right next door! Doors open every night at 6:00 p.m.

THE BAGGOT INN
82 West 3rd Street (between Thompson & Sullivan Streets), New York NY 10012. 212/477-0622. **Website:** http://www.thebaggotinn.com. **Description:** Located downstairs from the Boston Comedy Club (see separate listing), The Baggot Inn offers a great Irish pub experience in the heart of Greenwich Village. They offer live music every night of the week at prices that cannot be beat. If admission isn't free (it often is), cover charge is minimal. And, while you might expect to only find Celtic bands in such a place, The Baggot Inn offers a variety of other events for your listening pleasure: blues and funk are just a few of the various styles. They even offer open mike nights, where you can see some of the city's struggling (and stumbling) artists do their thing! On Saturday afternoon, you can catch their well-known Unnamable Poetry Reading. Another great thing about The Baggot Inn is their drink prices. Monday through Friday, until 7:00 p.m., you can take advantage of such money saving drink specials as $2.00 pints, $7.00 pitchers, and $2.00 mixed drinks. Cheers! Open Sunday, 12:00 p.m. - 2:00 a.m.; Monday through Friday, 11:00 a.m. - 3:00 a.m.

THE BITTER END
147 Bleecker Street, New York NY 10012. 212/673-7030. **Description:** One of the cluster of rock clubs at the end of Bleecker Street, near Houston, The Bitter End is one of New York's oldest rock clubs. Since it was first opened in 1961,

The Bitter End has offered a happy beginning to the careers of some of the best and most legendary acts in music. Performers who have graced The Bitter End stage include Les Paul, Joan Baez, Stevie Wonder, Curtis Mayfield, Miles Davis, Bob Dylan, Joni Mitchell, Van Morrison, and George Thorogood. Even easy listening favorites (you know, people your Mom listened to) like Anne Murray, Linda Ronstadt, Neil Diamond, and John Denver have played here. But The Bitter End wasn't always just about music: Some of the biggest and best names in comedy have tried their act here. Do the names Henny Youngman, Woody Allen, George Carlin, Steven Wright, Billy Crystal, or Bill Cosby ring a bell? On any given night, you're likely to find at least four live bands playing here. And, even with this obvious caliber of talent, they'll only charge you about $5.00 - $10.00 to come on in. The Bitter End prides itself on presenting talented performers who are likely to be the superstars of tomorrow. And you can say you saw them way back when... Open Sunday, 8:00 p.m. - 2:00 a.m.; Monday through Thursday, 7:30 p.m. - 2:00 a.m.; Friday and Saturday, 8:00 p.m. - 4:00 a.m.

CBGB

315 Bowery, New York NY 10003. 212/982-4052. **World Wide Web address:** http://www.cbgb.com. **Description:** This longtime institution, most widely-known as a founding father of the punk movement, still offers underground music-lovers the chance to catch to hear some great music. In one night, you're likely to hear a variety of different bands. Typically, CBGB is thought of as one of the city's wilder bars; so you might want to loosen up a bit before coming. Because of it's known all over the world, it's likely to house a mix of hard core musicians along side tourists and foreign travelers on any given night. One of the best things about the club is learning the history, which is easy enough to do by just reading the promotional posters that line the walls. All shows are open to ages 16 and over, and they will check for two forms of I.D. Drinking, of course, is reserved for those of the legal age of 21. On the average, cover is a mere $5.00 - $10.00. Open daily, shows start around 7:00 p.m.

CAFE WHA

115 MacDougal Street (between West Third & Bleecker Streets), New York NY 10001. 212/254-3706. **Description:** All the biggies seem to have played here including Bob Dylan and Hendrix. Now, you can go to the Cafe Wha and hear all types of bands. Monday night is the infamous Brazilian Dance Party! Best of all to hear cover bands on Wednesday and Sunday, there is no cover charge. The rest of the week the cover ranges from $5.00 - $10.00.

THE ELBOW ROOM

144 Bleecker Street (between Thompson Street & LaGuardia Place), New York NY 10013. 212/979-8434. **World Wide Web address:** http://www.elbowroomnyc.com. **Description:** This comfortable club epitomizes the term "shabby chic." With it's

comfortable setup and unpretentious atmosphere, it's a great place to kick back and here some live music. The Elbow Room features several rock bands each night, and even throws in some blues and funk performers from time to time. Located in one of the city's most prolific live music bar areas, one reason to choose The Elbow Room is, well, elbow room. There's a large dance floor, a full bar, and a lounge to relax in. Best of all, there's only one cover charge to see all these great performers and it's minimal at best. $10.00 should keep you covered. If you happen to be there after 11:00 p.m. on a Wednesday, prepare for their well-known karaoke party! To find out who's playing tonight, call or visit their Website.

THE KNITTING FACTORY
74 Leonard Street, New York NY 10013. 212/219-3055. **Description:** For the most progressive sounds in rock, jazz, world beat, and more, The Knitting Factory is a longtime fixture on the downtown music scene. Groove to the sounds of bluesman James Blood Ulmer, new wave country's Bela Fleck, and modern jazz artist John Zorn, as well as groups with names like "Drink Me," "101 Crustaceans" and "The Klezmatics." In one of the Factory's four listening rooms, you may hear "jazz rap," African drummers, or "industrial country." Cover prices start as low as $5.00 for two sets, and rarely top $10.00. Drinks are cheap here, too; at The Knitting Factory's "Progressive Happy Hour," Brooklyn Lager starts at just $1.00 from 5:30 p.m. - 6:00 p.m. and inches its way up to $2.00 by 7:00 p.m. Same scale for well drinks, from $1.25 - $3.50. Or enjoy coffees and herbal teas instead. The Knitting Factory also presents poets and performance artists at various times throughout the week. Even their weekend programs in the smaller space have tickets at $5.00 - $6.00 for live music. Entertainment here runs into the wee hours of the morning.

ROULETTE
228 West Broadway, New York NY 10013. 212/219-8242. **E-mail address:** info@roulette.org. **World Wide Web address:** http://www.roulette.org. **Description:** This TriBeCa gallery offers a concert series of what it calls "Experimental and Adventurous Music," featuring artists from around the country and some from around the world. You may hear a duo from Switzerland, accompanies by drums and saxophone; a pianist who's modified his instrument to play 24 notes per octave; or a composer's version of Debussy for "three harps, record turntables, sampling keyboard, electric percussion, and trombone.: Shows start at 9:00 p.m., primarily on Thursday through Saturday. Each series, fall and spring, consists of 25 different shows. Tickets are $10.00 for most concerts and free to members (join for $60.00 per year).

RYAN'S IRISH PUB
151 Second Avenue (at 9th Street), New York NY 10003. 212/979-9511. **Description:** Every Sunday starting around 8:00 p.m., Ryan's Irish Pub makes good on its name by sponsoring an open bluegrass jam session. If you feel, as Mr. C does, that

many great bands have become over-amplified and rock-oriented, you'll enjoy this primarily acoustic music. And if you play, of course, feel free to join in. It's an open-mike arrangement, and there is no cover charge. While there, you can also enjoy hearty food, from burgers to full dinners, at reasonable prices. Ryan's Irish Pub has great beers, naturally, as well as the rare and wonderful Woodpecker Cider.

ENTERTAINMENT
☞ Outdoors ☞

THE BRONX ZOO
Southern Boulevard (at 185th Street), Bronx NY. 718/367-1010.
World Wide Web address: http://www.wcs.org. **Description:** The
Bronx Zoo, which opened in 1899, is one of the earliest and
foremost zoos in the country. It has always been ahead of its time
in exhibit design and was one of the first zoos to recreate
naturalistic habitats for its animals. It's primarily a walking zoo,
but with 265 acres and over 6,000 animals, don't expect to see
everything in one day. The zoo has some rides in the summer
months including Zoo Shuttle, a tractor train which provides a
narrated ride from one end of the zoo to the other. Skyfari allows
visitors to see aerial views of the zoo's landscape. Also, don't miss
the Bengali Express Monorail, a round-trip narrated tour of Wild
Asia, where Siberian tigers, Asian elephants, and Indian
rhinoceroses roam free. Don't miss the World of Darkness, where
our nocturnal friends are awake during the daytime. The bison
range alone takes up a full three acres. And at the southern end of
the zoo are the African Plains and Wild Asia, two expansive
habitats in which large animals roam freely (don't worry, it's
perfectly safe). Speaking of animals roaming, the famous
Children's Zoo gives kids a chance to feed and pet all sorts of
furry farm critters. In June 1999, the zoo opened Congo Gorilla
Forest, a 6.5 acre African rain forest where you can come face-to-
face with lowland gorillas. Admission varies with the season, so
please check the Website or call ahead. Wednesdays are always
free and also popular, so expect crowds. There is an added fee for
car parking ($6.00) so walk or take the subway! There are also
extra fees for certain rides and exhibits.

BROOKLYN BOTANIC GARDEN
1000 Washington Avenue, Brooklyn NY 11225. 718/398-2400.
World Wide Web address: http://www.bbg.org. **Description:**
When New Yorkers refer to the Botanical Garden, they usually
mean the larger, more famous one in the Bronx. But don't overlook
this sister park, with its 50 acres of gorgeous flower beds,
Japanese landscaped garden, and the Steinhardt Conservatory,
which displays the flora of different temperate locales. Admission
is $3.00 for adults; $1.50 for seniors and students; children under
16 are free. Guided walking tours are also available. Open March
through October.

BRYANT PARK
Between 40th & 42nd Streets and Fifth Avenue & Avenue of
the Americas, New York NY. 212/983-4143. **E-mail address:**
bprc@urbanmgt.com. **World Wide Web address:** http://www.
bryantpark.org. **Description:** This lovely park behind the main

branch of the New York Public Library offers a variety of activities year-round. In the center of the park you'll find The Great Lawn, where you can kick back and relax on a sunny day. The Perennial Gardens, which border The Great Lawn, offers more than 100 different species of shrubbery for you to gaze at. You'll also find plenty of monuments here like the William Cullen Bryant Memorial, the Gertrude Stein statue, and the memorial to Jose Bonifacio de Andrada e Silva. There's even a number of chess boards set up for your competitive side. There's plenty of seating for the more than 10,000 people that visit the park everyday. Then again, with such a close proximity to some of Midtown's most treasured spots, is it all surprising? Bryant Park makes an especially good place to rest your feet as you trudge along the Fifth Avenue shopping drag.

CENTRAL PARK
World Wide Web address: http://www.centralparknyc.org.
Description: There's no address because it's kind of hard to miss. Now, you may know all about the events and activities that take place in Central Park (i.e. Shakespeare in the Park or the New York Grand Opera), but what about the park itself? Spending a morning or afternoon in Central Park is an enjoyable, relaxing, and *free* way to laze the day away. Created in 1858 by Frederick Law Olmsted and Calvert Vaux, Central Park covers more than 840 acres (of the already-small Manhattan), from 59th to 110th Street, between Fifth Avenue and Central Park West. Central Park is really the heart of Manhattan, separating the East Side from the West Side, and serving as the epitomizing New York backdrop for many films including several Woody Allen pictures, Terry Gilliam's *The Fisher King*, Rob Reiner's *When Harry Met Sally*, and Oliver Stone's *Wall Street*. Even animated films have brought this world-famous park to the big screen; 1995's *Balto* tells the story of the adventures of Balto the sled dog. If you'd like to get a real-life look at Balto (well, as close as you can get with an animated dog), visit the Balto statue in the southeastern part of the Park. Which brings me to the other attractions that Central Park has to offer: statues. Ludwig van Beethoven, Thomas Moore, Hans Christian Anderson, Alice in Wonderland, and Giuseppe Mazzini all have a statue of their likeness. The Bethesda, Untermeyer, and Burnett Fountains are all objects to behold as well. And don't forget to pay tribute to the 58 men of the 107th Regiment at the Civil War Statue located north of Tavern on the Green. Central Park hosts a variety of free, if not cheap, events throughout the year. The Central Park Conservancy operates four visitors centers that can offer you information on these activities (info can also be obtained on the Central Park Website): The Charles A. Dana Discovery Center (212/860-1370) is located at 110th Street & Fifth Avenue; North Meadow Recreation Center (212/348-4867) is located mid-Park at 97th Street; Belvedere Castle (212/772-0210) is located mid-Park at 79th Street; and The Dairy (212/794-6564) is located mid-Park at 65th Street). For as much fun as can be had in the park during the day, as nighttime creeps closer and darkness approaches, it is best to find a more heavily-populated, less

dangerous area. If attending one of the park's many tremendous and recommended nighttime events, just be sure to buddy up.

CENTRAL PARK ROWBOATS

Loeb Boathouse (East Side between 74th & 75th Streets), New York NY. 212/517-4723. **World Wide Web address:** http://www.centralparknyc.org. **Description:** For a refreshing pause amid city life, rent a rowboat or gondola for just a few bucks and paddle an hour or two away. It's a delightful, not to mention romantic pleasure and you don't really have to row very far. Bridges, fountains, and trees pass as you drift along. The cost is $10.00 for the first hour ($2.50 every 15 minutes after); split it with a companion and you've got a fun, cheap outing that'll energize you anew for returning to the daily grind. Just be prepared to leave a $30.00 cash deposit. Boating is available almost as soon as the lake defrosts in April, through the summer and fall.

CONEY ISLAND/ASTROLAND AMUSEMENT PARK

1000 Surf Avenue (at West 10th Street), Brooklyn NY. 718/372-0275. **Description:** This is it, kids, the original or what's left of it. Coney Island was one of the very first amusement parks in the country; a technological paradise meant to help people get comfortable with the Industrial Revolution. Today, though, we've gotten ahead of this kind of place, and it feels nostalgic. Still, you can have lots of fun here, on the rides or just strolling the three-mile boardwalk. (The Boardwalk offers free fireworks on Fridays in the summer.) It is a good idea to go during the daytime and keep a hand (your own) on your wallet; but police do maintain a strong presence, so you can enjoy yourself. For old-fashioned thrill-seekers, don't miss the Cyclone, circa 1927, one of the few classic wooden roller coasters left in America. If sand and surf are more your speed, sun yourself on the free beach. For $12.99 you can ride all the rides in Astroland. Or, if you prefer, you can buy tickets for individual rides for $1.75 - $4.00 per ride.

GATEWAY NATIONAL PARK

Floyd Bennett Field, Brooklyn NY 11234. 718/338-3799. **Description:** Did you know that Brooklyn has the largest urban park in the country? Gateway National Park is as wide open a space as you're likely to find anywhere in the metro area. In fact, its more than 26,000 acres extend out across the marshes of Queens, Staten Island, Brooklyn and Sandy Hook, New Jersey. The park offers a variety of activities year-round. For more information call 718/338-3688.

LASKER SKATING RINK

349 West 37th Street, New York NY 10018. 212/736-8700. **E-mail address:** info@laskerrink.com. **World Wide Web address:** http://www.laskerrink.com. **Description:** Located in Central Park, Lasker Skating Rink has been a well-kept secret -- much less crowded than the popular Wollman Memorial Rink. Adult admission is only $3.00, children's admission is $1.50, and skate rental costs

$3.50. Lasker doubles as a hockey rink, and also offers birthday parties. Open Monday through Thursday, 10:00 a.m. - 3:00 p.m.; Friday, 10:00 a.m. - 2:00 p.m.; TGIF (Live DJ), 11:00 a.m. - 9:00 p.m.; Saturday, 11:00 a.m. - 9:00 p.m.; Sunday, 11:00 a.m. - 6:00 p.m.

NEW YORK BOTANICAL GARDEN
200th Street & Kazimiroff Boulevard, Bronx NY 10458. 718/817-8700. **World Wide Web address:** http://www.nybg.org. **Description:** You like flowers? We've got flowers! The New York Botanical Garden is 250 acres of dazzling beauty and hands-on enjoyment, with 28 specialty gardens and plant collections including the Peggy Rockefeller Rose Garden and 40 acres of uncut forest. The garden's many different facilities offer hours of fun for everyone in the family. Take an ecotour of the world under glass in the Enid A. Haupt Conservatory, or let the kids explore nature in the Everett Children's Adventure Garden. The New York Botanical Garden offers a variety of money-saving passes including the Garden Passport, which includes grounds admission, the Conservatory, Rock and Native Plant Gardens, tram tour, and the Everett garden for $10.00 for adults, $7.50 for seniors and students, and $4.00 for kids under 12. If you prefer to buy admissions separately, grounds admission is $3.00 for adults, $2.00 for seniors and students, $1.00 for kids under 12 (kids under 2 are free). Grounds admission is free all day Wednesday, and on Saturday from 10:00 a.m. - 12:00 p.m. Conservatory admission is $3.50 for adults, $2.50 for seniors and students, and $2.00 for children under 12. The Everett Garden costs $3.00 for adults, $2.00 for seniors and students, and $1.00 for children under 12. Garden hours are Tuesday through Sunday and Monday holidays, 10:00 a.m. - 6:00 p.m. from April to October; and Tuesday through Sunday and Monday holidays, 10:00 a.m. - 4:00 p.m. from November to March. The Everett Children's Adventure Garden is open Tuesday through Friday, 1:00 p.m. - 6:00 p.m. from April to October; and Tuesday through Sunday, 10:00 a.m. - 6:00 p.m. from November to March.

NEW YORK CITY AUDUBON SOCIETY
71 West 23rd Street, Suite 606, New York NY 10010. 212/691-7483. **Description:** Go birding (yes, that's the word) with the best-known bird lovers in the world. Audubon Society adventures take place on the weekends to local sites, and occasionally to locations a day or overnight trip away. These are remarkably inexpensive. The society also offers slide lectures once a month, free and open to anyone interested. Call for details about upcoming events.

PROSPECT PARK/LITCHFIELD VILLA
95 Prospect Park West, Brooklyn NY 11215. 718/965-8951. **E-mail address:** prospect1@juno.com. **World Wide Web address:** http://www.prospectpark.org. **Description:** From the architects who brought you Central Park, 19th-century civic planners Frederick Law Olmsted and Calvert Vaux, Prospect Park has 526 acres and many of the same kinds of activities as its larger sibling.

On Prospect Lake, for instance, you can rent paddle boats for just $10.00 an hour with a $10.00 deposit; it's located near the Parkside and Ocean Avenue entrance, along the southern edge of the park. The famous Prospect Park Carousel is a fully-restored merry-go-round originally built in 1912, with a mighty Wurlitzer organ inside and 50 animals to ride on. It's like a magical time machine, and just $.50 a ride. Prospect Park is also full of great outdoor activities that are free or very inexpensive. In the winter you can skate in the Wollman Rink. Summer activities include fishing, bird watching, jogging, bicycling, walking tours, horseback riding, and inline skating, as well as live concerts and children's shows. Tour the park's two historic homes, Litchfield Villa and Lefferts Homestead, dating back to the 1800s and 1700s, respectively. Litchfield now also serves as the park's headquarters, where you can pick up more information. And this doesn't even get us to the Brooklyn Botanic Garden (see separate listing), which is yet another part of this magnificent park.

QUEENS WILDLIFE CENTER
111th Street & 53rd Avenue, Queens NY. 718/271-1500. **World Wide Web address:** http://www.wcs.org **Description:** Not quite The Bronx Zoo, but an adventure none the less. Queens Wildlife Center is located in Flushing Meadows Park and kids will love the interactive children's zoo and educational programs that are offered. Be sure to see the mountain lions, Roosevelt elk, and walk through the open aviary. Admission is $2.50 for adults, $1.25 for seniors, $.50 for children. Children under three gain free admission. Open daily, 10:00 a.m. - 4:30 p.m.

ROCKEFELLER CENTER
Midtown Manhattan (49th - 52nd Streets & Fifth - Seventh Avenues), New York NY. **Description:** You know, one of the great things about New York is that such everyday, prosaic buildings as your office or the local church can also be architectural masterpieces. Rockefeller Center is one such building. The buzzing that goes on here all day long makes it a wonder that any work gets done. Comprised of 19 buildings, Rockefeller Center is home to some of NYC's hottest attractions including NBC studios and Radio City Music Hall. NBC's *Today* show broadcasts from a storefront studio while you look on. Yet, Rockefeller Center also has much to offer in the way of art. Rockefeller Center is littered with mosaics and murals that could easily be found hanging in a museum. Be sure and snap a picture of the famed Prometheus and Atlas statues. And let's not forget two of Rockefeller Center's most famous images: the skating rink that takes over the dining area in the winter, and the gargantuan Christmas tree that could probably light up all five boroughs if given the opportunity. In that respect, winter travelers are getting an added bonus when visiting Rockefeller Center.

ROOSEVELT ISLAND TRAM AND PARKS
Second Avenue & 59th Street, New York NY. **World Wide Web address:** http://www.roosevelt-island.ny.us. **Description:** This

amusement park ride masquerading as public transit is one of New York's unique and cheap thrills. A mere $3.00 books you a round-trip passage in the completely enclosed gondola that glides up to a height of 250 feet above the East River, pulled along by giant gears. The trip is delightfully silent and gentle. Walk around from window to window: The majestic Queensboro Bridge rises alongside you to the south, while the Upper East Side stretches off to the north. Live the motorist's dream of floating above the traffic of First and York Avenues, a glittery sight at night. The ride lasts an all-too-short four minutes. Once you arrive on Roosevelt, explore its many activities, or hang out just a bit for the return voyage. On the island itself, climb aboard one of the red buses that link the Tramway Plaza with Octagon Park at the northern tip of the island. Geared as much to visitors as residents, it stops at several points of interest along the way. Or pick up a brochure at the bus stop for a self-guided walking tour of such features as Meditation Steps (photo-perfect views of passing ships, with Manhattan in the background). Nearby is the restored landmark Blackwell House, dating from 1796. This farmhouse is one of the oldest buildings left in New York City. To the north, Octagon Park's facilities include a soccer field, a baseball diamond, and six tennis courts, along with barbecue grills and community gardens. And further up is Lighthouse Park, built in 1872 from the island's own granite. Though it's no longer officially needed, the light still works. Indeed, you can spend a whole day on Roosevelt Island just four minutes to a getaway from the rat race.

STATEN ISLAND FERRY
One Bay Street, Staten Island NY 10301. 718/815-BOAT.
Description: Have a little time on your hands but no money in your pocket? It takes just half an hour to ferry from Battery Park, at the bottom of Manhattan, to the St. George terminal on Staten Island. Along the way, you'll pass the Brooklyn Heights promenade; the Statue of Liberty; Castle William and Fort Jay on Governor's Island; and of course, scenic New Jersey. Now you're probably saying to yourself, "Great idea. But how much money is it going to cost me?" Well, that's the great part: it's free! What a great way to while away a lunch hour, or to get away from the hustle and bustle of the city.

STATEN ISLAND ZOO
614 Broadway, Staten Island NY 10310. 718/442-3100.
Description: Hey, they've got one too! Much smaller than its famous Bronx counterpart, the Staten Island Zoo nevertheless makes the most of its compact size. This zoo is known across the country for its reptile collection, as well as its tropical forest, African savannah, and aquarium displays. There is no separate fee for entering the Children's Zoo, which is almost like a farm, with pony rides for the kiddies and opportunities to feed the animals. Admission is $3.00 for ages 12 and up, $2.00 for ages three to eleven, and free for kids under age three and zoo members. Wednesday afternoons from 2:00 to 4:45 p.m. are Donation Days, when you can pay what you wish to enter. They've even got free parking whether you've come by pony or Pontiac. Open daily.

WORLD TRADE CENTER OBSERVATION DECK

Two World Trade Center, New York NY 10048. 212/323-2340.
Description: Okay, so maybe it's not the cheapest place you could visit, but who can resist the adventurous lure of positioning yourself atop the world's highest outdoor viewing platform? If your stay is brief, visiting the World Trade Center Observation Deck can help maximize your sightseeing time: on a clear day, visitors can see more than 55 miles of pure New York City! There's even a recently installed exhibit that lets you take a simulated helicopter ride around the city. While calling itself the workplace to more than 50,000 people each day, the World Trade Center is also home to more than 70 restaurants and retail shops, so there's sure to be something to fit everyone's budget. The Observation Deck is open seven days a week (including holidays) from 9:30 a.m. - 9:30 p.m.; in the heavily-traveled summer months (June - August), the Observation Deck remains open until 11:30 p.m. Adult admission is $12.50; senior $9.50; children under 12 are $6.25.

ENTERTAINMENT
📖 Readings, Poetry, & Literary Events 📖

THE ACADEMY OF AMERICAN POETS
584 Broadway, Suite 1208, New York NY 10012. 212/274-0343.
World Wide Web address: http://www.poets.org. **Description:**
Founded in 1934, to support poets at all stages of their careers
and to foster the appreciation of contemporary poetry, The
Academy of American Poets is the country's largest organization
dedicated specifically to the art of poetry. Nationally, the
Academy sponsors a variety of programs and awards including the
Academy Fellowship for distinguished poetic achievement; the
Tanning Prize for outstanding and proven mastery in the art of
poetry; the Lenore Marshall Poetry Prize; the James Laughlin
Award; and the Walt Whitman Award. Each April, the Academy
coordinates National Poetry Month, an annual celebration of the
richness and diversity of American poetry. Throughout the year,
they host several poetry readings and other poetry events. To find
out about upcoming events, call or visit their Website.

ART IN GENERAL
79 Walker Street, New York NY. 212/219-0473. **Description:**
That's actually the name of an art gallery in the TriBeCa section,
very much a part of the hip world downtown. Along with its
exhibitions, AIG often presents free talks about the arts scene in
New York. Call to find out what's coming up.

BERNARD SHAW SOCIETY
AMERICAN-IRISH HISTORICAL SOCIETY
991 Fifth Avenue (at 80th Street), New York NY 10028. 212/288-
2263. **Description:** No, not the guy from CNN. For almost 50
years, lovers of the Irish bard have gathered periodically to read
out and listen to his many plays and essays. Afterwards there is
much animated discussion of the philosophical ideas brought out.
While membership only costs $20.00 a year, giving reduced-price
admission to the readings, these are also open to the general
public for $5.00 per person. For more details, your best bet is to
write to them at P.O. Box 1159, Madison Square Station, New
York, NY 10159-1159 and get on their mailing list.

COOPER UNION FOR THE ADVANCEMENT OF SCIENCE AND ART
Cooper Square, Third Avenue (at 7th Street), New York NY.
212/353-4195. **World Wide Web address:** http://www.
cooper.edu. **Description:** In 1859, Peter Cooper founded a noted
school of art and science and The Great Hall as a forum for public
education and culture. Great Hall speakers have included Abraham
Lincoln, Salmon Rushdie, Jane Addams, and Judy Chicago. To this
day, a distinguished slate of authors, poets, scientists, musicians,
and performers regularly share their talents with the public.

Recent events -- many of which were free -- have included such guests as Tibor Kalman, Bill Clinton, Barbara Cook, James Levine, and Tony Randall. Other events have included free walks of Greenwich Village and a recreation of the Astor Place Riots. If not free, programs rarely cost more than $15.00. Stop by and pick up a free brochure of upcoming events. While you're there, be sure and stop by their free historical exhibit "Great Moments in The Great Hall".

NEW YORK HISTORICAL SOCIETY

2 West 77th Street (at Central Park West), New York NY 10024. 212/873-3400. **World Wide Web address:** http://www. nyhistory.org. **Description:** The history of the New York Historical Society is almost as long and fascinating as the history of New York itself. Founded in 1804, the New York Historical Society houses a variety of permanent and changing fine and decorative art exhibits. The society's library is also one of the nation's oldest research libraries, calling itself home to 500,000 books and pamphlets; 2 million manuscripts; 10,000 newspapers; 10,000 maps; and hundreds of thousands of photos, architecture plans, and prints spanning more than four centuries. As might be expected, the society's dedication to exploring the history of New York extends to such educational programs as lectures and informal discussions with topics ranging from the architecture of NYC, to the impact of the publishing industry, to the city's strong sense of ethnic pride. New York Historical Society also offers occasional musical performances. Admission is a suggested donation of $5.00 for adults, and $3.00 for seniors and students. Open Tuesday through Saturday, 11:00 a.m. - 5:00 p.m.

NEW YORK PUBLIC LIBRARY

455 Fifth Avenue (at 42nd Street), New York NY 10016. 212/340-0849. **World Wide Web address:** http://www.nypl.org. **Description:** Where else to hear the written word spoken but the grand marble hall of the library's Celeste Bartos Forum, at the main branch? NYPL's Public Education Program brings a full slate of authors and lecturers to the auditorium. Recent guests have included Stuart Curran, expert on the poet Shelley; author E.L. Doctorow; and urban sociologist Robert Coles. These begin at 6:00 p.m.; call the number listed to get on the mailing list. Tickets are $10.00 for the general public, available in advance at the Library Shop (Room 116) or at the door if seats are still available. Many talks sell out; you can try the standby line, but success is not guaranteed. This branch also sponsors book discussion groups focusing on literary classics from Dickens to Stendhal, and are free of course; but space is limited, so you must register in advance. Among the many activities at NYPL's branch libraries, the Donnell Library Center at 20 West 53rd Street (212/621-0618) is another location for regular lectures and readings, as well as children's storytelling.

92^(ND) STREET YMCA

1395 Lexington Avenue (at 92nd Street), New York NY 10128. 212/415-5440. **Description:** This Upper East Side cultural and community center has long been famous for its concerts and literary readings. For over 60 years, the Y has been presenting such eminent authors as Kurt Vonnegut and Susan Faludi, along with adventurous series like the Native American Literature Festival. Prices range from $12.00 - $15.00.

NUYORICAN POETS CAFE

236 East 3rd Street, New York NY 10009. 212/505-8183. **World Wide Web address:** http://www.nuyorican.com. **Description:** This place embodies many of the best aspects of the revitalized East Village; it combines the beauty of words and music with the gritty realities of everyday life in a setting that is on the border of both. That border is the rough area of Alphabet City, a neighborhood that is catching up to the gentrification just across Tompkins Park. Here the barrio meets artists seeking lower rents, and they both meet the yuppies who flock to this exciting scene. The Nuyorican Poets Cafe presents dedicated, hard-working poets who read their works to appreciative audiences. Musicians are often on the bill as well, and the whole evening generally has a touch of various ethnic cultures. That, after all, is the New York experience. Nuyorican has even been the studio for live radio drama broadcasts. The cover charge for most shows is usually $10.00 or less, with no drink minimum. There can be two sets to an evening, which may mean an extra charge for the second show. And don't miss the annual Poetry Slam, a sort of competitive literary sport. The Nuyorican puts a modern twist on the coffeehouses of the 1960s; only back then, these were in the other Village.

THE POETRY PROJECT

St. Mark's Church, 131 East 10th Street, New York NY 10003. 212/674-0910. **World Wide Web address:** http://www. poetryproject.com. **Description:** Diagonally facing Second Avenue in the East Village, St. Mark's Church is well known among the arts community for its full schedule of theater, dance, and poetry readings. All of these take place in its large, airy theatrical space, with various performance times; but there seems to be something going on nearly every week. Call or stop by for flyers and schedules. Recent readings included Sherman Alexie, Robert Creeley, and Alice Notley. Admission is $7.00, $3.00 for students and members.

POETRY SOCIETY OF AMERICA

15 Gramercy Park, New York NY. 212/254-9628. **Description:** Since 1910, this organization has been presenting contemporary poets reading from their latest works as well as tributes to canonical writers in such wide-ranging locales as the New York Public Library, the United Nations, and Central Park. A recent program offered a Tribute to Octavio Paz at the Metropolitan Museum of Art. Admission to the society's events is free, unless otherwise noted. For a calendar of upcoming activities or membership information, call on any weekday.

POETS HOUSE

72 Spring Street, 2nd Floor, New York NY 10012. 212/431-7920. **E-mail address:** info@poetshouse.org. **World Wide Web address:** http://www.poetshouse.org. **Description:** An ode to Poets

House: Poets House is a comfortable and accessible place for poetry, a meeting place that invites poets and everyday Joes and Janes (like you) to step into the living tradition of poetry. Poets House offers a variety of resources and literary events that help to promote the long-lived poetic culture, and further stimulate the public's interest in and knowledge of poetry. Their 35,000-volume poetry library includes a variety of resources including books, journals, audio tapes, videos, and reference materials. Poets House is free to use and open to the public Tuesday through Friday, 11:00 a.m. - 7:00 p.m.; Saturday, 11:00 a.m. - 4:00 p.m.

THE WRITER'S VOICE OF THE WEST SIDE YMCA

5 West 63rd Street, New York NY 10023. 212/875-4124. **E-mail address:** WtrsVoice1@aol.com. **World Wide Web address:** http://users.aol.com/wtrsvoice1/files/WVintro.html. **Description:** The flagship of a national network of literary arts centers based at YMCAs. The Writer's Voice of the West Side YMCA offers writing workshops, a public readings series in the spring and fall, an international writing competition, and publishes the WV literary magazine. Come and hear emerging and noted authors, from free-for-all open-mike sessions to Nikki Giovanni. Readings take place in The Little Theater. Programs begin at 7:30 p.m. Admission is usually $5.00, though open-mike readings and other events are sometimes free. College students and senior citizens receive a reduced admission price, and children under 18 are admitted free.

ENTERTAINMENT
♈ Sports ♈

AMSTERDAM BILLIARD CLUB
344 Amsterdam Avenue (at 77th Street), New York NY. 212/496-8180. ♦ 210 East 86th Street (between Second & Third Avenues), New York NY. 212/570-4545. **World Wide Web address:** http://www.amsterdambilliards.com. **Description:** A billiards hall voted number one in the U.S.A. by *Billiards Digest*. If you are a beginner or just want to pick up the latest techniques, the club offers lessons. Pool Clinics include three lessons of an hour and 15 minutes for $24.00 and private lessons are $35.00 an hour. There is also Ping-Pong, a full-service bar, and big screen television. Opens everyday at 11:00 a.m.

AQUEDUCT RACETRACK
110th Street & Rockaway Boulevard, Queens NY 11420. 212/641-4700. **World Wide Web address:** http://www.nyra.com/aqueduct. **Description:** It's no wonder this place is referred to as Big A. With the capacity to hold approximately 90,000 people, Aqueduct Racetrack certainly is big! Aqueduct offers year-round racing and simulcast betting to all those who are daring enough to place a wager. Now, while in certain cases, a day at the track may cost more than the allotted Mr. Cheap cut-off, if you're looking for an exciting day where the chance to parlay your small savings into a minor fortune is actually possible, then this it. Pick your horses based on color, name, luck, or statistical formulas, it's up to you. A supervised playroom allows kids aged five - 12 to engage in a variety of arts and crafts projects and games. There is also an enormous video arcade located right outside the playroom. When the hunger hits, try one of the track's many dining establishments like the Big A Grill, Hello Deli, or The Man O' War Room. There is also a food court offering fast food for those on the go (or those on a budget). Throughout the year, Aqueduct also hosts a number of promotional events and activities including festivities for all the major races (Kentucky Derby, Breeder's Cup, etc.), and holiday fun (St. Patrick's Day, Thanksgiving, etc.). Grandstand admission is $1.00, clubhouse admission is $3.00, and skyline club admission is $4.00. Children under 12 are admitted free. Parking is also available for $1.00 - $5.00. Gates open at 11:00 a.m. everyday. For more information, give them a call. And when you hit that long-shot superfecta, don't forget who sent you!

BOWLMOR LANES
110 University Place (between 12th & 13th Streets), New York NY 10016. 212/255-8188. **Description:** Combine bowling lanes with funky dance music, artwork, and a bar with a waitstaff that delivers drinks to your lane, and you've got one hip alley. Now a city landmark that is known to attract some famous faces, the 42-

lane alley costs $4.95 - $6.45, plus $3.00 to rent shoes. The Lanes End Lounge serves several entrees as well as gourmet pizzas, burgers, sandwiches, and appetizers. Open Monday, 10:00 a.m. - 4:00 a.m.; Tuesday through Wednesday, 10:00 a.m. - 1:00 a.m.; Thursday, 10:00 a.m. - 2:00 a.m.; Friday and Saturday, 10:00 a.m. - 4:00 a.m.; Sunday, 10:00 a.m. - 1:00 p.m.

CHELSEA BILLIARDS
54 West 21st Street, New York NY. 212/989-0096. **Description:** If you want to shoot pool and nothing else, this is the place for you. Chelsea Billiards is open 24 hours and offers 44 tables, strong coffee, and the basics in food. Prices are between $8.00 and $10.00 and hour.

CHELSEA PIERS SPORTS & ENTERTAINMENT COMPLEX
West 23rd Street & the Hudson River, New York NY. 212/336-6666. **World Wide Web address:** http://www.chelseapiers.com. **Description:** Sports enthusiasts will find just about everything under the sun at Chelsea Piers. Here you can roller skate, bowl, hit the driving range, rock climb, or join a lacrosse league! There is something to suit everyone. One of the major draws here is the Sky Rink. Aptly named because it is 16 floors up, it seems as though you can skate right on into the heavens. With two indoor rinks catering to ice skating in all its many incarnations (including figure skating and ice hockey), and a 24-hour year-round schedule, a visit to Sky Rink is easy to fit into your daily plans. General skating fees are $10.50 for adults and $8.50 for children. If you forgot to pack your skates, you can rent a pair for $5.00. Call for times and further information. Check the Website for prices of individual activities.

CROSSTOWN TENNIS CLUB
14 West 31st Street (between Fifth Avenue & Broadway), New York NY 10001. 212/947-5780. **World Wide Web address:** http://www.tennisnetwork.com/crosstown. **Description:** This facility is one of the city's finest public tennis clubs. Because it is open to the public, there are no membership fees. Features include 18-foot back courts, four Championship DecoTurf tennis courts, and "true ball bounce." The club offers private, semi-private, and group lessons as well as private corporate, birthday, and children's parties.

GATEWAY SPORTS CENTER
3200 Flatbush Avenue, Brooklyn NY 11234. 718/253-6816. **Description:** Part of the Gateway National Park, near Floyd Bennett Field, Gateway Sports has a golf driving range with 100 practice tees; also, a full 18-hole miniature golf course, tennis courts, and baseball batting cages, all at reasonable rates. Call them for more information.

NEW YORK YANKEES
Yankee's Stadium, 161st Street (at River Avenue), Bronx NY 10451. 718/293-4300. **World Wide Web address:** http://www.yankees.com. **Description:** Want to get the ultimate New York experience? Travel the 20 minutes from Midtown to Yankee

Stadium where hometown pride ensues in an often-chaotic but always fun mix of hot dogs, beer, and baseball. Tickets will cost you anywhere between $8.00 for a bleacher seat and $29.00 for a field-level box. For senior citizens, the deal is even sweeter; tickets are just $2.00 on game day. Just remember that the cheaper the seat, the rowdier the crowd...but isn't that what adds to the excitement? For those of you with children, who would prefer to keep all their innocence intact, the Yanks offer family seating, where "non-alcoholic" is the key word. To keep your visit even cheaper, be sure to bring your own food and drinks. Though a hot dog can be tempting at any ball game, you'll save a lot by bringing your own food (and you won't have to spend any extra cash on a bottle of Tums either). And please, as a word of caution, I don't care how die-hard a fan you are, if you are NOT a Yankee fan, do NOT wear any opposing team paraphernalia!! Then again, this would save you the money of having to buy food and drinks, as fans will feel free to throw them at you. For tickets, you can call the Ticketmaster Yankee Hotline at 212/307-1212.

SoHo BILLIARDS AND SPORT CENTER
56 East Houston Street (at Mulberry Street), New York NY 10012. 212/925-3753. **Description:** A neighborhood place with SoHo pizzazz. Most rack 'em up before hitting the town. Rates are $7.00 per hour with an additional $2.00 per added person. Open daily, 11:00 a.m. - 3:00 a.m.

26 MAMMOTH BILLIARD
114 West 26th Street, Floor 1, New York NY 10001. 212/675-2626. **Description:** This is one of New York's largest indoor sports facilities, offering pool, Ping-Pong, billiards, snooker, and golf. Yes, golf. They actually have an indoor driving range, and there are even lessons available to help you perfect your swing here in town so you'll look better the next time you get out onto the course. It's also a great place for private parties, which can accommodate up to two hundred people. That should give you an idea of the size of this place. Open 24 hours a day, seven days a week.

WOLLMAN MEMORIAL RINK IN CENTRAL PARK
59th Street & Avenue of the Americas, New York NY 10019. 212/396-1010. **E-mail address:** wollmanrink@hotmail.com. **Description:** At the north end of The Pond, this is the city's largest outdoor rink, used for ice skating in winter (roughly, October through April) and inline skating in summer. Be warned that as one of the most well-known rinks in New York, Wollman Memorial Rink is also one of the most bustling. If you want to show off some of your near-Olympian toe loops or triple Axels, you may want to get up extra early and participate in one of the early-morning Figure Skating & Ice Dance sessions. Sessions are for advanced skaters only and you must bring your own skates. Join in the near-dawn fun Monday through Friday, 6:30 a.m. - 10:00 a.m.; and Sunday, 8:30 a.m. - 10:00 a.m. In the winter, the rink is open Monday and Tuesday, 10:00 a.m. - 3:00 p.m.; Wednesday and Thursday, 10:00 a.m. - 5:30 p.m.; Friday and Saturday, 10:00 a.m. - 11:00 p.m.; and Sunday 10:00 a.m. - 9:00 p.m. Winter admission is $7.00 for adults and $3.50 for kids under 12. Ice skate rentals

are $3.50. In the summer, the rink is open Thursday and Friday, 11:00 a.m. - 6:00 p.m.; and Saturday and Sunday, 11:00 a.m. - 8:00 p.m. Inline skates with accompanying safety gear rentals are $6.00. Also, the safety gear alone is available for rent for a mere $3.00 (a smart buy if you plan on enjoying any more of Mr. C's tips).

WORLD'S FAIR ICE SKATING RINK

New York City Building, Flushing-Meadows Corona Park, Queens NY 11368. 718/271-1996. **Description:** Queens borough is not to be left out in the cold when it comes to ice skating, either. This park, of course, is the direct descendant of the 1939 New York World's Fair. The 18,000-square-foot rink is open on weekends, with certain day and evening times during the week. Admission for all ages is $4.00 - $7.00, depending on the session; skate rentals cost $4.50. The rink requires children under 18 to get parental permission forms signed before they can skate.

ENTERTAINMENT
 ## Theater

JEAN COCTEAU REPERATORY
BOUWERIE LANE THEATRE
330 Bowery, New York NY 10012. 212/677-0060. **E-mail address:** cocteau@jeancocteaurep.org. **World Wide Web address:** http://www.jeancocteaurep.org. **Description:** At the small but stately Bouwerie Lane Theater, the Cocteau Reperatory has been staging critically acclaimed productions of the world's classics for two decades. Performances include *On The Razzle* by Tom Stoppard, *The Balcony* by Jean Genet, and *Medea* by Euripides. Don't worry about the troupe's French name, or its international slate of authors; everything's done in English. Tickets are $30.00, and preview performances are $24.00. Tickets for seniors are $24.00, and full-time students who bring a current ID can get discounted tickets at $15.00. Performances are Wednesday through Saturday, 8:00 p.m., and Sunday, 3:00 p.m.

DIXON PLACE AT VINEYARD 26
309 East 26th Street, New York NY. 212/532-1546. **World Wide Web address:** http://www.dixonplace.org. **Description:** Dixon Place at Vineyard 26 presents very progressive entertainment at rock-bottom prices. See staged readings of new plays still in the works, and wild experimental dance; hear the latest in poetry and fiction. Instead of stand-up comedians you may see a stand-up tragedian; and a variety of creative artists under that vague umbrella of performance art. Yes, the subject matter here tends to be... very liberal and open-minded. You should be too! Tickets are generally $0.00 - $12.00, depending on the show.

GENE FRANKEL THEATRE & FILM WORKSHOP
24 Bond Street, New York NY 10012. 212/777-1767. **Description:** Looking for an unusual night of theater? This is one of New York's top teaching studios, located in the lower corner of the East Village. Frankel, who has been teaching the school's major classes in acting, directing and writing for many years, is considered one of the founding fathers of the Off-Broadway movement (he's directed on Broadway, too). Among his grads are Judd Hirsch, Loretta Swit, Raul Julia, and Walter Matthau. Regularly throughout the year, his current classes present evenings of scenes and monologues in this unexpectedly lavish and professionally outfitted theater. Admission is free, but reservations are necessary. Call for the next showcase dates.

LA MAMA EXPERIMENTAL THEATRE
74A East 4th Street, New York NY 10003. 212/475-7710. **E-mail address:** office@lamama.org. **World Wide Web address:** http://www.lamama.org. **Description:** Over several decades, La MaMa has consistently presented the most daring and successful of modern theater's experimental artists. Works by playwrights

like Lanford Wilson and Sam Shepard have been developed here, as well as more avant-garde pieces by performance artists Meredith Monk, Ping Chong and more. A wide variety of troupes have been seen in La MaMa's three different flexible theater spaces. Ticket prices vary but are seldom higher than $15.00 and many performances allow Theatre Development Fund discounts (see separate listing). There is also an art gallery displaying the works of local painters and sculptors; the place is a real haven for the downtown arts community. For more information on upcoming shows, call or visit their Website. You can also send them an e-mail to get on their mailing list or call the box office to order tickets at 212/475-7710.

NEW DRAMATISTS
424 West 44th Street, New York NY 10036. 212/757-6960. **Description:** Dedicated, as you might guess, to the development of original plays, New Dramatists is one of those insider's finds; a place to discover a hit play well before it reaches Broadway, and at no cost. Yes, tickets are free for most of their showcases (don't expect much in the way of sets, lighting, or costumes), because the playwrights are seeking honest audience reactions to their writing. Tickets can be in great demand; so get your name on their mailing list.

OHIO THEATRE
66 Wooster Street, New York NY 10012. 212/966-4844. **Description:** If you're into downtown, avant-garde, in-your-face theater, this is a great place to find it. Ohio Theatre presents a variety of theatrical troupes, like House of Borax (gaining a reputation of its own for performing innovative plays in unusual locales like bars and dance clubs); TWEED, or TheaterWorks: Emerging/Experimental Directions; and many other dance and performance art groups. They've been doing so for over 15 years, a lifetime in these circles. The 75-seat house is in a loft space inside an old industrial building in the heart of SoHo. Tickets here tend to be in the $10.00 range, a small price to pay for certain adventure.

P.S. 122
150 First Avenue (at East 9th Street), New York NY 10009. 212/477-5288. **World Wide Web address:** http://www.ps122.org. **Description:** Once it meant Public School. Now it means Performance Space. On the outside, little has changed; but once you go in, you'll see things they never taught when you were growing up. Eric Bogosian played here in his early days, as did Spalding Gray. P.S. 122 specializes in the most outrageous of the avant-garde, simultaneously on two floors. Programs may range from new music to gay monologues to raucous dance performances. Admission is free; regular shows are between $12.00 and $30.00.

THE PERFORMING GARAGE
33 Wooster Street, New York NY. 212/966-9796. **Description:** The Performing Garage is a breeding ground for great

experimental theater and dance, and one of the best-known in the city. It is the home base of the performance ensemble The Wooster Group; Spalding Gray and Willem Dafoe are perhaps the best-known members of the company. As it has become one of the better-known downtown venues, it is now a bit pricier than it once was. Tickets range from $12.00 to $35.00, depending on the event.

PLAYWRIGHTS HORIZONS
416 West 42nd Street, New York NY 10036. 212/564-1235. **World Wide Web address:** http://www.playwrightshorizons.org. **Description:** If you love American theater, chances are you already know Playwrights Horizons. It's the only theater in New York City dedicated solely to the creation and production of new American plays and musicals. Playwrights Horizons, the cornerstone of Theater Row, provides an artistic home for playwrights, composers and lyricists--from the emerging newcomer, to the accomplished veteran--to work in an environment of trust, collaboration, support, and experimentation. Established almost thirty years ago, Playwrights Horizons has presented the work of over 300 writers, and has been the recipient of numerous awards and honors including Tonys, Obies, Outer Critics Award, and Pulitzer Prizes. To name just a few of the acclaimed plays that debuted on the Playwrights Horizons stage: Wendy Wasserstein's *The Heidi Chronicles*, Alfred Uhry's *Driving Miss Daisy*, William Finn's *Falsettos*, and Stephen Sondheim and James Lapine's *Sunday in the Park With George*. Purchase one of Playwrights Horizons' package plans, and save even more money on tickets. Call for the upcoming season schedule.

THE PUBLIC THEATER/NEW YORK SHAKESPEARE FESTIVAL
425 Lafayette Street, New York NY. 212/539-8750. **World Wide Web address:** http://www.publictheater.org. **Description:** What the late Joseph Papp started, with a bunch of actors performing Shakespeare for free in Central Park, has grown into a huge, year-round operation. Perhaps the anchor of the downtown theater scene, The Public Theater presents a full season of adventurous works by the world's leading artists. Shakespeare is still the main man here (NYSF is working its way through all of the Bard's plays, one or two each year); but this is also the place where *A Chorus Line* first kicked up its heels. In between you may see rare plays of Samuel Beckett, controversial and political performance artists, films, readings, and late-night cabaret. It's all at Off-Broadway prices; most shows are no higher than $45.00, about half of the top rates uptown. But there are even better bargains here. The Public offers Quiktix to most of its shows, subject to availability, at prices of $10.00 - $15.00. These are sold on a first come, first served basis at the box office 30 minutes before each show. There are occassional behind-the-scenes discussions with the playwrights, actors and directors, as well as Public Books, readings by noted authors (like Susan Sontag, Tama Janowitz, and Stephen Jay Gould). For most readings, there is a suggested donation of $5.00 and a general admission and members fee of $3.00.

PULSE ENSEMBLE THEATRE

432 West 42nd Street, New York NY 10036. 212/695-1596.
Description: For those whose interests lie beyond Broadway, why not try this small theater? Home to 40 ensemble performers the theater offers something for everyone. This past year, performances have included one man shows, *Juno & the Paycock*, a street version of *MacBeth*, and a look at the "real-life" *Kramer* (made famous on *Seinfeld*). Shows are Monday through Saturday from 2:00 p.m. - 10:00 p.m. and tickets are $12.00 - $20.00.

T. SCHREIBER STUDIO

151 West 26th Street, 7th Floor, New York NY 10001. 212/741-0209. **World Wide Web address:** http://www.t-s-s.org. **Description:** Like the *Gene Frankel Workshop* nearby (see separate listing), the T. Schreiber Studio allows you a peek into the creative processes by which actors and directors learn their craft. Notable actors who have emerged from the prestigious studio include two-time-Oscar-nominated Edward Norton, Annabella Sciorra, and Whit Stillman staple Taylor Nichols. From September through June, the Director's Unit stages new and little-known plays for four-week runs; admission is just $12.00. The artists on both sides of the footlights are students with varying degrees of professional experience; yet the overall quality is quite strong. Go on opening night, usually the first Saturday of the run, and you can attend the wine and hors d'ouevre reception afterwards (it's quite a spread). Rub elbows with the actors and talk about the work you've just seen, all for only $25.00. Call for schedules.

SHAKESPEARE IN CENTRAL PARK

Delacorte Theater, New York NY. 212/539-8750. **World Wide Web address:** http://www.publictheater.org. **Description:** This is where it all began for Joseph Papp and the now-mighty Public Theater. They haven't forgotten their humble roots; free Shakespeare in the park remains one of New York City's most joyous treasures. The New York Shakespeare Festival presents two or three different plays each summer on this large outdoor stage, with its elaborate scenery and lighting; usually, at least one offering is by Shakespeare, with other, more modern plays mixed in. The performers are Broadway's best, often with a Kevin Kline or an Patrick Stewart at the top of the bill. Getting a ticket, alas, is almost as hard as getting a Broadway audition. The shows are regular sellouts. So how do you get in on the act? You wait. Curtain time is 8:00 p.m., and they start distributing the free tickets at 1:00 p.m. at the Delacorte Theater, and between 1:00 p.m. - 3:00 p.m. at The Public Theater (425 Lafayette Street). Only two tickets are allotted per person and believe me, they don't last long. Folks start camping out early: they bring picnic baskets, set out blankets and lawn chairs, and have a jolly old time while waiting. It's all part of the whole experience. Oh, and don't forget to bring a parasol for the sun, or an umbrella for the rain.

THEATER DEVELOPMENT FUND

1501 Broadway, Suite 2110, New York NY 10036. 212/221-0013. E-mail address: info@tdf.org. **World Wide Web address:** http://www.tdf.org. **Description:** If you covet a life in the theater from the audience side, but can't afford to go as often as you'd like, consider joining this nonprofit agency. Theater Development Fund helps people in many low-paying professions save money on tickets to Broadway shows, Off-Broadway, and beyond. At the same time, of course, they're helping the theaters themselves by putting more fannies in their seats. To qualify, you have to be in the arts yourself; or a teacher, student, senior citizen, union member, clergyperson or member of the armed forces. If you're eligible to join, a $15.00 membership fee will magically entitle you to see Broadway shows, dance, and concerts for as little as $13.00 - $26.00 per ticket. You can also purchase special Theater Development Fund vouchers, just $28.00 per book of four, which can be presented for discounts or free tickets to many other shows for one year. Write to the address above for information on how to join.

THEATREWORKS USA
151 West 26th Street (between Avenue of the Americas & Seventh Avenues), New York NY. 212/647-1100. **World Wide Web address:** http://www1.playbill.com/twusa. **Description:** One of the nation's largest professional theater companies for family audiences. Shows are geared toward younger audiences, with stage performances of some of their favorite books and characters such as Ramona Quimby, Curious George, and Oliver Twist. From October through April, Theatreworks USA presents weekend performances at the Auditorium at Equitable Tower (787 Seventh Avenue) at 12:30 p.m. (with occasional 10:30 a.m. showings as well). Tickets are $19.00 each. During the summer months, the company presents its Free Summer Series for two weeks. Performances are free to children and their families and to out-of-town visitors. Performances are at 11:00 a.m. and 1:00 p.m. Call for specific shows and times.

TKTS BOOTH
Times Square (Broadway & 47th Street), New York NY 10036. ◆ 2 World Trade Center, Mezzanine Level, New York NY. **World Wide Web address:** http://www.tdf.org. **Description:** Not eligible to join the Theatre Development Fund? Don't despair. For everybody else, the organization runs the always-popular TKTS booths at three locations around the city, offering half-price tickets for Broadway and Off-Broadway shows. If a show has lots of seats available for that afternoon or evening's performance, they may send a batch of tickets over to the booths, where they sell at half their face value, plus a service charge of $2.50 per ticket. With top Broadway prices above $75.00, you can save a lot. Of course, you have to hope your show is listed on the daily boards at the front (always be armed with several choices). Available tickets are spread among the two outposts; but the Times Square branch is the most popular. Don't be daunted by the long lines, which, during tourist seasons especially, often double back on themselves. Once the windows open for business, workers at the front always keep

the lines moving very quickly. In the meantime, everyone seems to enjoy lots of showbiz chat. Another good tip from Mr. C: consider waiting until the last minute. When there's about half an hour to go before curtain, there are usually no lines but lots of shows are still available. Some actually release more tickets at this time, including hard-to-get seats up front; you may even find a mega-hit, which hadn't been on the boards all day, suddenly become available. You can buy tickets at Times Square from 3:00 p.m. - 8:00 p.m. for Monday through Saturday evening performances, and from 10:00 a.m. - 2:00 p.m. for Wednesday and Saturday matinees (no evening tickets sold before 3:00 p.m.!). Sunday hours are from 12:00 p.m. until the latest curtain time for available shows. Hours at the World Trade Center branch are Monday through Friday, 11:00 a.m. - 5:30 p.m., and Saturday, 11:00 a.m. - 3:30 p.m. *$Cash Only$*

WEST BANK CAFE
407 West 42nd Street (between 9th & 10th Avenues), New York NY 10036. 212/695-6909. **Description:** In its Downstairs Theatre Bar, this popular night spot presents an ever-changing variety of plays, cabaret, and comedy. On any given Wednesday through Sunday, you may find political dramas, risqué comedy revues, or just plain music. These shows feature professional actors and singers, many of whom work regularly on Broadway and Off-Broadway stages; they can use this stage rent-free, and so it's become an in place to try out new material or original plays. Admission is usually $10.00 or less. You never know what you may get then, but it's sure to be lively.

ENTERTAINMENT
🏃 Walks & Tours 🏃

ADVENTURE ON A SHOESTRING

300 West 53rd Street, New York NY. 212/265-2663.
Description: The name alone makes this a favorite. Not only does Adventure on a Shoestring offer the least-expensive walking tours in town, they have a huge, ever-changing selection of standard and unusual tours. They're also one of the originals in this business; Howard Goldberg founded the company in 1963, and he maintains a personal approach. Goldberg is clearly in love with New York. Along with the basic guided walks through areas like Chelsea, Long Island, and Little Italy, he's also taken people to the Little Odessa neighborhood at Brighton Beach. He's taken people across the Brooklyn Bridge on its birthday, backstage at the Met, and through a fortune cookie factory in Chinatown. And offbeat tours like Haunted Midtown or Haunted Greenwich Village lead you through those area's that are allegedly inhabited by the undead...I hope you don't scare too easily. Some tours have gone as far afield as New Hope, PA, but most take place in and around Manhattan. Often you'll meet with people who live in these areas; to get a personal flavor many tours wind up in coffee shops, chatting over a pastry. Most important of all, Goldberg knows the locations of just about every restroom on the island. Oh, and about the price: it's just $5.00 per person, virtually the same as it was almost 40 years ago. This is half-price (or better) than most other tours in town. Memberships are available for frequent walkers, reducing the prices even further to $3.00. Call to get on the mailing list.

BROOKLYN CENTER FOR THE URBAN ENVIRONMENT

Tennis House, Prospect Park, Brooklyn NY. 718/788-8500.
Description: This nonprofit organization runs inexpensive tours throughout the year, focusing on various neighborhoods around Brooklyn. Offerings can range from a noshing tour of Sunset Park to a trip into the lost subway of Atlantic Avenue. The average prices for tours are $6.00 for members, $8.00 for non-members, and $5.00 for students and seniors.

THE BROOKLYN HISTORICAL SOCIETY
BROOKLYN WALK AND BROOKLYN TALKS

128 Pierrepont Street (at Clinton Street), Brooklyn NY 11201. 718/624-0890. **World Wide Web address:** http://www. brooklynhistory.org. **Description:** Begun in 1863 as the Long Island Historical Society, back when Brooklyn was considered a city getaway, this organization grew into one of New York's foremost preservationists. Until early 2001, the Society will still be offering its Brooklyn Walks & Brooklyn Talks series. When Mr. C visited, the Society had scheduled a late morning tour of Sunset Park, a mid-day tour of Flatbush (oldest church in the City), and an evening slide show and discussion on the history of New York City.

Fees are $5.00 for members, $10.00 for non-members. Call to get a schedule of upcoming events and to make reservations. The Society also offers Brooklyn-related workshops and after-school programs for children.

CARNEGIE HALL & THE ROSE MUSEUM

Seventh Avenue & 57th Street, New York NY. 212/903-9790. **World Wide Web address:** http://www.carnegiehall.org. **Description:** How do you get to Carnegie Hall? Pay the price of admission. From September through June, interested music lovers can tour the famed hall and learn lots of the backstage gossip. The Rose Museum at Carnegie Hall furthers this musical tradition by housing some of the hall's most treasured memorabilia including photographs and letters. Carnegie Hall also welcomes families to come and bask in the glory that is music. Family concerts are held on Saturday afternoons throughout the season and include a variety of educational activities for kids and their parents to participate in. Tickets are only $5.00 each. For more information on Family Concerts, call 212/903-9670. Carnegie Hall tours run Monday, Tuesday, Thursday, and Friday at 11:30 a.m., 2:00 p.m., and 3:00 p.m. Admission is $6.00 for adults; $5.00 for students and seniors; and $3.00 for children under 12. The Rose Museum is open every day except Wednesday from 11:00 a.m. to 4:30 p.m. Museum admission is free.

EMPIRE STATE BUILDING

350 Fifth Avenue (at 34th Street), New York NY 10118. 212/736-3100. **Description:** Even though it's the second tallest skyscraper in New York, the Empire State Building is still the best bargain for mega-viewers. Visit the 86th-floor outdoor observatory, or the indoor version on the 102nd-floor. For a favorite activity among kids and adults alike, try the New York Skyride on the second floor; it's a Big Screen, thrill ride adventure that takes you on a citywide tour. General admission is $11.50; children ages four - 12 are $8.50; and children under four are free. Observation deck admission is $7.00 for adults; $4.00 for senior citizens, children under 12, and military personnel; free to kids under five. Observation hours are daily, 9:30 a.m. - 12:00 a.m. The last ticket is sold at 11:30 p.m. While you're here, why not do both? Discount admissions are available for combination tickets.

FEDERAL RESERVE BANK OF NEW YORK

33 Liberty Street, New York NY 10045-0001. 212/720-6130. **E-mail address:** FRBNYTOURS@ny.frb.org. **World Wide Web address:** http://www.ny.frb.org. **Description:** Want to see some money for nothing? Then take a free tour of New York's Federal Reserve Bank where, each day, approximately $331 million in currency is processed. With that kind of money, you wouldn't need me anymore. Tours will lead you through the Gold Vault and the Cash Area, and will let you enjoy some interactive fun with the FedWorks exhibit. Don't try any funny business either; cameras and bags must be left outside, and you will be asked to walk through the metal detector. Because tours are free, it is advisable to call or e-mail the bank a month or so ahead and let them know you are coming. You must be at least 16 years old to enter the

bank. Tours run Monday through Friday, every hour from 9:30 a.m. - 2:30 p.m., with each tour lasting approximately one hour.

JOYCE GOLD HISTORY TOURS OF NEW YORK

141 West 17th Street, New York NY 10011. 212/242-5762. **E-mail address:** nyctours@aol.com. **World Wide Web address:** http://www.nyctours.com. **Description:** Want to get an extensive lesson in the history of New York in only two to three hours? Then join Joyce Gold for one of her world-famous walking tours. From Harlem to Wall Street and every place in between, Ms. Gold will tell you all about the important and fun facts that make New York City such a cultural mecca. Tours trace the culture of many of New York's most bustling neighborhoods including, Greenwich Village, Fifth Avenue, Hell's Kitchen, TriBeCa, SoHo, and Chelsea. Tours start at 1:00 p.m. and cost $12.00 per person. Tours are usually given on weekends. Call or visit Joyce's Website for the most current tour selections and meeting places.

GENERAL GRANT NATIONAL MEMORIAL

Riverside Drive (at 122nd Street), New York NY 10027. 212/666-1640. **World Wide Web address:** http://www.nps.gov/gegr. **Description:** Quick, who's buried in Grant's Tomb? Sorry, couldn't resist. If you're really not sure, here's the actual place, way up on the Upper West Side. Modeled after ancient Greek mausoleums, it celebrates the great hero of the Civil War. Interestingly enough for 1897, the monument was completely funded by private contributions many of which came from African-Americans. While you're up in this beautiful, out-of-the-way part of town, take a stroll along Riverside Drive itself. This is a gently curving stretch of boulevard, lined with trees, old-fashioned gas lamps, and benches. The view across to New Jersey's Palisades is spectacular, while the buildings behind you will make you feel like a time-traveler to the 19th-century. Open daily from 9:00 a.m. to 5:00 p.m.; admission is free.

GRAY LINE NEW YORK

Port Authority, Eighth Avenue & 42nd Street, New York NY. 212/397-2600. **World Wide Web address:** http://www. graylinenewyork.com. **Description:** So you've tried and tried, but you can't seem to find your way around, and you definitely can't get that New York attitude. Well, as the old adage says, if you can't beat them, join them. Hop aboard one of the many Gray Line New York sightseeing and day trip tour buses and see all of New York's biggest attractions with a real New Yorker. No matter what you're looking to do, or how much time you have to spare, Gray Line is here to help you get around, at a very reasonable price. Take a complete city tour for only $35.00 for adults or $23.00 for children; after two days and one night, you will have seen almost everything the Big Apple has to offer including Lady Liberty herself, Ellis Island, Rockefeller Center, the Empire State Building, Wall Street, Lincoln Center, Times Square, the Museum Mile, and much more. If you're rather limited with time, take a three-hour tour of downtown and visit more than 20 sights. This truncated version costs only $22.00 for adults, and $13.00 for children. Take a day trip to the Woodbury Common Premium Outlets for only $33.00 for adults and $16.00 for children. Gray Line is bound to have a trip to meet your needs. FYI, Gray Line also offers an airport shuttle service between La Guardia, JFK, and Newark airports. One-way tickets run about $14.00 each (much cheaper than a cab). Stop by the Gray Line courtesy phone in the baggage claim or give them a call for more information.

HERITAGE TRAILS NEW YORK

61 Broadway, Suite 2020, New York NY. 212/269-1500. **World Wide Web address:** http://www.heritagetrails.org. **Description:** Heritage Trails is a nonprofit organization that helps to promote the history and culture of New York City through guided tours and special events. In keeping with this mission, the organization has mapped out several walking trails throughout the city that tourists and residents alike can follow to learn more about the history of the city. The free TrailsMaps can be picked up at more than 25 downtown locations, or by calling the organization. Each stop on the trail is explained in detail in the map so that, even without the aid of a tour guide, you can learn the significance of each of the designated buildings. If you would prefer the aid of tour guide, that can also be arranged. Just call Big Onion Walking Tours 212/439-1090. The organization also offers a few other guided tour options: take the two-hour World of Finance Tour and learn all there is to know about the city's deep involvement in the financial industry. Start at the Museum of American Financial History (28 Broadway) and follow your guide to the New York Stock Exchange and other financial landmarks. The World of Finance Tour runs every Friday at 10:00 a.m. Adult tickets are $15.00; Seniors, students, and kids under $12.00 are all $10.00. For more info on this exciting economic excursion, call 212/908-4519. Heritage Trails New York, in association with the Downtown Alliance, also offers Destination Downtown: New York Old and New. This 1½ hour tour is free and departs from the U.S. Customs House/Smithsonian's National Museum of the Indian every Thursday at noon. For more info call 212/606-4064.

LINCOLN CENTER FOR THE PERFORMING ARTS

70 Lincoln Plaza (between Broadway & Amsterdam Avenue on 65th Street), New York NY. 212/875-5370. **E-mail address:** visitorservices@lincolncenter.org. **World Wide Web address:** http://www.lincolncenter.org. **Description:** Do you love the glamour and intrigue of behind-the-scenes showbiz? Take the Lincoln Center tour and you'll see the world of backstage at three of the city's most respected theaters: the Metropolitan Opera House, Avery Fisher Hall, and the New York State Theater. You may even catch a glimpse of rehearsals, or the Met's famous revolving stage. All this is just $9.50 for adults; $8.00 for students and seniors; and $4.75 for children. Tours depart from the desk at the concourse level downstairs; they run every two hours from 10:30 a.m. - 4:30 p.m. If tour plans coincide with lunch plans, request the "Tour With a Bite" and grab a quick meal amidst all the excitement. Groups can enjoy private "Meet the Artist"

performances. Call ahead for more information and to make tour reservations at 212/875-5350.

MADISON SQUARE GARDEN ALL ACCESS TOUR
4 Pennsylvania Plaza, 16th Floor, New York NY. 212/465-5800. **World Wide Web address:** http://www.thegarden.com. **Description:** Sports fans should take advantage of this insider's, behind-the-scenes glimpse of The Garden. For just $14.00 (adults) and $12.00 for children under age 12, this one-hour tour takes you behind the scenes at the legendary arena and shows you how it all comes together. You can even visit the locker rooms of the Knicks and Rangers. After the tour, your ticket stub gets you 10 percent off all Garden merchandise and 10 percent off a lunch at The Garden Sports Restaurant, Play by Play, open weekdays from 11:30 a.m. - 2:30 p.m. Group discounts are available. Tours run at the top of every hour, Monday through Saturday, 10:00 a.m. - 3:00 p.m.; Sundays 11:00 a.m. - 3:00 p.m.

NBC EXPERIENCE STORE/STUDIO TOUR
30 Rockefeller Plaza, New York NY 10112. 212/664-4000. **Description:** Take a tour of the studio that calls itself home to many of your favorite programs, including the "Must-See TV" lineup. This one-hour tour begins with a history lesson and could include trips to the *Today* set, the *Saturday Night Live* studio, or the home of *Late Night with Conan O'Brien* (tour routes vary based on production schedules and studio availability). But where the real "experience" is is in the tour's interactive features: talk one-on-one with Jay Leno and tell him about all your latest movie deals, etc.; help prepare the Big Apple for upcoming storms and sunshine as an aid to Al Roker; or test your sports savvy against aficionado Bob Costas. Of course, everything is virtual, but stimulating nonetheless. Plus, you never know who your tour guide will be (one day). Former NBC pages who have run the show include Willard Scott, Ted Koppel, Regis Philbin, and Steve Allen. Tickets are $17.50 for adults and $15.00 for kids (ages six to 16). Group rates are available with advance reservations. Please note that, if you are toting some toddlers, children under six will not be allowed into the studio.

NEW YORK STOCK EXCHANGE INTERACTIVE EDUCATION CENTER
20 Broad Street, 3rd Floor, New York NY. 212/656-5168. **E-mail address:** iec@nyse.com. **World Wide Web address:** http://www.nyse.com. **Description:** Tour the inside of the New York Stock Exchange and look out onto the floor of the craziest, most chaotic scene in the world. If you can actually figure out what's going on, and how any important work gets done at all, you're doing well. Meanwhile, self-guided tours are absolutely free, which may be the best insider deal going. Open Monday through Friday, 8:45 a.m. - 4:30 p.m.

RADICAL WALKING TOURS OF NEW YORK
539 53rd Street, Brooklyn NY 11220-2722. 718/492-0069. **E-mail address:** brucewalk@igc.org. **World Wide Web address:**

http://www.he.net/~radtours. **Description:** If you're in the mood for something radically different, let political activist Bruce Kayton show you his New York. From Wall Street to Harlem, Radical Walking Tours offers 15 different tours that focus on contemporary revolutionaries and political movements. Malcolm X, Abbie Hoffman, Margaret Sanger, and Emma Goldman are just a few of the people Radical Walking Tours focus on. Learn about the political movements and minority groups that have shaped the current state of America including the anti-Vietnam War movement, the women's movement, the Greenwich Village Bohemian Era, socialism, communism, and anarchism. Learn how gay and lesbian, black, and labor histories have had an effect on New York City past and present. Tours average about three hours and cost $10.00 per person. Visit their Website or call for the latest tour schedule. For more information, you can also check your local bookstore for *Radical Walking Tours of New York City* ($12.95).

RADIO CITY MUSIC HALL
1260 Avenue of the Americas (at 50th Street), New York NY 10020. 212/247-4777. **World Wide Web address:** http://www.radiocity.com. **Description:** Ever wondered what it's like to be a Rockette? What this vast, 6,000-seat auditorium looks like from the stage? How the heck that gigantic organ works? Find out during an hour-long, behind-the-scenes tour of this Art Deco palace, which was totally restored to its original splendor in 1999. Tours cost $15.00 for adults, $9.00 for children under 12; and run seven days a week, starting from the main lobby. The schedule is sometimes cut short though when a new show is being put on, so call ahead for last-minute information. Hours are Sunday, 11:00 a.m. - 5:00 p.m.; Monday through Saturday, 10:00 a.m. - 5:00 p.m.

RIVERSIDE CHURCH
490 Riverside Drive (at 120th Street), New York NY 10027. 212/870-6700. **World Wide Web address:** http://www.theriversidechurchny.org. **Description:** The bell tower boasts 74 booming bells the world's largest carillon. That's New York, all right. The 400-foot tower also affords an even more dramatic view. Open daily from 11:00 a.m. - 4:00 p.m. Everything is free.

ST. JOHN THE DIVINE
1047 Amsterdam Avenue, New York NY 10025. 212/316-7540. **World Wide Web address:** http://www.stjohndivine.org. **Description:** Feast your eyes on one of the world's largest cathedrals, and go on a tour to learn all about its history and architecture. St. John the Divine is home to the Episcopal Diocese of New York and hosts a number of events and tours on the premises. Prices range from $3.00 for a basic, "Public Tour" to $10.00 for a "Vertical Tour" (this means you climb up 124 feet of stone spiral staircase for a great view). Other events include various plays and a Medieval Arts Workshop. Reservations are required for some events and tours. Call the tours line at 212/932-7347. Hours are Monday - Saturday, 7:00 a.m. - 6:00 p.m.; Sunday, 7:00 a.m. - 8:00 p.m. The "Public Tour" runs Tuesday through

Sunday, 11:00 a.m.; Sunday, 1:00 p.m. Call for the "Vertical Tour" schedule.

ST. PATRICK'S CATHEDRAL
Fifth Avenue (at East 50th Street), New York NY. 212/753-2261.
Description: As one of the nation's largest Catholic churches, St. Patrick's Cathedral sees thousands of visitors everyday. Whether taking a quick peek while making your way to Saks Fifth Avenue or coming to worship (amidst the masses, services are still held daily), this Gothic masterpiece is a must-see for anyone visiting the Big Apple for the first time.

TRINITY CHURCH
74 Trinity Place (at Broadway & Wall Street), New York NY 10006. 212/602-0800. **Description:** Come and take a guided tour of NYC's first Episcopal church, the burial place of Alexander Hamilton. If you happen to be in the area on a Thursday afternoon, drop by for some musical entertainment as Trinity Church offers a Noonday Concert. Concerts take place each Thursday at 1:00 p.m. For upcoming schedule information, call 212/602-0747. While concerts are free to the public, a $2.00 donation is greatly appreciated (and well worth it).

LODGING
🛏 Alternative 🛏

NOTE: *Throughout the year hotel rates can vary based on day of week, season, and special events/holidays. The prices listed in Mr. Cheap's are reflective of the average price you can expect to pay at each establishment. Please contact each location for specific rates.*

ABODE LIMITED
P.O. Box 20022, New York NY 10028. 212/472-2000. **Description:** An interesting idea that is worth looking into when a hotel room seems unlikely for logistical or financial reasons. Okay, okay, it's not really a place you can stay. (It was probably the P.O. Box that tipped you off, right?) This is a service that, by phone or mail, will connect you with short-term vacancies in apartments in residential buildings around the city, which Mr. C. considers to be a capital piece of creative thinking on someone's part. Although prices vary widely, it's safe to say that there is something here for just about every price range. Some rooms are available with a host on the premises; it's less expensive, but presumably less like having the place to yourself. Similar services are offered by City Lights Bed and Breakfast (212/737-7049), Bed and Breakfast Network of New York (212/645-8134).

AFFORDABLE NEW YORK CITY
21 East 10th Street, Suite PHW, New York NY 10003. 212/533-4001. **E-mail address:** Affordnyc@aol.com. **World Wide Web address:** http://www.innsites.com. **Description:** This is another agency that will do all the work for you. Affordable New York City is a bed and breakfast reservation agency representing over 100 B&Bs in the Manhattan area. Room prices are from $80.00 - $140.00 nightly.

ALADDIN HOTEL
317 West 45th Street, New York NY 10036. 212/977-5700. **World Wide Web address:** http://www.aladdinhotel.com. **Description:** This is the place for frugal backpackers and cost-conscious leisure travelers. The Aladdin Hotel runs more like a hostel than anything else. After a long journey by magic carpet, you will look forward to relaxing in this comfortable and homey atmosphere. Single or double rooms run between $75.00 and $85.00, while dormitory style accommodations are between $25.00 and $33.00.

BIG APPLE HOSTEL
119 West 45th Street, New York NY 10036. 212/302-2603. **World Wide Web address:** http://www.bigapplehostel.com.

Description: Another hostel in the Big City (actually Midtown Manhattan). Shared rooms with four beds are $30.00 and private rooms with double beds are $80.00. Features include a fully equipped kitchen and no curfew.

COUNTRY INN THE CITY
270 West 77th Street, New York NY 10024. 212/580-4183. **E-mail address:** ctryinn@aol.com. **World Wide Web address:** http://www.countryinnthecity.com. **Description:** This is one of the hidden treasure of the Big Apple. Country Inn the City is a renovated townhouse, offering a few beautifully decorated apartments. Each can be booked for both long or short-term stays and is filled with antiques, hardwood floors, and unique four poster and sleigh beds. As an added bonus, these rooms also include private baths with showers, kitchenettes, air-conditioning, and soundproof insulation so you can leave the hustle and bustle of the city behind. The environment is also smoke and pet free; so leave the cigars and Fidos at home. Rooms require a three night minimum stay with a maximum of two people per apartment. Rates are generally between $150.00 and $195.00 per night, but vary depending on season and availability.

GAMUT REALTY GROUP, INC.
212/879-4229. **World Wide Web address:** http://www.gamutnyc.com. **Description:** Gamut Realty Group provides well-maintained, furnished apartments and studios throughout the city for both tourists and professionals. Accommodations vary, but most include full kitchen, air conditioning, and free local phone service. Prices are dependent upon the neighborhood and length of stay, but average at $110.00 - $135.00 per night for a studio and $125.00 - $175.00 per night for a one-bedroom apartment. Apartments can also be reserved online.

HOSTELLING INTERNATIONAL
891 Amsterdam Avenue, New York NY 10025-4403. 212/932-2300. **E-mail address:** reserve@HInewyork.org. **World Wide Web address:** http://www.hinewyork.org. **Description:** If you relish the opportunity to meet people from all over the world and privacy is not an issue, hostels can be a very inexpensive way to travel. Hostelling International offers lodging for under $30.00 a night (credit cards are accepted). They can also help you find your way around the Big Apple through arranged walking tours and group outings to sports and entertainment events. Reservations are necessary June through October as well as December 25th through January 2nd.

THE LEO HOUSE
332 West 23rd Street, New York NY 10011. 212/929-1010. **Description:** The Leo House was originally established in the Battery Park area in 1899 by the St. Raphael Society, a group dedicated to aiding German Catholic immigrants. Today, at its West 23rd Street location, it serves as a Catholic hospice for out-of-state visitors. It is safe, clean, and ideally suited to visitors on

a tight budget...or at least, to those visitors on a tight budget who can plan their stay approximately three months in advance. (That's the estimated wait.) It perhaps bears repeating that the premises are meant for out-of-staters only, although people of all faiths and from all countries are welcome. Breakfast is served in the Leo's tidy little cafeteria every morning except Sunday; laundry facilities are available on the premises, as is a chapel, which holds daily Mass. Single rooms run between $62.00 and $72.00 per night; double rooms are priced from $70.00 - $78.00. Quite affordable indeed. The maximum stay is two weeks, although openings for short-term residencies do come up from time to time. Note well: You have to play by the rules at the Leo. Only registered guests are allowed in rooms, and smoking is restricted to a few common areas and the garden. This is certainly not your typical lodging establishment, but then you get the feeling that's just how the Sisters of St. Agnes, who have been running the place for the last century, like it.

MANHATTAN GETAWAYS
P.O. Box 1994, New York NY 10101. 212/956-2010. **World Wide Web address:** http://www.manhattangetaways.com. **Description:** If you'd like a home experience away from home, Bed & Breakfasts or short term private apartments are the way to go. Manhattan Getaways is a service that will help you find accommodations in a B&B room (where the owner/manager is always present) or in a private apartment. In fact, they will make the reservation for you! Most B&B room rates begin around $105.00 a night and private apartments begin around $145.00. Make sure to have your credit card handy because that is the only way to secure the reservation.

92ND STREET YMCA RESIDENCE
1395 Lexington Avenue, New York NY 10128. 212/415-5650. **Description:** If you're young (that means ages 18 - 26), you can stay here for extended periods of time at very low rates indeed. All they ask is that you don't make any jokes about the Village People. Seriously, though, the Y is a good inexpensive option to explore if you're going to be in town for a spell, although, to borrow a phrase from the world of advertising, certain restrictions apply. There is a minimum requirement to your stay that can vary from a few days to a year, depending on the time of year. Both single and double rooms are available, but you should apply well in advance by calling or writing in for a form. Security guards monitor all visitors.

URBAN VENTURES
38 West 32nd Street, Suite 1412, New York NY 10001. 212/594-5650. **World Wide Web address:** http://www. nyurbanventures.com. **Description:** Urban Venture has been providing travelers with B&B reservation services since 1979. They have been praised by *Travel & Leisure*, *Fortune*, and *The New York*

Times. They actually send a representative from the company to inspect each property they represent. Rates at the B&Bs range from $80.00 - $125.00 for one or two people.

LODGING
🔊 Hotels & Motels 🔊

NOTE: *Throughout the year hotel rates can vary based on day of week, season, and special events/holidays. The prices listed in Mr. Cheap's are reflective of the average price you can expect to pay at each establishment. Please contact each location for specific rates.*

ALLERTON HOTEL
302 West 22nd Street (at Eighth Avenue), New York NY 10011. 212/243-6017. **E-mail address:** AltHotel@aol.com. **Description:** In the heart of Chelsea, the Allerton Hotel features very affordable, modern rooms that feature air conditioning, private baths, and color televisions. Some rooms even include kitchen facilities as well. Single rooms start at just $81.00, studios start at $87.00, doubles from $104.00, and triples (which actually accommodate up to six people) can be had for as little as $126.00 a night.

THE AMSTERDAM INN
340 Amsterdam Avenue (at West 76th Street), New York NY 10023. 212/579-7500. **E-mail address:** info@amsterdaminn.com. **World Wide Web address:** http://www.amsterdaminn.com. **Description:** For rates this reasonable, you may be astonished by how comfortable and modern you'll find the rooms (equipped with the basic necessities such as air conditioning, TV, maid service, and phone). Shared bath single rooms are just $75.00 per night; shared bath double rooms are $95.00 per night; private bath single rooms are $115.00 per night; and private bath double rooms are $125.00 per night. Contact The Amsterdam Inn directly for special introductory rates and packages, or to make reservations.

THE BEACON HOTEL
2130 Broadway (at 75th Street), New York NY 10023. 212/787-1100. **Description:** Another affordable hotel on the Upper West Side, The Beacon Hotel is located within walking distance of Lincoln Center and Central Park. Rooms can get pricey, with the most expensive around $395.00. However, if you plan early and book ahead you can get rooms between $150.00 and $225.00. All rooms include two double beds and kitchenettes.

BEST WESTERN PRESIDENT HOTEL
234 West 48th Street, New York NY. 212/246-8800. **World Wide Web address:** http://www.bestwestern.com. **Description:**

The Best Western President Hotel boasts 400 rooms, including two deluxe penthouses and 12 executive suites. These last items are probably not the rooms you can secure for $109.00 a night, but they're no doubt close enough for some of the razzmatazz to rub off. This is quite a nice place, complete with coffee shop, atrium-style bar, and in-house Italian restaurant. It's also got a heck of an advantage over even some of the pricier places when it comes to location: the Best Western President Hotel is close to Times Square, the Museum of Modern Art, Rockefeller Center, and the Theater District, and within walking distance of the Jacob K. Javits Convention Center.

BEST WESTERN SEAPORT INN
33 Peck Slip, New York NY 10038. 212/766-6600. **Toll-free phone:** 800/468-3569. **World Wide Web address:** http://www. bestwestern.com. **Description:** This 19th-century guesthouse-turned-hotel offers fantastic accommodations at a great price. Each of the hotel's 65 rooms comes equipped with a refrigerator, in-room safe, TV, and VCR. Many rooms feature terraces and afford fantastic views of the nearby Brooklyn Bridge. Rooms range from $139.00 - $209.00 per night. You can even request a room with a balcony and whirlpool for as low as $189.00! Best Western Seaport Inn is within walking distance of many of Lower Manhattan's best attractions, including South Street Seaport and Battery Park. You'll also be situated less than a mile from Lady Liberty herself.

CHELSEA INN
46 West 17th Street, New York NY. 212/645-8989. **Toll-free phone:** 800/640-6469. **E-mail address:** reservations@ chelseainn. com. **World Wide Web address:** http://www.chelseainn.com. **Description:** Conveniently located just off Fifth Avenue, this small, affordable inn is within walking distance of such major shopping destinations as Barney's and Balducci's, as well as popular restaurants and theaters. The renovated 19th-century townhouse offers single suites with private bath for $179.00 - $199.00 per night, and two-room suites with a private bath for $219.00 - $259.00 per night. Guest rooms with private baths go for $139.00 - $159.00 per night, while guest rooms with shared baths go for $109.00 - $129.00 per night. As an added bonus, all rooms are equipped with kitchenettes. If you're looking to save money, this is a great way to do it. Forego the temptation of a restaurant for *one* night, and cook in instead. With markets as fresh and great as the one's in New York City, even an amateur cook can come off as a gourmet.

CHELSEA LODGE
318 West 20th Street, New York NY 10011. 212/343-4499. **Toll-free phone:** 800/373-1116. **E-mail address:** chelsealodge@ mindspring.com. **World Wide Web address:** http://www. chelsealodge.com. **Description:** This quaint, 22-room hotel was recently renovated and offers comfortable rooms at reasonable rates. Rates tend to increase on the weekends, but rooms are generally priced between $70.00 and $100.00 per night.

CHELSEA SAVOY HOTEL

204 West 23rd Street, Chelsea NY 10011. 212/929-9353.
Description: A new and worthy edition to the Chelsea neighborhood, the Chelsea Savoy Hotel offers affordable lodgings in the center of some of the city's most exciting action. With SoHo and Greenwich Village in walking distance, the Chelsea Savoy Hotel is also situated near the Empire State Building, and some of New York's favorite museums and Fifth Avenue shopping destinations. Single rooms start at a more than reasonable $99.00, with doubles and quads beginning at $125.00 and $175.00, respectively.

COSMOPOLITAN HOTEL

95 West Broadway (at Chambers Street), New York NY 10007. 212/566-1900. **World Wide Web address:** http://www. cosmohotel.com. **Description:** Revel in the comfort and intimacy of this reasonably priced hotel, located in the heart of trendy downtown TriBeCa. With 105 rooms, the Cosmopolitan Hotel offers rates starting at $109.00 for a room with one double bed, and $139.00 for a room with two double beds. And the location is fantastic; at the Cosmopolitan Hotel, you'll have an easy walk to Wall Street, SoHo, Chinatown, and Greenwich Village.

EDISON HOTEL

228 West 47th Street, New York NY. 212/840-5000. **World Wide Web address:** http://www.edisonhotelnyc.com. **Description:** Smack in the middle of the Theater District, the meritorious Edison Hotel offers some very competitive rates for an overnight stay. Singles start at just $130.00 per night, doubles at $145.00. The food at the Cafe Edison (located within the hotel) is a great bargain too, offering deli-style food in good portions and with relatively quick service. Cafe Edison is a great spot for a thrifty pre-theater meal or an inexpensive lunch, a rarity in this area. In addition to the cafe, the Hotel Edison also calls itself home to the fine dining establishments of Sofia's Restaurant, The Supper Club, and The Rum House. Still got food on the brain? Edison Hotel is a mere one block away from renowned "Restaurant Row" so, whatever you're craving, they've got you covered. Prepare to see a number of traveling business people in the hotel, as its prime location is just a short walk away from many of the city's largest financial and entertainment companies. The Art Deco style of both the lobby and the rooms (very similar to that of Radio City Music Hall) will be quick to delight the aesthetic in everyone.

THE GERSHWIN HOTEL

7 East 27th Street, New York NY. 212/545-8000. **E-mail address:** gershwinhotel@pobox.com. **World Wide Web address:** http://www.gershwinhotel.com. **Description:** Just off of Fifth Avenue sits one of the city's hippest (and most affordable) hotels, The Gershwin Hotel. As the name would suggest, the hotel caters to an artsy, predominantly European crowd, though all are welcomed with open arms. Each room is adorned in a medley of pastels and handcrafted murals. The hotel also offers a bar,

nightly entertainment, and an ever-changing art gallery. Prices generally range anywhere from $95.00 to $140.00 per night, depending on time of week and time of year. If you're willing to sleep in a dormitory-style room, bed prices are $27.00 - $29.00.

HABITAT HOTEL
130 East 57th Street (at Lexington Avenue), New York NY. 212/753-8841. **World Wide Web address:** http://www.stayinny. com. **Description:** Ever wanted to have breakfast at Tiffany's? Well now you can, as it's only a short distance from Habitat Hotel. Habitat Hotel offers money-conscious travelers a true New York City experience. What other notable sites are in the neighborhood? How about the Museum of Modern Art, CBS Studios, and Carnegie Hall? The Hard Rock Cafe and Planet Hollywood are just two local restaurants. For those who want to shop, Bloomingdale's and FAO Schwarz are also within walking distance. But not all of the Habitat Hotel's excitement takes place *outside* of the hotel; each room includes color cable television and Internet access. Single rooms start at just $105.00 per night, doubles begin at $120.00 per night.

HERALD SQUARE HOTEL
19 West 31st Street, New York NY. 212/279-4017. **Toll-free phone:** 800/727-1888. **World Wide Web address:** http://www. heraldsquarehotel.com. **Description:** The Herald Square Hotel is a clean, dependable place to spend the night in New York for very little money. The hotel boasts 120 rooms; with singles starting at just $60.00 per night, and doubles starting at $99.00. Or, invite a few other friends along, and pay only $130.00 per night for a triple room, or $140.00 per night for a quad.

HOLIDAY INN DOWNTOWN
138 Lafayette Street, Chinatown NY 10013. 212/966-8898. **Toll-free phone:** 800/465-4329. **Description:** A recognizable name and affordable rates...what more could you want from a hotel? The 14-floor Holiday Inn Downtown offers more than 200 comfortably appointed rooms, and a gorgeous marble lobby with Asian accents. Staying at the Holiday Inn Downtown puts you within walking distance of some of New York's most exciting neighborhoods including Chinatown, Little Italy, SoHo, and TriBeCa. Financiers will appreciate to hotel's close proximity to Wall Street. Room rates range between $169.00 - $229.00.

HOTEL LUCERNE
201 West 79th Street, New York NY 10024. 212/875-1000. E-mail address: lucerne@newyorkhotel.com. **Description:** A luxury hotel and New York landmark all rolled into one on the Upper West Side. While rooms start at just $150.00 a night, they can go all the way up to $450.00 a night. Be sure and book early so you can secure yourself one of the lower-priced rooms in this lavish hotel.

HOTEL 17
225 East 17th Street, New York NY 10003. 212/475-2845. **E-mail address:** hotel17@worldnet.att.net. **Description:** It has been said that the true mark of a venerable establishment in New York is

whether or not Woody Allen has chosen to film it. This said, Hotel 17 must be pretty highly-regarded. In addition to setting the scene of the "Mystery" in Allen's *Manhattan Murder Mystery*, Hotel 17 has served as the backdrop for several magazine and music video shoots. Both Madonna and David Bowie have visited the hotel for photo sessions. But just what is it that attracts these celebrities? The 160-room Hotel 17 maintains much of its old-world style and charm, while modernizing its attitude. Standard single rooms are $87.00; standard double rooms are $121.00; deluxe rooms (with air conditioning, cable, and maid service) are $138.00 or higher. Just don't forget that, as older buildings often go, you should expect to share a bathroom with your next door neighbor! *$Cash Only$*

HOTEL 31
120 East 31st Street, New York NY 10016. 212/685-3060. **E-mail address:** hotel31@worldnet.att.net. **Description:** While the building is over 80 years old, the features at Hotel 31 are anything but archaic. Set in the relaxed and quiet Murray Hill area of Midtown Manhattan, this small but refined hotel (and sibling to Hotel 17) offers 110 rooms and suites that start at just $85.00 per night. *$Cash Only$*

JOLLY MADISON TOWERS HOTEL
22 East 38th Street (at Madison Avenue), New York NY 10016. 212/802-0600. **Toll-free phone:** 800/225-4340. **Description:** This elderly but still quite appealing establishment can be found in the Murray Hill section, an oasis of relatively calm domesticity in the frenetic mix that is Business Manhattan. A weekend stay hereabouts will yield the opportunity for a welcome escape from the chaos of Midtown, without actually leaving it. Mr. C was attracted by the abundant supply of famous landmarks near the Jolly Madison; the United Nations, Grand Central Station, and those swanky Fifth Avenue boutiques are all within walking distance. When you're looking to relax after a day of sightseeing, the Jolly Madison's Whaler Bar and Cinque Terre restaurant afford you the perfect opportunity to do so. For a nominal fee, you can also soothe your aching bones with a trip to the third floor spa. Prices for nightly lodging can be as low as $198.00, but also as high as $350.00. Rates are seasonal, so it is advised that you call in advance.

MALIBU STUDIOS HOTEL
2688 Broadway, New York NY 10025. 212/222-2954. **E-mail address:** rooms@malibuhotelnyc.com. **World Wide Web address:** http://www.malibuhotelnyc.com. **Description:** Recently renovated, this budget hotel on the Upper West Side offers affordable rates and a location that can't be beat (just steps from Times Square and Fifth Avenue shopping). Rates start at just $49.00 a night for a room with a double bed and shared bath facilities, with prices escalating to a mere $79.00 with improved accommodations. If you want to throw in a continental breakfast, the prices rises to a slight $89.00. And with all the money you'll save, why not spend some more (or *win* some more) with a trip to Atlantic City? The

bus stops right across the street and takes passengers directly to the casinos.

THE MAYFLOWER ON THE PARK
15 Central Park West, New York NY 10023. 212/265-0060. **Toll-free phone:** 800/223-4164. **Description:** Great for both business and recreational travelers, The Mayflower on the Park is located right across from Central Park, and only a block from the always-animated Lincoln Center. Even after extensive renovations to the hotel, the rates remain some of the most reasonable in the city. With any room type, you have your choice of standard or "Park View." A standard guest room is $175.00 and the most expensive suite is $245.00 with a park view. If you're planning on driving into the city, The Mayflower on the Park offers parking for $25.00 a day.

METRO HOTEL
45 West 35th Street (between Fifth & Avenue of the Americas), New York NY. 212/947-2500. **Toll-free phone:** 800/356-3870. **Description:** Recently renovated, the Metro Hotel is a real insider's secret that few people know about. The lobby of this boutique-style hotel is an Art Deco wonder, with lots of vintage movie posters plastered along the walls for your enjoyment (be careful you don't mistake it for Radio City Music Hall). For even more personal enjoyment, check out the library at the Metro Hotel, where you can borrow books from an assorted collection throughout your stay. Rooms are clean and comfortable, and all rooms come with a tiny refrigerator. Metro Hotel also has a great gym that you are welcome to use, free of charge. Plus, you're just a short distance from lots of fun shopping in the Herald Square area or from a Knicks game at Madison Square Garden. One of the most exciting features of the Metro Hotel, however, is the Metro Grill and the rooftop terrace. Relax with a cocktail or a quick bite to eat as you gaze off at the looming Empire State Building. This is truly one of the better views in the city. Standard rooms were seen advertised from $215.00 - $250.00 a night. Check it out!

MURRAY HILL INN
143 East 30th Street, New York NY 10016. 212/683-6900. **World Wide Web address:** http://www.murrayhillinn.com. **Description:** Wedged in between Lexington and Third Avenue, the Murray Hill Inn offers the financially-challenged traveler a clean and friendly place to stay in the Big Apple. The Midtown location puts you in the center of it all, with treasured landmarks like the Empire State Building just a short distance away. If you're feeling adventuresome and are willing to share a bathroom, prices start at a mere $75.00 for a single room. Singles and doubles with a private bath will run you just $50.00 more, with a $125.00 price tag.

OFF SoHo SUITES HOTEL
11 Rivington Street, New York NY 10002. **Toll-free phone:** 800/OFF-SOHO. **E-mail address:** info@offsoho.com. **World Wide Web address:** http://www.offsoho.com. **Description:** If you're

traveling with a friend or with a group, Off SoHo Suites Hotel is a great choice for budget accommodations. An elegant, European-style hotel near the Financial District, Off SoHo Suites Hotel offers suites for two to four people. Choose an economy suite for two, with a master bedroom and full kitchen (complete with microwave, utensils, and flatware) for $97.50 - $109.00 a night. Deluxe suites, which sleep four and include all economy suite amenities plus a living room with a full-sized pullout sofa and dining area, can be secured for a paltry $179.00 - $219.00. The hotel also offers discount parking rates for those that choose to drive to the city (just $14.00 a day). Off SoHo Suites Hotel also offers a free fitness center for its guests. If you're planning an extended stay in New York, call Off SoHo Suites for even further discounts.

PICKWICK ARMS HOTEL
230 East 51st Street, New York NY 10022. 212/355-0300. **Toll-free phone:** 800/PICKWIK. **Description:** Location, along with price, is the main selling point of the 300-room Pickwick Arms Hotel. It's situated almost directly between Rockefeller Center (to the west), and the United Nations (to the east). It's a pleasant-enough place that offers some very impressive rates: just $70.00 per night for a single and $125.00 for a double.

THE PORTLAND SQUARE HOTEL
132 West 47th Street, New York NY 10036. 212/382-0600. **World Wide Web address:** http://www.portlandsquarehotel.com. **Description:** "ROOMS FROM $60.00 - $145.00 PER NIGHT!" That's the screaming headline on the brochures for the Portland Square Hotel, and it's true enough. The fine print on the rate card, however, will clue you in to the fact that the $60.00 rate (which is, granted, very nearly impossible to beat given the hotel's Times Square location), entails shared bathroom facilities for one person only. Certainly it's still an impressive deal, but the provisos are worth keeping in mind if you had visions of, say, taking a nice, long hot bath at your leisure. The standard one-person room, with shower, tub, and one bed, runs $99.00 a night; a double room (one bed) is $115.00. These are still pretty amazing rates for well-kept rooms in this locale. All rooms include color TV, voice messaging, and air conditioning. And that's about it. The Portland Square takes pride in its long-standing status as a classic, limited-service budget hotel. If you're up for that, and if you're looking for a good base of operations for a Broadway weekend, give The Portland Square Hotel a call.

QUALITY HOTEL AND SUITES MIDTOWN
59 West 46th Street (between Fifth Avenue & Avenue of the Americas), New York NY 10036. 212/719-2300. **Toll-free phone:** 800/848-0020. **Description:** Wondering how you can afford a vacation to the Big Apple for a family of four? This hotel chain features a great deal...children under the age of 18 can stay free with a parent or grandparent!! A room with one Queen-size bed is $159.00; two double beds are $169.00; and a King suite is $209.00.

THE ROGER SMITH

501 Lexington Avenue (between 47th & 48th Streets), New York NY 10017. 212/755-1400. **Toll-free phone:** 800/445-0277. **World Wide Web address:** http://rogersmith.com. **Description:** The Roger Smith refers to itself as an "urban bed and breakfast," and they sure do make you feel at home. Kids are welcome, and all those under 16 are invited to stay for free. And while prices here can go well up into the $300.00 range, The Roger Smith offers a number of budget-priced rooms with some great amenities. All rooms have a refrigerator and large writing desk, so you can be sure and keep your family and friends informed of all your Big Apple adventures. What Mr. C found most impressive about this hotel, however, was their free phone call policy. Unlike other hotels that charge as much as $1.00 or more for local, long distance, and toll-free phone access (yes, that's why your bill is always much higher than you expected), The Roger Smith offers absolutely free local calling and long distance accessing. The lobby also offers an online computer so that you can access your e-mail account throughout your stay. The hotel is decorated with beautiful artwork exhibits that continue to the Roger Smith Gallery (corner of 47th Street). When you feel the need for a good workout, The Roger Smith is more than willing to share their fitness center with you. Mr. C recommends checking the hotel's Website for rates. Discounts are available seasonally, as well as for corporate travelers.

WASHINGTON SQUARE HOTEL

103 Waverly Place, New York NY. 212/777-9515. **Toll-free phone:** 800/222-0418. **E-mail address:** wshotel@ix.netcom.com. **World Wide Web address:** http://www.wshotel.com. **Description:** The Washington Square Hotel doesn't stop trying to accommodate you during your stay. Sure, you've got a bed to sleep in, but what about entertainment? The hotel offers walking tours through Greenwich Village and a Tuesday night "Jazz Package" with free admission to one of the nearby Manhattan jazz clubs. Or get a similar deal on Wednesdays and Thursdays, when you can enjoy the sounds of a local jazz club, overnight accommodations, and dinner for two at the hotel's C3 restaurant. With so much to see in the renowned Greenwich Village area, who knows if you'll get to see the rest of the city. Single rooms are priced around $120.00 and double rooms and larger range from about $140.00 to $175.00.

WELLINGTON HOTEL

871 7th Avenue (at 55th Street), New York NY 10019. 212/247-3900. **Toll-free phone:** 800/652-1212. **World Wide Web address:** http://www.wellingtonhotel.com. **Description:** The Wellington Hotel is almost as bustling as the Midtown location it inhabits. With 700 rooms, two restaurants, a business center, ticket and transportation services, laundry/dry-cleaning facilities, and parking, it almost seems like there would be no reason to leave. But, with Carnegie Hall, Radio City Music Hall, Lincoln Center, Central Park, and the Museum of Modern Art all within walking distance, how can you resist? The Wellington Hotel offers a number of different room types and prices (all under $230.00). Rates change seasonally, so check the Website.

WOLCOTT HOTEL

4 West 31st Street (Fifth Avenue & Broadway), New York NY 10001. 212/268-2900. **Description:** Centrally located just three blocks from the Empire State Building, the 280-room Wolcott Hotel is a virtual tourist mecca. Bargain hunters will find a shopper's paradise only a few minutes away in Herald Square. For those who still have energy after seeing the sites and shopping, you can work out in the hotel's new fitness center. "Modest" rooms and suites are affordable at around $99.00 per night and the multilingual staff caters to budget and foreign travelers. Book early if you plan to stay between April and November, which is the hotel's busiest time of year.

RESTAURANTS
🍽 All Around Town 🍽

BLOCKHEAD'S
499 Third Avenue (between 33rd & 34th Streets), New York NY 10016. 212/213-3332. ◆ 1563 Second Avenue (between 81st & 82nd Streets), New York NY. 212/879-1999. ◆ 954 Second Avenue (between 50th & 51st Streets), New York NY. 212/750-2020. ◆ Worldwide Plaza, 322 West 50th Street (between Eighth & Ninth Avenues), New York NY 10019. 212/307-7070. ◆ 424 Amsterdam Avenue (between 80th & 81st Streets), New York NY. 212/787-5445. **Description:** Looking for a filling Mexican meal without too many pesos in your pocket? Then head on over to Blockhead's, where enormous entrees and mammoth margaritas are only part of the fun. Owners Don and Ken had your health in mind when they developed this Cal-Mex empire; lean meats, fresh veggies, tofu sour cream, and whole wheat tortillas are just a few of their health-conscious options. Start your meal out right with one of their many nacho plates (priced $3.95 - $9.95) or one of their delicious salads ($3.95 - $8.25). Then dig into the real treasures: The Blockhead ($6.95) burrito is a delicious 12-inch tortilla chock full of beef or chicken, beans, rice, Monterey Jack cheese, guacamole, and sour cream; vegetarians will be happy to opt for a variety of meat-less dishes including The Good ($6.75), The Vegetable ($6.95), The Fresh Spinach ($6.95), and the No-Dairy burritos ($6.75); more exotic burrito offerings include the Jamaican Jerk Chicken ($8.50) and the Carolina BBQ ($8.50). Blockhead's also offers a variety of fajitas ($9.95 - $10.95), tacos ($5.75 - $6.95), sandwiches ($6.25 - $7.75), and chilis ($5.75 - $6.75). Start out with a blank slate of a quesadilla ($3.50) and build from there, adding rice, beans, chili, and a variety of other ingredients. While the normal prices are definitely something to salsa about, Blockhead's offers fantastic lunch specials (including chips and salsa, and soda or iced tea) for $5.95 - $7.95. And don't forget about weekend brunch from 12:00 p.m. - 4:00 p.m., indulge in the unlimited champagne brunch for just $7.95 ($4.95 à la carte). Choose from a variety of specials including the Big Breakfast Burrito, huevos rancheros, omelettes, or a ham and egg quesadilla.

BURRITOVILLE INC.
1489 First Avenue (at 77th Street), New York NY 10021. 212/472-8800. ◆ 461 Amsterdam Avenue, New York NY. 212/787-8181. ◆ 166 West 72nd Street, New York NY. 212/362-0622. ◆ 625 Ninth Avenue (at 44th Street), New York NY. 212/333-5352. ◆ 352 West 39th Street (at Ninth Avenue), New York NY. 212/563-9088. ◆ 298 Bleecker Street, New York NY. 212/633-0249. ◆ 144 Chambers Street (at Hudson Street), New York NY. 212/964-5048. ◆ 1606 Third Avenue (between 90th & 91st Streets), New York NY. 212/410-2255. ◆ 141 Second Avenue (between 6th & 9th Streets), New York NY. 212/260-3300. ◆ 20

John Street, New York NY. 212/766-2020. ✦ 36 Water Street, New York NY. 212/747-1100. **Description:** Fast food, Mexican-style, is one of New York's latest rages. At Burritoville's many locations, you can really stuff your face for well under $10.00. Most of the menu items, in fact, are priced from $5.00 - $7.00. The ingredients for some of these are as unusual as their names: Davey Crockett's Last Burrito ($6.95) is filled with grilled marinated lamb, brown rice, beans, and cheese; the French Quarter Burrito ($7.50) is resplendent with sizzling shrimp; and the Vegged Out in Santa Fe Burrito ($5.95) contains, surprise, nondairy soy cheese, grilled vegetables, tofu sour cream, brown rice, and beans. (The Santa Fe may be one of the few things you can find in a fast-food restaurant that is both heavy and undeniably good for you). Burritoville also offers tacos from $2.50 each, fajitas for $7.95, and a bowl of good old chuckwagon chili for just $2.50. Burritoville prides itself on using no lard, no preservatives, and only fresh ingredients. There is no liquor license here, so if you want a beer, bring your own. There are also few tables at Burritoville; Mr. C. did not inquire as to whether diners could bring those, as well. Open daily, 12:00 p.m. - 12:00 a.m. Olé!

EJ'S LUNCHEONETTE

447 Amsterdam Avenue, New York NY 10024. 212/873-3444. ✦ 1271 Third Avenue (at 73rd Street), New York NY. 212/472-0600. ✦ 432 Avenue of the Americas (between 9th & 10th Streets), New York NY 10011. 212/473-5555. **Description:** What a wild scene this is. EJ's Luncheonette has grabbed hold of New York's passion for nostalgic diners, and has created a campy, funky joint that's like a time-warp to the 1950s. These establishments are covered with clocks, old-fashioned advertisements, ceiling fans, and the other accouterments for anyone interested in going back in time... and eating well along the way. The menu ranges all over the diner repertoire, but always with a modern twist. Breakfasts include a good-sized helping of EJ's buttermilk or multi-grain pancakes. These can be eaten alone -- with whipped butter and syrup, of course -- or with a variety of toppings including blueberry compote, chocolate chips, bananas and pecans, strawberries, or a variety of stewed fruits. Whatever you choose, prices are between $6.00 and $8.00. The same goes for EJ's Belgian waffles, which can be served with the same toppings. If eggs, toast, and homefries are your idea of breakfast, EJ's has got plenty of those dishes too! Two-egg plates start at right around $4.00 (and come with toasted challah and preserves). Omelettes are another popular dish at EJ's, and it's easy to see why with ingredients (gruyere, salami, ham, basil) and prices ($5.50 - $8.00) like these. For lunch, nary a thing reaches beyond $10.00. A variety of delicious and unique salads are available as are some great sandwiches. Tuna, chicken salad, turkey, and grilled chicken are just a few of the sandwich varieties. Priced right around $8.00 and under, EJ's serves up a mean burger: a whole half-pound to be exact! The basic model starts out at under $7.00, and toppings such as BBQ sauce, gruyere cheese, Canadian bacon,

and black bean chili can be added for just a bit more. Plus, what would a diner be without a soda fountain? Relive (or start creating) those malt shop memories with a milk shake, egg cream, or ice cream soda. Call it dessert! The result of all this is that EJ's is a monster hit; until the rage dies down, you may have to wait for a table (even in the middle of the afternoon). It'll be worth your while. They usually open early (8:00 a.m.) and close late (11:00 p.m.), but hours vary with location, so call first. *$Cash Only$*

JACKSON HOLE WYOMING

521 Third Avenue (at 35th Street), New York NY 10016. 212/679-3264. ◆ 1270 Madison Avenue (at 91st Street), New York NY. 212/427-2820. ◆ 232 East 64th Street (between Second & Third Avenues), New York NY. 212/371-7187. ◆ 517 Columbus Avenue (at 85th Street), New York NY. 212/362-5177. ◆ 1611 Second Avenue (between 83rd & 84th Streets), New York NY. 212/737-8788. **Description:** Burgers, burgers, burgers! That's the specialty at Jackson Hole, and they're huge. There are also over 30 different varieties to choose from. The basic beefburger starts around $4.50; the Texan burger comes complete with fried egg; a bacon pizza burger arrives with three strips of bacon on top; the Copsegmore features fried onions, tomato, ham, mushroom, and Swiss cheese. (Who knows what Copsegmore means? It's a full meal in itself.) All burgers range from $5.00 or $6.00 (more if you want a platter). Tired of burgers? It is possible to get something different at Jackson Hole, including a number of good Mexican dishes. Southern fried chicken is another good bet here, and Jackson Hole offers a wide variety of omelettes that start at just (such a deal!), as well as a full selection of sandwiches and salads. The atmosphere is lively and bright; the decor is best described as an exotic stainless-steel diner transported to a deserted stretch of two-lane somewhere in, well, Wyoming. The crowd, however, is definitely urban, and the lively, eclectic feel of the place is one of the best reasons to jump into Jackson Hole.

OLLIE'S NOODLE SHOP

200-B West 44th Street, New York NY. 212/921-5988. ◆ 2957 Broadway (at 116th Street), New York NY 10027. 212/932-3300. ◆ 1991 Broadway (between 67th & 68th Streets), New York NY 10023. 212/595-8181. ◆ 2315 Broadway (at 84th Street), New York NY 10024. 212/362-3111. **Description:** Ollie's gives you a ton of food at great prices in a lively atmosphere. In fact, they're so busy that waiting for a table is not uncommon during the dinner hour. The vast menu offers lots of different kinds of appetizers, which can become a whole meal in themselves. Be sure to get some kind of dumpling (you can watch them being made in Ollie's open kitchen while waiting for that table); whether meat, veggie, seafood, or shrimp, steamed in a green wrapper dough. Sesame wontons, scallion pancakes, and roast pork buns are some of the other fine specialties that Ollie's serves. Follow this with a heaping bowl of Cantonese wonton or Mandarin noodle soup, and you're all set. Most are between $5.00 - $6.00, packed with vegetables, strips of meat, noodles and all kinds of goodies; these enormous bowls are hard to finish! Of course, if you want to go on to a main dish, there is another huge selection to ponder.

PONGSRI THAI

311 Second Avenue, New York NY 10013. 212/477-4100. ♦ 106 Bayard Street, New York NY 10013. 212/349-3132. ♦ 244 West 48th Street, New York NY 10036. 212/582-3392. **Description:** With three locations in Chinatown and the Theater District, Pongsri Thai is one of the most recognizable names when it comes to traditional Thai food in the city. That tradition extends to the people that make Pongsri work as well, as it is the oldest family-run Thai place in town. Yet, with a fresh and fun menu, the folks at Pongsri Thai give a modern edge to their food. Take the Pongsri specialties for example, how traditional would you consider a dish known as Big Bird's Love Nest (chicken in chili and garlic with cashews, carrots, peppers, onions, celery, and pineapple)? Or what about Knight Kermit (garlic and pepper frog legs... sorry Kermit)? But, all *Sesame Street* allusions aside, the menu at Pongsri Thai is awash with your favorite Thai dishes. Try some Tomhka Gai soup (sliced chicken in coconut milk, galangar, onions, lime juice, and chili). Tease your appetite with the traditional satay or spring rolls, or the not-so-traditional Thai bean curd or Thai tempura (deep-fried shrimp and veggies). A number of fresh salads are not only delicious, but good for you too. Take the Som Tam salad with papaya, tomatoes, green beans, pounded peanuts, and dried shrimp; a meal in itself I tell you. Noodle dishes like pad thai and rad key moa are all priced around $9.00, with meat dishes averaging just a dollar more. Gang Pak (veggies and bean curd in coconut milk and curry) can be a vegetarian nirvana for under $8.00. Fish, duck, and steak entrees are all well-priced under $13.00. So what are you waiting for? Menu items and prices can vary at each location. Call ahead for specific location hours.

RESTAURANTS
🍽 Chelsea 🍽

Where? Bounded by the Hudson River, Avenue of the Americas, 13th Street, and 29th Street; includes the Fashion District and the Meat-Packing District.

Best Known For: The Chelsea Hotel (home to actors and playwrights), Chelsea Market, Chelsea Piers, and the Flower Market.

Insider Tip: Joni Mitchell's, *Chelsea Morning* was inspired by the Chelsea Hotel. Rumor has it, Chelsea Clinton was named for the song.

BENDIX DINER

219 Eighth Avenue (at 21st Street), New York NY 10011. 212/366-0560. **Description:** The Bendix is a fine example of New York's many retro diners, places that tend to offer campy fun and good food at affordable prices. The look here is a sort of Neo-Deco in bright colors, with original canvases on the walls fitting for the traditionally artistic neighborhood. Unlike some of the city's other diners, though, the menu here is as eclectic as Chelsea itself. Yes, there is authentic diner food, from omelettes to meatloaf. Good, strong coffee too, by the way. But the description of the grilled half-chicken tips you off to the style here: Marinated with Thai herbs and spices, Jewish style... Hmmm. The menu goes on to such wide-ranging items as chili con carne, fried tofu with ginger, yaki soba. Not to mention Po' Boy sandwiches, turkey melts, soups, salads, and burgers. Can they do so many different foods well? The answer appears to be yes. The food is homemade, cooked to order, and colorful. Sandwiches are on thick-cut fresh bread; French fries are done in the style of home-fry wedges, brown and crispy; Oriental dishes are served over brown rice, with crunchy vegetables. In fact, each platter that goes by your table looks so delightful that you want to come back and try them all. Ditto the homemade desserts! Open daily, 8:00 a.m. - 11:00 p.m. This restaurant has no liquor license but you are welcome to bring your own.

CHELSEA COMMONS

242 Tenth Avenue (at 24th Street), New York NY 10001. 212/929-9424. **Description:** Way up in the far reaches of Chelsea, this old-time neighborhood spot is as comfortable a hangout as you could want. Done up in dark wood decor, with ceiling fans, hanging plants and a fireplace, Chelsea Commons offers up good food and drink in a relaxed setting. The not-as-large-as-it-looks room is neatly divided into several areas by low wooden partitions, making each section more intimate and, therefore, good for quiet conversation. You can even sit at the large, old-fashioned bar up front where you'll watch them serve up some of your favorite

beers like Sam Adams and Guinness; they also serve wines by the glass. The large menu ranges from casual snacks to full meals. Among the appetizers, in the $4.00 - $8.00 range, are guacamole and chips, chili, nachos (and super nachos), chicken wings, chicken satay, and fried artichoke hearts with horseradish dressing. A variety of salads ($4.00 - $8.50) include spinach with avocado, mushrooms, eggs, and bacon; Caesars with blackened chicken and avocado strips; and chunk white tuna or tarragon chicken atop a mesclun salad. You can find a large menu of worthwhile burgers and sandwiches too! Good, fresh, half-pound hamburgers start just $6.00, and various toppings (or burger bases -- like turkey or bean) only crank the price up to $8.00 for a deluxe. Sandwiches, like the Philly cheesesteak, the sliced steak sandwich, and the Santa Fe chicken with guacamole and salsa, are appetizing too. The main entree menu offers up some traditional American favorites with a distinct gourmet twist. The most expensive finds were the three steak dinners, and even these were well priced at $16.00 (with all the fixings). Various chicken dishes, including a sizzling plate of fajitas, a chicken pot pie, and a Cajun-baked half chicken, were priced between $8.00 and $12.00. Seafood dishes are some of the more expensive entries, with a pan roasted filet of salmon topping the menu at $14.00. Chelsea Commons offers a number of good pasta dishes too, with most priced right around $10.00. Choices include linguini with hot and sweet sausage, shittake mushroom ravioli, and linguini with Scottish smoked salmon. Service is friendly and laid back, in keeping with the general atmosphere of the place. Speaking of atmosphere: When the weather's nice, they open up the garden courtyard in the back, making this a real oasis in the city. Open daily, 12:00 p.m. - 4:00 a.m.

EIGHTEENTH & EIGHTH

159 Eighth Avenue (at 18th Street), New York NY. 212/242-5000.
Description: Just up the street from the Bendix Diner (see separate listing) is another funky coffee shop, taking a modern approach to old-fashioned cooking. Smaller (read: cramped) and more sparsely decorated than the Bendix, Eighteenth & Eighth takes as its logo a steaming cup of coffee. Indeed, this is a fine place to hang out over a cup of fresh-brewed hazelnut (or whichever is the coffee of the day, same price as regular) and a piece of their extraordinary sour cream apple walnut pie ($4.50). Plenty of teas, espressos, and cappuccinos too, in regular and decaf. While on the subject of beverages, unusual milk shakes are another specialty of the house. The Energizer ($3.95) combines yogurt, brewer's yeast, wheat germ, honey, banana, soy milk, and spirulina protein. It'll keep you going, and going, and going. There are lots of other contemporary touches to the menu, interesting ingredients and garnishes. Sandwiches are a bit on the pricey side, most being $6.50 - $8.50; but they are served on big, fresh breads with red potato salad and pickles on the side. Egg dishes are more reasonable, with two eggs, crispy home fries, toast and a slice of melon for just $3.50. At the other end of the day, dinners

are also a good deal. Try the curry-mango chicken and rice, stuffed roast pork or one of the daily specials, all served with a choice of fresh salad or soup of the day, from $12.95 - $17.95. Sidle into one of the few seats at the tall counter, or squeeze into a table seat next to someone trendy, and dig in. Open Sunday through Thursday, 9:00 a.m. - 12:00 a.m.; Friday and Saturday, 9:00 a.m. - 12:30 a.m.

EMPIRE DINER
210 Tenth Avenue (at 22nd Street), New York NY 10011. 212/924-0011. **Description:** If you know anything about the late night dining scene in and around New York, you certainly know about Empire Diner. The Empire Diner has been a Chelsea institution for several decades now and is well-known as a prime spot for exciting people-watching (though late night dining yields the most interesting crowd). Empire Diner offers all the comfort foods you would expect to find: lots of fried treats like onion rings and French fries, salads, pastas, burgers, and tons of breakfast foods. Though they do stick to the traditional diner regalia, they do offer up some more modernized versions of the typical fare when things like lentil burgers and hummus pita pockets wedge themselves in between meatloaf sandwiches and bacon burgers. Most entrees are priced at $14.00 or under while nary a sandwich makes its way past the $10.00 mark. Breakfast dishes like eggs, omelettes, and French toast start at around $6.00 a plate. Open 24-hours a day (closed Tuesday from 4:00 a.m. - 8:30 a.m.).

FABULOUS CAFE
291 Seventh Avenue (between 26th & 27th Streets), New York NY 10001. 212/206-8283. **Description:** If you happen to be staying at one of the inexpensive hotels I've already told you about in the Chelsea area (or, if you're doing anything in Chelsea really), Fabulous Cafe is a great way to get your day started. This quaint little cafe offers some delicious baked goods, coffees, and sandwiches throughout the day -- allowing you a tasty and inexpensive breakfast, lunch, or coffee break. Each morning they bake up fresh batches of muffins, danish, and scones. They brew up a great cup of coffee too, and it's one of the few places in the city where you can get specialty drinks like a cappuccino or latte for under $3.00! For lunch, they combine fresh ingredients and unique recipes to make dining here an experience. Try the balsamic chicken breast sandwich with roasted red peppers and arugula or the sliced turkey with sun dried tomatoes and pesto mayonnaise for a real treat. Heartier entrees include lasagna and chicken parmesan. The health-conscious will appreciate the good-sized helpings of fresh salad with toppings like Thai chicken, fresh avocado, and smoked turkey. As the cafe is kind of a serve-yourself kind of place, everything can be made to go and barely an item is more than $7.00. This is one place that really lives up to its name! Open Monday through Friday, 7:00 a.m. - 7:00 p.m.; Saturday, 8:00 a.m. - 5:00 p.m.

FLIGHT 151 BAR AND RESTAURANT
151 Eighth Avenue (at 17th Street), New York NY 10011. 212/229-1868. **Description:** After leading a successful bombing run behind

enemy lines (or perhaps through the crowds at nearby Barney's), return to base by touching down at Flight 151. This fun Chelsea hangout is decorated with all sorts of World War II memorabilia; the folks here have even concocted an intricate story about the flight that purportedly gave the restaurant its name. Keen observers may conclude that the name would seem to have more to do with the address of the restaurant than anything you're likely to see in a *Time-Life* video series, but never mind. The place is lively and very casual, serving up burgers for $5.95 as well as tuna melts and chili dogs for the same price. These all come with crispy French fries. Step up to a grilled chicken sandwich ($6.95) or fog up your goggles over the soup of the day, which on Mr. C's visit was Manhattan clam chowder ($2.95). The bar features lots of great beers and good prices on mixed drinks. They also offer bar specials from 7 p.m. - 1 a.m. most nights, such as Tuesday, or "Flip Night," where they flip a coin, and if you guess it correctly, you get the drink free. Adding to the fun atmosphere are bowls of popcorn, a rowdy jukebox, pinball machines, and all kinds of old-time posters and advertisements on the walls. In addition to booths and tables, the restaurant opens its front to the sidewalk during warm months for al fresco dining. Flight 151 is open for both lunch and dinner; on weekends, be sure to check out the All-U-Can-Eat Buffet Brunch; just $6.95, Saturdays and Sundays from 12:00 p.m. - 4:00 p.m. Open daily until 4:00 a.m.

INTERMEZZO

202 Eighth Avenue (between 20th & 21st Streets), New York NY 10011. 212/929-3433. **Description:** Like so many restaurants that have popped up in Chelsea, Intermezzo sports an elegant uptown look. The uptown prices, however, are nowhere to be found. The cuisine is Italian, and from the high-toned atmosphere, white linen tablecloths, and sparkling glassware, frugal diners can be forgiven for a moment of panic upon being led inside. Trust Mr. C, though: you'll get out of here without having to roll up your sleeves and wash the dishes. The menu, which includes pasta, meat, and seafood, is reasonably priced throughout; nevertheless, the pasta dishes present the greatest opportunity for bargain dining. Pasta entrees range from $6.00 - $13.00, with nearly 20 enticing items to choose from. So what dishes make Mr. C's recommendation list? Penne puttanesca (tomatoes, capers, gaeta olives, and anchovies), fusilli norcia (with hot and sweet sausage and tomato), and gnocchi verde (those delicious spinach and potato dumplings with tomato and basil) all top the list for a) being fantastic and b) being priced at under $10.00. Meat and seafood entrees run somewhat higher, though there's plenty to choose from in the $8.00 - $14.00 range; you can get shrimp and calamari sautéed with tomato, avocado, and jalapeño peppers, or chicken primavera for under $11.00. In addition you can more than 15 different varieties of antipasti, including a delicious cold roasted veal with artichokes, olives, and onions; or a yellowfin tuna roll with wasabi mayonnaise. Most of these items are under $8.00. Nice price, but the best deal at Intermezzo is probably its $5.95 - $7.95 lunch, served Monday

through Friday, between 12:00 p.m. and 4:00 p.m. You start off with some soup or a mixed salad, and then move on to one of several main dishes such as fusilli boscaiola, chicken marsala, or salmone alla griglia. There's well over a dozen dishes to choose from and $10.00 should have you covered. The savings continue into the weekend, only then they call it brunch. Weekend prices range from $2.50 - $7.00 for more breakfast-oriented foods like eggs Benedict and pancakes. Intermezzo is the kind of place Mr. C loves to discover: a restaurant that is elegant without being greedy and overpriced.

MARY ANN'S CHELSEA

116 Eighth Avenue (at 16th Street), New York NY 10011. 212/633-0877. **Description:** Here's a popular Mexican restaurant with a long-standing reputation for good food at good prices. Mr. C sampled several different items and found no cause for argument. Lunch plates are a particular bargain, with two dozen choices between $5.00 and $10.00. Salsa and chips start you off, complimentary for the table. For an appetizer, try the tomato and avocado salad, a nice accompaniment for the chips. For entrees, daily specials are often the best values. How about this one: burritos filled with shrimp and scallops sautéed in garlic butter, topped with tomato sauce and served with rice and vegetables. All for $6.95. The food is homemade, so it's hard to go wrong. Atmosphere is casual, and sometimes boisterous; the decor is just enough to be authentic without seeming to try too hard, as some competitors do. *$Cash Only$*

TROIS CANARDS

184 Eighth Avenue (between 19th & 20th Streets), New York NY 10011. 212/929-4320. **Description:** Okay, so maybe prices at Trois Canards can and do go over Mr. C's normal dining budget. But, eating at a place as hip and chic as this is worth the extra dollar. Trois Canards offers exceptional French food in a fantastic and intimate bistro setting. But, instead of offering an always-pricey menu, the folks here are nice enough to afford Cheapsters like us some pretty generous savings. Stop in for their weekend brunch from 11:00 a.m. - 4:00 p.m. For just $10.95, you'll be able to stuff yourself silly with everything from homemade biscuits to crab cakes florentine. Warm duck salad and roast beef hash with poached eggs are a couple of other things you might want to try. Plus, you'll get coffee or tea and (if you're old enough, of course) your choice of a bloody Mary, mimosa, bellini, or a glass of wine) of which they have a fantastic selection). Weekends aren't the only time to save here: Everyday from 5:00 p.m. to 7:00 p.m., Trois Canards offers a prix-fixe dinner ($21.95) for the theater crowd. You'll start with a succulent salad or appetizers, then move on to a spectacular entree (choices include... grilled Norwegian salmon, beef bourguignon, bay scallops, veal scallopine, roast leg of lamb, or stuffed breast of chicken; all with fresh vegetables), finish it off with a sinful homemade treat from their dessert cart.

It's a great way to save a bit of money before heading off to that show you paid $100.00 to see! Open Sunday, 11:00 a.m. - 4:00 p.m.; Monday through Friday, 12:00 p.m. - 11:00 p.m. (until 12:00 a.m. on Friday); Saturday, 11:00 a.m. - 12:00 a.m.

RESTAURANTS
🍽 East Village 🍽

Where? Bounded by the East River, Broadway, Houston, and East 14th Street; includes NoHo and Alphabet City.

Best Known For: Astor Place, St. Mark's In-the-Bowery, Tompkins Square, Bohemian hangout.

Insider Tip: The East Village plays host to many Off-Off-Broadway productions.

ANGELICA KITCHEN

300 East 12th Street (First & Second Avenues), New York NY 10003. 212/228-2909. **Description:** Angelica's has to be one of the nicest vegetarian restaurants in the city. Inside the atmosphere is warm, friendly, and handsomely decorated, with natural wood tables and an open kitchen. The food is all organically grown, and prepared fresh daily. A variety of starters and sides start at just $1.50. Interesting edibles include the Angelica pickle plate, walnut-lentil pate, and mashed potatoes with brown rice gravy or parsley-almond pesto. One of the more exotic ways to start out a meal at Angelica is with a loaf of bread. Sure, it doesn't sound so unique, but when you get a look at the spreads they offer to go with the bread, you'll see what I mean: miso-tahini, ginger-carrot, and onion spreads are available for just about $1.00 extra. Trust me, it's so good you'll want to take a container home... and you can! Salads are prepared with only the freshest ingredients and, again, it's what you top them with that will make them so memorable. The house dressing is a delightful puree of tahini, scallions, and parsley; their oil free dressing is made up of brown rice gravy, scallions, and shoyu; and the creamy carrot dressing is flavored with ginger and dill. Angelica really takes healthy eating to a new echelon of gourmet cooking. And we haven't even gotten to the main dishes yet. But maybe that's because they're hard to capture on paper. Main courses tend to change daily at Angelica, so you always have to look at the menu insert to see what's cooking. If you're ordering a la carte, entrees will cost you about $12.00 apiece. Mr. C suggests you splurge a bit and pay the $14.25 and add two of Angelica's "basics" (tempeh, beans, sea vegetables, soba noodles), or a cup of soup. They also offer an unchanging variety of sandwiches everyday, like a marinated tofu sandwich and a warm tempeh reuben. A popular specialty of the house is the Dragon Bowl, a heaping salad of rice, beans, tofu, sea vegetables, and steamed veggies ($8.50). For an extra $4.00, you can add a cup of soup and bread to your order. Dragon Bowls can also be ordered in half sizes for $5.00 ($9.00 with soup and bread). There is also a daily selection of desserts made with organic ingredients (no refined sugars or dairy products). If things sound complicated, or if you're not fluent in vegetarian, don't worry! Your waiter will practically join you at your table and explain as many items on the menu as you need, and even make recommendations, if you wish. Like many other

Manhattan restaurants, Angelica Kitchen offers an amazing lunch deal: Drop in on a weekday between 11:30 a.m. and 5:00 p.m. and take advantage of their $6.75 deal that include a cup of soup, a slice of bread with your choice of spread, a small house salad, and a cup of tea. Although the foods sounds light and airy, you'll leave Angelica Kitchen just as full as you would from any carnivore's den. Plus, you can rest easy knowing that there's healthier food in your gullet and more cash in your wallet! Open daily, 11:30 a.m. - 10:30 p.m. *$Cash Only$*

BENDIX DINER

167 First Avenue (between 10th & 11th Streets), New York NY 10009. 212/260-4220. **Description:** The Bendix is a fine example of New York's many retro diners, places that tend to offer campy fun and good food at affordable prices. The look here is a sort of Neo-Deco in bright colors, with original canvases on the walls fitting for the traditionally artistic neighborhood. Unlike some of the city's other diners, though, the menu here is as eclectic as Chelsea itself. Yes, there is authentic diner food, from omelettes to meatloaf. Good, strong coffee too, by the way. But the description of the grilled half-chicken tips you off to the style here: Marinated with Thai herbs and spices, Jewish style... Hmmm. The menu goes on to such wide-ranging items as chili con carne, fried tofu with ginger, yaki soba. Not to mention Po' Boy sandwiches, turkey melts, soups, salads, and burgers. Can they do so many different foods well? The answer appears to be yes. The food is homemade, cooked to order, and colorful. Sandwiches are on thick-cut fresh bread; French fries are done in the style of home-fry wedges, brown and crispy; Oriental dishes are served over brown rice, with crunchy vegetables. In fact, each platter that goes by your table looks so delightful that you want to come back and try them all. Ditto the homemade desserts! Open Sunday through Thursday, 8:00 a.m. - 11:00 p.m.; Friday and Saturday, 8:00 a.m. - 12:00 a.m. This restaurant has no liquor license but you are welcome to bring your own.

BENNY'S BURRITOS

93 Avenue A (at 6th Street), New York NY. 212/254-2054. **Description:** Benny's has to be one of the liveliest, hippest spots in the East Village, serving up great Californian- and Mexican-style food in full platters for low prices. Obviously burritos are the specialty of the house; they come wrapped in a fresh 12-inch flour tortilla, making a burrito you shouldn't even try to pick up with your hands. Most are in the $5.00 - $6.00 range. These bargain meals include such exotic varieties as the Super Vegetarian, filled with vegetables, beans, rice, cheese, guacamole, and fresh salsa; and an interesting nondairy burrito made with a whole-wheat tortilla and filled with beans, brown rice, tofu, sour cream, and guacamole. Lest you think Benny's caters exclusively to the vegetarian crowd, there's a magnificent grilled shrimp burrito that comes with cilantro and garlic sauce. At $8.50, it's a notch or two over some of the other entrees price-wise, but it is a wonderful change of pace. Benny's also features tacos, enchiladas,

quesadillas, and chili, all of which come in beef, chicken, and vegetarian varieties. Most dishes include your choice of black beans or pinto beans. (As you have probably deduced by now, Benny's is very health-conscious.) Desserts at Benny's are special, too; different homemade delicacies such as orange flan are offered daily. If you like Benny's as much as Mr. C did, you may find yourself wishing you could buy ingredients from them in bulk so you can make your own versions of their dishes at home. Well, you can. The good folks at Benny's will be happy to sell larger quantities of their no-lard, no-preservatives, no-MSG fixings but be warned that the people here have had a lot of practice, and you may find it tough to match their standards. And besides, if you make the stuff at home, you'll miss out on the glorious and unapologetic boisterousness that is a nightly attraction at Benny's. *$Cash Only$*

CUCINA DI PESCE

87 East 4th Street (between Second & Third Avenues), New York NY 10003. 212/260-6800. **Description:** This East Village haunt has long been one of Manhattan's most popular and enjoyable Italian restaurants. The prices are extremely reasonable, with pasta dishes starting at just $6.95 for a large plate of vegetarian lasagna; and the same price for a plate of fusilli with sun-dried tomatoes and gorgonzola cheese, served up in a cream sauce. Other pasta dishes include linguine with fresh clams in white or red sauce and shells stuffed with calamari and anchovies in spicy red sauce. Main course entrees start at $6.95 for such dishes as grilled breast of chicken with sautéed mushrooms and garlic, or eggplant parmigiana. Going up the scale a little bit, you'll find veal marsala at $8.95, grilled tuna topped with peppers, olives, onions, and capers for $10.95. Even for these more expensive entrees, the prices are quite attractive indeed when you consider that each meal comes with spaghetti marinara. There are a number of good choices when it comes to appetizers. Try the escarole sautéed in a garlic and olive oil. Another good bet is the antipasta with fresh mozzarella and sun dried tomatoes. As you may gather, Cucina di Pesce adds a nouvelle twist to traditional Italian food. They must be doing something right, because crowds flock to this lively, urban restaurant. *$Cash Only$*

DOJO EAST

24 St. Mark's Place, New York NY 10003. 212/674-9821. **Description:** If you live in either Village and like inexpensive healthy foods, you probably know about the two Dojo restaurants. They take Japanese and other Eastern culinary methods as a point of departure, mixing them with more American-style dishes with intriguing results and at super-cheap prices. First and foremost, Dojo is home to the soy burger, served in a whole-wheat pita pocket with lettuce, tomato, and carrot. The hijiki tofu sandwich is another interesting selection, combining seaweed with tofu to form a patty that is served burger-style in pita bread with a teriyaki sauce. Another great sandwich -- the one that Mr. C chose to indulge in -- was the hummus pita pocket, stuffed with avocado,

tomatoes, cucumbers, and sprouts. There are lots of vegetable plates including vegetable curry, stir-fried vegetables over brown rice, and vegetable tempura. Salads will run you about $5.00 and offer a wide choice of Eastern and Western approaches. Dojo also serves hamburgers (and turkey burgers, for that matter), chicken or beef curry, and a variety of seafood dishes. Dinner entrees, like grilled salmon and barbecued chicken, are under $8.00. In fact, I don't think I saw a thing on the menu for more than $8.00. There is a wide selection of beverages here, including a number of fascinating imported juice and mineral water selections, wine, and good beer on tap. Freshly made desserts can be had, too, in varieties both ennobling and as close to decadent as this crowd gets. In true New York style, Dojo serves up breakfast right up until the dinner hour, and again from 11:00 p.m. until closing. The raisin French toast with fresh strawberries is particularly good, and it's just $2.95. Whatever time of day or night you go, the place is likely to be crowded, so be prepared to grab a drink at the bar and wait for a table. Open Sunday through Thursday, 11:00 a.m. - 1:00 a.m.; Friday and Saturday, 11:00 a.m. - 2:00 a.m. *$Cash Only$*

FLOR'S KITCHEN

149 First Avenue (between 9th & 10th Streets), New York NY 10003. 212/387-8949. **World Wide Web address:** http://www.florskitchen.com. **Description:** If you've never tried Venezuelan food before, Flor's Kitchen is a great place to start. With authentic foods that are always fresh and carefully-prepared, a dining experience here is like eating in the kitchen of a friend. The just over 10-seat setup in this bright and colorful establishment adds to the intimate feeling. For starters, try one of Flor's Venezuelan corn cake specialties. Arepas come filled with beef, chicken, ham, tuna, cheese, vegetables, or tofu for just $3.00 to $3.50; deep fried empanadas (empanadas criollas) are filled with beef, chicken, cheese, or beans for $2.75 an order. Another house specialty is cachapas (pure corn pancakes) with cheese ($5.50) or ham and cheese ($6.00). Flor's Kitchen prepares a variety of fresh salads, adding such stomach-pleasing ingredients as green bean, potato, carrot, cauliflower, mango, and avocado, for around $6.00. Another great dish to try is a cup of the Chupe soup, which is a delicious medley of chicken, potatoes, corn, white cheese, and milk. If you're looking for a heartier entree, Flor's delivers, with the most expensive meal costing only $13.00. Try a helping of Pabellon Criollo (shredded beef, rice, plantains, and black beans) for $9.00, and a plate of beef or vegetable lasagna for just $8.00. With no liquor license to speak of, Flor's Kitchen gets very inventive with the beverages they do offer: mango, passion fruit, papaya, and strawberry shakes will taste great; Guarapo de Papelon is a tasty mix of sugar cane and lemon; or try the rice-based Chicha. Flor's also offers a variety of regular and specialty coffees, fresh juices, and soda. And if, after all that, you've saved room for dessert, the Quesillo (caramel pudding) or Dulce Tres Leches (translation: three-milk-cake) will keep you going. For a friendly meal in the not-always-so-friendly-

big-city, Flor's Kitchen is as flavorful in taste as it is in atmosphere. Open Sunday, 10:00 a.m. - 10:00 p.m.; Monday through Thursday, 11:00 a.m. - 11:00 p.m.; Friday and Saturday, 11:00 a.m. - 12:00 a.m.

GREAT JONES CAFE
54 Great Jones Street, New York NY 10012. 212/674-9304. **E-mail address:** info@greatjonescafe.com. **Description:** Way down below Cooper Square, just off the Bowery, you'll find this cozy little bar/cafe (look for the banner overhead, or you could miss it). That puts it near such diverse musical homes as the Amato Opera and the rock club CBGB's, as well as the Jean Cocteau Repertory Theater and La Mama all inexpensive entertainment options. The cafe, meanwhile, is a great little hangout if you're in on the young art scene. The music in here is as different from one song to the next as the clubs outside, wandering from blues to zydeco to hard rock. The food takes its cue from that Cajun beat, though, and stays there; great jambalaya, spicy but not too, served with homemade jalapeño cornbread for $7.95. Blackened catfish ($10.95) comes with the jambalaya on the side (or your choice of two sides) and a big, fresh salad. For simpler eats, rustle up some Creole wings ($3.95) or one of several varieties of big, thick burgers from $5.25 for the basic to $6.95 for a bacon cheeseburger and $7.25 for a chiliburger. Nice, crispy French fries, too. There are plenty of good beers on hand, like Anchor Steam and other microbrews and imports. Great Jones also has a $8.95 brunch on Saturdays and Sundays. *$Cash Only$*

HELENA'S
432 Lafayette Street, New York NY 10003. 212/677-5151. **E-mail address:** Tapas432@aol.com. **Description:** As I've said before and will undoubtedly say again, one of the best ways to save money while experimenting with new foods is to go tapas! Whether you're meeting one friend or 10, tapas restaurants allow you to sample a variety of foods for (usually) very little money. Helena's, an authentic Spanish restaurant in NoHo, certainly understands this philosophy. Helena's even offers a number of group tapas specials that will certainly fill you and your companion(s) up for as little as $15.00 per person. You'll be introduced to such new and tasty foods as aceitunas (Mediterranean olives) and boquerones (anchovy fillets). The atmosphere is hip, fun, and festive... shouldn't you be too? Open daily, 5:00 p.m. - 3:00 a.m.

LANZA'S RESTAURANT
168 First Avenue (between 10th & 11th Streets), New York NY 10009. 212/674-7014. **E-mail address:** SalAnthon@aol.com. **World Wide Web address:** http://www.salanthony.com. **Description:** When you're in New York and are thinking Italian, think Sal Anthony. As one of the city's largest Italian restaurateurs (he owns several restaurants and Italian markets), Sal Anthony's restaurants are known for authentic Italian dining in a casual atmosphere. And while prices can sometimes go a bit beyond Mr. C's spending limit, a number of prix fixe options make dining an

affordable as well as enjoyable experience. For lunch (until 3:00 p.m.), Lanza offers a fantastic menu of filling foods for just $10.50 per person. You can even watch as the cooks prepare your delicious meal. Make it there in time for the fixed price dinner (Monday through Saturday, 4:00 p.m. - 6:30 p.m.; Sunday, 3:30 p.m. - 6:30 p.m.), and you can enjoy your choice of appetizer (sweet melon and prosciutto, clams oreganata), entree (chicken breast with fennel and cream, fusilli with tomato and prosciutto), dessert (black and white chocolate cake, spumoni), and coffee, tea, espresso, or cappuccino for just $17.50. Didn't make the 6:30 p.m. cut-off? If you can hold out until 9:00 p.m., Lanza will be at it again. Drop in daily after 9:00 p.m. and you can partake of their Late Night Pasta Dinner for just $13.95. This includes all the same goodies listed before: appetizer (arugula salad, mozzarella and roasted peppers), pasta entree (capellini primavera, rigatini toscana), dessert (cannoli, cheesecake), and an after dinner rejuvenator (coffee, tea, espresso, cappuccino). This is one place where you're definitely getting more for your money. Open daily.

LIFE CAFE
343 East 10th Street (at Avenue B), New York NY 10009. 212/477-8791. **World Wide Web address:** http://www. lifecafenyc.com. **Description**: If you're a fan of Broadway theater, you've probably heard of Life Cafe. A pivotal scene in the smash hit Rent played out at this very place. Now you can experience Life for yourself, and at an affordable price no less. Life Cafe offers fantastic and healthy American food, with a focus on vegetarian dining. A good way to start out the meal is with one of their salads like the house specialty, the Life Salad. It's chock full of tofu, vegetables, rice, and beans over mixed greens and is well worth the less than $7.00 price tag. Lots of entrees are available for under $10.00 and include such meals as grilled pork chops, Thai vegetable stir fry, and Southern fried chicken. Life Cafe also serves breakfast, lunch, and brunch (on weekends). Anytime you come, you're bound to find a number of dishes that are delicious, affordable, and wholesome. Open Sunday through Thursday, 11:00 a.m. - 1:00 a.m.; Friday and Saturday, 11:00 a.m. - 3:00 a.m.

OLD DEVIL MOON
511 East 12th Street (between Avenues A & B), New York NY 10009. 212/475-4357. **Description:** No, you don't have to drink that old bourbon and cointreau concoction to eat here, but you do have to leave all ideas of a diet at the doorstep. Old Devil Moon offers honest-to-goodness, down-home Southern cooking in a casual East Village setting. While many people claim it is the sinful pies that keep the cash register ringing (the owner/chef actually sells these pies for further distribution at a number of other local eateries), others keep coming back for the too-good-to-be-true $8.00 brunch. Whatever the case and whatever your preference, you would be hard pressed to find any other food that is quite so filling and rich. Appetizers include shrimp chipotle ($6.50), sweet potato scallion hash ($4.95), and fried green tomatillos ($4.50). Vegetarian plates, which include chicken fried tofu ($8.50),

pepper crust tofu steak ($9.50), and jambalaya ($8.95) don't ever even reach the $10.00 mark. For those who aren't afraid to put a little meat in their diet, there's plenty here to satisfy the heartiest of appetites, like ribs ($10.95) and chicken fried steak ($10.95). From 5:00 p.m. until 7:30 p.m. everyday, catch the Moonrise special. For just $9.95, you can enjoy three course meal with salad, dinner (choice of catfish, BBQ chicken, brisket, or pasta), and dessert (pies, cakes, cobbler). My suggestion is to start out with some biscuits and gravy, move on to the catfish, and finish up with a slice of peanut butter pie. Neither your stomach nor your wallet will be disappointed. Open Sunday, 10:00 a.m. - 11:00 p.m.; Monday through Thursday, 6:00 p.m. - 11:00 p.m.; Friday, 6:00 p.m. - 12:00 a.m.; Saturday, 10:00 a.m. - 12:00 a.m.

PASSAGE TO INDIA
308 East 6th Street, New York NY 10003. 212/529-5770. **Description:** One of the best-loved Indian restaurants along the East Village's Curry Row, Passage to India is like a brief trip to a far-off land. Its interior is quite pleasant, with natural wood decor and candlelit tables. Sitar music fills the room, but gently enough to permit conversation. The outstanding feature here is the restaurant's tandoor, a clay oven where a variety of breads are baked to golden perfection. Those breads, here called sundries, are terrific appetizers. There are a dozen kinds, from $1.25 - $2.95, each of which fills an entire plate, large as a record album. Other good appetizers include Mulligatawny Soup, a large bowl of spicy lentils with a handful of vegetable fritters on the side. Main courses are many; 10 or more choices each among chicken, seafood, vegetarian, or lamb and beef dinners. Curries start at just $5.25. Beef Vindaloo ($6.50) offers a super-spicy sauce. Portions are ample; indeed, you may well have trouble finishing. Service, like the spices, runs hot and cold but someone is always nearby to refill your tea. Passage also offers several complete dinner deals for $11.00 - $13.00, which gets you soup and fritters, one of several entrees, Indian pudding for dessert, and coffee. Good deal. The place fills up quickly, especially on weekends, so call ahead.

RECTANGLE
159 Second Avenue (at 10th Street), New York NY 10003. 212/677-8410. **Description:** One of the few truly authentic Israeli restaurants in the city. The menu is written in both English and Hebrew, and the tables full of diners speaking both tongues further attest to Rectangle's authenticity. As with the politics of that region, it's not easy to define the boundaries even of cuisine. The food is an eclectic mix of Israeli and Yemenite; world peace may be elusive, but hey, everyone has to eat. Rectangle starts with all the basics, like beef, lamb, and chicken kebabs, couscous and baba ghanoush. Their falafel ($4.25 for five) is dark and intense, well spiced and crunchy. But beyond that, you'll find appetizers like mlawach ($5.75), a sort of deep-dish layered bread that's sometimes known as a Yemenite pancake; and Moroccan Cigars ($5.50), ground beef rolled up in phyllo dough. On weekends they add extra Yemenite delicacies, such as jahnun ($4.75), another

rolled flour dough that is actually cooked slowly overnight. In the morning they add eggs for a unique brunch dish. Weekday lunch specials are a real bargain too; just $7.75 gets you the entree of the day, with a cup of soup to start, plus coffee or tea. Rectangle's has a long wooden bar. There are beers from over a dozen countries not just Maccabee from Israel, but plenty from England, Ireland, and Germany, and even Red Stripe from Jamaica. And be sure to finish off your meal with a marvelously thick, grainy demitasse of Turkish coffee, just $1.50. Open daily, 11:30 a.m. - 12:00 a.m. and until 1:00 a.m. on Friday and Saturday.

STINGY LULU'S

129 St. Mark's Place (between Avenue A & First Avenue), New York NY 10009. 212/674-3545. **Description:** Stingy Lulu's really typifies the "funky" atmosphere the East Village and it's dining establishments are known for. From the bright colors that meet you to the unique menu items, everything about Stingy Lulu's screams comfort and welcome. At the heart of Stingy Lulu's is a diner: they serve typical comfort foods like salads, burgers, and pastas until late, late into the night (or early in the morning, depending on your perception). Still, in keeping with the cutting-edge nature of the neighborhood it inhabits, Stingy Lulu's offers a distinctly twenty-first-century twist. Instead of the traditional chicken noodle or chili, Stingy Lulu's soup standard is always vegetarian. Forget the mozzarella sticks, here it's Turkish cigars (filo dough with feta parsley). Lulu's "Not So Stingy Salad" (smoked salmon, asparagus, mushrooms, and pink peppercorns over mixed greens) reigns over the more traditional Caesar salad (though they've got those too). Lulu's chicken sandwich with roasted tomato and olive tapenade is just one of the sandwiches that dares to be different. As for the main course, you'll find such well orchestrated meals as seared salmon with tarragon cream sauce for under $11.00. In fact, that's actually the most expensive dish on the menu. Then again, what else would you expect from a place that refers to itself as "stingy"? Open Sunday, 10:00 a.m. - 4:00 a.m.; Monday through Thursday, 11:00 a.m. - 4:00 a.m.; Friday, 11:00 a.m. - 5:00 a.m.; Saturday, 10:00 a.m. - 5:00 a.m. *$Cash Only$*

TERESA'S

103 First Avenue (between 6th & 7th Streets), New York NY. 212/228-0604. **Description:** First off, Teresa's is not the kind of restaurant that is all that concerned about making an impression; it's decidedly no-frills, and we like it that way! That's not to say that eating here doesn't make for an enjoyable experience. In fact, if it's good food and good prices you're after, Teresa's is one of the city's best. The enormous menu is comprised of lots of breakfast foods (served all day), sandwiches, and entrees. While considered a Polish eatery, there are plenty of items that aren't typical of Polish cuisine. In the morning, buttermilk pancakes with bananas, blueberries, and apple and walnuts are sure to get your engine revving for right around $4.00. Omelettes are another

great choice, with most priced under $5.00 (even after you add the cheese, veggies, ham, or kielbasa). For lunch, they offer a different soup for every day of the week. Ukrainian borscht, cabbage, and white bean are just a few of the varieties you'll find. Teresa's offers more than 10 kinds of sandwiches and burgers, most for under $5.00. Veal cutlet, pork chop, pastrami, and chicken salad are just a few of the things you can grab for take-out or sit in and eat. Prices on entrees fluctuate between lunch and dinner, but rarely will you see anything for over $10.00. Veal goulash, chopped steak, beef stroganoff, and kasha with sautéed onions are some of the traditional meals offered. Teresa's also serves up some worthwhile fish dishes (including sole and trout) for well under $10.00 a serving. And don't forget the pierogies, filled with cheese, meat, potato, or sauerkraut and mushrooms. Get them boiled or fried for under $5.00 a plate. Homemade blintzes ($3.25 - $6.75), are fabulous: crispy on the outside, sweet on the inside, and dusted on top with confectioners' sugar. Open Sunday through Thursday, 7:00 a.m. - 11:00 p.m.; Friday and Saturday, 7:00 a.m. - 12:00 a.m. *$Cash Only$*

TWO BOOTS

37 Avenue A (between 2nd & 3rd Streets), New York NY 10009. 212/505-2276. **Description:** What does Two Boots mean? It means that someone had the novel idea of combining food from Italy, a country shaped like a boot, with food from Louisiana, a state shaped like a boot. The result is wild, wacky, and extremely popular. Where else can you order something like penne jambalaya ($10.95), a spicy mix of shrimp, chicken, andouille sausage, and piquante sauce over penne? Or capellini leonetta ($8.95), pasta tossed with crawfish and sun dried tomatoes in a cayenne cream sauce? Two Boots offers lots of great salads and appetizers as well, most for under $8.00. But what has made Two Boots a recognizable name around town (and allowed them to open several branch locations) is their pizza. Named after such pop culture icons as *Seinfeld*'s Newman and Steve Buscemi's "Mr. Pink" character from *Reservoir Dogs*, it is obvious that Two Boots caters to the young and hip. Pizzas come in three sizes: individual, medium, and large. Prices range anywhere from $6.95 for an individual cheese, to $21.95 for a large orchida (five toppings). My personal choice? The Alphaville ($8.95 - $18.95) mix of goat cheese, sun dried tomatoes, and jalapeño pesto on a veggie crust keeps me feeling forever young. The boot motif even carries over into the shape of their frosted beer mugs, which gives you an idea of the ambiance here. The place is fairly raucous, painted in bright colors of red, yellow and blue. Casual foods, like Po' Boy sandwiches and calzones, add to the fun for groups -- especially those with kids. And let's not forget the homemade desserts, like peanut butter and pecan pie. Open daily, 5:00 p.m. - 12:00 a.m.

VESELKA COFFEE SHOP

144 Second Avenue (at 9th Street), New York NY 10003. 212/228-9682. **Description:** For a dining experience that is truly New York and Old World, Veselka is one of the best. You can stuff

yourself here for just a few rubles. The front of the joint is the coffee shop part, with lots of winding counter space. Cut through to the back and there are two rooms--up and down--with tables. Like all the Russian/Polish restaurants in the neighborhood, the fare at Veselka consists of borscht, pierogies, blintzes, stuffed cabbage, and the rest. Various combination plates allow you to sample lots of these. The deluxe meal combo starts with a cup of soup (several choices daily), and moves on to salad, a stuffed cabbage, grilled kielbasa, and three pierogies, (meat, potato, and cabbage). Hearty, to say the least. You can also have a vegetarian platter instead. If you have room, try a Polish poppyseed danish or one of their many pies with some fresh-ground coffee. With or without dessert, you'll definitely want to linger awhile before getting up.

YAFFA CAFE
97 St. Mark's Place (between First Avenue & Avenue A), New York NY. 212/674-9302. **Description:** Yaffa Cafe is an East Village landmark, serving a wide variety of food in their dark, cozy restaurant/bar, or out back in their walled-in garden. It's a scene just about any time of day, filled with artists, punkers, musicians, and young professionals. The food is fine, whether you nibble on a Yaffa Salad for $5.50 with pita bread on the side or fettucine marinara for $6.25. A chicken teriyaki dinner ($8.25) includes a green salad and bread. Yaffa also serves up a mean weekend brunch for just $7.95. Whenever you go, one thing's certain there will be plenty to look at and plenty to eat, and it won't take plenty of cash to enjoy it. Open daily, 24 hours.

RESTAURANTS
🍽 Gramercy Park & The Flatiron District 🍽

Where? Bounded by the East River, Avenue of the Americas, 13th Street, and 29th Street; includes Union Square.

Best Known For: Publishing, advertising, and graphic design firms, the Flatiron Building, and Greenmarket (an open-air fresh produce market in Union Square).

Insider Tip: President Theodore Roosevelt's birthplace is located in Gramercy Park.

BACHUE

36 West 21st Street (between Fifth Avenue & Avenue of the Americas), New York NY 10010. 212/229-0870. **Description:** Warning: Bachue is a strictly vegan restaurant! Now that we've gotten rid of all those who are scared off by such a concept, let's discuss the sundry dishes that Bachue has to offer. Everyday, Bachue offers an alternatively healthy choice for breakfast, lunch, and dinner. For breakfast, try some whole grain pancakes with pure maple syrup and tofu whipped topping, or scrambled tofu with walnuts and onions, a bagel, and home fries. For lunch, Bachue offers a number of light sandwiches and wraps including the highly-recommended Burrito Bandito. And just what is this concoction, you might ask? The Burrito Bandito is a whole wheat tortilla with beans, seitan, tofu, rice, roasted red peppers, avocado, cabbage slaw, salsa, and tofu sour cream (side salad included). Now that's what I call a meal! Dinner, which is served after 5:00 p.m., offers much of the lunch time menu, though the prices may change. But, before you dig in to your dinner, don't forget the appetizers. I highly recommend the blue corn chips and salsa, the cold soba noodles and peanut sauce, the nori rolls with pickled ginger and wasabi, or the fried plantains. (With an honorable mention going to the hummus). Open Monday through Friday, 8:00 a.m. - 10:30 p.m.; Saturday, 10:00 a.m. - 10:30 p.m.; and Sunday, 11:00 a.m. - 7:00 p.m. This restaurant has no liquor license but you are welcome to bring your own.

BAMIYAN

358 Third Avenue (at 26th Street), New York NY 10016. 212/481-3232. **Description:** If you've never had Afghani food, then I hope that you like the following three items: yogurt, mint, and mint yogurt. No matter what the dish, chances are it will be encased with the stuff. Bamiyan offers authentic Afghani food at great prices and in good portions. For an appetizer, try one of their amazing dumplings, like Aushak, a scallion dumpling with (you guessed it) mint yogurt sauce. Most appetizers like Boulanee, turnovers with scallions, potatoes, and spiced pumpkin, are around $4.00. Another great appetizer is the Fesenjan, chicken with walnuts and pomegranate juice. Yet, Afghani food also showcases a variety of pasta dishes, like Asheh Gooshti, noodles with meat

sauce and (mmm hmmm) yogurt; or Asheh Keshida Lubia, noodles with red kidney bean sauce and (that's right) yogurt. Bamiyan has a fairly extensive list of kabobs, most fairly priced between $10.00 and $15.00. For the vegetarians at your table, try one of Bamiyan's fresh mixed salads or one of their many vegetarian specialties. If you're looking for even more authenticity, take a seat on the comfortably-pillowed floor. Call ahead for hours.

CAFFE ADELINA
119 East 17th Street (between Irving Place & Park Avenue South), New York NY 10003. 212/674-6677. **E-mail address:** SalAnthon@aol.com. **World Wide Web address:** http://www.salanthonys.com. **Description:** Caffe Adelina is an added bonus for those who work or live in the Flatiron District. Whether dining out or eating in, this Italian deli has got your craving covered. For breakfast, try one of their delicious baked goodies like a muffin, cinnamon roll, apple turnover, or a fresh bagel. A variety of pastries are available for under $2.00. Try one of their delicious panini sandwiches like smoked salmon with mozzarella and tomato ($4.65) or grilled vegetable ($4.65). Like any good Italian market/cafe, Caffe Adelina will serve you up a big stone oven pizza for $13.50 or under. If the normal pizza is a bit more than you were looking for, individual pies can be had for $3.50 - $4.95. Light entrees include penne with sun dried tomatoes ($4.25) and stuffed eggplant ($4.25). Yet, my favorite part of Caffe Adelina is the desserts: cream puffs, eclairs, tiramisu, apricot sponge cake, chocolate dipped strawberries, cookies, and all the rest of your favorite treats ($.85 - $3.25) are definitely worth a vacation from your diet. Open daily, 7:00 a.m. - 11:00 p.m.

CHEZ GOURMET
281 Fifth Avenue (at 30th Street), New York NY. 212/213-9366. **Description:** Talk about cheap!! Every breakfast item on the menu is priced under $3.75. There are more than 120 sandwich choices including: Mexican egg salad, Arizona-style chicken salad; eggplant parmigiana; grilled vegetable, crab meat salad, cracked pepper turkey, Texas roast beef with BBQ sauce, and prosciutto. All sandwiches are priced around $4.00 - $6.00.

THE GAMUT BISTRO LOUNGE
102 East 25th Street (at Park Avenue South), New York NY 10010. 212/598-4555. **World Wide Web address:** http://www.gamutnewyork.com. **Description:** Cute and sophisticated at the same time, this bistro offers gourmet sandwiches, salads, and pastas. Mr. C recommends the delicious chicken and fresh fruit salad (the chicken is poached in apple sauce) for $8.50; pan-seared tuna nicoise $14.00; and sweet and sour pineapple sesame chicken tenders $7.00. Open daily, 11:00 a.m. - 10:00 p.m.

HEARTLAND BREWERY
35 Union Square West, New York NY 10003. 212/645-3400. **Description:** Just when you thought you couldn't find an affordable brew pub in the city, along came Heartland Brewery.

Come for the beer and stay for the food. The beer list offers five standards year-round: Cornhusker Lager, Harvest Wheat, Indiana Pale Ale, Red Rooster Ale, and Farmer John's Oatmeal Stout. There are also seasonal favorites like Indian River Ale and Smiling Pumpkin Ale. More than just your typical pub fare is the order of the day here. The menu includes hummus and eggplant caponata, jerk chicken, fresh Maine crab cakes, salmon or catfish sandwiches, and buffalo burgers. Main dishes range from $12.00 - $20.00, appetizers and sandwiches $8.00 - $12.00.

L'ANNAM

393 Third Avenue, New York NY. 212/686-5168. **Description:** If you don't mind waiting in line, L'Annam is a culinary experience everyone should try. While the interior is not as delightful as one might hope for, the food is. The Vietnamese restaurant came highly recommended by the *Daily News*, *Zagat's*, and friends. The menu includes over 50 dishes from calamari salad ($5.75) to sautéed Saigon noodle ($6.25). From 11:30 a.m. - 4:00 p.m., try one of L'Annam's 20 luncheon specials for just $4.95. Lunch entrees include sautéed chicken with ginger sauce, sautéed shrimp with broccoli, stir-fried veggies with bean curd, oxtail soup, rice vermicelli with your choice of topping, and rice crepe with cucumber and sprouts. The large menu includes appetizers (spring rolls for $2.45, lemongrass chicken for $4.25, and combo platters for $6.75); soups (curry shrimp for $2.95); salads (chicken for $4.95, calamari for $5.75); curry dishes from $7.95 - $12.95; noodle dishes, soups, and platters from $5.50 - $7.95; and a variety of chicken, pork, beef, and vegetarian dishes that do not top $10.00. Don't forget to wash all your savings down with a refreshing glass of coconut juice ($2.50) or ginger iced tea ($1.50).

MOLLY'S PUB

287 Third Avenue, New York NY 10010. 212/889-3361. **Description:** Sometimes, nothing hits the spot like a traditional Irish feast; shepherd's pie ($8.25), lamb stew ($8.25), and corned beef and cabbage ($8.50) are just a few of the Celtic treats that you can indulge in at Molly's Pub. For lunch and dinner, Molly's offers a mixture of typical pub fare and Irish classics. Salads, like The Continental--a bed of mixed greens topped with chicken breast and walnut dressing--are priced between $4.95 and $7.75. Sandwiches, including an enormous turkey club, corned beef on rye, and grilled chicken breast, are all served with french fries and seldom priced over $6.25. You can't think of a pub without thinking of burgers; Molly's serves up a variety of toppings on their juicy 10-ounce patties, all reasonably-priced from $5.75 - $6.50. Besides the previously-mentioned, entrees include a vegetarian platter ($6.95), pork chops with apples and onions ($9.95), and flaky-crusted chicken pot pie ($8.95). The fact that the most expensive thing on the menu (10-ounce New York sirloin) is only $13.95 should assure you that your wallet is in good hands at Molly's. Just be sure not to overdo it on that other Irish delicacy--beer! Molly's is famed for its delicious Guinness pints

(just $4.00), as well as its extensive draught beer list that includes ales from Murphy's, Bass, McSorley's, and Harp. So curl up by the fireplace at one of New York's most cherished Irish pubs. Open Monday through Saturday, 11:00 a.m. - 4:00 a.m.; Sunday, 12:00 p.m. - 4:00 a.m.

NOODLES ON 28
394 Third Avenue (at 28th Street), New York NY 10016. 212/679-2888. **Description:** Noodles on 28 is popular with the locals because it is fast, cheap, and good. Every noodle under the sun is available as well as soups, dim sums, fried rice and oodles of other Chinese dishes. Most dishes can be served over noodles for $1.00 extra. Lunch is a real bargain. There are 20 lunch specials for $4.95 and 25 "popular lunch specials" for $5.95. These are served from 11:30 a.m. - 4:00 p.m. Open Sunday through Thursday, 11:30 a.m. - 11:30 p.m.; Friday and Saturday, 11:30 a.m. - 12:00 a.m.

OLD TOWN BAR & RESTAURANT
45 East 18th Street, New York NY 10003. 212/529-6732. **Description:** Lower midtown is well-known for its many 19-century saloons: all dark wood, brass, and hearty food. Most of these, alas, can also be fairly expensive, especially if you figure in a hefty liquor tab. For this reason, many such bars can also be mistaken for a Brooks Brothers showroom. One alternative that just about anyone can afford is the Old Town Bar. It's a long, high-ceilinged place with two floors of that same turn-of-the-century New York charm and a great place to hang out over beers and a simple menu of inexpensive fare. These are mostly sandwiches, whether cold deli varieties such as smoked turkey, bacon, and muenster cheese or a hot fish sandwich made with fried flounder ($7.25). You can also get a bowl of chili for under $6.00, and a fresh, plump burger for under $7.00 (with French fries or new potato salad). The beer, of course, is not so cheap, but that's where they make their money. If you're really watching your wallet, nurse a Ballantine Ale and enjoy the food and the bustling atmosphere. It is, to say the least, a popular (read: crowded) watering hole, especially after 5:00 p.m. The place also has the distinction of being immortalized in the minds of late-night television viewers everywhere; it's the bar you used to see every night during the opening of David Letterman's show. The intro has since changed, but let's hope this Gotham landmark never does. Open daily, 11:30 a.m. - 1:30 a.m.

REPUBLIC
37 Union Square West, New York NY 10003. 212/627-7172. **Description:** For a quick and delicious meal, Republic urges you to "think noodles"! This narrow, sophisticated space offers plenty of seating and food until late at night. It's a great place to grab a healthy meal on the go. Best of all, dishes range from about $6.00 - $8.00 each. While the menu, predominantly, is Asian-influenced, you can find plenty of other cuisines represented as well. The pad thai, for example, is a well-known dish from Thailand; can you guess where the Vietnamese vegetable noodles originated? The point is, Republic takes the philosophy of a noodle shop one step further and offers tastes for a variety of palates. Open Sunday

through Wednesday, 12:00 p.m. - 11:00 p.m.; Thursday through Saturday, 12:00 p.m. - 12:00 a.m.

SOTTO CINQUE
417 Third Avenue, New York NY 10016-8174. 212/685-2037. **Description:** How can you beat this? For those of you who don't speak fluent Italian, Sotto Cinque means "under five" and they're not talking about age here, they're talking about dollars! This basic pasta house offers about 10 different pasta dishes for (you guessed it) under $5.00! Choose from penne pomodoro, ravioli marinara, spaghetti puttanesca, gnocchi sorrentino, and penne ortolane. If there's nothing on the "under five" menu that gets your pulse going, there are more than 15 specialty pastas that are specially priced at $7.95. On this more advanced menu, you'll find things like manicotti with tomato sauce, penne romano, baked rigatoni with sausage, and vegetarian lasagna. There are also lots of appetizers and antipasti such as minestrone soup, stuffed mushrooms, and fresh mussels. The same value-pricing goes for sandwiches and desserts. At lunch time, they offer an even better deal: an appetizer (bruschetta, salad, or soup) and an entree (sandwich or pasta dish) for just $6.95. Sotto Cinque is especially good for quick and easy take-out, and the restaurant also offers free delivery. Open Sunday through Thursday, 11:00 a.m. - 11:00 p.m.; Friday and Saturday, 11:00 a.m. - 12:00 a.m.

SUNFLOWER DINER
359 Third Avenue (at 26th Street), New York NY. 212/532-8171. **Description:** The Sunflower Diner is like a shining ray of light on Third Avenue, as its charmingly yellow exterior can be seen for blocks. The selection is amazing at this diner. The seven page menu brings you back to the 1950s era with milk shakes, ice cream sodas, and an endless choice of burgers. Breakfast offerings are standard (eggs, pancakes, waffles). Most dishes are reasonably priced but you will pay more for dinner entrees like veal, shrimp, and surprisingly some of the pasta dishes. Most lunch items are under $8.00.

RESTAURANTS
🍽 Greenwich Village 🍽

Where? Bounded by the Hudson River, Broadway, Houston
Street, and 13th Street.

Best Known For: Beat and Punk Rock movements, New York
University, Washington Square.

Insider Tip: Edgar Allan Poe, Walt Whitman, Mark Twain, and
Edna St. Vincent Millay once occupied the narrowest
house in the city on 75½ Bedford Street.

BAGEL BUFFET

406 Avenue of the Americas (at 9th Street), New York NY 10011.
212/477-0448. **Description:** Talk about your Village institutions.
The place is clean and bright, if nothing fancy, with lots of small
tables; and best of all, it's open 24 hours a day. They hand-roll 19
varieties of bagels on the premises, including all the basics, along
with vegetable, honey, wheat, and even spinach bagels. Obviously,
breakfast is a big deal here. You can choose any of their 17
different types of omelettes, pancakes, or French toast, or a
platter of two eggs, potatoes, coffee or tea, bagel or toast, and
the choice of bacon, ham, or sausage for $3.55. Beat that with a
stick. Add a homemade muffin (six different flavors) for $1.25 or
a yogurt muffin for $1.65. Meanwhile, you can, of course, get just
about anything on a bagel including eggs, green olive cream cheese,
sliced lox, or hot corned beef. How about a Bagel Buffet tuna melt
for $4.25 or grilled chicken sandwich for $3.65? And this doesn't
even begin to touch the dinner specials like homemade baked
potato with melted muenster cheese on top or lasagna (meat or
vegetable) served with a bagel or roll for $3.25. This place has
everything under the sun! Open 24 hours daily. *$Cash Only$*

BAR SIX RESTAURANT

502 Avenue of the Americas (between 12th & 13th Streets), New
York NY 10011. 212/691-1363. **E-mail address:** barsix@aol.com.
Description: This cozy neighborhood bistro, which resembles a
Parisian cafe from the 1920s, serves French-Moroccan cuisine and
draws a predominantly young crowd. Specialties include bisteeya
(Moroccan chicken pie for $13.75) and tagine of chicken ($13.00 -
$14.75). Other entrees include grilled salmon, steak frites, and
mussels provençale. Entrees start under $10.00, though they can
work their way up to just under $20.00. For lunch, Bar Six offers
a variety of freshly-made sandwiches, from the traditional (B.L.T.
and tuna salad) to the non-traditional (grilled veggies with sheep's
milk ricotta and smoked salmon and egg salad), all priced between
$7.00 and $8.00. Theatergoers will enjoy the pre-theater prix
fixe dinner menu which, for $18.50, includes soup, salad, your
choice of entree (sautéed skate, roast chicken, grilled leg of lamb,
or penne), your choice of dessert (ice cream, sorbet, crème brûlée,
or lemon tart), and coffee or tea. Nightly dinner specials, all
priced at a flat $15.00, change throughout the week and include

such elaborate and tasty dishes as grand aoli broiled cod, homemade gnocchi with manila clams, and grilled poussin. And don't forget about Bar Six for brunch, with a weekend menu serving a variety of egg and omelette dishes ($5.50 - $8.50), entrees, and appetizers. The kitchen is open late, serving until 2:00 a.m. during the week and 3:00 a.m. on the weekend, so there's really no excuse for not stopping by.

CORNER BISTRO
331 West 4th Street, New York NY 10014. 212/242-9502. **Description:** The Corner Bistro serves up what are arguably some of the best burgers to be had in the Big Apple. Other establishments may claim their fair share of partisans but in Mr. C's opinion, said partisans couldn't have visited Corner Bistro yet. Monstrously sized burgers of freshly packed ground beef, served on an equally fresh roll, start at just $4.00. Nice. You can add an overflowing plate of crispy French fries for just $2.00 more. Alternatively, you might choose to pick up a chili burger for $5.25 or the Bistro burger topped with cheese and fresh bacon, all for a mere $5.00. If you don't want a burger, no problem: go for the grilled cheese and bacon sandwich, just $3.75. Add a bottle of Brooklyn Beer for $3.25, or a mug of Yuengling Dark for $2.00. Yes, the menu is simple and the atmosphere old-fashioned, the back room is composed of quaint wooden booths, but if you like good cheap food in an unassuming (okay, down-and-dirty) environment, this is the place. *$Cash Only$*

CUSTARD BEACH
33 East 8th Street (at University Place & Boardwalk), New York NY. 212/420-6039. **Description:** On a hot summer day there's nothing quite like a cone of frozen custard! This unusual treat was actually developed in the 1930s and is catching on again. This location of Custard Beach, the first in the franchise, opened in 1994 and has been churning out new batches every day since. It's similar to ice cream but not as cold and much creamier. For the traditional there are chocolate and vanilla flavors and for the more daring, peach cobbler, crème brûlée, and apple pie. Custard Beach will also custom make flavors to order. Even more intriguing...Ice Caps (frozen custard and Italian Ice swirled together) or Belgian waffles topped with custard. Prices range from $2.15 - $3.40. *$Cash Only$*

DOJO WEST
14 West 4th Street, New York NY 10012. 212/505-8934. **Description:** If you live in either Village and like inexpensive healthy foods, you probably know about the two Dojo restaurants. They take Japanese and other Eastern culinary methods as a point of departure, mixing them with more American-style dishes with intriguing results and at super-cheap prices. First and foremost, Dojo is home to the soy burger, served in a whole-wheat pita pocket with lettuce, tomato, and carrot. The hijiki tofu sandwich is another interesting selection, combining seaweed with tofu to form a patty that is served burger-style in pita bread with a

teriyaki sauce. Another great sandwich -- the one that Mr. C chose to indulge in -- was the hummus pita pocket, stuffed with avocado, tomatoes, cucumbers, and sprouts. There are lots of vegetable plates including vegetable curry, stir-fried vegetables over brown rice, and vegetable tempura. Salads will run you about $5.00 and offer a wide choice of Eastern and Western approaches. Dojo also serves hamburgers (and turkey burgers, for that matter), chicken or beef curry, and a variety of seafood dishes. Dinner entrees, like grilled salmon and barbecued chicken, are under $8.00. In fact, I don't think I saw a thing on the menu for more than $8.00. There is a wide selection of beverages here, including a number of fascinating imported juice and mineral water selections, wine, and good beer on tap. Freshly made desserts can be had, too, in varieties both ennobling and as close to decadent as this crowd gets. In true New York style, Dojo serves up breakfast right up until the dinner hour, and again from 11:00 p.m. until closing. The raisin French toast with fresh strawberries is particularly good, and it's just $2.95. Whatever time of day or night you go, the place is likely to be crowded, so be prepared to grab a drink at the bar and wait for a table. Open Sunday through Thursday, 11:00 a.m. - 1:00 a.m.; Friday and Saturday, 11:00 a.m. - 2:00 a.m. *$Cash Only$*

THE EMERALD PLANET
2 Great Jones Street, New York NY 10012. 212/353-WRAP. **Description:** Okay, so maybe it *is* just a wrap and smoothie joint, but you can't go wrong there, can you? Emerald Planet serves up a variety of delicious wraps all day long. They offer a pretty large menu consisting of chicken, beef, seafood, and vegetarian concoctions. The Bangkok (my personal favorite) is a great mix of chicken, veggies, and rice in a ginger and Thai-style peanut sauce. For seafood lovers, there's the Honolulu with snapper, salsa, and avocado; and the New Orleans with blackened shrimp and mango salsa. Carnivores will love the Seoul, a mix of steak, soy sauce, and rice on a wheat tortilla. But vegetarians, fear not: the Berkeley (tofu, sprouts, veggies, and rice) is just *one* of the meals that aims to please you! You should expect to pay between $5.00 and $8.00 for one of these rolled delights. Now, while some might say that this is a bit high for a sandwich, The Emerald Planet is all about atmosphere. Especially if you're exploring the city on your own, it's a comfortable and attractive place to sit and eat by your lonesome. Don't forget to wash it all down with one of their extraordinary smoothies ($2.50 - $3.50). Open Sunday, 12:00 p.m. - 8:00 p.m.; Monday through Friday, 9:00 a.m. - 10:00 p.m.; Saturday, 12:00 p.m. - 10:00 p.m.

JOHN'S OF BLEECKER STREET
278 Bleecker Street, New York NY 10014. 212/243-1680. **Description:** A fabulous place to grab a pizza in the Village. Most large pizzas go for $11.00 and a bottle of the house wine is $13.00. Other tasty entrees include ravioli, ziti, meatballs, and traditional Italian cuisine. Just like everything in the city, the service is fast paced, but there can be a wait for tables. *$Cash Only$*

THE TEMPLE IN THE VILLAGE

74 West 3rd Street (between La Guardia Place & Thompson Street), New York NY 10012. 212/475-5670. **Description:** Temple in the Village is a modest-sized eatery near NYU. It's a simple, quick, eat-in-or-take-out spot specializing in macrobiotic and vegetarian food. The specialty of the house is the large and extensive buffet of vegetables, rice dishes, and a wealth of other vegetarian items, all available at under $5.50 a pound. Take as much as you like. There are more than 60 things to choose from, and everything takes your health into account. Whether you're a strict vegan or a "sometimes vegetarian," The Temple in the Village can cater to your needs. All food is prepared with no sugar, no dairy, no MSG, and no preservatives. Dishes are also low in fat and salt and high in fiber. If The Temple in the Village sounds like the kind of eating you could enjoy everyday, they'll be happy to do that as well. For $89.00, you can purchase an All-You-Can-Eat Meal Plan ticket, entitling you to 10 all-you-can-eat meals. Think about it, that's less than $9.00 a serving. Plus, you can take food home with you, and they'll throw in a hot cup of tea with each meal. The decor is spare (after the Japanese, with rice paper decorations and such). Classical music plays over the sound system; the tables are small and plain. In other words, this Temple is nothing fancy. But, if you're in the area and looking for a quick and simple meal, this is a great spot to park. Open daily, 11:00 a.m. - 9:30 p.m.

RESTAURANTS
🍽 Lower East Side & Chinatown 🍽

Where? The area below Houston Street and between Lafayette
Street and the East River; includes Little Italy.
Best Known For: Diverse ethnic population (Chinese, Italian, and
Jewish), Orchard Street Market, great food.
Insider Tip: Don't miss Little Italy's week-long Festa di San
Gennaro in September.

BO KY

80 Bayard Street (between Mott & Mulberry Streets), New York
NY 10013. 212/406-2292. **Description:** If it's a genuine
Vietnamese kitchen you're looking for, Bo Ky is the answer. Though
the menu is largely incomprehensible, it *does* contain some 30
dishes, so you're bound to find something to your liking. Generic
entree names like "Special Beef Flat Noodle Soup" or "Country
Style Duck" might not provide as much description as you were
hoping for, but don't be afraid to take a chance and order it
anyway. Being open-minded and willing to stray from your normal
comfort zone are definite pluses here. Another great way to
decide your edible fate is to check out what everyone else is
ordering and point! As this place is always busy, there's sure to be
plenty to look at. And with nearly everything priced under $10.00,
you can afford to be adventurous. Open daily, 8:00 a.m. - 9:30 p.m.
$Cash Only$

IL FORNAIO

132-A Mulberry Street (between Grand & Hester Streets), New
York NY 10013. 212/226-8306. **Description:** Making your way
through the maze of eateries in Little Italy can be daunting, not
to mention expensive. Il Fornaio is one place that dares to be
different, offering super-cheap, good food in a clean, bright cafe.
Their white-tiled open kitchen cranks out brick-oven-baked pizzas
and calzones, along with a plethora of pasta dinners. In the more
cozy room beside the kitchen, you can chow down in a casual
setting. Individual-sized pizzas start at $5.00, with an extra
$1.00 tacked on for each topping you choose. Calzones are another
dependable and inexpensive choice, starting at just $4.00. As is
usual in any restaurant, pasta can be the way to go if you're not
looking to shell out too much cash. Il Fornaio brings inexpensive
pasta to a new level with the majority of the nearly 20 choices
being priced under $8.00. All your favorites are here; lasagna,
spaghetti and meatballs, and fettucine alfredo are some of the
least expensive offerings. Il Fornaio also serves up several
chicken, veal, and seafood dishes, and it's a rarity to see anything
over $10.00. Shrimp parmesan, chicken al forno, and veal marsala
are some of the dishes you'll be tempted to try. There is also a
chalkboard of daily specials, including soups and salads (all of
which are à la carte) for a truly inexpensive and quick alternative
to the bigger showplace restaurants. Open Monday through

Thursday, 11:30 a.m. - 11:00 p.m.; Friday and Saturday, 11:00 a.m. - 12:00 a.m.

KATZ'S DELI

205 East Houston Street, New York NY. 212/674-3270. **Description:** Noted as one of the best deli's in town, Katz's has been serving hand-carved pastrami sandwiches ($9.40) for decades. And, if you remember Katz's from the famous diner scene in *When Harry Met Sally*, you can just imagine how good the food is. Open Sunday through Tuesday, 8:00 a.m. - 10:00 p.m.; Wednesday and Thursday, 8:00 a.m. - 11:00 p.m.; Friday and Saturday, 8:00 a.m. - 3:00 a.m.

NEW YORK NOODLE TOWN

28½ Bowery (at Bayard Street), New York NY 10002. 212/349-0923. **Description:** If you can divert your attention from the sight of a windowful of roasting animals to the menu at New York Noodle Town, I am willing to bet you will find one of the city's tastiest and cheapest noodle shops. To state the obvious, New York Noodle Town has a menu full of terrific noodle dishes, with just about everything under $8.00. But what keeps people coming back again and again (chances are, anyone you ask in this place would consider themself a "regular") is the deliciously crisp, salt-baked seafood dishes. From squid to shrimp to soft-shell crabs (which many consider to be the absolute best in the city), you will not walk away disappointed. If these ocean-dwelling dishes do not strike a craving (try some anyway), there's plenty of standard Chinese fare here, like dumplings, duck, and pork. Even more amazing than how filling the food is, is how inexpensive it is. *$Cash Only$*

NHA TRANG

87 Baxter Street (between Bayard & Canal Streets), New York NY 10013. 212/233-5948. **Description:** What Nha Trang lacks in decor and prettiness, it certainly makes up for in authenticity. One of the best things about this restaurant (besides the food, of course) is the fact that it is kind of set apart from the normal tourist-traveled road of Chinatown eateries. Still, for those who know good food, Nha Trang is considered a top choice. Start out with one of their rice noodle soups, which can be made with beef, flank, fish balls, chicken, and veggies. They're quite a bargain at just $3.75 a bowl. A number of delicious rice dishes include barbecued pork with steamed egg and rice; chicken, chili, and lemon grass; and curry squid. On the weekends, Nha Trang offers up a rarely-seen delicacy, pig's legs. Plus, they offer all the most popular Vietnamese dishes like spring rolls, fried butterfly shrimp, and frogs legs. There's barely an item on the menu that makes its way toward the $10.00 mark. In fact, it can actually be quite difficult to spend more than $15.00 or so on your entire meal. Open daily, 10:00 a.m. - 10:00 p.m.

VEGETARIAN PARADISE

33-35 Mott Street, New York NY 10013. 212/406-6988. **Description:** For more than 30 years, Vegetarian Paradise has been just that... a paradise for vegetarians! The food comes in heaping quantities and is carefully prepared to culinary perfection. Sure, the menu reads like any old Chinese restaurant, with chicken and beef dishes making the menu, but rest assured that these are really soy-based and other vegan concoctions. Some of the tantalizing dishes spotted for under $10.00 included honey pepper chicken, ginger chicken with black mushrooms, spicy lotus root mushroom, and braised pipa bean curd. A wonderful selection of dumplings and appetizers are available to start out the meal too; try the fried turnip cakes or the walnut and sesame biscuits. Because this place is well-known throughout the city, it might be a good idea to make reservations. Open Monday through Thursday, 11:00 a.m. - 10:00 p.m.; Friday and Sunday, 11:00 a.m. - 11:00 p.m.

WONG KEE
113 Mott Street (between Hester & Canal Streets), New York NY 10013. 212/226-9018. **Description:** If you want to impress someone with your knowledge of the best Chinatown eateries, Wong Kee is a great place to go. Wong Kee is a small, family-style restaurant; the no-frills decor may be a bit off-putting, but the accompanying menu prices and excellent fare more than make up for it. Prepare yourself for a boisterous dining experience as, during the dinner hour especially, the place is filled with kids. The food, however, will calm you right down. Order a heaping platter of Wong Kee's Special Chicken or pineapple roast duck, both around $8.00. There is also a good selection of soups. Service is prompt, the restaurant is quite clean, and the clientele is diverse, all good signs. *$Cash Only$*

RESTAURANTS
🍽 Lower Manhattan 🍽

Where? The area below Chambers Street; includes Battery Park
and the Financial District.
Best Known For: Famously photographed skyline, New York
Stock Exchange, World Trade Center, Statue of Liberty
and Ellis Island.
Insider Tip: This area really comes alive during the bustling
9:00 a.m. - 5:00 p.m. workday hours.

BENNIE'S THAI CAFE
88 Fulton Street, New York NY 10038. 212/587-8930.
Description: Variety is the spice of life at this great Thai eatery,
as the menu is almost as big as the restaurant. You've had pad
Thai, what about pad-see eiw (flat rice noodles with broccoli, egg,
and your choice of beef, chicken, or pork) or pad-voonsen
(vermicelli noodles with egg, scallions, and sprouts)? All these
dishes are $6.95. For starters, try a curry fish cake, shrimp
fritters, or fried bean curd ($3.95 - $5.95). For noodle-lovers,
there is goy see mee (sautéed egg noodles with chicken, bamboo
shoots, mushrooms, scallions, and gravy) for $6.95; Singapore
noodle (thin rice noodles with yellow curry, chicken, egg, and
veggies) for $6.95; or noodles in soup for $4.95. For those with a
spicier appetite, try a bit of the pla-lad-Phrig (deep-fried fish
topped with hot chili and garlic) for $13.95; or the pla-merk-pad-
ped (sautéed squid with onions and peppers in a hot and spicy
sauce) for $7.95. For an even better deal, stop by Bennie's during
the week for their luncheon special (Monday through Friday, 11:00
a.m. - 3:00 p.m.). For as little as $4.50, you'll be treated to one of
more than five entrees, served over a plate of rice. You can't go
wrong for less than $5.00! (Unless you're a vegetarian -- luncheon
specials seem to cater to a meat-eating crowd) Still, all in all,
vegetarians and meat-lovers alike will find plenty of entrees to
suit their tastes, and all at prices that suit Mr. C's taste. So
whether you're in the mood for beef or tofu, Bennie's Thai Cafe is
the answer to your lower Manhattan hunger pains. Open Sunday,
12:00 p.m. - 9:00 p.m.; Monday through Friday, 11:00 a.m. - 9:00
p.m.; Saturday, 12:00 p.m. - 10:00 p.m.

JOHN STREET BAR & GRILL
17 John Street (between Broadway & Nassau Street), New York
NY 10038-4010. 212/349-3278. **World Wide Web address:**
http://www.johnstreet.com. **Description:** While the name may be
colorless and nondescript (except when it comes to location), this
place is anything but. From the Harley Davidson-inspired logo, to
the colorful cast of clients and staff, this is one place you don't
want to miss. Mixing the traditional with the nontraditional, the
result is an extensive food and bar menu that makes this place one
of the biggest draws to the sometimes ghost town-like Lower
Manhattan area. Start out your night with a bang and try one of

John Street's spicy appetizers like a basket of hot wings ($4.95 - $6.95), a plateful of nachos ($6.95), tequila poppers ($6.95), or some chicken fajita spring rolls ($7.95). Next up on the food to-do list is one of their main entrees that span all food categories, from burgers and sandwiches, to veggies and fish, to pork and steaks. Traditional sandwiches (burgers, grilled chicken, BBQ pork) will run you anywhere between $7.00 and $8.00; while herbivores can try the unique twist on an all-veggie meal with a delicious Szechuan stir fry ($9.95). Heartier appetites have a wide range of choices, from a grilled tuna steak with wasabi soy sauce and ginger ($14.95), to a full rack of baby back ribs, complete with slaw and cornbread (for a reasonable $14.95). But neither the fun nor the savings are limited to the dining room. John Street Bar & Grill boasts a huge selection of beers with an especially good microbrew list. With nearly 20 beers on tap, hops-fan or not, you're bound to find one to your liking. Come in for the John Street's free hot buffet and join in some of their drink specials: on Monday, John Streeters will choose a bottled beer of the day and sell it for half price until there is no more to be drunk (or until you are). On Thursday, $10.00 will get you all-you-can-drink from 5:00 p.m. - 8:00 p.m.; get your Friday night started at John Street with $5.00 Bud pitchers. While you're drinking up a storm, while away the hours in this spacious brew pub with a friendly game of pool, or strut on over to the jukebox and see if they don't have your favorite tune. (Come in on a Saturday or Sunday for free all-day pool and jukebox play). Open daily, 11:00 a.m. - 2:00 a.m.

MENCHANKO-TEI WORLD TRADE CENTER

5 World Trade Center Concourse, New York NY 10048. 212/432-4210. **Description:** This fantastic and quick Japanese delight, always brimming with businesspeople, has some of the best noodle soups in town. Try some Menchanko, the house specialty; served in an enormous cast-iron bowl, this egg noodle soup is one of the restaurant's most popular and talked about items for $8.75. A variety of appetizers include saba shioyaki (grilled mackerel), steamed or fried gyoza (pork dumplings), yakitori (skewered chicken and scallions), or vegetable spring rolls. For a great meal, made to order, order off the Oden menu (which they refer to as "Japanese Hodgepodge") from such items as ganmodoki (mixed veggie in a fried tofu cake), satsuma age (fried fish cake), daikon (Japanese white radish), and atsuage (fried tofu). Order à la carte for $1.85 each, or five pieces for $8.50. If you're looking for lighter fare, Menchanko-Tei offers a variety of salads including ika kari kari salad (fried calamari atop greens with miso dressing), nasu ginger itame (stir fried eggplant with ginger), or nozawana shirasu (diced and pickled mustard greens with baby white fish). Entree offerings include nira liver itame (liver with Chinese chives with sautéed bean sprouts), grilled yakibuta (Japanese pork in soy sauce), and tori kara age (fried chicken). Ramen noodle soups ($7.75 - $10.25) include such ingredients as Korean hot pickles and simmered pork; udon and soba noodle soups ($5.00 - $5.95) aren't complete without fried bean curd and vegetable tempura. Onigiri (delicious balls of rice, wrapped in seaweed) are all priced at just $2.00. So, if it's noodles that you are craving, stop by this

Financial District sanctuary. Open Monday through Friday, 11:30 a.m. - 9:30 p.m. (closed between 4:00 p.m. - 5:00 p.m.).

NATHAN HALE'S BAR & GRILL
6 Murray Street, New York NY 10007. 212/571-0769. **Description:** While the Captain himself will long be remembered for his "only regret that I have but one life to lose for my country" before being hanged, this namesake restaurant and bar will long be remembered for its great prices. A full menu, consisting of soups, salads, sandwiches, pasta, and steaks rarely goes over $10.00. You can devour a sirloin steak for just $10.95, two pork chops in an apple brandy sauce for just $9.95, grilled salmon for $9.95, or stuffed filet of sole for a guiltless $10.95. Now how many other places in the city can you say that about? If you're not really feeling the dinner thing, try a cup of homemade French onion soup ($3.95), one of their fresh salads ($4.95 - $8.95), or an appetizer like the stuffed mushrooms with crabmeat ($5.95). Everyone is treated like a hero at Nathan Hale's; try a Haleburger (an eight-ounce burger topped generously with mozzarella cheese, bacon, onions, and mushrooms) for just $7.50. Okay, so your arteries might not thank you, but your wallet certainly will! If you prefer to lean on old time favorites, order up the fish and chips ($7.95) or the bangers and mash ($7.25). To give you just a taste of Nathan Hale's bar specials, stop by on a Monday night (5:00 p.m. - 8:00 p.m.) for $1.50 Miller Genuine Draft and Miller Lite bottles; or pop in on a Thursday night (6:00 p.m. - 8:00 p.m.) when, for $10.00, you can challenge your liver to an All-You-Can Drink battle with an extensive beer list that includes Bass, Guinness, Harp, and Fosters. If you'd prefer to take it easy, drop by for their Saturday brunch (10:30 a.m. - 3:00 p.m.) where a less-than-$10.00-meal and two-for-one drink specials will help to start the weekend out right! Open Monday through Wednesday, 10:00 a.m. - 12:00 a.m.; Thursday through Saturday, 10:00 a.m. - 2:00 a.m.

NORTH STAR PUB
93 South Street, New York NY 10038. 212/509-6757. **Description:** Everything about this place screams England! From the traditional brick-front exterior, to the hearty food and drink menu, you just may forget that you're in the South Street Seaport area. For starters, try a plate of grilled Cumberland sausage with sliced apple and pickle ($2.95) or some ale-battered scallops ($5.25). A variety of sandwiches include an ale-battered fish filet ($7.95); a succulent steak sandwich with onion gravy and chips (9.25); or a Stilton burger with lettuce, tomato, onion, and chips ($8.25). Traditional British entrees include a savory shepherd's pie ($9.50) and bangers and mash ($9.95). Additional North Star specialties include Lorry Driver's Special (Cumberland sausages, beans, and chips) for $9.95, Ploughman's Lunch (cheddar or Stilton or pâté forestiere with mango chutney, apple, pickled onion, Branston pickle, and bread and butter) for $8.95, and Fishmonger's Combo (fish, scallops, shrimp, chips, and tartar sauce) for $12.95. For a daily variety, check the board for the Pub

Pie of the Day (though it's *always* steak and kidney on Monday). After such a filling meal, you'll need something to wash it all down with. Be sure to try one of the North Star Pub's 75 single malt scotches, or one of their delicious British ales. Open Monday through Saturday, 11:30 a.m. - 12:00 a.m.; Sunday, 12:00 p.m. - 12:00 a.m.

SOUPERMAN
77 Pearl Street, New York NY. 212/269-5777. **Description:** Tired of ham and cheese? Peanut butter and jelly isn't your style? Why not try something different for lunch...soup. I'm not talking chicken noodle or tomato soup here; our hero Souperman has uniquely changed the face of soup. A sampling of varieties include wild mussel, cold-carrot-cilantro, Thai free-range chicken, and chicken orzo with pasta. For under $10.00 you get soup, fresh bread, fruit salad, and a mint. Now that's tough to beat.

RESTAURANTS
🍽️ Midtown Manhattan East 🍽️

Where? The area east of Avenue of the Americas and between
29th and 59th Streets; includes Murray Hill.

Best Known For: Radio City Music Hall, Rockefeller Center, New
York Public Library, Empire State Building, Trump Tower,
Museum of Modern Art, St. Patrick's Cathedral.

Insider Tip: After 65 years and $20 million in restoration fees,
the famed Rainbow Room announced that it would be
closing before the new millennium due to a dispute over
the lease.

BLOOM'S DELICATESSEN CAFE
350 Lexington Avenue, New York NY 10016. 212/922-FOOD.
Description: Now this is what being a New York Deli is all about:
huge selection, enormous portions, and good prices. While it may
seem that the prices at Bloom's Delicatessen Cafe are a bit higher
than you'd expect to pay at any corner deli, this is simply because
Bloom's is not your average deli. The gigantic menu, comprised of
gourmet sandwiches, heroes, triple deckers, and salad plates,
definitely has something for everyone. Many of the sandwich
choices are numbered; the fact that there is actually a "number
51" lets you know the sheer magnitude of this menu. Mr. C had the
Mediterranean hero, a delightful blend of grilled chicken, grilled
vegetables, feta cheese, oregano, and olive oil vinaigrette. I was
absolutely astounded by the size of the sandwich as it approached
the table; I even had to develop a strategy on how I was going to
consume it, as it was so large! Sandwich choices run the gamut
from traditional (turkey club, chicken salad, roast beef and
cheese) to the not-so-traditional (black forest ham with provolone,
salami, and sweet pimentos; Swiss, cheddar, brie, and gouda
cheeses with lettuce and sweet pimentos). Sandwiches start
around $3.50 and work their way up to just under $12.00. Bloom's
also serves breakfast, and offers a variety of lunch and dinner
specials. Dinner specials are served from 5:00 p.m. on and are all
priced right around $9.00 - $10.00. Entrees include grilled chicken
breast in a mushroom sauce on a bed of lettuce, broiled salmon
steak, and linguine bolognese. Open daily, 6:00 a.m. - 10:00 p.m.

CINEMA RESTAURANT/CAFE
505 Third Avenue (at 34th Street), New York NY 10016.
212/689-9022. ◆ 1325 Second Avenue (at 70th Street), New York
NY 10021. 212/772-6400. **Description:** Movie-lovers rejoice at all
of the Hollywood-themed restaurants in Manhattan. Cinema
Restaurant is one of the more popular choices. They offer a
better quality of food than what you might expect from a diner,
but these are certainly diner prices! There are plenty of burgers
and sandwiches to choose from like grilled cheese, B.L.T.s, and
tuna melts. They also offer a variety of great specialty sandwiches
like a grilled vegetable melt on focaccia, chicken souvlaki, and a

marinated flank steak. A fantastic array of salads dare to venture beyond your typical Caesar or mixed greens: couscous with roasted vegetables, grilled salmon Niçoise, and a Mediterranean salad with grilled chicken and fresh mozzarella are just a few of the options. For dinner, Cinema Restaurant/Cafe offers some worthwhile chicken and seafood dishes like grilled rosemary chicken and fillet of sole. Seafood prices can be a bit higher, but when you consider that they come with a salad, potato, and side of mixed veggies, they're well worth the extra dollar. Another inexpensive option is to order up one of the pasta dishes like angel hair alla pignoli, linguni seafood marinara, or penne with chicken and broccoli. Chef's specials are an ever-changing mix of good food at good prices. On weekends, the diner opens early for breakfast where they serve all your traditional early morning favorites: eggs, omelettes, pancakes, and french toast. Why not be a true cineaste and, when sitting down to reflect on a movie you just saw, sit here! They even offer daily movie screenings in the restaurant itself. Open Sunday, 8:00 a.m. - 12:00 a.m.; Monday through Thursday, 11:00 a.m. - 12:00 a.m.; Friday, 11:00 a.m. - 1:00 a.m.; Saturday, 8:00 a.m. - 1:00 a.m.

EVERGREEN SHANGHAI
10 East 38th Street (between Madison & Fifth Avenues), New York NY 10013. 212/448-1199. **World Wide Web address:** http://www.nydelivery.com/evergreen.html. **Description:** The best time to savor the menu at Evergreen Shanghai is at lunch time. Monday through Friday, from 11:30 a.m. - 3:30 p.m. lunch specials are offered for $5.95. You can choose from some of your favorites including General Tso's chicken, chicken in curry sauce, and double-cooked pork. Japanese lunch specials include sushi, California rolls, and sashimi. While any time you choose to dine here, you will find tons of dishes on the menu, the weekday lunch specials will afford you the best savings.

LE CAFE CREME MADISON
165 Madison Avenue (at 33rd Street), New York NY 10016. 212/679-8077. **Description:** One of the great things about dining in New York is the number of culinary heritages you can experience. For lovers of French food, the difficult thing can be finding a good and affordable place to dine. At any time of day, Le Cafe Creme Madison is a good place to consider for an affordable experience. Sure, they've got some dishes that approach the $20.00 mark but, if you look elsewhere around town, you'll find this is still pretty reasonable. Yet, Mr. C is dedicated to finding you the best possible options at the best possible prices, and Le Cafe Creme's three-course dinner special is one you should certainly take advantage of. Every night, from 5:00 p.m. - 10:00 p.m., drop by to experience le food française at its most delicious (and most affordable). Start the menu out with a salad or appetizer: endive with walnuts, escargot de bourgogne, and fresh mozzarella and tomato are a few of the choices. Next, choose an entree from one of their seafood or poultry offerings. If there's still room afterwards, choose something from the dessert tray and call it an evening. How much to experience this divine

pleasure? Just $19.50 per person! Open Monday through Saturday, 11:30 a.m. - 3:30 p.m. & 5:00 p.m. - 10:00 p.m.

MENCHANKO-TEI MIDTOWN EAST
131 East 45th Street, New York NY 10017. 212/986-6805. **Description:** This fantastic and quick Japanese delight, always brimming with people, has some of the best noodle soups in town. Try some Menchanko, the house specialty; served in an enormous cast-iron bowl, this egg noodle soup is one of the restaurant's most popular and talked about items for $8.75. A variety of appetizers include saba shioyaki (grilled mackerel), steamed or fried gyoza (pork dumplings), yakitori (skewered chicken and scallions), or vegetable spring rolls. For a great meal, made to order, order off the Oden menu (which they refer to as "Japanese Hodgepodge") from such items as ganmodoki (mixed veggie in a fried tofu cake), satsuma age (fried fish cake), daikon (Japanese white radish), and atsuage (fried tofu). Order à la carte for $1.85 each, or five pieces for $8.50. If you're looking for lighter fare, Menchanko-Tei offers a variety of salads including ika kari kari salad (fried calamari atop greens with miso dressing), nasu ginger itame (stir fried eggplant with ginger), or nozawana shirasu (diced and pickled mustard greens with baby white fish). Entree offerings include nira liver itame (liver with Chinese chives with sautéed bean sprouts), grilled yakibuta (Japanese pork in soy sauce), and tori kara age (fried chicken). Ramen noodle soups ($7.75 - $10.25) include such ingredients as Korean hot pickles and simmered pork; udon and soba noodle soups ($5.00 - $5.95) aren't complete without fried bean curd and vegetable tempura. Onigiri (delicious balls of rice, wrapped in seaweed) are all priced at just $2.00. Open Sunday, 11:30 a.m. - 11:30 p.m.; Monday through Saturday, 11:30 a.m. - 12:30 p.m.

MOONSTRUCK EAST
449 Third Avenue (at 31st Street), New York NY 10016. 212/213-1100. **Description:** So many diners, so little time! In fact, the menu at this Murray Hill spot is a massive book in itself. Page after page listing breakfasts, salads, sandwiches, burgers, dinners, desserts, the works. There are more than 30 varieties of omelettes, and 20 types of hamburgers alone. One good deal is the mushroom burger ($5.45), a plump seven-ouncer (as they all are) piled high with equally plump grilled mushroom halves. Mr. C had a Victoria House sandwich ($7.95), grilled chicken breast on a bulkie roll topped with melted mozzarella and fried onions and served with fries, coleslaw, and pickle. You can get breakfast all day, full dinners, and, of course, Greek specialties.

ROMANTICA CAFE
373 Fifth Avenue (at 35th Street), New York NY 10016. 212/532-0044. **Toll-free phone:** 877/SO-YUMMY. **World Wide Web address:** http://www.romantica.baweb.com. **Description:** A light music soundtrack and flowers or a bottle of wine on each table set the mood for romance in this dimly-lit establishment, reminiscent of a Mediterranean villa. Morning, noon, and night, the friendly

staff will be more than happy to fill you up on falafel, tabouli, hummus, moudamas, or a variety of other Mediterranean delights. The large menu consists of a variety of fresh soups, salads, and sandwiches, as well as charcoal-broiled kebabs and pitas. Try one of their vegetarian sandwiches, like a baba ganush or tabouli and feta pita. For the meat-lovers out there, Romantica also serves up some pretty big and delicious (not to mention lean) burgers with a variety of toppings including grilled onions, peppers, feta cheese, and chick peas. A variety of kebabs and pastas make up the Romantica entree menu; the Kafta kebab is a delicious concoction of spiced ground beef, parsley, and onions. Chicken marinara, chicken bolognese, and shrimp scampi are just a few of Romantica's pasta dishes. Mr. C had the Pollo Romantica, a delicious mix of pasta, peppers, and mushrooms (served with salad and bread). Add to that an order of hummus, a glass of wine, and a generous-sized cappuccino to wash it all down with (topped with lots of foam and cinnamon, just the way I like it), and you've got yourself a great deal! Be sure to save room for dessert, as Romantica is well-known for their after-dinner delights. A rich chocolate mousse, creamy tiramisu, carrot cake, and baklava are just a few of the options offered. What's almost better than the food, however, is the prices. Most dishes don't reach over $10.00. From 12:00 p.m. - 4:00 p.m., Romantica also runs a lunch buffet for just $7.99 (including dessert). The buffet is served from a huge salad-bar-like fixture that almost runs the length of the restaurant. Don't worry if you happen to get there after 4:00 p.m., Romantica runs a Happy Hour from 5:00 p.m. - 7:00 p.m. where you can get a free glass of wine or soda with your meal. Open daily, 7:00 a.m. - 11:00 p.m.

SAM'S NOODLE SHOP & GRILL BAR
411 Third Avenue (at 29th Street), New York NY. 212/213-2288. **Description:** Sam's is another noodle shop with a huge selection and great bargain meals. Sam's offers you the chance to "Design Your Own Dish" by selecting vegetables and sauces for $7.75. The restaurant also has more than 25 different lunch specials which are served Monday through Friday, 11:30 a.m. - 4:00 p.m. for just $4.95. Selections include soy sauce chicken over rice, baby shrimp with broccoli over rice, and eggplant with garlic sauce over rice. Open daily, 11:30 a.m. - 11:00 p.m.

TASTE BUD
585 Third Avenue (between 38th & 39th Streets), New York NY. 212/889-4929. **Description:** The biggest problem you'll have eating at Taste Bud is deciding what to order. The menu is overflowing with choices; some are everyday selections while others are daily specials. Standards include poached salmon wraps ($7.75), grilled honey lemon chicken sandwiches ($7.50), and Greek spinach salad bowls ($7.75). Sandwiches require a choice from 12 breads and seven dressings. Vegetarians and the health-conscious can also find many options at Taste Bud (spinach rotelle and herbed goat cheese; carrot and snow pea Oriental salad). Be sure to save room for dessert...citrus sunshine cake with citrus

frosting, raspberry linzer torte, lemon mousse, and sinful chocolate cupcakes are just a few of the choices on the menu...my mouth is watering already. Open Monday through Friday, 7:00 a.m. - 6:00 p.m.

TIBETAN KITCHEN
444 Third Avenue (at 31st Street), New York NY 10016. 212/679-6286. **World Wide Web address:** http://www.potala.com/kitchen. **Description:** As I've said before, New York has at least one restaurant for every country in the world. Tibet is ably represented by this humble, quiet restaurant in Murray Hill. Just stepping in the door takes you into a serene world of soft lighting, Eastern music, and polite, attentive service. A pot of black Tibetan tea is brought without question and poured for you. The small room is simply decorated in dark wood, with a spiral staircase down to a second dining room with a bar. The menu divides almost evenly into vegetarian and meat dishes, most of which are priced between $7.00 and $9.00. Start with a tasty bowl of thang soup, a variation on egg-drop with spinach and a clear, light broth base. Move on to a plate of steamed dumplings filled with vegetables or beef ($7.50 - $8.25), which the menu notes as Tibet's most popular dish (a good tidbit to know in case you ever get on *Jeopardy*). Or, try a huge plate of tentsel ($8.25), sautéed peas with bits of fried egg and shredded beef. Tibetan chili chicken is $8.50; for anyone looking for a quick description of this cuisine, Indian food is probably the nearest relative. Another interesting curry dish, Himalayan khatsa ($7.50), consists of curried chunks of cauliflower, peas, and tofu, served cold and spicy on a bed of lettuce. By the time you leave, you're sure to feel warm and relaxed as though you'd been much further away from the hustle of the city than in Midtown. Open Monday through Friday, 12:00 p.m. - 3:00 p.m. and 5:00 p.m. - 10:30 p.m.; Saturday, 5:00 p.m. - 10:30 p.m.

TRE POMODORI
210 East 34th Street (between Second & Third Avenues), New York NY 10016. 212/545-7266. **Description:** This cute little midtown restaurant offers worthwhile Italian food in a casual setting. The large menu consists of a number of soups, salads, and antipasti. Pasta dishes include basic meals like penne with tomato sauce and mozzarella, cappellini and vegetables, fettucine Bolognese. Most are priced under $10.00. Even when you get to the more experimental dishes, like the whole wheat pappardelle with asparagus and chicken, prices still hardly top $10.00. If you're looking for something a bit heartier than a plate of pasta, Tre Pomodori offers a number of chicken, veal, and seafood entrees. The rosemary and white wine sautéed chicken breast and the Dijon mustard salmon were two of my favorite choices. Entrees are around $10.00 - $12.00. Tre Pomodori is a great little spot to know about when you're looking for a restaurant that is consistently good and affordable. Open Sunday through Thursday, 12:00 p.m. - 10:30 p.m.; Friday and Saturday, 12:00 p.m. - 11:30 p.m.

WATERFRONT ALE HOUSE

540 Second Avenue (at 30th Street), New York NY 11201. 212/696-4104. ◆ 155 Atlantic Avenue (between Clinton & Henry Streets), Brooklyn NY 11201. 718/522-3794. **Description:** Who wouldn't want to visit a restaurant that deems itself the home of "warm beer, lousy food, and an ugly owner"? Waterfront Ale House is a homey establishment with an ample beer selection and a plethora of drink specials. The menu's entrees include half barbecued chicken, spicy beer shrimp, and a "German Wurst Platter" (with brockwurst, bratwurst, and baurenwurst). Various sandwich choices, like pulled pork and bratwurst & sauerkraut are sure to please as well. As for the ale: draft beers are $3.00 - $4.50, bottled beers are $3.00 and up. Open Sunday through Wednesday, 11:30 a.m. - 10:30 p.m.; Thursday through Saturday, 11:30 a.m. - 11:30.pm

WRAP-N-RUN

788 Lexington Avenue, New York NY 10021. 212/888-7781. **Description:** For a quick bite while you're on the run, Wrap-N-Run is an excellent choice. Healthy and delicious, Wrap-N-Run offers breakfast and sandwiches all day long. For breakfast, try a Mexican omelette with onions, tomatoes, and jalapeño peppers for $3.40; or stick with the standard two eggs, meat, homefries, and toast for only $2.25. To drink, choose from a variety of juices including celery, carrot, banana, melon, or strawberry ($1.95 - $3.45); or non-fat frozen yogurt smoothies from $2.65 - $3.65. Breakfast sandwiches are just over $1.00 (after 11:00 a.m., breakfast prices rise anywhere between $.10 and $1.00). Wrap-N-Run offers a variety of burgers including those of the turkey, veggie, and beef variety ($3.65 - $6.15). Entrees include chicken, fresh roasted turkey, pork chops, and steak, all reasonably priced from $6.45 - $10.95. More than 15 different sandwiches are all priced under $6.00 (some *well* under), and a fresh salad will run you right around the same price. Finally, we come to the wraps for which the restaurant is named: Thanksgiving, Pasta Lover, Mexican Fisherman, Grecian, and Vegetarian are just a few of the nearly 20 wraps sold, all priced between $3.95 - $5.95. Don't skip dessert; Wrap-N-Run has a bakery case and counter filled with all sorts of tasty cakes, cookies, pies, cheesecake, and frozen yogurt.

RESTAURANTS
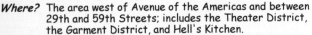 **Midtown Manhattan West**

Where? The area west of Avenue of the Americas and between 29th and 59th Streets; includes the Theater District, the Garment District, and Hell's Kitchen.

Best Known For: Herald Square, Times Square, Madison Square Garden, Broadway, Penn Station, Carnegie Hall, Macy's.

Insider Tip: Restaurant Row in Hell's Kitchen, (named for a tenement located at 54th Street and Tenth Avenue) has recently become *the* place to affordably dine before or after a night (or day) at the theater.

CABANA CARIOCA
123 West 45th Street (between Avenue of the Americas and Seventh Avenue), New York NY 10036. 212/581-8088. **Description:** Take a look at the menu at this popular Brazilian restaurant and you just may wonder what it's doing in this book. It's just outside of Times Square, where everything is expensive. The dinners (steaks and fish, mostly) are around $15.00 and up. Ah, but wait! The best time to get bargains is lunch time. Everyday for $9.95, it's an all-you-can-eat extravaganza. Don't miss the feijoada, which the waiters simply call the Brazilian National Dish to save time and embarrassing pronunciation questions. And here comes your plate, a thick dark stew piled atop a mound of white rice, garnished with orange wedges and more salad on the side. The stew consists of large chunks of grilled pork, slices of mild sausage, and black beans. There are half a dozen other choices on any given day, such as garden beef stew, codfish, and pot roast. Open Monday through Thursday, 11:30 a.m. - 11:00 p.m.; Friday through Sunday, 11:30 a.m. - 10:00 p.m.

THE CARNEGIE DELI
854 Seventh Avenue (between 54th & 55th Streets), New York NY. 212/757-2245. **Description:** When one envisions the typical New York deli, The Carnegie Deli is the place that they are thinking of. From the wee hours of the morning 'til the wee hours of the next morning, The Carnegie Deli packs in a constant flow of hungry celebrities and civilians alike, and everyone is treated alike (I said *alike*, I did not say *well*). Start your meal out with one of the enormous, fresh pickles that await you at your table. Next, try one of their world-famous pastrami or corned beef sandwiches on for size (or try a delicious combination of both under the guise of the Broadway Danny Rose). While the prices may seem a bit higher than your average deli, it's all proportionate to the serving sizes. If you've ever recited one of those "I'm so hungry I could eat a horse" or like clichés, test your hunger with the Number 13, which consists of a pound of turkey, a pound of corned beef, and a pound of Swiss cheese (you do the math)! Don't let the close quarters deter you from saving room for dessert; The Carnegie Deli serves the kind of cheesecake you'll be hankering for at 4:00 a.m. (due to

the addictive nature of these cravings, they've even been nice enough to set up a 24-hour cheesecake hotline, 800/334-5606, where you can order their baked goods from anywhere in the country, any time of day). While The Carnegie Deli is happy to take reservations up to one year in advance, it is an unlikely occurrence that you would have to wait more than a few minutes for a table. But while you *are* waiting, be sure and check out the Carnegie Wall of Fame and realize that, with both the food and the clientele, you are in the presence of true greatness. *$Cash Only$*

CLINTON GRILLE
637 Tenth Avenue (at 45th Street), New York NY 10036. 212/315-4690. **Description:** Clinton Grille is a comfortable and cozy neighborhood cafe and bar, and a very nice place to end up if you find yourself wandering aimlessly around the Hell's Kitchen area of town. This place is *definitely* a step above the rest of the neighborhood. You'll find good beers (Guinness, Foster's Lager) on tap, plenty of snacks, and substantial meals, all at very good prices. Appetizers include New England clam chowder ($4.00) or Maryland crabcakes with Creole mustard and horseradish cocktail sauce ($8.00). Also available are a variety of fresh salads for as little as $4.00, and some delicious pizzas. Pizzas start at $7.00 for a basic model and can cost you up to $10.00 once you fill it with toppings; still not a bad deal for this 10-inch, gourmet delight. At lunch (Monday through Friday, 11:00 a.m. - 4:00 p.m.), Clinton Grille has got plenty of reliable burgers and sandwiches, too. A chicken parmesan hero, flame-grilled hamburger, and grilled black forest ham and brie are a few of your options for $7.00 or under. Tortilla wraps are similarly priced -- if not a bit lower -- and include stuffings like grilled veggies, tuna salad, and chicken salad. Want a full dinner? There are a number to choose from, like lemon pepper chicken, chicken stir fry, wild mushroom ravioli, and oven roasted pork loin. Prices start out at under $10.00 and can range as high as $16.00; but don't worry, there are plenty of great things to choose from while still keeping your *Cheap* radar on! The atmosphere is informal, relaxed, and even a little artsy, but never pretentious.

CUPCAKE CAFE
522 Ninth Avenue (at 39th Street), New York NY. 212/465-1530. **Description:** Want to impress people with a real insider's discovery? Just a block down from the Port Authority, amidst the terrific seafood shops and butchers is a hidden treat. From across the street the Cupcake Cafe looks like any old bakery, but inside it has a handful of small tables, where you can sip herbal teas or rich coffees while nibbling away on some delicious sweets and other palatable delights. The cupcakes, of course, are wonderful. They come in small and large sizes ($1.50 - $2.50), and in such flavors as chocolate with mocha frosting and maple walnut with maple frosting. The cafe also offers an array of other goodies like chocolate chip cookies ($.50 each), lemon poppyseed muffins ($1.25), homemade quiche ($3.00), and individual pizzas with fresh toppings ($3.00). The surroundings are strictly no-frills; that's

part of the bohemian charm. The bakery is at the back of the store, and you can watch the freshest batches of treats being carted out to the counter. Open Sunday, 9:00 a.m. - 5:00 p.m.; Monday through Friday, 7:00 a.m. - 7:00 p.m.; Saturday, 8:00 a.m. - 7:00 p.m. *$Cash Only$*

FILM CENTER CAFE
635 Ninth Avenue (at 44th Street), New York NY 10036. 212/262-2525. **Description:** Here's a very cool place to hang out. If you're a showbiz fan, Film Center Cafe will make you feel like you're in *Chinatown*... Roman Polanski's version, at least. Walk in through the dark, laid-back bar, past a genuine wooden telephone booth, into the dining room at the back. The walls are painted with the trademarks of the major film studios (Paramount's peak, MGM's lion, etc.). These are illuminated by special lights that create the look of venetian blinds, as if you're in sunny L.A. with the shades drawn. Hollywood illusion may be the backdrop, but the food is perfectly real and deserves top billing. Dinner entrees, like chicken Kiev and shell steak, can reach up into the $12.00 - $14.00 range. For a better deal, stick with something like the burgers or the vegetarian plate of steamed veggies over rice with a Thai peanut sauce; better yet, try the cafe at lunch, when the same menu is offered at much more budget-friendly prices. The atmosphere is fun, and makes this a unique experience.

HAMBURGER HARRY'S
145 West 45th Street, New York NY 10036. 212/840-2756. **Description:** This eatery offers up good, dependable burgers and fries, along with other dishes at reasonable prices. The burgers (more than 15 varieties) are made from seven ounces of fresh ground beef, and cooked to order over a charcoal and wood grill. $7.95 will get you your basic burger with a variety of cheeses (American, cheddar, Monterey jack, or Jarlsberg) adding just another $.50 to your bill. But why settle for an everyday burger when you're at such an extraordinary place? Obviously, burgers are the specialty here. So, rightfully, there should be an assortment from which you can choose. Harry's specialty burgers encompass such delightful names and flavors as The Hollywood, with slices avocado and alfalfa sprouts; Bernaise, topped with a tarragon and shallot sauce; South of the Border you'll find guacamole and pico de gallo; while North of the Border there's Canadian bacon and cheddar cheese. Harry's turkey and vegetable burgers are two of the more health-conscious choices. Burgers come with curly fries or homemade potato salad. No matter what you get atop this meaty monstrosity, it shouldn't run you more than $10.00. Harry's also offers other kinds of fun food like salads and appetizers, soups and chili, beef and chicken fajitas, burritos, and a variety of dinner entrees. While the entrees are good, they can run you as much as $16.00. Still, why would you want an entree at *Hamburger Harry's* when you can have a hamburger?

HEARTLAND BREWERY
1285 Avenue of the Americas, New York NY 10019. 212/582-8244. **E-mail address:** beernyc@aol.com. **Description:** Just when

you thought you couldn't find an affordable brew pub in the city, along comes Heartland Brewery. Come for the beer and stay for the food. The beer list offers five standards year-round: Cornhusker Lager, Harvest Wheat, Indiana Pale Ale, Red Rooster Ale, and Farmer John's Oatmeal Stout. There are also several seasonal favorites like Indian River Ale and Smiling Pumpkin Ale. More than just your typical pub fare is the order of the day here. The menu includes hummus and eggplant caponata, jerk chicken, fresh Maine crab cakes, salmon or catfish sandwiches, and buffalo burgers. Main dishes range from $12.00 - $20.00, appetizers and sandwiches are priced between $8.00 and $12.00.

ISLAND BURGERS & SHAKES
766 Ninth Avenue (between 51st & 52nd Streets), New York NY 10019. 212/307-7934. **Description:** If you like burgers, you'll love Island Burgers & Shakes. They lay it all on the table for you (not literally): this is not some fancy eatery; it's a burger joint, and mighty proud of it! But this isn't any old restaurant where they throw meat on a bun and call it lunch. Island Burgers & Shakes offers a number of options when it comes to preparing your meal: First, they start out with a half-pound of fresh and delicious beef; next, it's time to start constructing your masterpiece. Island Burgers & Shakes offers seven kinds of cheeses and six different breads. Burger varieties include the Hippo (curried sour cream, bacon, cheddar cheese, sautéed onions, scallions, and guacamole), the Princess Grace (ham, boursin, onions, mushrooms, peppers, and ciabatta), and the Black & Bleu (blackened with bleu cheese). All burgers are $7.25 and under. If hamburgers aren't your thing, they offer just as much variety when it comes to building a chicken churasco (a grilled chicken sandwich for those who aren't hip to the lingo). The Mad World is blackened chicken with Swiss cheese, pesto, relish, and salsa; Duke's sandwich has blackened chicken with jalapeño and jack cheese; while Vito's sandwich combines roasted red peppers, mozzarella, and ciabatta. Churascos, on the average, are about $.50 more than the burgers, and can be made the exact same way. Island Burgers & Shakes is an especially good place to drop by if you're visiting with finicky kids. What child has ever been known to dispute a burger? Open Sunday through Thursday, 12:00 p.m. - 10:30 p.m.; Friday and Saturday, 12:00 p.m. - 11:30 p.m. *$Cash Only$*

MOMS BAGELS
15 West 45th Street, New York NY 10036. 212/764-1566. **Description:** This is what a midtown quick-food joint *should* be like. Whether or not there is a Mom actually making the bagels, bialys, and onion breads, they are made fresh on the premises under religious supervision. That means kosher dairy; there is no meat on the menu, though they do serve fish. You can't have a bagel without lox, after all, or without smoked whitefish for that matter. A basic bagel and cream cheese is $1.70; fancier cheeses include walnut and raisin, blueberry, and others. The bagels themselves don't go far beyond the familiar, but they're good. Sandwiches on a bagel or bialy (sort of a filled-in, flatter bagel) include tuna salad ($4.75), sable ($5.95), gouda cheese ($3.35),

and many others. All of these are also available as platters, with your bread on the side, for a few dollars more; nothing tops $7.95. Moms Bagels also makes other old-world treats like cheese blintzes and potato pancakes ($4.95 each), apple-noodle pudding ($2.50), and homemade soups. And, until 11:00 a.m., you can get a breakfast special of scrambled eggs, home fries, coffee, and a bagel or bialy for $2.36. Being a breakfast and lunch kind of place (catering largely to the business crowd), Moms Bagels closes by 6:00 p.m. Being kosher, they close at 2:30 p.m. on Fridays, and their only weekend hours are Sunday, 9:30 a.m. - 3:30 p.m.

RESTAURANTS
🍽 SoHo & TriBeCa 🍽

Where? SoHo is south of Houston Street and TriBeCa refers to the triangle below Canal Street.

Best Known For: Cast-iron architecture, art galleries (Museum for African Art, New Museum of Contemporary Art), trendy-artsy reputation.

Insider Tip: New Yorkers pronounce Houston Street as *Hows*ton Street.

BASSET CAFE

123 West Broadway, New York NY 10013. 212/349-1662. **E-mail address:** bassetcafe@aol.com. **Description:** What more could you want in a hang out? This cafe has dogs, coffee, tea, and even fresh buttermilk biscuits!! Whether it's breakfast, brunch, or dinner you crave, the Basset Cafe can fill the order. Breakfasts range from $6.00 - $10.00 and include something for everyone (French toast, fruit plate, bagels and smoked salmon). Brunches at the Basset Cafe are a bit more on the more exotic side. How about trying the shrimp sea island Caesar salad for $12.95 or the warm goat cheese salad. Traditional offerings include macaroni and cheese for $6.95 and eggs Benedict for $8.75. Craving a late night treat? Why not drop in for vegetarian lasagna, hound dog salad (fennel, sun-dried tomatoes, mixed greens, goat cheese, and herbs), or shrimp and sausage jambalaya. All entrees include a side dish and fresh-baked bread and average about $10.00 per dish. Open Monday through Friday, 7:30 a.m. - 10:00 p.m.; Saturday and Sunday, 9:00 a.m. - 6:00 p.m.

BROOME STREET BAR

363 West Broadway (at Broome Street), New York NY 10013. 212/925-2086. **Description:** From its vantage point at the corner of Broome and West Broadway, this cozy SoHo joint serves up tremendous burgers and sandwiches. Considering the price levels at the other restaurants in the area, the Broome Street Bar's offerings are very cheap indeed. Burgers are priced from $6.50 - $7.50 and, in an interesting twist, come served in pita bread. Potato chips and pickles are served on the side. There are a number of appealing burger varieties to choose from. Sandwiches are in the $5.00 - $8.00 range, and the categories here (ham, turkey, tuna) are relatively familiar; sandwiches are served with lettuce, tomato and chips. You may opt instead for a crispy grilled cheese sandwich, which is in the same price range, or an omelette. This last selection, just $5.00, is a particularly good weekend brunch choice. Don't miss out on the chili; it's mild but tasty and will run you $3.25 for a cup and $5.00 for a bowl. As you would expect, there are plenty of great beers available here at Broome Street Bar, including Foster's Lager and Brooklyn Brown Lager. This place has been serving up burgers and beers in high style for almost 30 years and, in this case, that's a definite plus. There's a

very funky jukebox in the back with plenty of vintage rock and soul tunes; the hanging plants also lend a commendable coziness to the proceedings. Interestingly enough, although it can be very difficult to secure a table during the dinner hour, the crowd seems to peter out about 9:00 p.m. This makes the Broome Street Bar an easy top-notch choice for a late-night snack.

BUBBY'S

120 Hudson Street (between Franklin & North Moore Streets), New York NY 10013. 212/219-0666. **Description:** If you want to be in with the TriBeCa in-crowd, the key is to find out where locals like Robert De Niro and Harvey Keitel eat. In keeping with that rule, Bubby's must be the place, as they are just a few of the locals that frequent this popular eatery. For those of you who thought Bubby's was a pie company, you're right....partly. Before opening the restaurant, owners Seth Price and Ron Crimson peddled their pies around town, making such delicacies as the Mile High Apple Pie a household name. With the demand escalating, the future restaurateurs decided to open their doors to the public. Today, Bubby's offers a huge menu of great comfort foods, all baked from scratch, that are as healthy for your wallet as they are for your body. Entrees start at just $9.95 and, while they can go as high as $21.95, there is plenty to choose from in the Cheapster range. Try the creamy macaroni and cheese with a salad ($9.95), the grilled chicken burrito ($11.95), or the homemade meatloaf ($12.95). The lunch menu consists of much of the same food (at even better prices), alongside great soup and sandwich menus; the chicken noodle soup is sure to bring back memories of grade school. Kids will love the peanut butter and homemade strawberry jam sandwich ($3.95 - $5.95), while Mom or Dad can curb their hunger with the mozzarella, tomato, and basil on foccacia ($4.95 - $8.95). Many think the weekend brunch at Bubby's is among the best in the city (though it can also be among the *busiest*). Breakfast treats include sour cream pancakes with bananas and berries, omelettes, and smoked trout and egg scramble. Besides a menu full of tempting treats and delectable desserts (don't forget about the pie that made this all happen), Bubby's has a large bar that serves up a great collection of microbrews like Checker Cab Blond Ale. Drop in during Happy Hour (Monday through Friday, 4:00 p.m. - 7:00 p.m.) for a two-for-one special. What is best about Bubby's is that through all the hype, the original concept for the restaurant (a comfortable, family-style restaurant) has stayed true, regardless of the neighborhood's newfound trendiness. While Bubby's is happy to cater to the celebrity set and corporate honchos, they're even happier to see you and your kids there. Open Sunday through Tuesday, 9:00 a.m. - 11:00 p.m.; Monday through Wednesday, 8:00 a.m. - 12:00 a.m.; Thursday through Saturday, 8:00 a.m. - 3:00 a.m.

FRANKLIN STATION CAFE

222 West Broadway (at Franklin Street), New York NY 10013. 212/274-8525. **Description:** This casual French/Malaysian bistro is one of the few places left in the TriBeCa area where you can

grab a great meal for under $20.00. Basic fare includes a variety of delicious sandwiches like fresh roasted turkey with lettuce, tomato, and Dijon mustard; smoked salmon with mascarpone cheese; and avocado and tomato with lettuce and smoked gouda. For salads, Franklin Station Cafe offers a bed of mixed greens with your choice of roasted turkey, grilled chicken, baked ham, smoked salmon, goat cheese, portabello mushroom, or tuna salad for under $10.00. At the Malaysian end of the bistro, look for great dishes like satay chicken with peanut sauce, coconut-curried squid, and rendang chicken (roasted with coconut and ginger). Noodle dishes (ranging from $7.00 - $10.00) include vegetable soba with watercress, mushrooms, carrots, and tofu; shrimp udon with watercress and carrot; and shrimp, squid, and salmon udon. Like any good cafe, Franklin Station rounds out the menu with some delicious homemade desserts (fruit tarts, rice pudding, cakes, and cookies) and a plethora of specialty coffees. Open Monday through Friday, 11:00 a.m. - 10:00 p.m.; Saturday and Sunday, 10:00 a.m. - 10:00 p.m.

GLORIA'S TRIBECA
107 West Broadway (between Reade & Chambers Streets), New York NY 10013. 212/766-0911. **Description:** In the oh-so-trendy TriBeCa area, finding a decent place to eat affordably can be quite a challenge. Gloria's TriBeCa is one of the few restaurants that couples modest food with modest prices. Not to mention, it's a whole lot of fun! The menu doesn't vary much between lunch and dinner, but the prices can increase by about $1.00. This Mexican gem offers traditional starters like nachos, chili, and chicken taquitos. Lighter eaters will appreciate the selection of salads like the grilled shrimp with tomato, jicama, and pumpkin seeds. Everyone's favorite flaming entree -- fajitas -- come in beef, chicken, and vegetable varieties. A number of burrito and quesadilla selections are well-priced under $11.00. Try the Santa Fe burrito with sirloin, salsa, and beans; the spinach kind with potato hash; or the shrimp quesadilla with crushed garlic and wine sauce. Steak and seafood entrees can get up there in price ($15.00 - $17.00), but they're still reasonable. Especially when you consider the portion sizes. Gloria's is a fun stop for lunch or dinner, but fun can also be had at Happy Hour. Stop by for their daily Happy Hour and indulge in one of their traditional or fruit margaritas for just $3.50 - $4.50. Nothing tastes better with Mexican food! Open Sunday, 12:00 p.m. - 10:00 p.m.; Monday through Saturday, 12:00 p.m. - 11:00 p.m.; Friday and Saturday, 12:00 p.m. - 12:00 a.m.

LE GAMIN
50 MacDougal Street (between Houston and Prince Streets), New York NY 10013. 212/254-4678. **Description:** For those of you who need to brush up on your French, Le Gamin means "The Kids." And the kids and the adults alike come from all over SoHo to sample the crepes, croque monsieurs, and cafe au lait. C'est manifique! Expect to get an entire meal and beverage for under $20.00. Bon appetit! Open daily, 8:00 a.m. - 12:00 a.m. *$Cash Only$*

MOONDANCE DINER

80 Avenue of the Americas (between Grand & Canal Streets), New York NY 10013. 212/226-1191. **Description:** At any time of day or night, the sight of a diner is a sight to behold for those managing to eat on a budget. SoHo's Moondance Diner is a particularly pleasing sight in an area that is well known for its high prices. They serve typical diner fare with a distinctively Manhattan twist (you wouldn't find a hummus and pita platter at any old greasy spoon elsewhere in the country). You can certainly choose from all of your favorite comfort foods like burgers and salads, but Moondance gives you the option of choosing a turkey or veggie burger as well. Entrees include home cooking staples like meatloaf and fried chicken at prices that rarely exceed $10.00. The Moondance pasta dishes are a particularly good deal at $6.95: you choose the pasta (angel hair, penne, linguine) and the sauce (marinara, alfredo, olive oil and garlic, tomato vodka). For a few dollars extra you can even top it with some chicken, sausage, bacon, or all of the above. Of course, eggs and other breakfast specialties are always available too at prices that are hard to beat: two-egg plates start at $3.95. When you're hungry and roaming around the SoHo neighborhood, it's always a marvelous night for Moondance. Open Sunday through Wednesday, 8:30 a.m. - 12:00 a.m.; Thursday through Saturday, 24-hours a day.

PICCOLA

594 Broadway (at Houston Street), New York NY 10012. 212/274-1818. **Description:** Right on the border of SoHo and NoHo, this eatery is an outstanding example of fast-food that isn't junk food. Piccola bakes up tasty individual pizzas in its brick oven, which takes up one wall of this large but narrow space, giving it a homey feel. As you walk your tray along the cafeteria-style counter, you can also survey freshly-made sandwiches, salads, and full entrees, all very good and all very cheap. The pizzas come in a dozen varieties, from good old pepperoni to a white pizza topped with only mozzarella and ricotta cheeses. Or you can build your own pizza for just $4.99, with $1.00 for each additional topping. Freshly-made sandwiches, served on more of that brick oven bread, are just $4.79; and the dinners (all large-sized platters) start at $5.99 for your choice of freshly-made pasta with marinara sauce. How about some baked ziti for $6.99? Mr. C loved the frilled chicken over pasta, smothered in a thick tomato and vegetable sauce. All entrees come with bread and butter. Be sure to check out the daily specials for an even heftier bargain, and don't forget to peruse the large beverage menu with a variety of soda, mineral water, coffee, cappuccino, beer, and wine offerings. For those of you early-risers out there, skip on over to Piccola for their full-course breakfast served weekdays from 7:30 a.m. - 11:00 a.m.; and until 12:00 p.m. on Saturday. Open Monday through Thursday, 7:30 a.m. - 9:00 p.m.; Friday, 7:30 a.m. - 10:00 p.m.; Saturday, 9:00 a.m. - 10:00 p.m.; Sunday, 12:00 p.m. - 8:00 p.m.

SOHO KITCHEN & BAR

103 Greene Street, New York NY 10012. 212/925-1866. **Description:** The SoHo neighborhood may be one of New York's

highest rent districts, but SoHo Kitchen & Bar is decidedly one of the city's coolest and most affordable places to get a great meal in posh surroundings. This American bistro serves a good selection of casual, well-priced foods to both the rich and famous and the cheap and hungry (like us). The menu consists of a number of hearty salads and sandwiches like a goat cheese salad or a smoked salmon sandwich for barely more than $10.00. A number of pasta dishes, including a wild mushroom ravioli with pesto, are also well-priced at $12.00 or less a plate. 10-inch pizzas range in price from $9.00 - $11.00, and are well worth every penny with such great toppings as Thai chicken. Since their opening in the mid eighties, SoHo Kitchen has not increased their price on their always-popular New York sirloin. You'll get 14 ounces of choice, aged meat with plenty of sides for just $16.75. And let's not forget about the wine list, as that is what SoHo Kitchen is most known for. SoHo Kitchen & Bar offers more than 100 different kinds of wine. Sure, prices can range up to almost $25.00 per glass, but there are plenty of options that are delicious and affordable enough to keep everyone happy!

YAFFA'S TEA ROOM
353 Greenwich Street (at Harrison Street), New York NY 10013. 212/274-9403. **Description:** You know that you've found Yaffa Tea Room when you are greeted by the sight of a zebra print-framed door. As one might imagine from this initial introduction, anything goes in this wildly eccentric TriBeCa hotspot. While it is claimed that the theme here is Mediterranean, the eclectic menu would lead one to believe otherwise. For breakfast, Yaffa serves up lots of traditional breakfast fare like eggs, omelettes, and waffles. A number of fresh salads and light sandwiches comprise the lunch menu. But for dinner, let your imagination run wild as the menu is experimental, unpredictable, and fun. In the nicer weather, try and get a seat outside to fully absorb the TriBeCa culture. If you can divert your attention from the funky furniture and decor, you can feast your eyes on the live entertainment that Yaffa offers. Open daily, 8:30 a.m. - 11:00 p.m. The bar serves food Monday through Friday, 11:00 a.m. - 1:00 a.m.

RESTAURANTS
🍽 Upper East Side 🍽

Where? The area above 59th Street to the east of Central Park.
Best Known For: Madison Avenue, Bloomingdale's, Barney's, Metropolitan Museum of Art, Guggenheim Museum, Millionaire Mile.
Insider Tip: The Upper East Side houses the wealthiest postal district in America.

AFGHAN KEBAB HOUSE EAST

1345 Second Avenue (between 70th & 71st Streets), New York NY. 212/517-2776. **Description:** Of all the ethnic restaurants one can sample in New York, the Afghan Kebab House is frequently singled out for good food and value. If you've never tried Afghan cuisine, it's sort of a cross between Greek and Indian; lots of grilled meats, cooked with spices, and served with rice. There aren't many dishes that top $10.00 here. Half spiced chicken (that's half a chicken, all of which is spiced) offers up plenty of food, as does the spicy fish kebab plate; for vegetarians there's palau baudinjan, grilled eggplant with onions, tomatoes, peppers, herbs, and spices. Meat dishes are grilled over wood charcoal to a delicious and mildly spicy taste. All plates come with brown basmati rice, a side salad with a mint-yogurt sauce, and a slice of warm Afghan bread (similar to pita bread) over the top. For appetizers, try the mishawa soup (lentils and vegetables) or the aushak (boiled dumplings with scallions and herbs that can be topped with a mint-yogurt sauce and ground beef as well). The decor is minimal, but offers some authentic touches from the Far East. So if this your first try at Afghan cuisine, you're in for quite a treat. This restaurant has no liquor license but you are welcome to bring your own.

ANGELS RISTORANTE ITALIANO

1135 First Avenue, (between 62nd & 63rd Streets), New York NY 10021. 212-980-3131. **World Wide Web address:** http://www. angelsnyc.com. **Description:** It seems that just about every prestigious restaurant magazine and survey is singing the praises of these Angels. One of my favorite ways to start out a meal here is with the gorgonzola bread: it's a loaf of delicious garlic bread that sits swimming in a pool of gorgonzola cream. The hard part comes when it's time to make up your mind regarding your entrée: do you go with the San Giovanni (angel hair pasta with chicken and mushrooms in a white wine garlic sauce), the San Thoma (fettucine with broccoli, mushrooms, and eggplant), or the tri-color tortelloni. With more than two dozen pasta dishes to choose from, your waiter is sure to understand your indecisiveness. Best of all, there are tons of choices in the $7.95 - $9.95 range. Angels also offers a good number of sandwiches for under $8.00.

THE BREAD FACTORY CAFE

785 Lexington Avenue (at 61st Street), New York NY. 212/355-5729. **Description:** Twenty-four hours a day, this cafe bakes up desserts, pizzas, and sandwiches in their large stone hearth oven. Their not-your-basic-New York bagels in more than 10 varieties are just $.65 each; and any of their fresh cream cheeses (lox, veggie, walnut raisin, kalamata olive, and more) can accompany for just $1.30 more. Croissants, danish, and muffins are priced between $1.40 and $2.50; cookies, biscotti, baklava, and babka are all priced under $1.75. For a lunch time treat, try one of their more than 20 bagel sandwiches such as smoked turkey breast and brie, baked salmon, hickory smoked tuna, or Philly cheesesteak, all priced between $3.50 and $8.95; or try a homemade wrap for just $5.95. The Bread Factory Cafe offers a variety of deli sandwiches, salad plates, and stone oven pizzas as well. Of course, they also serve bread, in more than 15 varieties, including a line of yeast-free breads, priced between $1.65 and $4.25 a loaf. Drop by, day or night, for a snack or meal, or just grab yourself a delicious cup of coffee ($.75), cappuccino ($1.95), or fresh-squeezed juice ($1.95).

CANDLE CAFE

1307 Third Avenue (at 75th Street), New York NY 10021. 212/472-0970. **Description:** For as fashionable an area as the Upper East Side is, they don't boast much in the way of vegan eateries. Candle Cafe is one of the few no dairy- no meat spots and, thankfully, it's one where you can catch a break on the price. Their extensive menu offers a wide variety of your organic favorites, at prices that are quite reasonable! While it is often an assumption that eating healthy means missing all of those usually guilt-ridden favorites, this couldn't be further from the truth, as Candle Cafe proves. Start your meal out with a Mezze Plate; hummus, tabouli, and babaganoush served with oven baked pita chips. Candle Cafe offers a good menu of salads, like the Sea Salad; kombu, arame, and hijiki with cabbage and carrots, tossed in a miso mirin dressing. They even offer you a choice of two delicious breads: a supremely delicious garlic bread or a sourdough or five-grain with a carrot butter spread. For your main course, try a Candle Cafe Burger. Other good sandwiches include the open-faced portabello on rustic bread and the Pocketful of Miracles (a whole wheat pita stuffed with harvest salad and served with ginger dressing). Main courses include an As You Like It stir fry, a grilled seitan steak, and a vegan lasagna. All entrees run right around $12.00 - $15.00. While that might be a bit pricier than other vegetarian haunts about town, let's not forget where we are. Plus, Candle Cafe offers some great little extras that are hard to find elsewhere, like a kiddie menu. Start your kids out on the road to good health by letting them chow down on a plate of pasta with plum tomato sauce or a grilled soy cheese sandwich on sourdough bread. While they might not think so, it beats McDonald's any day! To drink, Candle Cafe concocts a good number of healthy cocktails and smoothies too. Plus, they've got some deliciously un-sinful desserts on hand to finish the meal out right like a carrot-apricot cake, couscous pie, and banana cream pie. Give your kids the vanilla fudge brownie and they just might be surprised at how savory healthy eating can be! Open Sunday, 11:30 a.m. - 9:30 p.m.; Monday through Saturday, 11:30 a.m. - 10:30 p.m.

EL POLLO
1746 First Avenue (at 90th Street), New York NY 10128. 212/996-7810. **Description:** South American cuisine, a basic, unadorned style of cooking that often yields exquisite results, has been gaining a foothold in the city for a couple of years now. El Pollo is a Peruvian restaurant with a simple but elegant atmosphere that specializes in a barbecue-style chicken, grilled with a mild blend of spices and seasonings. The prices here are phenomenally low for the Upper East Side, and the portion sizes are more than adequate. A whole chicken is $8.75; a half-chicken only $5.00. You can get a hefty breast and wing for a mere $2.75. These are all à la carte, so you'll need to add side dishes, and there are some wonderful ones at El Pollo. Mr. C encourages you to try the thin curly French fries ($2.50), fried sweet plantains ($2.50), or a nice house salad ($4.00). For dessert, try the flan ($3.00) or a helping of quinua pudding, a sort of South American rice pudding flavored with raisins, cloves, and cinnamon. Lunch specials (served weekdays from 11:30 a.m. - 3:00 p.m.) offer all of the above choices at slightly lower prices. Open Monday through Friday, 11:30 a.m. - 11:00 p.m.; Saturday and Sunday, 12:30 p.m. - 11:00 p.m.

LUKE'S BAR AND GRILL
1394 Third Avenue (at 80th Street), New York NY 10021. 212/249-7070. **Description:** With a not-too-overpriced menu of simple food in a casual setting, Luke's Bar and Grill is a welcome addition to the Upper East Side. It's like an upscale Ground Round, green walls and brass decor, with a handsome wooden bar up front. The bar, by the way, features Foster's Lager, Sam Adams, and Beck's beers on tap. The food includes lots of appetizers, sandwiches, and dinners too (let's not forget, Luke's *is* a bar after all). A variety of appetizers -- including guacamole and salsa with chips, buffalo wings, mozzarella sticks, and stuffed mushrooms -- are priced under $6.00 each. Lighter appetites will appreciate a diverse salad menu that includes salad appetizers and salad entrees. Whichever you choose, it's doubtful that you'll be charged any more than $9.00. Varieties include mozzarella, tomato, and basil; shrimp and avocado; and beef carpaccio. Luke's has got a number of hearty and delicious sandwiches as well, priced between $5.00 and $8.00. They take many traditional bar food favorites and add a distinctive twist, like the grilled chicken breast with guacamole or the B.L.T.A. (the 'A' is for avocado!). Luke's is well-known for their big and juicy burgers too! As for their entrees, most are priced under $10.00. These include a marinated and poasted half chicken with ginger and hoisin sauce; sauteed cubes of chicken with mushrooms, sun dried tomatoes, and leek au jus; chicken paillard; and meatloaf with mashed potatoes. Even without their low prices, Luke's Bar & Grill would be a great find on the Upper East Side, as there aren't too many places with this kind of atmosphere and attentive service. Open daily, 11:30 a.m. - 2:00 a.m. *$Cash Only$*

MOCCA

1588 Second Avenue (between 82nd & 83rd), New York NY 10028. 212/734-6470. **Description:** If you've never tried Hungarian food, be warned: it is very filling! If ever there were a cuisine to match the hunger you experience on a cold and wintery East Coast day, this is it. For more than 15 years, this neighborhood institution has been serving up big and hearty portions at tiny little prices. Drop in for their lunch special and you can indulge in a soup, entree, dessert, and coffee (trust me, you won't finish!) for under $7.00. They offer similarly great deals at dinner, when you can get a salad, appetizer, entree, dessert, and coffee or tea for a fixed price of under $15.00. Upper East Siders and native Hungarians swear by the authenticity of this place and claim its old-world charm is one of the biggest reasons it has survived so long. If you're curious as to what kinds of food you'll find here goulash and weiner schnitzel are two popular choices. Many of the dishes are chicken, veal, or pork based and paprika is definitely the seasoning of choice. Although it's easy to fill up on all this great food, make sure to save some room for dessert: homemade apple, cherry, and cheese strudels are on the menu. Call ahead for hours.

PIG HEAVEN

1540 Second Avenue (between 80th & 81st Streets), New York NY 10028. 212/744-4333. It's been praised by all the New York biggies: *The Times*, *New York Magazine*, *Wall Street Journal*... even *Forbes*. That said, now it's my turn. Pig Heaven is a great little place on the Upper East Side where you can get a delicious meal and not spend half your paycheck in doing so. As you might guess, pork is the specialty here, though they offer plenty of seafood, poultry, meat, and veggie dishes too. One of the best ways to start a meal here is with the shui-mai or any kind of dumpling -- fried, boiled, or steamed. For the most part, pork dishes can be had for under $10.00 and include such good ones as sautéed sliced pork with hoisin sauce, twice-cooked pork, and shredded pork with bamboo shoots. Though there are plenty of other interesting and delicious dishes (citrus shrimp, three glass chicken, sesame beef, and dry-cooked string beans for example), for a true Pig Heaven experience, it's best to stick with the specialty of the house! Open Sunday through Thursday, 11:30 a.m. - 11:15 p.m.; Friday and Saturday, 11:30 a.m. - 12:15 a.m.

SHIP OF FOOLS

1590 Second Avenue (at East 82nd Street), New York NY 10028. 212/570-2651. **World Wide Web address:** http://www.shipoffoolsnyc.com. **Description:** Get on board for good food, games, and entertainment. Ship of Fools offers reasonably-priced pub fare until 4:00 a.m., seven nights a week. Snack on one of their many appetizers like nachos for $5.95, chicken fingers for $5.95, or a Fools Platter of three appetizers for $12.95. Main dishes are all around $8.95 - $9.95. This friendly bar and restaurant is the place to be during Happy Hour (weekdays, 4:00 p.m. - 7:00 p.m.) when you can get a beer for $2.00 and a frozen margarita for $1.00 more!! Or drop in anytime for a $12.50 "Bucket of Beer". Entertainment is provided by satellite televisions, pool tables, and dart boards. Open Monday through Friday, 4:00 p.m. - 4:00 a.m.; Saturday and Sunday, 12:00 p.m. - 4:00 a.m.

SOTTO CINQUE

1644 Second Avenue (between 85th & 86th Streets), New York NY 10028. 212/472-5563. **Description:** How can you beat this? For those of you who don't speak fluent Italian, Sotto Cinque means "under five" and they're not talking about age here, they're talking about dollars! This basic pasta house offers about 10 different pasta dishes for (you guessed it) under $5.00! Choose from penne pomodoro, ravioli marinara, spaghetti puttanesca, gnocchi sorrentino, and penne ortolane. If there's nothing on the "under five" menu that gets your pulse going, there are more than 15 specialty pastas that are specially priced at $7.95. On this more advanced menu, you'll find things like manicotti with tomato sauce, penne romano, baked rigatoni with sausage, and vegetarian lasagna. There are also lots of appetizers and antipasti such as minestrone soup, stuffed mushrooms, and fresh mussels. The same value-pricing goes for sandwiches and desserts. At lunch time, they offer an even better deal: an appetizer (bruschetta, salad, or soup) and an entree (sandwich or pasta dish) for just $6.95. Sotto Cinque is especially good for quick and easy take-out, and the restaurant also offers free delivery. Open Sunday through Thursday, 11:00 a.m. - 11:00 p.m.; Friday and Saturday, 11:00 a.m. - 12:00 a.m.

TONY'S DI NAPOLI

1606 Second Avenue (at 83rd Street), New York NY 10028. 212/861-8686. **Description:** Although Tony's Di Napoli has been around since 1959, it has only recently brought family-style dining to the Upper East Side. While the price of a single entree is rather expensive, that's because it is actually a huge, central plate that has enough food to serve two to three people (or that one cheapie who wants to take it all home and not have to cook for a month). There are about 20 pasta dishes to choose from, ranging from $12.00 for your basic spaghetti and linguine marinara, to $18.00 for spaghetti or linguine with shrimp or seafood. Try eating anything else after that! Several chicken and veal dishes, on the average, will run you about $18.00 - $22.00, including chicken scarpiello and veal and eggplant. Seafood dinners (mostly shrimp) cost about the same, topping out at $32.00 for a mixed plate of lobster tail, shrimp, clams, and mussels (don't forget, you'll be getting enough to start your own ocean.) The restaurant covers a couple of storefronts with a bright, spacious interior, natural wood, and the ever-so-popular red and white checkered tablecloths. Tony's Di Napoli also accepts food orders by phone which you can then pick up for an instant and inexpensive party buffet. Open Sunday, 2:00 p.m. - 10:00 p.m.; Monday through Friday, 5:00 p.m. - 11:00 p.m.; Saturday, 2:00 p.m. - 12:00 a.m.

TRIANGOLO

345 East 83rd Street, (between First & Second Avenues), New York NY 10028. 212/472-4488. **Description:** Of the East Side's

many affordable Italian restaurants, Triangolo is one of the most appealing for its simplicity and great food. Sometimes Mr. C just likes a simple, quiet restaurant for a special meal without the hype. This is it. Triangolo is small, spare, and elegant inside; the walls are painted in rich Mediterranean colors but remain undecorated. The staff is extremely attentive and friendly, watching over you without creating any pressure. The menu features over a dozen pasta dishes priced under $11.00 (apart from daily specials) and the antipasti are around $6.00 - $9.00. The pastas are beautifully cooked, whether you go basic or fancy. One of Mr. C's companions made the real find on the menu: Rotolo di pasta Montanaro ($11.00) features dark porcini mushrooms sautéed in virgin olive oil and rolled up in a large pasta tube; this is then sliced into four sections, which are cooked flat and smothered in sauce. The mushrooms are so rich and tasty, you'll think it's a meat dish. Other good dishes for under $11.00 included the caserecci affumicati (pasta with peppers, artichokes, and smoked mozzarella); and rigatoni contadina (rigatoni with chicken, eggplant, tomato, and mascarpone). Portions are very big, so be prepared to take something home; it tastes just as good the next day. Triangolo offers a few chicken and veal entrees as well, and their reasonably priced between $13.00 and $15.00; but, for the best deals, it's a good idea to stick with the pasta dishes. They're just as filling (if not more so) and equally tasty! Triangolo is a good place for a romantic, quiet date. Because the place is small, reservations are a good idea on the weekends. *$Cash Only$*

RESTAURANTS
🍽 Upper West Side 🍽

Where? The area above 59th Street to the west of Central Park.
Best Known For: Metropolitan Opera House, Lincoln Center,
   Columbia University, Juilliard School of Music.
Insider Tip: If you're strolling along Broadway, stop by
   Symphony Space, a performing arts center that presents
   occasional twelve-hour music marathons for FREE.

AFGHAN KEBAB HOUSE WEST
764 Ninth Avenue (at 51st Street), New York NY 10019. 212/307-
1612. **Description:** Of all the ethnic restaurants one can sample in
New York, Afghan Kebab House is frequently singled out for good
food and value. If you've never tried Afghan cuisine, it's sort of a
cross between Greek and Indian; lots of grilled meats, cooked with
spices, and served with rice. There aren't many dishes that top
$10.00 here. Half spiced chicken offers up plenty of food, as does
the spicy fish kebab plate; for vegetarians there's palaw
baudinjan, grilled eggplant with onions, tomatoes, and peppers.
Meat dishes are grilled over wood charcoal to a delicious and mildly
spicy taste. All plates come with brown basmati rice, salad with a
mint-yogurt sauce, and a slice of warm Afghan bread (similar to
pita bread) over the top. The decor is minimal, but offers some
authentic touches from the Far East. So if this your first try at
Afghan cuisine, you're in for quite a treat. This restaurant has no
liquor license but you are welcome to bring your own.

CAFE MOZART
154 West 70th Street, New York NY 10023. 212/595-9797. **E-
mail address:** cafemozart@aol.com. **Description:** If you're looking
for an intimate evening of upscale entertainment (food, wine,
music, and frivolity), Cafe Mozart is a great choice. They offer a
delicious array of lunch and dinner items for those with a more
discerning palate: Niçoise salad, duck pâté, and Viennese schnitzel
are a few of the items you'll find here. The best time to visit is
for dinner, when Mozart orchestrates a delicious prix fixe meal
for $19.95. The meal starts out with salad or an appetizer and
really gets going with your entrée, which includes such meals as
grilled tuna, sautéed salmon, and filet mignon. The fixed price
menu begins at 4:00 p.m. If you're willing to shell out just $10.00
more, you can get all of the above courses plus a glass of wine and
one of Cafe Mozart's famed desserts. Anyone who has ever been
to Cafe Mozart will be sure and tell you all about their desserts;
they've got one of the finest selections around, not to mention one
of New York City's largest. Plus, amidst all the food, you'll be
entertained by the compositions and sounds of some of the city's
most talented classical and jazz musicians. This is a great place to
get together with friends and enjoy a good cup of coffee or a spot
of tea! Open Sunday, 10:00 a.m. - 1:00 a.m.; Monday through

Thursday, 8:00 a.m. – 1:00 a.m.; Friday, 8:00 a.m. – 3:00 a.m.; Saturday, 10:00 a.m. – 3:00 a.m.

88 NOODLE & ORIENTAL HOUSE

565 Columbus Avenue (between 87th & 88th Streets), New York NY 10024. 212/501-9360. **Description:** You may not have noticed the 88 Noodle & Oriental House in Columbus Avenue's restaurant section; that's the price you pay for being in a non-descript building on a non-descript block, well above the main stretch. But one of Mr. C's foremost restaurant experts says he dines here almost once a week, and with over 200 different items to choose from, it's easy to see why. This is a full Chinese menu with all of the standard options, from sweet and sour chicken to mu shu pork and orange beef. However, Mr. C always recommends that you go with the specialties of the house, which means starting with something like an order of cold sesame noodles, or spinach or whole-wheat noodles. Among the many other noodle dishes are lo mein and chow fun, of course; mei fun, the wonderful thin rice noodle dish, is worth looking into as well. You can order them here with chicken, beef, pork, or vegetables. Try sampling noodles from many parts of the Far East, such as Hong Kong-style chicken wonton tommen soup. There are plenty of vegetarian options here, as well. The only time the menu approaches more than $10.00 is when it comes to the Chef's Specialties, and even these are great deals! And, of course, 88 Noodle & Oriental House, like most Chinese restaurants, offers a fantastic lunch deal (served daily, 11:30 a.m. - 3:30 p.m.). The deal starts out with your choice of soup (wonton, egg drop, hot and sour, miso tofu); appetizer (egg roll, vegetable roll, shui mai); and rice (white, brown, or vegetable fried). Now comes the hard part: picking your entree. With more than 25 different meals to choose from, you'll certainly never lack variety. 88 Noodle & Oriental House is a terrific example of your basic no-frills, good-food, not-a-lot-of-bucks noodle joint, and heaven knows we need more of those these days. Open Sunday, 12:30 p.m. - 11:00 p.m.; Monday through Thursday, 11:30 a.m. - 11:00 p.m.; Friday, 11:30 a.m. - 12:00 a.m.; Saturday, 11:30 a.m. - 11:00 p.m.

FIREHOUSE

522 Columbus Avenue (at 85th Street), New York NY 10024. 212/787-3473. **Description:** If you want to hang with a rowdy crowd, head over to Firehouse. Red siren lights flash and bounce off the walls, and a raised area of tables at the rear offers monitors and a giant-screen TV showing sports, but don't expect to hear any of the play-by-play; this place packs them. During the warm months, you can also grab a patio-style table out front. What's good here? All sorts of bar foods including a variety of wings (Buffalo, BBQ, Jamaican jerk, boneless, etc.); homemade 10-inch pizzas, with crispy, thin crusts and such toppings as pineapple, chicken, Oriental shrimp, or grilled veggies. There are plenty of salads, burgers, and sandwiches to go around too. The place is cute and there's a great outdoor seating area that fills up in the warmer weather.

HARRIET'S KITCHEN

502 Amsterdam Avenue (at 84th Street), New York NY 10024
212/721-0045. **Description:** Harriet's Kitchen is just that, a take
out place that strives to be just like your own kitchen at home (or
better). Like their slogan says "You provide the home, we'll do the
cooking." All the food is fresh and homemade, with an eye toward
healthy preparations like skinless chicken fried in cholesterol-free
vegetable oil. Chicken, in fact, is the main item here, in such
entrees as a barbecued half-bird with corn bread, boneless lemon
chicken with linguine, and Harriet's famous chicken pot pie; as well
as in main-course salads like mixed greens with sliced chicken
apples, walnuts, and Swiss cheese. If you're not after the things
with wings, don't despair. There are six-ounce hamburgers and
homemade meatloaf with real mashed potatoes and gravy. Plus
appetizers from chicken noodle soup to zucchini sticks with
horseradish sauce, vegetable side dishes, and desserts too. Rarely
does an item come close to $8.00 on this menu. Extra bargains are
the family meals, with enough chicken, potatoes, coleslaw, and corn
bread to feed four to six people for under $20.00. Throughout
the week, they offer some pretty sweet deals as well: Tuesday
night, pick up a 1/4 grilled or roasted chicken with mashed
potatoes and gravy, green beans, and cranberry sauce for under
$6.00; on Wednesday nights, a 1/2 grilled chicken with a 1/2 pint
of mashed potatoes and another 1/2 pint of herbed corn is just
$7.95. Just remember, there's barely a bench to speak of here,
nevermind a dining area. They'll be happy to deliver it to you if you
live in the area, or you can drop by and pick it up! Open daily, 4:30
p.m. - 11:00 p.m.

HI-LIFE BAR AND GRILL

477 Amsterdam Avenue (at 83rd Street), New York NY 10024
212/787-7199. **Description:** Definitely one of the hipper spots on
this restaurant-packed stretch of Amsterdam, Hi-Life feels like a
scene out of some 1950s movie. From the martini-glass sign
outside, to the black leather upholstered walls inside (try to get
the cozy booth just inside the front door), this is a good old
fashioned lounge. There should be a beaded curtain, through which
you would hear some torch singer crooning away. And yet there is a
slightly modern skew to the decor; check out the bizarre lamps
for instance. Hi-Life is kind of small, adding to the intimate
atmosphere, although they compensate by squeezing in as many
tables as they can. Once you're seated though, the food makes it
all worthwhile. The menu is modern and eclectic, with burgers
pastas, steaks, salads, and desserts. The prices are at the top of
Mr. C's budget range, particularly the daily specials; but you get a
lot of delicious eats, and after all, it's an experience. Among the
lower-priced dinners are chicken pot pie for $8.95, with good
mashed potatoes and a vegetable of the day. Big, juicy burgers
range from $5.50 - $7.50, and are served with the traditional
fries and pickle. Pastas are also a good bet, in the ubiquitous large
white bowls for $11.00 - $12.00. Brunch runs all day on the
weekends; otherwise lunch is not served at Hi-Life. Just dinner
from 5:00 p.m. - 12:00 a.m. No respectable lounge lizard would be
up and out any earlier.

THE HUNGARIAN PASTRY SHOP

1030 Amsterdam Avenue (at 111th Street), New York NY 10025. 212/866-4230. **Description:** In the Columbia University area, folks know about this extremely laid-back establishment, famous for its coffee and pastries. It is also known as a spot where you can literally sit all day over refills while dawdling over Dostoevsky. If anyone bothers you at all, it's likely to be the be the cafe's cat. In short, the Hungarian Pastry Shop offers a mellow and pleasantly homey scene. Service is mellow too, which some of the more uptight patrons may be tempted to read as minimal, but then again, sometimes you just want to be left alone. A variety of simple pastries, cookies, tarts, etc. are all priced around $5.00 and under. Wash it down with a bottomless cup of fresh-brewed coffe that can give you energy for the entire day. Open Sunday, 8:30 a.m. - 10:30 p.m.; Monday through Friday, 8:00 a.m. - 11:30 p.m.; Saturday, 8:30 a.m. - 11:30 p.m. *$Cash Only$*

INDIAN CAFE

201 West 95th Street, (between Amsterdam Avenue & Broadway), New York NY 10025. 212/222-1600. ✦ 2791 Broadway (at 107th Street); New York NY 10025. 212/749-9200. **Description:** Of New York's many, *many* Indian restaurants, the Indian Cafe has often been singled out by reviewers as a pleasant and dependable eatery for good food on a budget. Mr. C confirmed this on his own visit to the 95th Street branch. The interior is small but comfortable, the atmosphere subdued, and the service very attentive and quick. The menu offers a wide variety of chicken, beef, seafood, and vegetarian dishes, with barely an item priced above $10.00. All of the food is delicious, so it's pretty hard to go wrong. The standard practice here is to walk on the mild side unless you request otherwise; if you like your food hot, be sure to ask for it. Meanwhile, the portions are nice and large. For an inexpensive entree, curried rice pilaf and mixed vegetables with shredded coconut and almonds is hard to beat at under $6.00. Other entrees that priced out at under $8.00 include lentils with spinach, sliced tandoori chicken with curried rice pilaf and broccoli and bell pepper, and your choice of chicken or beef curry. Plus, the cooks at Indian Cafe are no slouches when it comes to being creative. If there's a particular dish you're craving but don't see on the menu, just ask: if they can, they'll prepare it! To drink, the restaurant offers some great and authentic Indian beers. Especially worth noting is the lunch menu, which offers no less than 10 different entrees from vegetables to beef, lamb, and even goat curry, along with an appetizer, salad, rice, and chutney for only $4.95. And, unlike many such luncheon deals, it's available from 11:30 a.m. right up to 4:00 p.m. Open daily, 11:30 a.m. - 11:30 p.m. The Broadway location stays open until 12:00 a.m.

LA CARIDAD

2199 Broadway (at 78th Street), New York NY 10024. 212/874-2780. **Description:** New York is known as one of the few places in the world where you will find a wealth of Cuban-Chinese restaurants, and La Caridad is one of the city's best. Most dinners, whether Hispanic or Oriental, are priced well under $10.00 and come in staggering quantities on heaping plates. The arroz con pollo, for instance, is indeed beautiful to look at; a large mound of saffron-colored rice in bright orange, laced with large chunks of chicken and topped with green peas and pieces of red pepper. It tastes great too, and there's plenty of it; this is one selection that will not leave you hungry. On the Oriental side, fried rice plates start at $4.00. Chop suey, chow mein, and lo mein dishes start out right around $6.00. With a menu that's comprised of more than 175 items, I guarantee you'll find something unique and to your liking... today, tomorrow, and each time you come back. Sit at the counter, find a table, or just grab some take-out. The atmosphere is bustling at La Caridad; it has a reputation as a good place for a quick, tasty, and inexpensive meal, and it well deserves it. *$Cash Only$*

PUCCINI CAFE (Italian)
475 Columbus Avenue (at 83rd Street), New York NY 10024. 212/875-9533. **Description:** Dining at Puccini is like a quick trip to Europe -- all of it. The decor could be that of any bright, clean cafe in Paris or Rome; Spanish guitar music plays on the sound system, and the menu ranges from pasta to pizza to delicious seafood entrees. The food is all fresh and attractive, and the atmosphere is lively and bustling. It's the light nature of the foods offered that keeps this trendy-looking place affordable; salads and sandwiches are the main fare, though there are some larger entrees too. More than a dozen pasta dinners are priced under $12.00 including pasta primavera; pasta melanzanna (eggplant and mozzarella); and pasta toscana (mushrooms, artichokes, asparagus, and ricotta cheese). The large variety of salads are equally well-priced in the $8.00 - $10.00 range. The arugula salad is a great choice with arugula (obviously), endive, radicchio, sun dried tomatoes, roasted red peppers, and warm goat cheese. There's also a great salmon concoction that's made with mesclun lettuce, plum tomatoes, and onions. Individual sized pizzas are a filling meal and a worthwhile one at that; toppings include roasted peppers, sun dried tomatoes, and calamata olives. When it comes to the main entrees, these are much pricier, though still not bad considering the area you'll be dining in. And just try to keep from looking at the long pastry case, with such delights as flan, profiteroles, and cappuccino mousse cake. These are pricier too, but worth the splurge!

ZABAR'S CAFE
2245 Broadway (at 80th Street), New York NY 10024. 212/787-2000. **World Wide Web address:** http://www.zabars.com. **Description:** If you're one of the many who love shopping at Zabar's for their fresh-baked breads and pastries, cream cheeses, smoked fish, and so forth, but you can't wait to get home to tear into this great food, stop into Zabar's Cafe. It's right next door to the main market and provides both stand-up counter eating and take-out service. Here, you'll find all the bagels and cream cheeses you've come to love, as well as muffins, pastries,

and the like. The cafe also has a number of breakfast specials. On Mr. C's visit, one of these was a fresh-made omelette croissant (choose from ham and egg, or egg and cheese) plus coffee and orange juice, for just $2.00; quick, hard to beat price-wise, and a great way to start the day. There are a number of similar specials at Zabar's Cafe, including their terrific home-style soups. Be forewarned: There's almost always a line to get to the counter, but it moves quickly. Like any good New Yorker, you should too. With any luck, you'll be able to find an open stool at one of the side counters; otherwise blend in with the rest of the natives and eat while you walk to your next destination.

· Rain

· Calle Ocho

RESTAURANTS
🍽 Outer Boroughs 🍽

⋆BROOKLYN⋆
The most popular of New York's boroughs, few places welcome visitors and residents alike with such splendor as the Brooklyn Bridge. **Check out: Carroll Gardens, Prospect Park, Coney Island, and Brighton Beach.**

⋆QUEENS⋆
Geographically, the largest of the boroughs and a true melting pot. Queens is home to a huge Greek population in Astoria, high numbers of Asians in Flushing, and a substantial Indian community in Jackson Heights. Most people visit Queens because both La Guardia and John F. Kennedy International Airports are located here. **Check out: Shea Stadium, Queens Museum, and New York Hall of Science.**

⋆THE BRONX⋆
The city's northernmost borough, The Bronx is beginning to rise above it's crime infested past by creating a more community focused landscape with the planned addition of walking trails and bike paths. **Check out: Yankee Stadium, The Bronx Zoo, and New York Botanical Gardens.**

BENFAREMO - THE LEMON ICE KING OF CORONA
52-02 108th Street (at Corona Avenue), Queens NY. 781/699-5133. **Description:** This family business offers 25 varieties of homemade ices. Yummy flavors include lemon, peanut butter, and cantaloupe. Benfaremo is only open during the summer but does stay open until 12:00 a.m. during those months. Prices are under $2.00.

COUSIN JOHN'S CAFE AND BAKERY
70 Seventh Avenue, Brooklyn NY 11217. 718/622-7333. **Description:** With their location in Brooklyn's up-and-coming Park Slope district, Cousin John's Cafe and Bakery offers simple fare for a snack or light meal. Order three eggs, any style, with a croissant (fresh-baked on the premises) and a salad for just $4.75. Or try the soup of the day (Mr. C was impressed by the hearty vegetable variety offered on the day of his visit) that comes with a salad as well, and is just $5.50. The ingredients are fresh, the food is quite tasty, and the prices are tough to beat. If you're not in the mood for a meal, check out the pastry counter. There's plenty to choose from, and coupled with an herbal tea or a cappuccino, one of these can make for a nice midmorning or mid-afternoon snack. All in all, a good spot for a quick, cheap bite between window-shopping visits to those entertaining shops on Seventh Avenue.

GOODFELLA'S
9606 Third Avenue, New York NY. 718/833-6200. **World Wide Web address:** http://www.goodfellas.com. **Description:** You don't have to worry about mobsters hanging out at Goodfella's, although the food would make the Corleone family proud! Goodfella's offers traditional Italian meals with old world flavor. A trip here would not be complete without a sampling of their specialty brick oven pizza. Prices range from $6.50 to $12.00+ depending on how many toppings you can handle. Gourmet varieties include Pizza a la Vodka, famous for its tomato cream vodka sauce; The Goodfella, donning peppers, sausage, and garlic; and taco pizza featuring salsa, ground beef, and Monterey Jack cheese. But the menu doesn't stop there and neither should you. Give one of their reasonably-priced entrees a try (veal parmigiana, chicken marsala, penne primavera, shrimp romulus, and fettuccino... just to name a few). Or nibble on a meatball hero or a grilled chicken club. And to end the evening on a sweet note, your grand finale should be one of the many sumptuous desserts like tiramisu, cheesecake, or Snickers pie.

GRIMALDI'S
19 Old Fulton Street, Brooklyn NY 11201. 718/858-4300. **World Wide Web address:** http://www.grimaldis.com. **Description:** In the shadow of the Brooklyn Bridge, on the Brooklyn side, there are several fine restaurants offering great food with dramatic views of Manhattan. Unfortunately, if you're reading this book, you may not be able to afford the dramatic prices they charge. But because you are reading this book, you're in luck. There are less expensive, just as delicious, alternatives. Tops on this list has to be Grimaldi's. Pizza here is thin-crusted, coal-oven-baked, and topped with the freshest ingredients. This means a pie that is crisp, not oily or greasy, on which sauces and cheese are placed, not smeared on. The mozzarella is homemade, the tomatoes are freshly crushed. It's good stuff. Grimaldi's is a restaurant, not a sub shop; the decor is bright and clean. A 1940s-style jukebox plays plenty of Sinatra, and his picture adorns the pastel-colored walls. Beer and wine are served, and the place is open daily until 11:00 or 12:00 p.m. You cannot order slices here; whole pies only. At $12.00 for a small pie, and $14.00 for a large, this is not the cheapest pizza in town. But two people can share the small, three can share the large, and don't forget the superior quality or the location.

JUNIOR'S RESTAURANT
386 Flatbush Avenue Extension (at DeKalb Avenue), Brooklyn NY 11201. 718/852-5257. **Description:** Junior's Restaurant may perhaps symbolize the transition that takes place in so many of New York's neighborhoods. This huge, sprawling establishment, opened in 1929, is a wacky mix of old-time Jewish coffee shop and modern urban barbecue house. The clientele is similarly made up of African-Americans, Hispanics, and Jews, all chowing down on blintzes, chopped liver, Buffalo wings, and ribs. The atmosphere is bright and boisterous, with lots of groups out for big dinners. The

waitstaff is attentive and efficient, setting out onion rolls, pickles and coleslaw upon arrival, the tradition of a good Jewish deli. Indeed, for those looking for the best bargains, the overstuffed sandwiches are the winners. There are over 40 options, ranging from egg salad and bacon ($6.50) to Nova Scotia salmon, sliced tomato and Bermuda onion ($9.25). Mr. C, however, seeing that the Old World side was in good hands, ordered a platter of barbecued baby back ribs ($11.95). What promptly came out was about a rack and a half of meaty, juicy ribs smothered with a tangy sauce, along with a baked potato and more coleslaw. It was too much to finish. Saving room for dessert, though, is important. Of the two dozen treats offered, many baked in-house, the cheesecake ($4.25 a slice) is a big winner. Huge is more the word for this creamy slab with a cookie crumb crust. Have it topped with strawberries. If you didn't leave room, you can always pick some up to take home from Junior's retail bakery. In fact, the cheesecake is the restaurant's calling card; you can have one shipped anywhere in the country. Junior's has a separate cafe lounge with a full bar and more tables for dining. Open seven days a week.

MONIKA
643 Fifth Avenue, Brooklyn NY 11215. 718/788-6930. **Description:** Walking into this tiny storefront restaurant is like walking straight from the street into someone's dining room. Monika is a Polish restaurant that, in the end, leaves both your wallet *and* your stomach full. There's barely a thing on the menu that costs more than $6.00. The best way to start out a meal at Monika is with one of their freshly made soups. There's always more than a dozen to choose from with varieties like chicken, sauerkraut, barley, tripe, borscht with egg, and cold cucumber tempting your palate. On the average, soups are under $2.00 for a good-sized helping. Some other great Polish delicacies to try are pierogies. You can try them with meat, cheese and potato, or cheese and sauerkraut for as little as $3.00 a helping. Of the nearly 20 entrees offered, the most expensive I spotted was the baked duck for $7.50. Baked chicken, beef goulash, pork chops, Polish kielbasa, stuffed cabbage, and baked turkey were all under $5.50 a plate. Cheese blintzes, already an inexpensive delicacy at so many Polish restaurants in Manhattan, are priced even lower here: just $4.00. They make an intriguing dessert, not unlike an Italian cannoli, but you may end up considering them a meal in themselves. Another dessert option is cheesecake or rice pudding for $1.50. When was the last time you got dessert at that price? They'll take good care of you here; the servings are ample, the ingredients are the genuine article, and the prices are "bardzo tano" (loosely translated, "surrealistically low"). Open daily, 12:00 p.m. - 8:00 p.m.

SGT. GARCIA'S
70-09 Austin Street, 2nd Floor, Forest Hills NY 11375. 718/575-0007. **Description:** When you want some good Mexican food, without the hassle of going all the way into the city, head over to Sgt. Garcia's. The lively and bright Tex-Mex decor is sure to get you tapping your tamales. Every dish is prepared to your

specifications, so if you like it hot, they will spice it up for you. Choose from mouthwatering appetizers (all about $5.00 - $7.00) including quesadillas, scallops sautéed in red sauce, three alarm chili, or gazpacho. Specials may include anything from paella to roast pork to seafood kebabs. Or pick from one of the numerous standards like Mexican pizza, tacos, arroz con pollo, fajitas, or enchiladas mole poblano. Most of these are priced around $15.00 and are sure to please. Sgt. Garcia also likes to let loose by offering special promotions like "Monday Madness" when mango margaritas are a mere $3.00. They even offer a children's menu with dishes for $5.95. Open Sunday, 3:00 p.m. - 10:00 p.m.; Monday through Thursday, 11:30 a.m. - 11:00 p.m.; Friday, 11:30 a.m. - 11:00 p.m.; Saturday, 11:30 a.m. - 11:30 p.m.

TRIPOLI
156 Atlantic Avenue, Brooklyn NY 11201. 718/596-5800. **E-mail address:** trablus@tripolirestaurant.com. **World Wide Web address:** http://www.tripolirestaurant.com. **Description:** A long-time landmark in Brooklyn's Middle Eastern district, Tripoli is a large and lavish restaurant and bar that looks a lot more expensive than it actually is. The decor features a nautical theme, with wood-paneled walls and ornate seafaring decorations. Even the very high ceilings have been painted with blue skies and puffy white clouds. These sailors must have gotten a bit confused on the voyage to Brooklyn, though Tripoli offers foods originating not in Libya, as the dutiful map-consultant might expect, but in Lebanon. The extensive menu offers many traditional Lebanese foods and dozens of entrees. Most of these main dishes are priced between $7.00 and $14.50. Kibbee Mishwiye ($9.75) is lean and finely ground leg of lamb mixed with cracked wheat and further stuffed with chopped nuts and onion, then charcoal broiled. Or try Minazli ($9.00), which is sautéed eggplant stuffed with ground lamb and pine nuts, cooked in a spicy tomato sauce and served over rice. In addition to the lamb dishes you will find chicken, steak, and seafood entrees such as Sumuk B'tahini ($12.00) sautéed fish filet cooked in a spicy tahini sauce made with almonds and walnuts and served with rice. The vegetarian entrees are even better bargains: most run between $7.00 and $8.75. The Kibee B'ziat ($7.00) is a platter of cooked potatoes and onions stuffed with walnuts and raisins; the whole mixture is then baked in olive oil. A most exotic offering! After your meal you can choose from dozens of desserts, all priced at $2.50 or less, including baklava, rice pudding, and other treats. Tripoli has a full bar, including a fairly extensive and reasonably priced wine list. The downstairs function room is available for private parties, and can seat up to 100 people. For those wishing to enjoy Lebanese entertainment and belly dancing, they are both available for an extra charge.

UNCLE GEORGE'S
33-19 Broadway, Queens NY 11106. 718/626-0593. **Description:** Of all the Greek tavernas along these few blocks of Broadway, Uncle George's is clearly the favorite of many. Racks of lamb and spits of whole chickens are turning above open fires as you walk in.

A large diner with long, family-style tables, George's is open 24 hours a day and is regularly packed. The natives know a good deal when they see one. The menu is large, too, with most entrees under $10.00. Choices range from traditionaul favorites like roast leg of lamb ($7.00, with orzo or vegetable) and a barbecued half-chicken with potatoes ($5.00) to such seafood delicacies as a platter of baby smelts ($7.00). Then there is the Pandora's Box of daily specials which may include stuffed squid for $6.00; roast pork with spinach rice for $5.00; or rabbit stew with onions, $7.00. Whether your tastes are basic or exotic, you're sure to find something yummy. Portions here are enormous so bring your appetite.

ALPHABETICAL INDEX

W

Y

Z

CASH ONLY

ANGELICA KITCHEN • 238
BAGEL BUFFET • 253
BENNY'S BURRITOS • 239
BO KY • 257
THE CARNEGIE DELI • 270
CORNER BISTRO • 254
CUCINA DI PESCE • 240
CUPCAKE CAFE • 271
CUSTARD BEACH • 254
DOJO EAST • 240
DOJO WEST • 254
GREAT JONES CAFE • 242
HOTEL 17 • 222
HOTEL 31 • 223
THE HUNGARIAN PASTRY SHOP • 289
IDEAL CHEESE SHOP • 113
ISLAND BURGERS & SHAKES • 273
JOE'S DAIRY • 113
JOHN'S OF BLEECKER STREET • 255
LA CARIDAD • 289
LE GAMIN • 277
LUKE'S BAR AND GRILL • 282
MARY ANN'S CHELSEA • 236
McSORLEY'S OLD ALE HOUSE • 141
MOCCA • 283
NEW YORK NOODLE TOWN • 258
NHA TRANG • 258
STINGY LULU'S • 245
TERESA'S • 245
TRE POMODORI • 268
TRIANGOLO • 284
WONG KEE • 259

BRING YOUR OWN

Is your favorite cheap spot missing?
Do you have comments or suggestions?

New York City has a lot to offer. If you've got a
bargain-priced store, restaurant, hotel, or entertainment
activity, let us know about it!!
Or drop us a line to let us know what you
do or don't like about the book.

CHAPTER HEADING:

_____

NAME OF BUSINESS/ORGANIZATION:

_____

ADDRESS:

_____

_____

PHONE:

_____

WHAT'S SO GREAT ABOUT THIS PLACE?

_____

_____

_____

_____

COMMENTS:

_____

_____

_____

YOUR NAME & ADDRESS:

_____

_____

Clip this page and send to:
Mr. Cheap's® New York
c/o Adams Media Corporation
260 Center Street
Holbrook, MA 02343
E-mail: mrcheap@adamsmedia.com